URBAN DEVELOPMENT IN CENTRAL EUROPE

INTERNATIONAL HISTORY OF CITY DEVELOPMENT

VOLUME I: *Urban Development in Central Europe*

VOLUME I

URBAN DEVELOPMENT IN CENTRAL EUROPE

E. A. GUTKIND

The Free Press of Glencoe
Collier-Macmillan Limited, *London*

For information, address:
The Free Press of Glencoe
A Division of The Macmillan Company
The Crowell-Collier Publishing Company
60 Fifth Avenue, New York, N. Y. 10011

Collier-Macmillan Canada, Ltd., Toronto, Ontario

Library of Congress Catalog Card Number: 64-13231

As the title implies, the *International History of City Development* is an attempt to present a world-wide survey of the origin and growth of urban civilization. Throughout history, cities have been the power stations of new ideas and the seismographs on which the impact and the transformation of these ideas can be read.

The *International History of City Development* endeavors to describe and to analyze this continually renewed interplay of adaptation and readaptation, of challenge and response, which has made cities in all parts of the world the most significant agents of renewal and decline, of expansion and contraction.

With a few exceptions, all the important countries are represented. Those few that are missing had to be excluded because no or only insufficient co-operation from their governments or local administrations was forthcoming, in spite of sustained efforts and repeated approaches to the heads of state. Without this assistance, the standards aimed at in this work could not have been maintained. It is to be hoped that these shortcomings can be eliminated in a later edition.

The countries are arranged according to geographical regions. Within each volume, the material has been grouped as far as possible under the following headings:

The Land
Historical Background
Rural Settlement
Urban Settlement
City Survey

The sequence of the countries included in this work is as follows:

Central Europe
Austria, Switzerland, Denmark, Norway, Sweden
Greece, Italy, Spain, and Portugal
France, Belgium, The Netherlands, and Great Britain
Finland, Poland, Czechoslovakia, Hungary, Bulgaria,
    Roumania, Union of Soviet Socialist Republics, Mongolia
Near and Middle East and Africa
China, Japan, Korea, Ceylon, Pakistan, Nepal, Sikkim, India,
    Southeast Asia, and the Antipodes
The Americas
General Conclusions

Since the present geographical boundaries of some countries are not identical with their historical development, a certain overlapping in the treatment of relevant material was unavoidable.

Preface

The City Surveys are selective, rather than encyclopedic, presentations of restricted numbers of cities and towns. They should be viewed in their entirety as a mosaic in which each small piece is part of the whole; only all together can they give a complete picture. The periods covered in the City Survey sections and the lengths of description of individual cities differ considerably according to the importance of the historical evolution and to the significance of the relevant data for the *History* in general, apart from the desirability of avoiding repetition where the origin and development of several cities were, in many respects, similar.

The comparative analysis of city planning during the last 100 years, from about 1850 to the present, has been reserved for the concluding volume. During this period, many national characteristics were disappearing. A nondescript uniformity was spreading over the world, with all the disadvantages of standard solutions to the pressing, but not clearly understood, problems of rapidly advancing urbanization. The projects for replanning cities in the second half of the nineteenth century can be summarily dealt with. With hardly any exception, such projects were unimaginative, coinciding with the nadir of city planning in its almost 5000 years of historical evolution.

Certain basic problems, such as the changing ideas of space and scale, are discussed in the first volume only. Reference is made to this discussion in the subsequent volumes, however. The number of footnotes has been kept to a minimum. Complete acknowledgment of references to sources is, in any case, impossible in a work of this kind, nor am I convinced that innumerable footnotes are a proof of scholarly competence.

The bibliographies for each country are fairly comprehensive, although by no means complete. Completeness would have been not only unattainable but also undesirable, especially since many of the books mentioned in the bibliographies contain full lists of works on the general history of the respective countries and on the local history of individual cities.

In a history of city planning, old plans, maps, drawings, and engravings of general and detailed aspects of cities are the most valuable primary sources. The documentation for each volume therefore includes a considerable number of reproductions of this type of material, apart from ground and aerial photographs of historically important views. As far as possible, no city, town, or even village has been described in the text without relevant visual documentation. Where such documentation is missing— and such cases are very rare—it is because difficulties in procuring the material were insuperable. Each volume contains between 400 and 500 illustrations.

The preparation of this *History* has occupied me for several decades, interrupted by work on city planning and building projects.

I am greatly indebted to Dr. Martin A. D. Meyerson, then at the University of Pennsylvania, who played the role of *deus ex machina* when he surprised me on my first visit to the United States in 1955 with the suggestion that I join the faculty of the University of Pennsylvania and produce the *International History of City Development* under the auspices of the Institute for Urban Studies.

An initial grant was made by the Rockefeller Foundation in 1956 on the recommendation of Mr. Edward F. D'Arms, now at the Ford Foundation, to whom must go my most cordial thanks for his interest in the work and his understanding of its importance.

The American Philosophical Society of Philadelphia made several personal grants to me for translations from material contributed by the governments of Poland, Hungary, Bulgaria, and other countries of Eastern Europe and by the Chairman of the Architectural and City Planning Department of the Academy of Sciences of the U.S.S.R., Professor A. V. Bunin.

The Wenner Gren Foundation also made a personal grant in aid of research for the volume on the development of indigenous settlements in Africa, Oceania, and the Americas. I wish to express my thanks to both institutions for their invaluable help in my work.

The Mary Reynolds Babcock Foundation has generously supported the project by two grants to the University of Pennsylvania, which enabled us to accelerate the research and preparation of the volumes for publication. I gratefully acknowledge its help and encouraging interest, without which the *History* could not have been continued on anything like the planned scale and with the intended speed.

I take this welcome opportunity to express appreciation to the governments, government agencies, public and private institutions, and especially the mayors of numerous cities who have supplied comprehensive documentation consisting of local histories, photographs, old plans, maps, and books. Without their ever-ready willingness to respond to my repeated requests and without their assistance, which I hope not to have taxed unduly, the *History* could never have been written.

I owe a special debt, which I am particularly glad to acknowledge, to my colleagues, Professor G. Holmes Perkins, Dean of the Graduate School of Fine Arts, and Dr. William L. C. Wheaton, now at the University of California at Berkeley. I have not merely enjoyed their assistance, but, above all, I have had the benefit of their great administrative experience, which they placed unhesitatingly at the disposal of the work and which piloted it through financial and organizational difficulties. It is not only this assistance but the freedom of research compatible with the highest standards of academic independence that I have valued most sincerely.

I must also record my obligation to Mr. B. H. Jacobson, Librarian of the Fine Arts Library, whose untiring help in unearthing even almost inaccessible material was matched by his marvelous knowledge of the subject and his kindness in translating and extracting from foreign language sources, especially from Dutch books, all the information that I could possibly wish to have.

My thanks go to numerous individual persons and experts who have given valuable assistance in this work. I cannot mention all of these helpers by name, but I wish to express in a general, though no less sincere, manner my great obligation to them, as well as to all those writers without whose contributions to the literature of city development, this *History* could never have been completed.

Finally, I owe more than I can express to my daughter, Gabriele M. E. Gutkind, now our research assistant, for the unflagging patience with which she has sorted out the sometimes chaotic mass of material and has gone over the manuscripts again and again. Her considerable knowledge of the subject and her conscientious persistence in weeding out mistakes and improving the text cannot be valued too highly. Her work deserves public thanks.

The *International History of City Development* has been sponsored by and produced and published under the auspices of the Institute for Urban Studies. But the responsibility for its scope and character, for possible mistakes, and for sometimes very personal opinions is exclusively my own.

At the time of the publication of the first volume, the next two or three volumes will be in the hands of the publishers and the subsequent volumes have been so far advanced with regard to the preparation and drafting of the manuscripts that publication should continue steadily.

E.A.G.

May, 1964
University of Pennsylvania

viii

Acknowledgments

I wish to express my sincerest thanks to all municipal administrations and especially to the mayors of the numerous towns and cities that have been represented in this volume. They have co-operated most readily and supplied documentary material consisting of plans, maps, and photographs. If no other acknowledgment has been made, it may be assumed that my thanks are due to the mayors of the respective towns and cities. In addition, I wish to extend my gratitude to the governments of some of the German Länder, to government agencies, and to semi-official institutions, all of which have assisted generously in the collection of the documentary material.

I owe special thanks to the Hirmer Verlag, Munich, and to the publishing house of Julius Hoffmann, Stuttgart. Both have not only allowed me to make use of their excellent publications, *Deutsche Reichsstädte* by R. Schmidt and *Lebendige Städtebauliche Raumbildung* by W. Rauda respectively, but have also lent some of their original photographs.

Contents

City Survey 233

List of Illustrations

XV

xvi

INTRODUCTION

TO THE *INTERNATIONAL HISTORY OF CITY DEVELOPMENT*

The new mentality is more important even than the new science and the new technology.

A. N. WHITEHEAD

THIS IS THE INTRODUCTION to the whole *International History of City Development*, rather than simply to the first volume.

Does a work of so ambitious and comprehensive a character as this need a particular justification or explanation? I think it does; first of all, because I believe the reader has a right to share in the thoughts that occupied me for many years and which finally prompted me to embark on this enterprise; and second, because the first reaction to the publication of this History is almost certain to be the question: Why do we need an "International History of City Development?"

I

The reasons are many, the less important of which can be given briefly: There is no history that deals with the problems of city development on an international scale, and this gap has to be filled. All we have are individual studies on the structure of settlement of individual countries, written mostly by geographers and often buried in not too well-known periodicals; we also have an incalculable number of local descriptions of cities and towns; a few publications dealing with the historical development of cities in individual countries; numerous and widely scattered articles on one or another feature of urban or rural problems; various articles, reports, and pamphlets on selected periods and aspects of cities; and several incomplete histories of urbanism restricted to Europe, as though the rest of the world did not exist. But none of these quite fills the gap.

However cogent this reason may be, it is of secondary importance only. The need for an "International History of City Development" rests on broader and firmer foundations. A detailed examination of the manifold and interrelated aspects which, combined, make the publication of this History imperative is therefore indispensable; and I also think that an initial discussion of the whole field of inquiry will make it easier for the reader to understand my general approach to the intricate and complex problems of city development.

It is no casual coincidence that during the last decades there have appeared a number of general, comparative histories dealing with particular subjects on an international basis. Histories of science and technology, of art, and of philosophy and culture and general historical surveys have been, or are being, published. The reasons are obvious. The world is shrinking at an unprecedented rate. Countries that only a few decades ago seemed to lie outside the main stream of knowledge are now within easy reach. The understanding is growing that no country exists in isolation and that what happens in one country affects the others. Consequently, our desire to know more about other countries is increasing, and comparisons between one's own country's past and present achievements with the contributions of other parts of the world toward cultural changes are attracting more and more attention. This steadily accelerating trend explains the international character of the recent histories.

Europe, where most of the earlier histories were written, is no longer the "center of the world"—which it was in the imagination of the pretwentieth-century provincial Europeans. The majority of these historians wrote European histories for Europeans. It is difficult to decide whether this parochialism was mere shortsightedness or the result of insufficient knowledge, or whether it came from sheer arrogance, the view that other peoples were inferior and uninteresting beings who lived on the fringes of the civilized world. But since the beginning of the twentieth century, a new and wider appreciation of the interdependence of all countries has been emerging, and with it has come the desire to compare, to understand, and to evaluate the international scene. And as the rigid barriers between countries have been losing their meaning in the political and cultural spheres, so the frontiers of the mind, which had forced scholars into the strait-jacket of an almost exclusively analytical search for knowledge and understanding, have been leveled. This has opened the way toward a synthesis and an integrated appraisal of the past and present.

Analysis and synthesis belong together. They are component parts of the same whole. As Goethe said, "A century which relies only on analysis and seems to be afraid of synthesis is not on the right way, for only both together like breathing-in and breathing-out form the essence of science"—and, we may add, of every scholarly work. This widening-out in space and thought is one of the most hopeful signs of our situation and is an antidote to the dangerous "Cult of the Expert," which retards the development of full man in favor of fractional man. This international trend explains the ever-growing tendency toward a general stocktaking and evaluation in the intellectual field, toward a universal character of historiography, and also toward large-scale studies in different spheres of learning.

Ever since secularization of human existence in the sixteenth century, the powers of unification have been evident, unconsciously at first, but slowly rising to the surface until in our time the veil behind which they were hidden has begun to dissolve and they now emerge in their irresistible strength and appeal. Our generation is witnessing the painful emergence of universal ideas and the unwilling retreat of national idols —still so dear to the eternal laggards and still defended with a narrow stubbornness. All these trends work toward a re-appraisal of the past as the teacher of the present if its lessons are applied wisely. They demand that this reappraisal proceed on a wide front and with a synoptic view that opens new vistas and enables us to understand not only the "What" but the "Why" and the "How" of history. These manifold factors are operative in broadening the approach toward historical problems and consequently toward the composition and writing of international histories.

In the particular field of city development the same prin-ciples are at work. The role of cities in the history of mankind has generally been a constant one, despite the varying fortunes of each in particular. Cities have been standard bearers for most of the decisive changes in thinking and history-making. This is true in spite of the fact that the majority of the world's people were, and are still today, country-dwellers. The in-numerable revolts of those countrypeople against the cities have left hardly more than a passing influence upon the latter. The country-dwellers broke out many times in opposition to unbearable conditions imposed by the cities or feudal lords, but they did not change the basic fabric of city life and mentality.

On the other hand, rural populations were the protagonists of such great migrations as the west–east colonial movement during the early European Middle Ages or the expansion of China from her earliest small nucleus; and in this capacity they were directly or indirectly the founders of many cities that grew up from rural settlements. But once the cities had gained self-confidence and strong footholds, they turned against the countryside, forgetting their early rural affinities and sup-pressing the peasants in their own selfish interests.

About 5000 years have passed since the Urban Revolution and about 180 generations separate us from the origins of the first cities. But neither the purpose nor the structure of cities has changed basically in these five millennia. What have undergone transformation are the complexity of city life and the size of urban communities. When men first cut out a little space from the surrounding land, enclosed it with a wall, and formed a place where they could live without tilling the soil themselves, they gave up their intimate solidarity with nature. A new type of human being was born and with it, from the very beginning, began the antagonism between the country-people and the townspeople. I am aware how problematical it is to speak of a decisive turning point in any sphere of human history. But I do maintain that, in this case, the original conception of a city—a conception that has lasted for 5000 years with only minor modifications—is now approaching its end.

The first cities were small enclosures with small numbers of inhabitants. They were limited in conception and size and reflected on earth man's vision of a limited universe that, like his city, sheltered him. But just as our conception of the universe has changed from the limited geocentric one to the still limited heliocentric ideas of Copernicus, so, over the centuries, the urban scale has widened, and the limitations have disappeared. Now that the universe is conceived of as unbounded yet not infinite, something similar has happened to our cities: Their scale and their size have grown beyond all expectations. They have spread their tentacles over vast dimensions into the open country. They have burst their organic coherence and invaded a no man's land that is neither urban nor rural but a mongrelized anomaly. The old scale has lost its meaning. Our new conception of space now has to reconcile two seemingly diametrical opposites: expansion and restriction, corresponding to our conception of an expanding, unbounded, yet not infinite universe.

Here, perhaps, a short explanation is needed: The world of Copernicus, Galileo, and Newton is today a microcosm—a thousandth part of a light-year in comparison with a thousand million light-years of the universe, as contemporary astronomers conceive it. We can compare our new conception of space to a sphere, the extension of which is without boundaries; yet it is not infinite since it has a definite size conditioned by its radius. We have to attune ourselves to such new conceptions. This does not mean that like children we should try to imitate this picture dangling before our eyes; but we should be aware that our ideas about space have undergone vast changes and that these changes will be reflected in our earthly works, consciously or unconsciously. We are reaching for the moon; we send satellites to orbit around the earth. Can we escape the urge to apply these tremendous transformations in our thinking and acting to our attitude toward our environment, of which cities are not a negligible part? The twilight of cities as mankind has known them for millennia is spreading over all countries, and it is our task, at once inspiring and terrifying, to begin a new chapter in the history of human settlement. This task demands understanding of and insight into the development and destiny of cities; and they cannot be gained without knowledge of what cities have been in the past and of the disintegrating forces in the present. Here we have the most important reason for writing an *International History of City Development*.

1. Erbil in Mesopotamia, on a site that has been permanently inhabited for almost 5000 years.

Now that the decision has been made, it is essential to determine "How" to write such a history. Historiography is one of the disciplines that is now going through a period of violent controversy. Is it a branch of the humanities, or can it claim to be an exact science? The answer I would give to that question is unequivocal: History is a humanistic discipline; therefore, this work has been written accordingly. As Pope said, "The proper study of mankind is Man."

As I see it, historiography's ambition to emulate the exact sciences is not only misdirected but impossible. It expresses an inferiority feeling that has arisen from the fear of "not being up-to-date" and "not being taken seriously" unless a history is a vast compilation of old records, documents, state papers, codices, and statistics—in short, a vast storehouse of so-called "facts." By fostering a pseudoscientific attitude and by reducing everything to such "facts," the human prerogative of revolting against facts is threatened, apart from the fact that a pursuit of useless details is not conducive to a unitary outlook. As Professor Trevor-Roper said in his inaugural lecture, *History Professional and Lay*, at Oxford in 1957:

We may know, or be able to know, what every unimportant official in a government office did every hour of his day, what every peasant paid for his plot in a long extinct village, how every back-bencher voted on a private bill in an eighteenth century parliament. Our libraries may groan beneath volumes on mediaeval chamber administration and bed-chamber administration. But to what end?

What can these facts tell us about the life of a people, about their desires and ambitions, their successes and failures, and their relations to their fellow men? Nothing whatsoever! Factual evidence as such is meaningless. It does not, and cannot, give a clue to the intricate web of crosscurrents, and hardly ever can it tell us how and why these facts have come about. It cannot explain the unpredictable vagaries of human nature, the irrational impulses, and the historical incidents that have all been operative in city building and development. Man is the agent who, with all his inadequacies, with all his complacent credulity, and with all his self-deception, *creates* these seemingly incontestable facts. But in the words of Alexander Pope, Man,

> Plac'd on this isthmus of a middle state,
> A being darkly wise and rudely great;
> With too much knowledge for the Sceptic side,
> With too much weakness for the Stoic's pride,
> He hangs between, in doubt to act or rest;
> In doubt to deem himself a god or beast;
> In doubt his mind or body to prefer;

Born but to die, and reas'ning but to err;
Alike in ignorance, his reason such,
Whether he thinks too little or too much:
Chaos of thought and passion, all confus'd;
Still by himself abus'd or disabus'd;
Creator half to rise and half to fall;
Great lord of all things, yet a prey to all;
Sole judge of truth, in endless error hurl'd;
The glory, jest, and riddle of the World.

Tolstoy, too, was aware of the influence of these imponderables when applied to writing history. So he shows in *War and Peace* when he speaks of the "illogical phenomena . . . of which we see the causation but darkly, and which only seem the more illogical the more earnestly we strive to account for them"; or when he says of Kutuzov that this old man used "quite meaningless words that happened to enter his head . . . [for he had] by experience of life reached the conclusion that thoughts, and words serving their expression, are not what move people."

Can we ever hope to fathom the real motives that move people to build cities, transform them, or let them decay? Only by intense mental effort and imaginative experience can we try to read in the location of a city, in the street pattern, in the circumstances of its foundation, and in numerous other aspects something of the true nature of city life and city development. Artistic short cuts may be more fruitful than compiling the "facts" or reducing the history of city planning to differences among the layouts of streets, to a classification according to site, or to any other single characteristic. For all this is misleading if it is not related and subordinated to the human factor, to the life of the individual in relation to his community, and to his attitude toward his environment at a particular period and in a particular place.

Whether I have succeeded in writing this work in this spirit, I do not know. But I do know that it is neither a textbook nor a technical compendium, neither an economic treatise nor a sort of manual for surveyors. I do not claim that it is a history of the ideas that have been shaping the cities of the past, although I have tried to show the creative power of ideas that have produced different languages of form in different countries. A history of city development, like any other history, is a prophesy in reverse, and like all prophesies it is susceptible to uncertainties and fertile errors out of which a fuller knowledge may grow. But it is sterile to be too afraid of being inexact or wrong, thus losing the enthusiastic urge in the quest for understanding and interpretation.

9

A history of city development must derive its material from more than written documents. It is favorably distinguished from other histories in that it can, in very many cases, rely on visual evidence. The visual documentation now available in the form of aerial and ground photographs, supplemented by old drawings and old maps, provides an almost perfect guide to the subsequent stages of urban development and life. These data, when used carefully in combination with relevant written evidence, are the "facts" on which this work has been based. To discard this visual documentation, as has often been done, as "unreliable" or "easily misleading" because we "cannot trust our eyes" merely proves that those who cling to such out-dated ideas know nothing of the great advances which the interpretation of photographs, especially aerial ones, has made during the last decade. Moreover, is the interpretation of written records *not* liable to mistakes or different explanations? The recent archaeological evidence gained from aerial photographs has often revealed facts no written records could have supplied.

While this work must rely on the spadework of innumerable people who have diligently investigated individual cities, types of settlement structure, and many other relevant factors, the history itself had to be written by one author. Without in the least minimizing the work of the individual researchers and their invaluable and devoted labors, it would be seriously mis-judging the character of this work to believe that it should, or could, have resulted from teamwork, from a number of individual minds each preoccupied with its own rigidly circum-scribed field of research. However valuable such individual studies might have been, neither the danger of bureaucratizing the work as a whole nor the risk of organized irresponsibility could have been avoided. Teamwork is hardly the best way to bring out the continuity or discontinuity of ideas, trends, and changing directions as a thread running through the work as a whole. Nor have the ideas or the vision and the spirit that hold a work together ever been produced by a committee. Only the free mind of an individual, his conscience and enthusiasm, can provide the ideological unity essential in holding together innumerable strands and in demonstrating the unity of man-kind and the fact that only differences of degree and not of principle distinguish peoples—one of the main objectives of this history.

The belief that a work of this kind could be "scientifically objective"—whatever this term may mean—is pathetic. It is, moreover, a confusion of thinking: Certain data can be ob-jectively ascertained—such as years of foundation, location, ex-tension, or destruction of a city—but the interpretation of the fluctuating fortunes, of the small or great changes in the lives of cities, will always differ according to the various outlooks of different authors. Were this not so, the result would be a dull and compromising uniformity and a history without interest. The past should be interpreted with relevance to our own problems, and since this interpretation is obviously open to a considerable variety of judgments, it is essentially each author's personal affair. The personal touch is indispensable to such a work, and the more *engagé* the writer, the more valuable the personal touch—provided it is free of narrowness and political partisanship.

As I have said already, this history is a prophesy in reverse that tries to fathom the deep and irrational fountainheads of humanity. I am fully aware of the risk that such an ambition involves; but whether this effort has been successful or unsuccessful is of only secondary importance in this particular connection. What is important is the realization that the search for the mainsprings of human actions, for the social ideals that alter societies, is not a suitable subject for the compromising mind of a committee or for research workers acting as a team.

The appreciation of city building as an art, not as a technique, is one of the clues to understanding urban life, which itself should be viewed as an artistic activity. A city's physical appearance or its cathedral can tell us more about medieval society than can volumes on its municipal administration or legal privileges. A history of city development is therefore an artistic enterprise and is implicitly a medium through which we can look at the past as a whole. Such an approach to the spirit in which this history should be written is an efficient defense against the fragmentation, so widespread today, that has overtaken history. Unless we have a universal conception of history, history will cease to be universal. In our case this means that unless we have a unifying conception of the history of city development as an integrated whole, the indissoluble interaction of all the manifold trends that have shaped cities in the past will not reveal itself to us. It is this wholeness, this antifragmentary appraisal, that infuses an artistic element into the conception of this history. Wholeness is the essence of art and fragmentation the essence of technology. It is obvious that this artistic wholeness can be achieved not by a group of minds but only by imagination and insight gained in personal isolation.

The questions why and how an *International History of City Development* should be written beg the third question: *What* is to be represented in this work? The answer is that the world is one, and therefore all countries, not only Europe and perhaps America, are included. The difficulties involved were considerable, but they constituted a challenge that had to be faced; otherwise it would have been better to abandon the whole project. There is either total internationality or none; and since this history is international the choice was obvious. The position that, in the past, the world was not one and that certain countries had no connection with each other is untenable: We have to look at history from our own vantage point.

The choice between encyclopedic completeness and representative selection of cities posed another problem. An attempt has been made to strike a sensible balance between these two possibilities. In any case, encyclopedic completeness had to be ruled out. This work is not a glorified gazetteer. On the other hand, the selection of representative cities depends on what is regarded as representative and what criteria are applied. It has to be admitted that the number, as well as the type, of cities selected as representative of different countries varies considerably. Choices, therefore, were influenced by difficulties in collecting material from each country and by the need to keep the work within practicable limits. It is hoped, however, that each country has been represented as far as possible.

A main consideration was to show the perennial transformation through which cities have passed. Consequently, special attention has been given to illustrating the subsequent stages of a city's development by using old maps from different centuries and completing the story by using present-day plans and aerial photographs of the existing conditions; and, in the case of ancient cities and other settlements of which nothing or only parts are still visible, by using archaeological air views. Because development means change, it was essential to investigate and to show the limitations and expansion, the systematic and deliberate growth, and the spontaneous and uncontrolled transformations of cities and their changing relations to the regions of which they were parts. For these factors are all dependent on man's attitude toward his environment and the formative ideas that have modified the physical appearance of cities. These imponderables have been given a prominent place, although it should be added that, to avoid repetition, they have not been dealt with separately in each part. They were frequently similar in different countries and different periods.

The social structure of a city and its economic concomitants determine not only its physical layout and type of buildings but create a particular atmosphere characteristic of that city. It is this social space that, together with the architectural space, expresses more than anything else the character and purpose of an urban community. As far as possible, the interrelation of these factors has been documented and explained in its influence upon layout, streets and houses, size, growth, or stagnation of cities.

Finally, the physical structure of a city—its streets, squares, houses, parks, and gardens, hitherto the only "recognized" subjects of city-planning investigations—has been given considerable space in this work. It is the final result, as it were, the sum total written in stone and mortar of all the other factors already mentioned. To treat it in isolation, as has been done in the past, is superficial and has led to the debasement of city planning, which has, in many cases, become a purely technical and utilitarian activity with a few irrelevant crumbs of criticism of style thrown into the bargain.

These, then, are the main aspects of city development represented in this history.

II

When and why have cities come into existence? Perhaps their original rise is easier to explain than their subsequent development. The first cities arose where and when agriculture was sufficiently advanced to supply food, not alone for the actual producers, but also for those who were not engaged in agriculture. This was the basic prerequisite, for artisans, craftsmen, soldiers, and traders who congregated in cities—often, though by no means always, around the court of a ruler—had to give their time to their professional pursuits; and even if they owned fields outside the city or gardens within it, they produced hardly more than a welcome portion of the food they needed in addition to the supply from full-time farmers. This interdependence of city and surrounding country had far-reaching consequences, which will be dealt with at length in the following volumes. Here it is pertinent to mention merely some of the reasons that have induced men to create within the vast expanse of cultivated or even uncultivated lands an enclave where they took up their abode for short or longer periods of time and where generations after generations were born, died, worked and begot children, and became the protagonists of ideas and the disseminators of material goods.

The intimate relationship between city and country was the original beginning of regionalism. This aspect of city development has played hardly any role in the existing works on city planning. It is a mistake to assume that this interdependence has been weakened in the course of time and has now almost completely disappeared. Yet this notion has, at certain times, found a wide acceptance. Apparently it arose from mistakenly identifying the antagonism between city and country with disengagement from one another. Antagonistic interests and attitudes do not necessarily lead to mutual independence; certainly they have not done so in this case. The decisive question is: Can city and country live without each other? Needless to say, they cannot; today they cannot even *try* to do so since agriculture is becoming more and more a branch of chemistry and technology and is losing the romantic appeal of previous centuries. The mentality of farmers all over the world is changing. The spirit of the cities penetrates the land; and farmers of all lands are on the move, more than ever aware of their indispensability to the life of the nations.

These considerations are offered because there is still considerable reluctance to admit the inevitable consequences of these developments. In previous centuries, men were more openminded in this respect. The cities had no inhibitions against acquiring "their" hinterlands either by force or by legal means. City and surrounding country formed one unit. When communications improved and the scale of action widened, this urban "ownership" of the hinterland came to an end, for food could be supplied from more distant regions. Today, this possibility is self-evident. The bonds between city and the neighboring country have not been broken, a fact that has not yet found its practical expression in planning a city and region as one coherent whole. The notion of regionalism is still anathema to many governments and even to professionals who should know better; but being "city planners," they obviously cannot look beyond the chaotic fringes of their cities.

The Urban Revolution, which began 5000 years ago, has been perennially shaping and reshaping the face of the earth. It has united city and country into an antagonistic whole from which neither can escape at free will. This unity, this mutual dependence, was one of the most powerful forces making the emergence of cities possible, although not the only one. Out of this unity developed the *polis* and the city-states of Greece, the Roman cities as nodal points of the imperial administration, the cities and towns of the Middle Ages with their often cruel suppression of the countrypeople, the cities of China as seats of the emperor's representatives, the cities of Japan with their tremendous attraction for the peasants, and many other urban settlements of the past. All had in common the inescapable dependence on the surrounding countryside, which they dominated and regarded as their particular sphere of influence. All were small compared with the present-day megalopolis. All were more or less self-contained entities and, together with their hinterlands, self-sufficing food producers and food consumers. And all were the fountain springs of ideas and ever-renewed social and economic changes.

Why did men come to the cities? Many factors have been operative, not only in generating the first impulse to create an urban space, but in maintaining the magnetic power that makes men captives of the urban way of life. When men moved to the new urban environment, it was in flight from insecurity and isolation, from the spiritual dangers of Nature, from her demons and her unforeseeable powers. This new environment opened the floodgates of man's creative mind to the adventures of art and philosophy, of civic life and technical progress. We may broadly distinguish two trends—one general, the other composed of a number of intimately related functional needs and activities—that in varying degrees have attracted men to city life.

The first is most evidently expressed in the gregarious instinct that lures man away from the isolation and dullness of the country, an instinct strengthened by the need for political organization and the desire for an active participation in (or at least a greater nearness to) communal activities. The urge that makes the countryman restless and causes him to long for freedom and a better life, that induces him to abandon his rural surroundings, is almost as strong as the pull that life in cities exerts on the inarticulate feelings of those for whom the country ceases to be the whole world. These motives, alive in the conscious and subconscious sphere and working from two different poles, could become operative only when agriculture had reached a stage of development where it was able to support a sufficient number of people engaged in pursuits other than agriculture and who could supply certain of the countrypeople's needs.

The second trend consists of a group of motivations, including a variety of causes that range from communal to individual activities and aspirations. These motivations may be grouped as follows:

1. Protection against weather and men (oasis towns and fortified places).
2. Worship (temple and cathedral cities).
3. Kingship (residence and castle towns).
4. Politics (administrative centers).
5. Industry (industrial and craftsmen's towns).
6. Trade (trading and road centers).
7. Expansion (colonial and satellite towns).

15

16

3. The town of Shibam in the Hadhramaut.

2. *Opposite:* Aerial view of the oasis town of Ghardaia in Algeria.

18

4. *Opposite:* The cathedral city of Mainz.

5. Regensburg. Detail of a woodcut by Michael Ostendorfer, 1558.

These causes for the rise of cities have remained valid throughout history and are still at work in some parts of the world today. What has changed in the course of millennia is the language of form in which these various motivations are expressed, a change resulting from the transformation of social and religious ideas, from widening conceptions of space and scale, from improved technical skills, and from the growing complexity of individual and communal needs. But it should be emphasized that none of these trends worked in isolation; all, together, formed an intricate web of forces that made cities in all lands and at all times the exponents of a revolutionary spirit and the standard bearers for art and architecture.

III

In the last book of the *Metamorphoses,* Ovid puts into the mouth of Pythagoras the wonderful words that express his anxiety to make his fellow men aware of the permanence of change. We, the heirs of innumerable generations and the progenitors of innumerable future generations, should always keep these words in mind when we try to understand the involved ways of history and, in this particular case, the development of cities.

Nothing is constant in the whole world. Everything is in a state of flux, and comes into being as a transient appearance. Time itself flows on with constant motion, just like a river: for no more than a river can the fleeting hour stand still. As wave is driven on by wave, and, itself pursued, pursues the one before, so the moments of time at once flee and follow, and are ever new. . . . Nothing in the entire universe ever perishes, believe me, but the things vary, and adopt a new form. . . . Though this thing may pass into that, and that into this, yet the sum of things remains unchanged. For my part, considering how the generations of men have passed from the age of gold to that of iron, how often the fortunes of different places have been reversed, I should believe that nothing lasts long under the same form. . . . Troy was great in wealth and men . . . Sparta too was famous once; once the great city of Mycenae flourished. . . . Now Sparta is a tract of worthless land, lofty Mycenae has fallen, what but a name is Oedipus' city Thebes? What remains of Pandion's Athens but a name? Even to-day, rumor has it that a Trojan city, Rome, is rising close to the river Tiber, that flows down from the Apennines, rising to support a vast structure. This city, too, alters her form as she grows, and will one day be the capital of the wide world.[1]

In this never-ending, changing transformation, man is the creative agent whose relation to the group and the environment determines the trend and character of the perennial revolution

1. Translation by M. M. Innes. Penguin Classics. 1955.

through which the cities have been passing. It is from this interaction that the best criteria for the evaluation of city development can be derived. The relationship between the individual and the group has been, and still is a formative factor of the first order in the changing pattern of urban development. City life had a weakening effect on the biological group, on the narrow and the extended family, and on the clan. It created a new set of values that furthered elective affinities and resulted in new groups of common interest held together by religious, social, and professional attachments. As in almost all spheres, the scale within which even this most personal affiliation had to live, has widened. Balzac concludes his story, "Abbé Birotteau," with words meaningful for all times:

The circle within which men act out their lives has insensibly grown larger. The mind which can embrace and synthesize it will never be anything but a magnificent exception; for, ordinarily, in the mental sphere as in the physical, an impulse loses in intensity what it gains in range. Society cannot base itself upon exceptions. Once, a man was simply and solely a father, and his affections were warm and active, concentrated in the circle of his family. Later, he lived for a clan, or a small republic; and from that relation sprang the great historical acts of devotion of Greece and Rome. Then, he was the man of a caste or a religion, in the service of whose greatness he often showed himself to be sublime; but there the range of his interests was extended by all the intellectual fields. To-day his life is bound up with that of a vast stretch of country; soon his family will embrace, so they say, the entire world. But is this conception of the cosmopolitanism of the soul, the hope of Christian Rome, not a sublime mistake? It is so natural to believe in the realization of a noble chimera, in the brotherhood of men. But alas! the human machine is not made on such a divine scale. Souls great enough to embrace a noble sentiment which only the great can feel will never be those of simple citizens or family men.

But the family was not completely displaced by these new values; it lost its unique place as the sole cause of group activity. Henceforth the small family units were absorbed into the larger units of classes, fraternities, religious communities, and guilds—the principal forces of the cities' transformation in fact and in spirit. These units were instrumental in the formation of that union of the individual and the general will from which a group consciousness evolves. As Sir Herbert Read says about architecture in *The Grass Roots of Art* (and his observations are, of course, also valid for the sister art of city building) :

The greatness of great architecture is not to be explained by national greatness: its secret is not to be found in race, not in blood, not in soil, not even in religion, but in a certain social structure animated by a spirit which may be religious or may be practical but which essentially owes its efficacy to its integrity—its wholeness and smallness, its all-over-ness and intimacy. The generation of enthusiasm is the necessary postulate; but the means come from relatively simple factors, which, because they are simple, have generally been overlooked—from mutual aid, from the social cohesiveness of small groups, from unity of sentiment and unity of aim. . . . Whatever the positive connection between the form of social organization and the quality of architecture, it is certain that in the negative direction the loss of social unity always involves a stylistic decadence. . . . The group is more powerful than the individual, not only in the physical sense, but in spiritual potentiality. It has this power only in virtue of achieving group-consciousness, which is not the same thing as consciousness-of-being-a-group. When a psychological unity of consciousness is achieved by a group, then that group has reached the highest evolutionary level, and its artists are inspired to works of art which are an expression of its vital achievements.

Biological groups have been, in numerous cases, the originators of small rural settlements, especially in early times and under primitive conditions; nevertheless, clans and tribes whose consanguineous bonds embraced less homogeneous groups were frequently the agents of rural and even urban developments, as in Mohammedan countries, for instance. Even the early *synoikism* of the Greeks had a strong biological component which did not prevent the rise of the *polis* but actually furthered it. Until recently, Chinese villages were biologically more or less homogeneous, and the same holds true for indigenous villages of Africa. But what should be clearly understood is that the more cities grew in complexity and size and the more their self-confidence increased, the more the biological family had to give way to groups based on elective affinities as the formative agents of city life. As these groups superseded the family, the state superseded the city, and the early identification of city and state as we know it from Antiquity disappeared.

The spatial development of the cities of early Antiquity in relation to the surrounding country and the territory of the state culminated in such enormous city enclaves surrounded by mighty walls as Babylon, into which, as it were, the state contracted and for which the open country was merely a sort of glacis to be evacuated in times of war; state and city were identical. A similar process took place in China, India, and other countries. The Greek *polis* is the classic example of the identity of city and state: The open country was merely an extension of the city for which it produced men and food. Rome is the high point of this identification of city and state: Taking

6. The village of Bari in the Sudan. The relationship between man and man and between man and nature is intimate and direct. It is a reciprocal "I-Thou" relationship.

the whole Roman world as one entity, the provincial cities were almost like distant suburbia of Rome, and the open country stretching between them was virtually nonexistent as an independent factor.

The representative of the early European Middle Ages was the peasant; only in the course of the general development did the burgher appear. The cities and towns forced the surrounding countryside into political and economic dependence. Innumerable autarchic, dwarf, economic units developed, but they lasted only as long as the state remained relatively weak. As soon as the state grew in strength, in administrative coherence, and in efficiency, the narrow domain of municipal self-sufficiency dissolved. The state spread its influence over these innumerable cells, accelerating this process by taking over such functions previously fulfilled by the cities as defense and certain industrial activities. Then the time came when the bonds

23

between towns and their immediate hinterlands grew more lax and the centralizing tendencies of the state gradually replaced the equal status of numerous towns by a kind of hierarchy and specialization. The importance of widely dispersed fortress towns decreased until finally they lost their significance when the fortified frontier became the state's first line of defense.

Cities are primarily social products. Economic considerations are secondary. Social—that is, human—forces are the dominant elements. In all periods, whatever the social coherence of the different strata has been, the structure of society is like a pyramid. One personality, or a small group of personalities, is always at the apex of this pyramid—often in a purely imaginary sense. This personality was always more or less believed to dominate the mass of individual beings who make up the social pyramid, although in fact it was quite ineffective. Here I have to add a warning. These so-called leaders are not necessarily the men who make history. On the contrary, as Tolstoy says in *War and Peace,* the higher such a man "stands on the social ladder, the more numerous the fellow-beings whom he can influence, the more absolute his power, the more clearly do we perceive [that] those who are known as great men are really name-labels in history; they give their names to events, often without having so much connection with the facts as a label has." Nor should we necessarily subscribe to fatalism and predestination or cyclical movements in history. These men standing at the apex of the social pyramid were ordinary human beings not independent of the vagaries of historical evolution, although we have to accept the fact that they are regarded as symbols of supreme power by their societies. If this pyramid is destroyed by force, by war, by revolution, or simply by natural events, or if it falls to pieces by its own weakness or insufficient evolutionary efforts, it always reverts to its original pyramid form. The social pyramid has remained constant throughout history, and this fact should, with all reservations, be kept in mind when examining the development of cities.

I believe that no better commentary on these facts could be added than the text of a letter buried in the grounds of the New York World's Fair in 1939, which Albert Einstein addressed to the peoples of the year 6939—that is, 5000 years hence:

Our time is rich in inventive minds, the inventions of which could facilitate our lives considerably. We are crossing the seas by power and use power also to relieve humanity from all tiring muscular work. We have learned to fly, and we are able to send messages and news without any difficulty over the entire world through electric waves. However, the production and distribution of commodities is entirely unorganised so that everybody must live in fear of being eliminated from the economic cycle in this way suffering from the want of everything. Furthermore, people living in different countries kill each other at irregular intervals so that also for this reason anyone who thinks about the future must live in fear and terror. This is due to the fact that the intelligence and character of the masses are incomparably lower than the intelligence and character of the few who produce something valuable for the community. I trust that posterity will read these statements with a feeling of proud and justified superiority.

IV

As man's attitude toward the group, the community, and the society of which he is a member has been changing throughout known history, so his reaction to his environment has passed through successive stages of transformation. Cities have played an important role in this process, which consists of a never-ending dialogue between challenge and response and which derives its strength and continuity from elementary thoughts of mankind—religion, exchange of ideas and goods, and need for protection and gregarious living. For millennia human efforts have been directed, as far as cities are concerned, toward the same goal. Always and everywhere the basic elements of cities have been the same—dwelling houses, public buildings, the space between them. But the form and its meaning have changed, for both express the spiritual and intellectual conception of the universe that men have made for themselves.

The fight sways between magical union with nature and the urge toward a detached interpretation and rational use of it. Magical trends, more or less deeply embedded in and dependent on natural phenomena, have been present in all those epochs when the universe was limited and men were aware of their insignificant role in the general order of things. This magical identification with environment and the cosmic order is evident in the indigenous settlements of Africa and the South Seas, in Mesopotamia, in the *polis,* in Rome, in medieval towns, and even in the cities of the Enlightenment. This bond has created an integrated and systematic order that we do not yet fully understand. The growing independence and clarification of mind, on the other hand, make man believe that he is free and that in freedom he can conquer the universe and adapt it to his own needs. Up to the present this freedom has produced a great disorder because the idea of the unbounded but limited universe, conceivable speculatively but not visually, is still too new, still too great for man to confront it systematically with his own works. What we are witnessing today, in its most outspoken form, is the violent clash between

7. Mining town in the Pas-de-Calais, France—the "I-It" relationship at its worst.

the sense of reality and the sense of possibility. But what is real and what is possible?

This is the fatal query that mankind has always addressed to the universe and the earthly environment—and one to which a different answer has always been given. And its ever-changing answer has shaped the different forms of human creation. To fathom this oscillation of ideas, this insubstantial power behind man's past and present work is no easy task. It necessitates an approach that is not to the liking of eternal realists, for whom ideas are thin air, "such stuff as dreams are made on." But ideas are more potent forces than material achievements. We may quote in this connection Alfred North Whitehead, who says in his *Adventure of Ideas:*

In each age of the world distinguished by high activity there will be found at its culmination some profound cosmological outlook, implicitly accepted, impressing its own type upon current springs of action. This ultimate cosmology is only partly expressed, and the details of such expression issue into derivative specialized questions of secondary generality which conceal a general agreement upon first principles almost too obvious to need expression, and almost too general to be capable of expression. In each period there is a general form of the forms of thought; and, like the air we breathe, such a form is translucent, and so pervading, and so seemingly necessary, that only by extreme effort can we become aware of it.

These "first principles" are what we must try to understand, to formulate, and to apply to the development of cities if this history is to be more than a collection of so-called "facts."

The underlying trends of this development form an indivisible unity in space and time, provided we apply the right yardstick—that is, a long-term and large-scale evaluation.[2] Then chains of transformation become visible, and something like an organic and integrated process of development emerges from the ever-renewed adaptation of the environment to human needs and of man to his environment.

In broad outlines three principal chains of transformation can be distinguished. The most general is the change in the interaction of man and environment from an "I-Thou" to an "I-It" relationship. The second chain is more explicit in character; it shows man's reactions to his environment in successive stages, ranging from fear and defense to confidence and aggressiveness and, finally, to growing understanding and responsibility. These reactions are always guided by the two complementary forces of instinct and reason, and they result in man's conscious or unconscious control of his efforts toward systematization. The third chain represents the widening scale and the changing experience of space, the latter intimately related to the notion of the universe.

These three chains of transformation illustrate, together and each in its own right, the fulfillment of the basic human needs for shelter, food, work, and social intercourse. Consequently, the significance of each chain should be evaluated in relation to these four basic needs. The three principal chains of transformation and the four basic needs of human nature form an indissoluble whole; and, since human nature is everywhere fundamentally the same, they produce in similar conditions similar results, although for an inexperienced eye they may seem to differ considerably.

There are, of course, still other ways of systematizing the transformation through which the interaction of man and nature has passed and is likely to pass in the future. But as we shall see, those just suggested are the most comprehensive and the most formative of relations between the two contestants.

2. The remainder of this section is based on my Introductory Paper to the International Symposium on Man's Role in Changing the Face of the Earth. Published by the University of Chicago Press as part of a book with the same title.

1. The transformation from an "I-Thou" to an "I-It" relationship is evident in the changing interdependence of man and nature and of individual and group. These two aspects belong together, and the results of this unity and of this change can still be seen today. The layout of tribal villages and old towns in Europe and Asia, the ancestral graves interspersed between the settlements of the living generation in China, the pyramids and temples in Egypt, Mexico, and the Far East, the rival symbols of church and castle dominating the skyline of medieval towns all bear witness to the intimate and direct "I-Thou" relationship between man and nature and man and man. When this relationship became indirect and estranged, when it turned into an "I-It" relationship, disintegrating the symbolic and magical bonds between man and environment and upsetting the oneness of man's functional and personal life, the growing abstractness and the ensuing disunity produced the amorphous character of all modern towns and villages and a harsh and purely utilitarian attitude toward nature.

As long as man was deeply embedded in nature and every natural phenomenon had a symbolic significance, the man-environment relationship was more a mutual adaptation than a one-sided conquest of nature by man. The replacement of natural features was more a modification as defense against external dangers than a deliberate attempt at dominating nature in a spirit of aggressiveness. If nature threatened to get out of hand, magic was expected to help. It was an "I-Thou" relationship, with all the ups and downs inherent in even the closest association. It was also a total relationship, in which man was dependent on the universal character of the environment, being himself an integral part of nature and dimly aware that there was nothing that could not influence in one way or another his own existence and attitude to the surrounding world. Ever since the Scientific Revolution, nature has been depersonalized, and the awareness of the total relationship between man and nature has been fading.

During the first 3000 years of recorded history, man remained deeply embedded in his natural environment. Nature and man, human and cosmic events, were merged into one, and man's experience was immediate and personal. The symbolic significance of events and phenomena was equated with actual reality. This equation produced a particular concept of causality and of space and time that established between man and the phenomenal world an intimate and reciprocal dependence. The external world was a great "'Thou" to early man. He did not search for impersonal laws behind the goings-on of the universe. Consequently, his approach was not analytical.

Today, the world of primitive man is still a living reality and still immersed in magic and animism. It is a world that has no development as we understand it; for change means a break in the established and reciprocal relationship between man and environment and would destroy the unity between him and the natural phenomena. In his world, two spheres, the macrocosm and the microcosm, pervade each other. His effort is directed toward a fusion of the two by means of magical contacts that make the universal and the social space coalesce.

Ancient Greek thought was also permeated by an experience of nature that, as Professor Butterfield has expressed it somewhat controversially in *The Origins of Modern Science*, "has the door half-way open to spirits." In spite of the fact that man's interpretation of the universe had shifted from unquestioning belief to the search for truth, the Greek relationship to nature remained tinged with the conviction that it was an eminently personal world in which one had to find his way. The great "Thou" still lingered on despite the brilliant unfolding of individualistic thought and reason. The legacy of the past was still too strong for the Greeks; they had not completely shaken off the fetters of mythical limitations. Macrocosm and microcosm were firmly interwoven, and man symbolized the general in his individual being. Greek symbolism was very concrete, very direct; it came to life in visible form, not through complicated analogies. Thus the classical and even the Hellenistic *polis* became the symbolic expression of the ideal structure of society, the only correct form of its synthesis with the supermathematical cosmic order. The *polis* was limited in size and character, and its scale was fixed by human standards. Thus, life had not become abstract, and the relations of men to their town remained concrete.

Somewhat the same thing applies to the towns of old China. The walls, the most sacred part of the town, were erected first. The town was conceived as a whole from the very beginning, and the space created by the enclosing walls was only gradually filled with houses and official buildings. Although quite a number of Chinese towns extend over a large area and their streets and houses seem to form an inextricable mess, they are yet systematic and attuned to the human scale. Life was not deprived of its immediate and personal character. Magical considerations played an important part: The layout of a town was not only based on practical conditions, it was dependent on geomantic rules—part of the magical ideas that have dominated Chinese thinking from early times. If we look from the air at a Chinese town that has retained its old character, we

8. Aigues-Mortes, Gard, France, an example of the narrow-wide world of the medieval burgess.

see the sharp line of the walls enclosing a seemingly chaotic agglomeration of houses in their protecting embrace. The direct and intimate relation between man and nature is still at work.

The burgher of the medieval town was direct successor to the citizen of the *polis:* The narrow living space of his town was the center where his whole life converged, his spiritual and practical activities being confined to this limited sphere. Family, guilds, religious orders, and confraternities enfolded him. The town was a community, a union in the sense of brotherhood.

Christianity tended to break up the magical bonds and links of taboo that formed the basis of blood relationship in China, India, Japan, and Islamic countries. Elective affinities assumed equal rights with consanguineous relationships. The voluntary association gave a new security and created essential preconditions from which an urban community could grow.

Religion was the great "uniter" of medieval life; it guided men into the spirit of genuine communities and made life direct and personal. Work and family life were one, and they proceeded under the same roof. Natural man-made environments retained their intimate character, and man still felt that he, like the earth, was the center of the universe. Nature was on a par with man. In the words that Pico della Mirandola puts into the mouth of the Creator when he is speaking to Adam: "In the middle of the world have I placed thee that thou mayst the more easily look about thee and see all that is therein contained."

After the Scientific Revolution, man's awareness of his total relationship with nature began to fade. Life gradually became more abstract, and the relations between men lost their personal directness. Religious man receded into the shadows of the past, and economic man appeared on the horizon. Group consciousness weakened; the interaction of general and individual will melted away until, in the Baroque period, only a small minority was supreme, the majority having been leveled down to an inarticulate mass of obedient subjects of the rising state. The strong social and religious bonds that had enveloped and held the small communities together, that had created a union of individual spontaneity and communal spirit, were broken, and the way was open to the social disintegration of the present. The new order had a far-reaching effect on the relationship between the places in which men lived, worked, and traded. Family life and business life fell apart. Work became the center

9. View of Venice, showing compactness, close proximity, and open space for social intercourse.

around which everything else rotated, until it swallowed up the whole of man's thinking and feeling and dictated the cycle of his daily life—until fragmented man, the finished and dangerous product of our time, resulted.

This growing disintegration can be seen in the loss of homogeneity of urban and rural settings and in the unrelated attempts to exploit the natural resources. The new "I-It" relationship between man and nature has destroyed the continuity of the intimate and personal contact between man and environment—and also the unity of thought linking everyday events and the immediate environment to the order of the universe. Only about ten generations separate us from the beginning of the Scientific Revolution, but this short period has created conditions of life that challenge the very essence of our existence. We face the disruptive impact of an "I-It" relationship that extends not only to things but also to persons.

2. The second chain of transformation consists of four stages in man's changing attitude to his environment, all of which can be observed today, sometimes in close proximity

10. Disintegration and ugliness.

to one another. The first stage is one of fear and longing for security—fear of nature's unpredictable and unknown forces and longing for protection against these forces and the hostility of men. Particularly under primitive conditions, this results in careless displacement of the natural features of the land, which often leads to collective work and is accompanied by the gradual formation of integrated groups. Man feels himself a part of nature, and cosmic and earthly events are for him inextricably interwoven. His orientations in space and time are concrete, not abstract, concepts. He solves his practical problems in an empirical manner, and his attitude to the external world of things and men is permeated by an "I-Thou" relationship full of symbolic and personal meaning. All this is evident in the works of early and primitive man, to be observed today in the windscreen settlements of the Bushmen, in the pile dwellings of the South Seas and other parts of the world, in the careless displacement of the natural conditions for shifting agriculture, in the *kraals* of the Bantu Negroes, in the *zadrugas* of Old Bulgaria, and in many other institutions and works.

The second stage is one of growing self-confidence and increasing observation, leading to a more rational adaptation of the environment to differentiated needs. Elementary protection develops into purposeful reshaping of the environment, and displacement of nature is followed by replacement. The objectives are complex and interrelated; they widen in scope and character. Man accepts the challenge of nature in the guise of disciple and reformer; the "I-Thou" relationship persists, although man fashions it in a different way. This relationship remolds the interrelationship of individual and group and the appreciation of the cosmic and earthly phenomena correspondingly. During this stage all activities bear the same mark of immediacy and reciprocal adjustment, manifest in such works as rice terraces and fields in China, the geomantic adaptation of Chinese towns to environmental conditions, the regulations of the rivers and irrigation of the fields, and in the social and religious significance of the layout of Indian, African, and other towns, to mention only a few of the innumerable examples.

The third stage, which has led to our present situation, is one of aggressiveness and conquest. Adjustment to the environment develops into exploitation. The objectives are unlimited; they grow in diversity but also in disunity. With the ruthlessness of a pioneer, man expands his living space, and, with a complete disregard for the danger of a primarily quantitative expansion, he deludes himself into the role of an omnipotent remaker of his environment. Neglect and exploitation of the natural resources, rural isolation, and urban expansion have produced an unexampled disunity of the social and economic structure. The physical expression of this third stage is evident in practically all of modern man's works. Man failed to see, to use once more Pope's wonderful words, that

> All are but parts of one stupendous whole . . .
> All nature is but art unknown to thee;
> All chance direction, which thou canst not see;
> All discord harmony not understood;
> All partial evil universal good:
> And spite of pride, in erring reason's spite,
> One truth is clear, whatever is is right.

This third phase of aggressive ignorance is drawing to a close, and the fourth stage in the interaction of man and environment is slowly taking shape. Faintly the outlines of this new epoch are discernible. It will be an age of responsibility and unification. Expansive ruthlessness is gradually merging into a careful adjustment to environmental conditions and new possibilities. Man is beginning to be aware of his real responsibility and of the limitations that the closing frontiers of the world impose upon him. His objectives are gaining precision, foresight, and coordination. Unity in diversity and unification are emerging as the main tasks in the next stage of development, in which man must act as a coordinator guided by social awareness and insight into the workings of nature.

3. The third chain of transformation represents man's changing experience of space in relation to the conception of the universe and the widening scale of human activities. Through the whole of known history the ideas of space that man accorded to the universe reflected his changing attitude toward the environment and vice versa. And with different ideas the scale widened; large and comprehensive operations replaced small and isolated activities.

a. During the first phase, man was the center of life on earth, as the earth was center of the universe, conceived of as finite and consisting of concentric spheres. This is Aristotle's system, which dominated man's thought for 2000 years. Similar conceptions, though slightly modified, developed in other parts of the world. While this conception lasted, all of man's activities were undertaken in relation to it: they aimed at stability and were limited in scope and character. Nature was experienced as a multitude of concrete orientations, and, therefore, a concrete bodylike property was the essential quality of all human works. As far as these conceptions still exist, this conformity between the conception of universal space and man's earthly

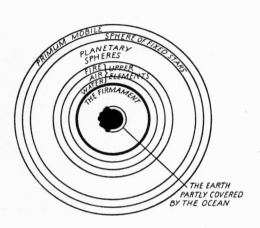

11. The Aristotelian universe.

works is unmistakable. This identity does not result from a deliberate and conscious adaptation of the environment to the ideas of universal space—such a notion would belong to the dream world of retrospective fabrications—but, rather, expresses the latent spiritual forces which unite all man's thoughts and works in one great scheme. Whitehead, whose words we repeat in this connection, said that this expression is the "profound cosmological outlook, implicitly accepted, impressing its own type upon the current springs of action." The fortified walls erected to protect and enclose the great empires of the Incas, the Romans, and the Chinese are outstanding examples of this spirit. The towns within these empires are built from outside in, as are also those of the European Middle Ages (though with some modifications) and some in other parts of the world. Such towns are conceived of as limited units for a self-contained and stable life.

b. The heliocentric universe of Copernicus was still finite, since it terminated in the sphere of the fixed stars; but instead of the earth, the sun was the center. A new feeling of space developed, the relegation of the earth to a secondary role in the universal system engendering tensions that made the ancient conception of the universe meaningless. With the earth, man was moved to the periphery. Slowly but irresistibly his whole outlook changed. He and his earth lost their central position, and he was forced into accepting a totally different view—a

12. The Copernican universe.

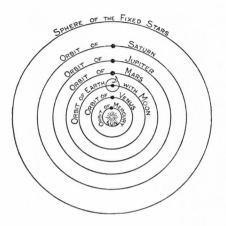

13. The Great Wall of China.

14. **The military engineer takes over—elaborate fortifications at Naarden near Amsterdam.**

15. *Opposite:* **The grand perspective view at Karlsruhe, Baden, Germany.**

view from the periphery toward a new center, the sun. A wider and more dynamic outlook resulted. The compact empires of the first period were superseded by scattered possessions and an outburst of expansion set in. The towns of Europe began to expand; simple walls were replaced by complicated fortifications for defense against long-range firearms. The perspective view was introduced as an element of town planning, and the external appearance of the houses gained in importance. The extrovert dwelling place became the general rule, and a new feeling of space and spaciousness began to be expressed in all of man's works. Of this period we still have numerous examples that bear witness to the tremendous tensions arising from this new attitude toward life and from thinking and planning on a larger scale.

c. The third phase led eventually to our conception of space that, like the universe, is unbounded and yet not infinite. Like the sphere mentioned earlier, the size of the universe depends on its average curvature. The first rudiments of this modern cosmology can be traced back to the Renaissance. Giordano Bruno was first to assert that the universe is infinite and without a creator—for an infinite universe cannot be created from outside. After the beginning of the seventeenth century, the evolution of the feeling of space became more or less identical with a quest for expansion, with the breaking down of limitations, and with the belief in a progress that is almost automatic. Today we are face to face with the confused results of this mode of thinking. We have reached the limits of expansion. The earth is fully known. Protective frontiers and walls are now recognized only as historical incidents and as useless demonstrations. Our towns are shapeless and flow over into the country.

At present we are in a particularly dangerous, but also particularly formative, period of transformation. The old ideas of space are still strong, and the new conceptions have not yet found a concrete expression. This confused state of mind is visible in all parts of the world. The illusion of infinite spread and the conviction that individual and unrelated actions will produce a coherent whole are fading away. So far, the new feeling of space seems merely to be a cult of bigness. Its true implications still await their expression in a language of form that grows out of the deep layers of human creativeness.

d. The widening scale of man's transformations suffers from the same facile deception that bigness is identical with large enterprises. The situation is much more complex and will not be solved by the immature and blind boosters of quantity or by adherence to the dogma that quantity turns into quality if and when the quantitative increase of change has reached an overwhelming scale.

Moreover, scale, like many other notions, is relative. When we fly from England to Japan, the gradual change of scale is perhaps the most striking impression. Scale is small in the British Isles, increases over Europe, grows to large dimensions over Russia, only to decrease again over Japan. This is not exclusively the result of geographical factors, although these play a not entirely negligible role. It is more the outcome of the inhabitants' changing attitude toward their respective environments. However, the varying scale is manifest in many things that are far removed from the direct and physical influence of the environment. Here are a few examples. For the western European, a garden is a collection of beautiful flowers and plants arranged as pleasingly as possible—or rigidly as are the ornamental gardens of Spain or France, or with modest variety as are the peasant gardens of Austria and Switzerland. But for the Japanese, the garden is a microcosm consciously created out of nature's overwhelming diversity as a "concentrated" nature within a limited space. The houses differ too: Broadly speaking, they are small in England, generally larger in Europe and Russia, but distinctly smaller in Japan. This applies of course only to the indigenous and old buildings, not to the Europeanized monstrosities dotted over the whole route.

What, then, is the correct assessment of scale and its gradually widening character? The answer can be given succinctly. Today we must reconcile two diametrically opposite aspects: the infinitely large and the infinitely small. This means, therefore, not merely an extension in space, but also a limitation. The new scale does more than express a transformed environment as such. It is an intellectual adventure into the totality of phenomena and conditions that surround us. As a matter of fact, this has always been so. It is evident in a Zulu *kraal*, every part of which is within easy walking distance and which can be taken in as a whole at a glance. We also see it in the small fields of Europe; in the small and compact settlements in oases; in hilltop towns of Italy, Spain, and Switzerland; in medieval towns of Europe; and even in the large cities of old China.

City development is therefore to be interpreted not as an assessment of formalistic irrelevancies but as a chain of transformations in all spheres of the life of cities. That one can merely add together details, though they may accrue to a seemingly coherent whole, is an erroneous proposition. The proper study of cities should relate the organic—or for that matter the unsystematic—growth of a city in all its innumerable aspects to the language of form characteristic of a given period and a given place. This identity of time and space permeates everything. The awareness of this fact in historical studies of cities is an unerring guide that binds everything together, including the past and the future. Everything has both a cause and a consequence that reach backward or project forward. The continuity stretching backward and forward over wide spaces and long periods is beyond mere historical data, beyond subjective "taste"; it comes near objectivity.

It is thus essential to view causality from two different aspects. To modern man it means that general laws are at work in the phenomenal world. To primitive man, and to a certain extent ancient man, it means peculiar and individual events; he does not ask how this or that event has happened but who has brought it about—an eminently personal view based on actually experiencing the event. Space also has to be looked at from two different aspects. Modern man is able to conceive of it as a system of abstract relations, but primitive and ancient men have to experience it by concrete orientations dependent on localities that arouse a direct emotional participation. Consequently, our approach to the settlements and cities of primitive and ancient men must differ from our approach to those of modern man. In the former case, cities, like all other works, are manifestations of the interdependence of earthly and celestial order and of a society deeply embedded in nature. Such cities belong to the era of the "I-Thou."

This protecting shell of immediacy and concrete orientation was broken by the Ionian philosophers, although the audacity of their thoughts had no immediate results and had still to wait for many centuries before men were ready to accept and to emulate them. The Ionian philosophers assumed that the universe was intelligible as a whole and that a lasting and simple principle pervaded the *modus operandi* of the whole world. But they were not yet entirely free from the fetters that bound them to a nature still inhabited and moved by anthropomorphic beings. The veil had not yet fallen from their minds; it still hid the grand scheme of things that worked independently of man-made gods. This period was an interlude foreshadowing the distant future, and, though it had no direct effect upon the conception and building of cities, its early contribution to later developments should not be overlooked.

v

Within the framework of these primary criteria of city development, a group of secondary criteria exists. Since they will be dealt with in the following volumes, it is not necessary to go into a detailed description of the many other factors that have shaped and reshaped the urban environment. But it may be pertinent to discuss briefly one problem that shows with special clarity the alternating character of the interdependence of city and country. The first industrial activities were concentrated in the village, each village being a self-contained economic unit. Consequently, industries were dispersed over the whole country, and each village contained many different types. The craftsman and artisan worked only for the small community to which they belonged. Therefore, the problem of the localization of industry did not arise.

A new factor was introduced when the *villa,* and later the manor, concentrated all industries needed for self-sufficiency. Thus, two closed economies existed side by side: the village economy and the *villa* and manor economy. Under such conditions, the lord of the manor had to move his household from one of his domains to the other in order to consume the products and to supervise production—the consumer had to go, as it were, to the product, rather than vice versa. Like village economy, *villa* and manor economy comprised all types of production needed for all the inhabitants of the domain. A rudimentary localization of industry existed only insofar as industries were concentrated in the manor in the center of the domain. Gradually, however, with the expansion of the domains and the increase in security, industries began to move out and to be dispersed over the territory of the lord. The needs of the domain were, in these early periods, still small and simple; the cultivation of land and the production of goods for the household and of tools for agriculture, building, and other activities were still closely related and carried on by doing part-time work in both: hence the trend toward the gradual dispersion of industries.

Urban industries developed along similar lines: They were first concentrated in the cities and towns, which formed with their hinterlands self-sufficient economic units; like the *villa* and the manor they included all industries needed for all inhabitants of the urban community. But here the similarity ended: The city, like the manor, was surrounded by an agricultural "domain," but this urban domain, the hinterland of the town, produced certain goods apart from the purely agricultural ones. These elementary rural industries catered to the villagers' basic needs, such as the making and repairing of agricultural tools, building and carpentry, constructing simple furniture, and supplying household needs. However, the monopolistic tendency of urban economy and the political ambitions of the burghers were antagonistic even to these remnants of independence. The cities tried to suppress or at least to reduce to a minimum the still existing rural industries and to concentrate them within their own urban areas. From this tendency a certain localization developed: Trade was mostly carried on in the center, in the market square, or in the workshops of the craftsmen and artisans. Later, shops were introduced, but this development was slow and mainly restricted to the larger cities. This gradual dispersion of trade and commerce within the cities led in many cases to the restricted use of the market square as the center of food supply. Trades were "localized" in streets and quarters. The more the diversity and productive capacity of urban industries increased, the more pressing the need to find new and larger markets for their products. Thus urban economy grew into a national economy with the two branches of home industries and factories.

At this juncture the complicated process of modern industrialization set in, and the hitherto relatively simple relationship of the urban structure to the countryside underwent repeated and far-reaching transformations. Two movements began to overlap: Some industries left the city and dispersed over the country as home industries; others concentrated in the city in factories. Simultaneously, individual industries tended to congregate in certain regions. With their exodus to the country as home industries, production and commerce began to separate. However, the commercial center remained in the city.

41

The cheaper production costs of the country were an added attraction. This exodus of industries, which in Europe was considerable between the fifteenth and eighteenth centuries, proceeded against strong opposition from the cities. The textile (above all the wool) industry was the first to move out and establish itself in villages and farms. Agriculture and home industry were once more united. This general trend toward decentralization continued as long as water was used as motive power.

Steam had the opposite effect: Industries concentrated again in the cities. This process progressed rapidly and soon led to the decline of the home industries. But the high urban rents and the growth of the cities first pressed the industries out of the center to the suburbs and then farther out beyond the boundaries of the built-up urban area. Electricity has generally strengthened this decentralizing process. With regard to the second movement, the local concentration of certain industries, in the early stage of this development every city tried to attract as many different industries as possible. In the period of an expanding national economy, local specialization of industries set in because better communications over long distances made the exchange of goods easier. In the period of international commerce, this local specialization continued with a concentration of similar principal and auxiliary industries in a few places, regions, and countries.

The development described above refers mainly to Europe; but many of its features also pertain to other parts of the world. The industrial pendulum that was swinging to and fro between city and country may be taken as a symbol of their inescapable interdependence and of the alternating importance of rural and urban economy. This oscillation is like a breathing-in and a breathing-out of cities and villages. It is a concentration and a dispersal that accompany or follow one another: Industry concentrated in the manor and village is dispersed over a larger area; with the developing urban economy it moves back to the towns; with revived home industries it returns to the country; and with the factory system it leaves the country and concentrates in the cities, first in or near the centers, then on the peripheries. Today the pendulum is again swinging back and decentralization is gaining momentum.

In these periodical changes, two main principles are evident: The centrifugal forces decentralize the structure of settlement in general, and the centripetal forces increase the size of cities. Both result in a widening scale of activities, and both are intimately connected with man's attitude to his work. Either they unite working place and living place, or they separate them.

They unite when there are home industries and small trades; they separate when larger establishments and specialization develop. In the first case, worker and work remain, in general, united from the beginning to the end, and an eminently personal attitude to the work persists during the whole time of production. In the second case, worker and work are increasingly alienated from each other; only parts of the working process are executed by the same worker, and an impersonal attitude results.

The separation of working place and living place has had the most far-reaching effect on the structure of urban settlement. It has created problems still unsolved after several centuries except by an ever more unmanageable traffic. The separation of working and personal life has produced the most crucial enigma of our time: how to prevent human beings from being swallowed up by routine and loneliness; how to redress the victory of fractional man over full man; how to subordinate the expert, the idol of our time, to the demands of a morality that puts human values, not technical knowledge, above everything else. All these factors have had profound effects upon the varying fortunes of cities, upon their rise and decay, and upon their status, whether as genuine communities or haphazard conglomerations of heterogeneous multitudes.

VI

If we look back over the vast field of city development in the past and survey the present situation, we are faced with a seemingly chaotic variety of cities, towns, and smaller urban and rural communities. This bewildering manifoldness has a not too surprising effect upon the tidy minds of those who believe that life cannot hold out any hope nor offer any security unless it is systematically divided and subdivided into neat categories. This pigeonholing is sometimes called classification and sometimes, by less benevolent observers, a labor of Sisyphus. Whatever the motives of these filing clerks of history may be, they are wrong. Neither life nor history—nor city development for that matter—can be reduced to a narrow and rigid filing system. Life, history, and city development are complex entities, and it reveals a profound misunderstanding to use one or two or even more single factors as a basis of classification. We need the "courage of uncertainty"—that is, we must dispense with all classifications as crutches of appraisal. Such an approach is neither theoretically possible nor even a useless pastime; it is an entirely unrealistic attempt. It is unrealistic because its tacit assumption is that cities are static entities.

What else can it mean to speak, for instance, of roadside cities, hilltop settlements, fortress towns, residence cities, and many similar categories? Cities are living and ever-changing organisms, and one function or one characteristic that was possibly important at one time may have lost its meaning at another time. Or what does it mean to group cities according to their layout as square or circular types? Or as gridiron, radial, or concentric cities? Or according to functions as commercial, cathedral, or administrative? All these groupings are entirely meaningless: They refer to one or a few functions only. Rather we should understand that in all lands and at all times urban and rural settlements have grown up different in character and layout, in spite of the fact that their initial development may have been similar and may have proceeded on the same physical prerequisites as location on a river, on a hill, in a valley, on the coast, on a plain, in a pass, or on any other natural site. There are innumerable cities, towns, and villages that were the product of colonization and were built according to the needs of the time and of the colonization movement. They all began in more or less the same manner, either as street or ring-fence villages, fortified strongholds in good defensive positions, military camps with rigid street patterns, or small enclosed enclaves in hostile territory. But only very rarely was the subsequent development of these places, which had been founded under similar conditions and on similar sites, the same. Historical incidents; irrational actions; social and economic forces; trade and commerce; war and peace; natural influences like desiccation, flooding, or moving coastlines; reclamation of land—to mention only a few—have turned their development in different directions.

Nor is it justified or possible to differentiate between a few great cities and a majority of less important ones if we want to arrive at a genuine understanding of city development. Our understanding should derive from a great variety of cities, large and small, and from an ever-present awareness that even "eternal" cities can die and new ones come into existence in all periods. Cities have been the power stations of integrated cultures from which creative forces radiated in invisible waves, spreading knowledge and skills, religion and philosophy, art and ideas over large regions. Culture and its emanations are independent of size, and small cities have in certain periods made greater contributions to culture than the big and powerful ones—just as a powerful nation need not be a great nation, and a technical civilization need not be a great culture.

Another problem that is less easy to dispose of is whether there are any national characteristics that could serve, not as a basis of classification, but perhaps to explain certain features and each city's particular atmosphere. Here we enter the sphere of imponderables; but, I believe, this is no reason not to try to sense how this atmosphere has pervaded the actual appearance of a city. It is not fashionable nowadays to call on the *Zeitgeist,* or the spirit of a locality, to help toward understanding a work of art. These unsubstantial yet, as I see it, significant or symbolic emanations of the human mind are anathema to the strange species of "fact-finders" who sincerely believe that statistics and questionnaires if "correctly" interpreted can tell us everything about any given problem. To them the world of the irrational is a closed book, and it is useless to remind them that this world does exist and that out of this world the most powerful motivations of mankind have drawn strength and inspiration. I maintain that unless we try to raise these imponderable values into the light of consciousness, our understanding of art, architecture, and city building will remain piecemeal and will lack the wholeness that is the essential property of all artistic creation. The atmosphere of a city belongs to this sphere of insubstantiality. It is a "baseless fabric of a vision," and, because it cannot be touched or weighed, it is all-pervading and envelops us in its wholeness—a wholeness, to repeat Whitehead's words, "so translucent, and so pervading, and so seemingly necessary, that only by extreme effort can we become aware of it."

Cities are basically the same everywhere. They are pieces of land cut out from the surrounding country. They remove men from the inescapable rhythm of nature to which the countrypeople are chained. They consist of buildings and the spaces between them. They are either walled in or without walls. These are the primary elements of every city. But within this wide framework there are a number of distinguishing characteristics of which two are, in this connection, particularly significant: the conception of a city as a complex and limited entity or, for that matter, as an unlimited and haphazardly growing product of human unpredictability; and certain stylistic elements characteristic of a period or of a country.

To take the second point first, stylistic details include parts of architecture and city building and are expressed, to mention only a few, in the ornamental treatment of a façade, the relation between solids and voids, the shapes of the towers of churches, the forms of squares, the street furniture, and the relation of houses and streets. All these factors are concrete and substantial and can easily be perceived and apprehended. They are the factors that have been the delight of art historians, who use them as material for their stylistic analyses. There is no need to go into a detailed description of this approach; the method and results are known and have sometimes produced interesting and useful insights. Nevertheless, it is often rather awkward to have to find one's way through the mass of cross-references and to be faced with the author's obsession to explain almost every work of art by referring to influences from other works of art, until in the end it is difficult, if not impossible, to discover the original and spontaneous vision in the midst of a welter of unrelated details. Certainly, the stylistic characteristics of a country and a period are distinguishing marks of city building and architecture, and they contribute toward the particular atmosphere of a city; but they are not the only ones, and they are by no means the most important. They depend, to a degree, on the traditional legacy of a country and above all on the awareness of this legacy as a formative force—that is, if the tradition is one of depth rather than of the surface. The former is like a never-ending thread twisted together with the innumerable fibers of our being. It is this tradition in depth that, in the past, has brought forth nationally characteristic architecture and city building and that has given a particular atmosphere to a city. This subconscious tradition is overlaid by a tradition of the surface, which resembles a tapestry woven from narratives of recorded events and which is hung up on the walls of the narrow passage through which our life proceeds. Although it need not be so, this tradition of the surface can be in the truest sense "superficial"; then it is nothing but the unimaginative imitation of details and forms. It is invariably the sign of a decaying civilization that has lost the vision and the strength to evolve an independent language of form out of the raw materials of its own time. This all too conscious tradition contributes nothing of any value to the atmosphere of a city. It makes it hypocritical, embarrassing, and vulgar.

Whether or not a city has been conceived from the very beginning as one complex entity is of infinitely greater importance. It is not the fact that the walls of such a city have been an ever-present reminder of its limitation that creates a particular atmosphere; it should not be forgotten that in numerous large cities of the past, such as Peking, Babylon, Cologne, or Paris, a wall was not visible in all parts of a city as it was in smaller towns. What is essential is that the inhabitants of these limited cities were always aware of living within an unalterable enclave that protected them against the outside world and to which they had to attune their existences. This does not mean that their existences were "static," but it does mean that life had to be concentrated, not diffused; intensive, not sporadic; and balanced, not hectic. Living in a compact, narrow, and limited space brings out other facets of the human personality than does living in an unlimited space as we do today.

Walls are not the indispensable prerequisite of this attitude or of the particular atmosphere of limited cities. The ideal conception of a Greek city did not rely on walls; walls were added later for purely practical reasons. The city was held together by its conscious restriction to a small area beyond which the city was not supposed to grow. Limitation was voluntary and essential to a Greek life that achieved unity in diversity without the solid enclosure of walls. What held the inhabitants together was the common purpose of a life lived out to the full, which did not need unlimited expansion.

Something similar is still evident today in many Spanish cities, with the exception of metropolitan centers like Madrid, Barcelona, and Valencia. The walls have fallen, but the spirit of containment has remained. Most Spanish cities end abruptly at the peripheries, as though the old walls still separated them from the country. There are no straggling suburbs; there is no transitional no man's land. And within this invisible limitation an atmosphere of directness and intimacy is the supreme characteristic. The streets and squares are open-air interiors; short vistas, rather than long perspectives, impose awareness of restriction on the minds and senses of the inhabitants; and innumerable small street widenings, stairs, and irregularities of an entirely unsystematic street pattern are invitations to intimate social intercourse. Why is this so? The Spaniard demands immediate results. He shuns abstract relations and prefers direct contact with men and things and complete absorption in one object, in one idea. He does not want to be lost in the infinity of space. It is the complex of all the mental characteristics so peculiar to Spaniards that has kept their towns limited and made them vessels of social directness. For Spaniards the spaces between the buildings, the streets and squares, are extensions of their homes; and their homes mean shelter and protection within a narrow space. The absence of limitations is therefore alien to Spanish towns.

The cities of China were entirely different, but they achieved similar results. They were conceived as limited entities. The walls were built first, and the gates determined the number and layout of the main streets. Between them the secondary streets and lanes formed an almost inextricable maze. Here the human scale was preserved; here the houses were the primary element; here life remaind immediate and personal. This combination of systematic organization and life-centered, personal intimacy is a unique accomplishment that was possible because the life of the inhabitants of old China was deeply embedded in religious and magical symbolism. All this did not create a community spirit as we know it in other countries; yet Chinese cities were living organisms that did not and could not grow beyond a certain size. Far beyond their utilitarian purpose, the walls were the symbol of this deliberate restriction.

Indigenous settlements in Africa were likewise limited, sometimes enclosed by fences and sometimes not. They too were restricted in their growth by religious and magical symbolism. But these limiting influences were reinforced by social homogeneity and by blood relationship that excluded any outsiders, which therefore kept the settlements small in size and homogeneous in character.

To interpret these remarks as a glorification of small towns for small-town folk, would be a profound misunderstanding. Rather, I want to prove that living within self-imposed limits demands and creates a supreme confidence that enables man to evolve a pattern of living within a narrow compass. This introverted attitude is in no way inferior to the extroverted ambitions of the present: It has been the source of great works of art and of great cities far superior to our amorphous megalopoleis. It is an essential ingredient of every genuinely artistic nature. To regard limitation as inimical to creativity is an untenable proposition; yet there are many people who believe that unlimited expansion is the panacea for all our frustrations and ambitions. Both limitation and expansion are needed today: We need small and organic communities that cannot grow beyond a certain size and that are, at the same time, constituent parts of a large region over which they are systematically dispersed, each one serving a definite and different function. Thus, limitation and expansion can both be made living realities. They are not exclusive of one another, but complementary.

I believe that these characteristics, which I can mention only briefly in this introduction, but which I will try to explain in their significance for the development of cities in the following volumes, are the best criteria and that the forces that have caused limitation or expansion are the same as those that have created the unique atmospheres of particular cities. These characteristics are molded by influences rooted in individual countries and in individual periods; that is to say, they are the composite results of space and time both working together toward the same end: the creative unity of the feeling of space, of the attitude to the environment, and of group consciousness. Altogether, they are the underlying and imponderable qualities out of which the atmosphere of a city emanates.

VII

Architecture and city building are one. They differ in scale but use the same media: space and space relations. The artistic style of a period is the same in architecture and city building, although the latter develops more slowly owing to greater practical obstacles. Both are equal partners in man's struggle with his environment. A city is not a mere utilitarian structure, nor can a history of city development be conceived and written as though a few showpieces could explain a city's nature and appearance. But it is precisely this attitude that has so far dominated the work of most city historians. The main function of a city is to provide a space where men can live and work; and, if there happen to be a few good public buildings, so much the better for the inhabitants. The vast majority of buildings are for people to live in, and they are what gives a city its character. This self-evident truth has been almost completely absent from the minds of historians who have been interested in city development. They tell us something about churches and temples, palaces and castles, fortifications and streets; they may even mention the architecture of the dwellings of the well to do. But they keep silent about the houses of "the people," their excuse being that we know next to nothing about the humbler quarters of the "masses." In many cases, this is not true; and where time has destroyed these quarters there is usually other evidence available from which relevant conclusions can be drawn.

A city, like a house, is the germinating cell of the whole civilization of a country and a period. In a great civilization, home, house, city, and landscape are in perfect harmony. City building, like architecture, is not utilitarian, not even a biological necessity, but a moral obligation; and both are links in the long chain that binds past and present to the reality of life. After what has been said before, however incomplete and condensed it has had to be in this introduction, there is no need to repeat in detail that a city is one of the most complex works ever produced by man. The history of this development can be written from different angles, but it should always be centered on man as the creative agent rather than on details. For man is the master mind, the ἀρχιτέκτων, the chief builder of the houses and cities that he creates in harmony with his ideas and ambitions, his skills and experiences, his needs and knowledge.

The last volume of this work will deal with the place of cities in our present civilization. Emerging trends seem to be opening a way out of the chaotic impasses into which the breakdown of our loyalties has led us. The more the state has assumed responsibilities, not only for the material side of its citizens' life, but also for their spiritual and intellectual guidance, the more the loyalties that have given coherence to society have faded away. Remote control of our lives through officially appointed committees is the order of the day in all countries. But men refuse to extend their loyalties to committees; thus the growing alienation between the many and the few combined with the impersonal "I-It" spirit have drawn all civilizations into a quest for security in all internal and external relations. This security, not understood in a political sense, is found in the longing for an attachment to what is familiar and customary and to what can easily be understood and applied. It undermines originality in thought and action and leaves the field free for a morally unhampered science and technology. What we are witnessing today is a withdrawal from responsibility, a contracting out of society, and a devil-may-care attitude that seeks refuge and fulfillment in an easy satisfaction of material comfort. Can we expect under these conditions to revitalize our cities and to instill a spirit of community out of which a new pattern of urban life can grow? Can we expect a few well-meaning but unrelated reforms to produce a new and integrated way of urban life?

The laudable optimism of the very small minority of enlightened city officials and city planners is, alas, not contagious. Their efforts are still restricted to the old conception of cities and to purely utilitarian improvements, however architecturally excellent they may be in detail. If we survey the whole field of present city building, the most conspicuous fact is a general leveling-down, an almost indistinguishable similarity of virtually all development schemes in all parts of the world. Everywhere we see metropolitan empires arising, suburbia spreading, traffic dehumanizing life, and slum clearance proceeding without definite and coherent goals. Possibly, all this could be accepted with benevolent toleration in the hope that it is an ephemeral trend and is recognized as a sort of expedient "solution." But this is not the case. The vast majority of men take it to be an entirely natural and justifiable development. They are proud of the bigness of their cities; they are content with their subtopias; they glory in the number of automobiles they have; and they believe in the efficiency of removing a few slums.

Condemning this attitude is not to long nostalgically for the past; it is not to retreat from progress. But it is an assertion of the belief that these efforts are misdirected and consequently in vain. For they do not touch the more deeply lying causes that have brought about this development. In recognition, awareness, and understanding of these causes lie the germs of a new beginning. No sensible person expects anyone responsible for the building or administration of cities to revolutionize urban life. But it would be a great advance and a source of optimism if these experts would look beyond the narrow confines of their professional work and become aware of the fact that it is impossible to create a new and fertile pattern of urban life out of the existing structure of our cities. If these experts would cease to explain the present situation by pointing to the increase in traffic, the growing population, the decay of houses, and all the innumerable material factors that have made our cities what they are and, instead, begin to understand that in a disjointed society their work can at best be provisional and at worst a patchwork of alleged remedies—then they would strive for membership in the open conspiracy of those who are trying to understand the genuine causes for our situation and for city decadence, who are striving to show the direction in which we and our work should be moving. This is the greatest challenge to all of us who are concerned with the problems that have accumulated in our cities, problems that have to be solved on a much more comprehensive scale and in a much more penetrating way than is generally assumed. Then we will find the right answer to the question, "Can our cities survive?" They can*not* survive.

This answer will not be demolished by the usual retort that cities are here to stay, that they are a permanent part of our civilization. This is only too true—but is our civilization permanent? I do not propose to discuss such problems here; they will be dealt with in the appropriate place. I will say only this: There are faint tendencies, still submerged, that seem to work toward new possibilities. As I have mentioned repeatedly in the foregoing pages, the scale of our thinking and acting is widening; decentralization and dispersal are beginning to be accepted as promising potentialities; a far-reaching redistribution of population and industry seems to be at least a debatable proposition; and, above all, revulsion for the routine and loneliness of urban life is spreading. The twilight of cities as mankind has known them for five millennia means the rise of communities—of an environment dominated by human values that will cease to be the confused expression of a life centered on work, on traffic, on material achievements, and on pride in quantity not quality.

Here I take leave of my subject at a point where the introduction merges into the actual work. Much more could have been said about general principles and particular aspects of city development. The purpose of an introduction, however, is to prepare the reader for what is to follow, to provide a yardstick by which he can judge the author's approach to his subject. If, on the preceding pages, my ideas have been explained clearly enough, the reader will understand that I regard the *International History of City Development* to be not a compilation of so-called "facts" and more or less dead documents, but a survey of the dynamic interplay of numerous forces and of the changing sensibility to and awareness of the pre-eminence of human values and aspirations.

CENTRAL EUROPE

16. *Opposite:* Tübingen.

CHAPTER 1

GERMANY, together with the Scandinavian countries, Switzerland, and Austria, forms, generally speaking, a cultural entity. The large extent of this region has produced a certain cultural differentiation which is, however, considerably counterbalanced by numerous common factors—above all by the fact that it was the scene of an almost homogeneous spread of settlement and interdependent migrations. The differences in settlement types and in their origin and development were no greater than, for instance, the difference between the northern and the southern provinces of China; however different in detail, common features retained the essential characteristics of the civilization shared by all who lived within this vast area.

The ice sheet that covered northern Europe in prehistoric times extended, during its greatest advance southward, as far as Ireland and Scotland and in England as far south as the Thames. Eastward, it went from Scandinavia across the European plain from the present mouth of the Rhine to the Vistula and beyond. Simultaneously, glaciers moved from the Alps northward but did not meet the ice sheet advancing from the North: Between them remained a fertile belt of varying width not buried under ice, extending from Picardy in France, across the southern part of the German Plain, through Poland, and into Russia; it was covered with loess, a light and sandy soil, which made it a rich agricultural region. After its final retreat, the ice sheet left behind the clays, sands, gravels, rocks, and boulders that the advancing glaciers had carried with them.

The three main physical divisions of central Europe are the Alps, the Central Uplands, and the Northern Lowlands. These three zones run more or less parallel from west to east and give the whole region a considerable variety of physical structure and geographical features. Further subdivisions consist of the Alpine Foreland, the Upper Danube Basin, the basins of the Main and the Neckar, the broken highlands of mid-Germany, and the Vienna Basin. The rift valley of the Rhine also forms a subdivision that runs from the south to the north.

The northern part of the Alps, as far as they lie in Germany, stretch roughly from Constance to Hallein. The main rivers in this region are the Iller, the Lech, the Isar, and the Inn, tributaries of the Danube. The northern fringe of the Alps, which includes the Bavarian Plateau, is a zone of fairly high altitudes. It widens between the Alps and the Danube and continues in the East into the Vienna Basin. The Upper Danube Basin is traversed by the Danube, which rises in the Black Forest and is enclosed by Lake Constance and the Bavarian Alps in the south and by the Alpine Foreland and the southwestern part

The Land

Physical Division

of the Bohemian Massif in the north. The Danube flows through the northern half of its basin, leaving Germany at Passau. The area is strewn with morainic and alluvial material that was deposited by former glaciers and carried by postglacial rivers. The soils are fertile and support a diversified agriculture. The Swabian Jura forms part of the boundary between Bavaria and Württemberg. The basins of the Main and the Neckar, both tributaries of the Rhine, are situated to the north and west of the Jura ridge. Between Basle and Mainz, the rift valley of the Rhine forms, on the eastern side, the western slope of the Black Forest up to Karlsruhe in the north. On the western side, the valley is contained by the Vosges in France. The banks of the river are rough, and only a few towns are situated along its southern course. However, towns are numerous from Speyer northward.

The Central Uplands, the *Mittelgebirge,* extend from the Vosges and Ardennes to the Sudetes. In central Germany, this area consists of the Thuringian Forest and the Harz Mountains. In the west it is cut by the Rhine gorge between Bingen and Bonn. The Hunsrück, the Eifel, the Taunus, and the Westerwald form the western and northwestern end of the Franconian Jura, and the Erzgebirge and the Böhmerwald form the eastern zone. This region is of a moderate altitude and has a fairly smooth relief consisting of plateaux, scarped lowlands, and small disconnected plains. It is drained to the north by the Rhine, the Weser, and the Elbe. The Thuringian Lowland, drained by the Saale, is in its center around Erfurt a fertile loess area.

The Northern Lowlands stretch from Artois in France to the Pripet Marshes in Poland, and beyond into central Russia. Along its northern boundary extends the Loess Belt. The Rhine, the Weser, the Saale, the Elster, the Elbe, and the Oder are the main rivers of this region in Germany. Apart from the foothill zone, the main features in this area are morainic hills, running more or less parallel to the Baltic coast, and numerous small lakes. The morainic belts west of Berlin generaly extend west-northwestward, with many lakes in Mecklenburg and Schleswig-Holstein and between the lower Elbe and the Aller and the Weser.

The Vienna Basin is Austria's only lowland area that extends to the east into the Lesser Hungarian Plain and to the north into Czechoslovakia. The eastern Alps separate into southwestern and northeastern ranges. These are formed by low chains and are traversed by the Danube. They form the Vienna and Bratislava Basins in Czechoslovakia. In the southwest, the Karawanken and Julian Alps stretch through a limestone zone that is linked to the Dinaric Mountains in the western Balkans.

The Scandinavian Peninsula is mainly an elevated plateau of ancient and denuded rocks. Its only lowland area of any significance lies in southern Sweden, and is a detached part of the Northern Lowlands of continental Europe. Ice was the most effective agent in wearing away the surface of this land. Its highlands rise steeply from the sea in the west and slope gradually as wide terraces to the Baltic in the east, reaching their greatest height and extension in the southwest in the Jotun and Hardanger Fjelds. The main water-shed lies near the west coast, and from it descend short and swift streams to the west, and longer ones to the southeast as far as the Baltic, forming large lakes and numerous falls. The Atlantic coast is fringed with innumerable islands and indented with fjords. The Swedish coast is lower than the Norwegian coast, and its relief much less broken.

Denmark comprises the larger part of the Jutland Peninsula as well as some islands at the entrance to the Baltic. With the exception of the island of Bornholm, it is an undulating or flat country, and is part of the Northern Lowlands. The west coast of Jutland is fringed by sand dunes and has few good harbors. The east coast has numerous openings.

Switzerland consists of four natural regions: the Alps; the Jura; the plateau between these two zones, the *Mittelland;* and the southern part, the Ticino. Longitudinal valleys with numerous rivers separate the Alpine ranges. The Rhine, the Rhône, the Po, and some of the tributaries of the Danube rise in the Alps. The Alps are crossed by numerous passes, and rise to almost 16 thousand feet, Mont Blanc being the highest peak. During the ice age, the valleys were filled with large glaciers that spread their morainic material over the lower parts of the country. They are mostly U-shaped depressions with flat floors enclosed by steep cliffs, the upper parts, the original V-shaped valleys, gradually rising above them. This formation resulted from the ice-age glaciers, which "overdeepened" the valleys into the troughlike U-shaped depressions. The gently sloping side valleys (called hanging valleys) are covered with glacial debris that provides a fertile soil with rich pastures, the alps.

The fold ranges of the Jura are separated, like those of the Alps, by longitudinal valleys. The valley floors are broad and used as meadows, whereas the steeper slopes are clad with pines, above which are the Upland Pastures. The wedge-shaped plateau, the *Mittelland,* narrows toward the western end of Lake Geneva where the Alps and the Jura converge. It extends northeastward toward Lake Constance and the Rhine. It is an undulating region of 1200 to 2400 feet altitude, and has numerous hills of morainic material but few larger stretches of level land. The main river is the Aar, which drains the Lakes of Neuchâtel, Lucerne, and Zurich into the Rhine. The Ticino stretches from the southern slopes of the Alps to the northern end of Lake Maggiore and Lake Lugano. The Alps shelter these valleys from the north winds, making their climate mild and favorable for vines and other southern fruits.[1]

Climate

The climate of the whole region varies considerably. In Germany it ranges from the oceanic to the continental climates of western and eastern Europe respectively. No hills or mountains in the northwest intercept the warmer winds from the Atlantic. The summers are warm and have a moderate rainfall. The winters can be very cold, especially in the East. In general, rainfall is heaviest in the Bavarian Tableland and the hilly parts of western Germany. The southwest winds, which blow against the steep mountain ranges of the western part of the Scandinavian Peninsula, cause a heavy rainfall, whereas the East, in the rainshadow of the mountains, is fairly dry. The prevailing southwest winds drive the warm water of the North Atlantic Drift along the west coast, making the climate very mild.

The eastern regions, on the other hand, have an extreme climate, while such a country as Switzerland occupies an intermediate position between the climates of northern Europe and the Mediterranean, and belongs, according to the prevailing winds, either to the maritime climatic zone of the West or to the continental zone of eastern Europe. For this reason, climatic differences are very great in this small region. The main part, however, has a climate similar to the harsher one of central Europe, with strong oceanic influences. In general, west winds prevail, although they often alternate with northeast winds, especially in the plateau between the Alps and the Jura.

Austria's climate varies considerably, even within short distances. Broadly speaking, the northern part is influenced by west and northwest winds that carry a modified Atlantic climate deep into the interior along the Danube Valley and the side valleys running from south to north. This results in the absence of a definite dry season. On the other hand, eastern influences make themselves felt in the valleys of the eastern borderlands, in the Burgenland, and in east Styria.

The Clearing of the Forests and the Progress of Settlement

The spread of settlement in central Europe and adjacent regions was dependent on the clearing of the forests. At first, only those areas free of forest or immediately adjoining the marginal belts of the woodland were settled. The early settlements were therefore sporadic, isolated, and small; and the clearing proceeded from many centers at the same time, gradually widening the open spaces and turning them into pastures and

1. A detailed geographical description is given in connection with the individual countries.

fields. But in many cases the clearings were not permanent; the woods crept back and new clearings had to be made. The natural landscape of neolithic central Europe was an almost continuous cover of forest. Only the higher mountains, where they rose above the tree line, interrupted this vast wooded area.

The early settlers set in motion

... an economic and scientific revolution that made the participants active partners with nature instead of parasites on nature. The occasion for the revolution was the climatic crisis that ended the pleistocene epoch; the melting of the northern ice sheets ... converted the steppes and tundras of Europe into temperate forests.[2]

Man's relation to nature was determined by his aggressive attitude. He initiated the conquest of a continent when he began clearing the woodlands, producing new food supplies and new tools, and caring for flocks and herds.

The neolithic populations of Europe ... are normally found living in small communities—villages or hamlets. When fully explored these have been found to cover areas from 1½ to 6½ acres. ... Such spatial aggregates formed social organisms whose members all co-operated for collective tasks. ... Many neolithic villages in western Europe and in the Balkans are surrounded by ditches, fences or stockades, as a protection against wild beasts or human foes, and these, too, must have been erected by collective effort. ... The arrangement of the dwellings along definite streets ... gives expression to some form of social organization. ... But there is no need to assume any industrial specialisation within the village apart from a division of labour between the sexes. On the analogy of modern barbarians each neolithic household would grow and prepare its own food, make its own pots, clothes, tools and other requisites. ... Each village could be self-sufficing. ... This potential self-sufficiency of the territorial community and the absence of specialisation within it may be taken as the differentiae of neolithic barbarism to distinguish it from civilization and the higher barbarisms of the Metal Ages. A corollary therefrom is that a neolithic economy offers no material inducement to the peasant to produce more than he needs to support himself and his family and to provide for the next harvest. If each household does that, the community can survive without a surplus.[3]

However, a certain intercommunity contact did exist. It is probable that the hunters brought back from their hunting trips knowledge of other groups and implements and that the neolithic community was only seldom absolutely sedentary. Thus the neolithic revolution produced to a certain extent a pooling of practical experience and traditional rituals. However, "there is no 'neolithic culture' but a limitless multitude of neolithic

2. Gordon Childe. *What Happened in History*. 1952, p. 48.
3. *Ibid.*, pp. 59, 60.

cultures,"[4] each with its own individual cultivation or animals, its own characteristic siting and layout of settlements, and its own tools and rites.

The woods were cleared either by ax or by fire. Although the areas of settlement did increase during the Bronze and Iron Ages, these extensions were generally rare. Rather, the development seems to have moved toward a more intensive use of the clearings that had already been made.[5] The reason for this continued occupation of the same areas was that the peasant did not possess a heavy-wheeled plow until the close of prehistoric times. The heavy and ill-drained clay soil remained, therefore, covered by woods for a long period.

Roman Period

Little is known of the clearings during Roman times, or of what happened to them during the great invasions of the Germanic tribes into the lands that had belonged to the Roman Empire. It was a tribal society organized in local groups which began to move westward. Economically, this society rested on a primitive agriculture and on flocks and herds that were moved perennially from summer to winter pastures. Such conditions were not conducive to settled town life. As Tacitus remarked, "There are no towns in the whole of Germany," but there did exist permanent rural settlements consisting of compact villages or scattered farmsteads. However, the forests spread again over many of the cleared areas, especially over those where the fields had been neglected.

Middle Ages

The actual and large-scale attack on the forest did not begin until the waves of the Folk Migrations came to rest. It was by no means a coherent or systematic process, but as a whole it proceeded steadily, resulting in spectacular feats of human endurance, determination, and perseverance. Two main groups of pioneering settlers may be distinguished: the east and the west German tribes. Both spread out from an area roughly comprising southern Scandinavia and the Baltic shores east of the lower Elbe. Urged on by the pressure of other Teutonic and Slavic tribes following them, they penetrated toward the Roman frontiers along the Rhine and the Danube.

In the fifth century A.D., the Franks and the Alemanni extended their raids into the lands of the Rhine Basin, while the Saxons, Bavarians, Thuringians, and Slavs advanced toward the line of the Elbe, the Saale, the Naab, and the Danube; there they were faced by the frontier established by Charlemagne. This remained the effective frontier between Germans and Slavs until about A.D. 1200. The early migrations were accompanied by an ever-widening clearing of the woodland, at first in isolated and scattered islands surrounded by vast tracts of forest and

4. *Ibid.*, p. 62.
5. For the following, see H. C. Darby. "The Clearing of the Woodland in Europe." In William L. Thomas, Jr. (ed.), *Man's Role in Changing the Face of the Earth*, pp. 183-210. The Wenner-Gren Foundation for Anthropological Research and The National Science Foundation, 1956.

marsh. But gradually, though very slowly, the isolated bits of land merged into coherent territories, each protected and separated by a belt of uninhabited forests called the *Mark*. In many cases, these forest belts retained the names of the tribes that had settled within the area the belts enclosed—for instance, Frankenwald, Böhmerwald, and Thüringerwald.

By the third century A.D., the Salian Franks had advanced to the Meuse. By the fourth and fifth centuries they had moved into the lowland of southern Brabant, the later Flanders, avoiding the *Silva Carbonnaria* ("Forest of the Charcoal Burners") and occupied it during the sixth and seventh centuries. The Ripuarian Franks settled in the Rhine Basin southward down to the northern end of the middle Rhine. The Alemanni continued farther south, along the middle Rhine and upper Neckar and around Lake Constance. The Bavarians occupied the Bavarian Plateau between the Lech and the Enns. The Saxons established themselves on the northern Loess Belt and the adjoining uplands to the south, and also on the fertile areas of the northern heathlands; their main strongholds were in the highlands between the Rhine and the Weser.[6] The Thuringians settled in the low-lying loess country of Thuringia, and the Frisians who had arrived in these parts as early as the fifth century B.C., struck roots in the marshy region and on the islands of the northern coast that extends from Holland to Schleswig-Holstein and Denmark. Their settlements were located on isolated mounds called *Warft-Wurt-Werf* which rose above the level of the tides.

At the beginning of the ninth century the forests were still regarded as the unlimited treasure of the country; as late as the thirteenth century the German poet Freidank wrote in his work *Bescheidenheit*, meaning literally "Modesty" but perhaps better translated as "practical wisdom":

> *Dem richen walt es lützel schadet,*
> *Ob sich ein man mit holze ladet.*[7]

And even much later, people still believed that the forests were seats of dark chthonian powers that deserved to be uprooted and destroyed. It was not until the fourteenth century that occasional complaints about a lack of wood could be heard.

In the first period of the clearing of the forests—that is, between the sixth and eighth centuries—the pioneers were groups of freemen who established settlements in the deep recesses of wooded valleys and on plateaux. But the more the clearings expanded and the old cooperative groups of the *Mark (Markgenossenschaften)*, of village neighbors, disintegrated, the more this

6. After R. E. Dickinson. *The German Lebensraum.* 1943, pp. 45-56.
7. "Little harm is done to the wealth of the forest if a man burdens himself with wood."

group aspect of settlement changed. Just as the freeman began to cultivate his fields and live in the village without depending so much on others, so his efforts in clearing the woods became more personal and more independent than before. Like a modern squatter he penetrated into the forest and built his lonely house on the cleared ground.[8] These activities were, of course, very irregular and still violent. The rulers often had to interfere with these settlers' activities for political and personal reasons and also because they wanted the profits from the clearings for themselves. A rather human testimony of this attitude toward clearings in the Thuringian Forest has been preserved. Markgrave Ludwig wrote the following to one of his retainers in about A.D. 1130:

If I did not esteem you particularly highly among my trusted followers, I had long ago shown myself as a severe lord to those who are clearing various parts of my forests and put themselves under your protection and had made them feel this bodily and economically. Remove them as soon as possible or I shall make my threat come true. . . .

And to the leader of those who were actively engaged in clearing the forest, he wrote:

You have to quit the forest immediately with all the woodcutters under your command. If this does not happen within the shortest time, I shall come myself. Your goods and chattels will be seized; your huts will be burnt down. It will cost your life.[9]

—plain language that certainly produced desired results.

The kings who still held title to all uncultivated lands therefore declared, in a number of solemn edicts, their rights to and possession of all forests, in particular of those in the mountainous regions. Thus, the Spessart, the Frankenwald, the Ardennes, the Hagenauer Forest, and others in high regions became imperial forests that could be cleared only by permission of the rulers. This royal prerogative devolved gradually on the dukes, markgraves, counts, and bishops, and finally, the clearings became almost the exclusive prerogative of the large manorial estates. By the end of the thirteenth century, this crusade—it can hardly be called anything else—had reached such proportions, and had been carried through so carelessly, that many settlements had to be abandoned because they were established on unproductive soil.

As an example of many similar cases, a report on the transfer of the Forest of Strelna between the Oder and March to the Order of the Premonstratensians by Henry, Markgrave of Moravia, in 1203, may serve here:

8. K. Lamprecht. *Deutsche Geschichte*, Vol. 3. 1904, pp. 52 ff.
9. F. Peek (ed.), *Monumenta Germaniae Historica, Epistolae Selectae V*, Nos. 94, 95. 1952.

We have conceded to the brothers all freedom to clear the forest and to establish villages, hamlets and towns. They may act as they like. They shall enjoy the same rights and privileges which their church possesses in its other estates. In order to remove right from the beginning all doubts the forest shall be surveyed and marked by boundary stones.[10]

However, the area of cultivation usually expanded, and many new villages were founded. The layout of each differed widely, and their field systems grew out of practical needs and social considerations.

Perhaps the greatest conquest of new territories was made by the movement of the Slavs east of the Elbe and the Saale. After the inhabitants of Mecklenburg, Holstein, parts of Brandenburg, and the Middle Elbe Basin, and the Wends and the Sorbs had been converted to Christianity and advanced into the regions formerly occupied by the Teutonic peoples who had settled in the old Roman provinces of the west, numerous villages and towns were founded in this part of central Europe. But most of these new settlements were not laid out by the Slavs. To the extent that they built any permanent settlements at all, they established one large place of refuge for each group and many smaller fortified castles.

Spread of Settlement

The occupation of the formerly German country by the Slavs seems to have proceeded everywhere under more or less similar conditions. They settled only on easily cultivable land; in general they were only able to plow the less heavy soils with their wooden, hook-shaped plows drawn by cows: bogs and marshes, forest and under-growth so common on the slopes of the Central Uplands and in the wide river valleys of the east remained mostly untouched and un-settled. Thus they established themselves in scattered groups which were separated from one another by thick woods and large marshes; this inaccessibility itself was regarded as sufficient protection. The marshes could be crossed only in winter—very often the attacks of the Germans were, therefore, undertaken in this season—while the forests were blocked by fortified lines of trees that had been cut down and were hidden by newly-grown wood and plants; only a few forest-gates led out into the open country. The settlement proceeded in families and clans. Each family or clan founded a village under the headman, the oldest member of the group (*Župane, starost*). The farmsteads were laid out in a circle or along a wide street facing the inner space. At the beginning the inhabitants shared as a community the work and the yields of their rural existence; only the great-grandchildren, the descendants of the third generation of the original and oldest settlers, used to divide and to establish according to the number of their grandfathers new and smaller communities which were . . . inherited in ever-repeated subdivisions by the following generations. It was a life that was intimately depend-

10. Boczek (ed.), *Codex diplomaticus et epistolaris Moraviae II*, Nos. 11, 219. 1836.

63

ent on the natural conditions of production and kinship; as far as it took common interests into account, they were related to the clan; unity was preserved by the absolute and patriarchal power of the actual elder. A change set in only when a prince of one of the ruling houses extended his sway over the clans of the individual settlements. This is the procedure that began to give to the civilization of the Slavs, particularly to the Poles and Czechs, a different character from about the tenth century onwards. The more the power of the prince extended over a growing number of groups, the more it laid claim to the frontier forests that had separated them and were now considered to be annoying obstacles; as *Občina*, as *res nullius,* this power opened their darkness to the clearings.[11]

However, the more spectacular achievements, such as the founding in this region of new towns and villages on a systematic scale, were the work of the advancing Germans who began to move southeastward in the tenth century and northeastward across the European plain after A.D. 1100. This colonial crusade proceeded irresistibly under the leadership of the Church, the nobility, and the merchants. To the western lands it added an almost equal territory of virgin country having a mixed population of Germans and Slavs. A second zone of settlement came into being, which included Pomerania, the Neumark, Silesia, and the upland borders of Bohemia. It was a peaceful penetration; the Slav rulers invited the German settlers to settle in their territory during the thirteenth and early fourteenth centuries. In general, it was an almost systematic colonization, in the course of which numerous villages were founded, surrounding cities and towns as their focal points.

Another zone of settlement developed further east in Poland and Bohemia. Here, German settlers were given special privileges to colonize regions that were to remain predominantly Slavic in population. Thus, German settlements extended over the mountain border of Bohemia into the low-lying heathland of this country, in the north into western Prussia and Posen and in the south into Silesia.

The Teutonic Knights conquered the Baltic provinces as far as the Gulf of Finland, and the Hanseatic League pushed its trading outposts far into Russia. In the course of this advance, rural and urban settlements were founded. The Teutonic Knights introduced town life to these predominantly rural parts of Eastern Europe, and built their fortified places on the lower Vistula and the coast of East Prussia.[12] Towns like Reval and Riga owe their origin to this period.

The Teutonic Knights were crusaders in the service of the pope. He enlisted them in the crusade against the Prussians that was preached throughout northern Germany and in the

11. K. Lamprecht. *Op. cit.,* Vol. III, pp. 335-336. (Author's translation)
12. Dickinson. *Op. cit.,* pp. 48-51.

countries of the eastern Slavs. In the spring of A.D. 1231, a small group of Teutonic Knights crossed the Vistula into hostile land. They stopped, so the legend goes, under an oak tree while one of this group climbed the tree and watched for enemies. Around this place they dug a wall and moat. This was the actual origin of the town of Thorn and of the colonial domain of the Order. It is characteristic that the colonization in this region began not so much with the rural settlement of the open country as with the foundation of urban places that soon grew into industrious traffic centers. This development was common to most regions that had been penetrated and opened up by civilizations with an already organized commerce and trade: the German immigrants, who had a higher living standard, needed all sorts of imports, such as herring and salt, linen and cloths, paints, wine, and pepper. Thus, populous towns sprang up very early in a relatively thinly-peopled country. This trend can be observed in all the German colonial lands east of the Elbe, but it is especially obvious in the domain of the Order of the Teutonic Knights, and explains the rapid rise of the Hanseatic League in the east during the following centuries.[13]

All these advances were accompanied by the clearing of woodlands. But this was not the only achievement of the pioneer settlers, although it was the most spectacular. The advances were followed by those of the Dutch, Flemish, and Frisians, who were called in to embank streams, drain marshes, and cut irrigation channels into the dry soils of part of the *Geest*.[14]

From Flanders and Holland, from Brabant and the Lower Rhine, from the most densely peopled regions of the Empire developed the origins of a free and systematic settlement of the east: from these parts streamed since the end of the eleventh century in ever growing numbers during almost two centuries the surplus of Germanic peoples toward the east. Their desire for independence and liberty, their agrarian order helped to a very great degree to create the type of a systematic and well-regulated settlement.[15]

About A.D. 1140, Albert the Bear, Markgrave of Brandenburg, began to colonize the lands east of the Elbe.

He held sway over many tribes between the Havel and the Elbe and subdued the rebels. As the Slavs finally decreased in numbers he sent to Utrecht and the Rhine, especially to the coast of the North Sea where the inhabitants, Dutchmen, Zealanders, and Flemings suffered greatly during the high tides. From these parts he had many brought to his own country, where he assigned to them, as their new home, fortified places and undefended hamlets in the Slav region. Especially the bishoprics of Havelberg and Brandenburg made big gains from these new settlers. The number of churches

13. Lamprecht. *Op. cit.*, Vol. III, p. 407.
14. Darby. *Op. cit.*, pp. 196, 197.
15. Lamprecht. *Op. cit.*, Vol. III, p. 357. (Author's translation)

increased and revenues from the tithe rose considerably. On the left bank of the Elbe Dutchmen settled: from Salzwedel to the Erzgebirge they occupied every marshy or flat piece of land. In former times, under the imperial family of the Ottos, the Saxons occupied these lands, as can still be seen near the old dikes . . . on the banks of the Elbe in the marshy lands of the Balsamians. But now . . . the Slavs have been pushed back and numerous and able settlers from the coast occupy the territory of the Slavs and build settlements and churches.[16]

This type of colonization repeated itself many centuries later when foreign settlers, experienced in reclamation, were also called in during the eighteenth century, especially under Frederick the Great. As his father had done before him, he invited settlers, Huguenots in particular, to reclaim lands in the eastern and northern parts of Old Prussia; there they drained marshes and helped to further colonization as well as to develop a new pattern of small settlements owned by peasants.

The Southeast Frontier

In the South, German or German-influenced penetration was of equal importance. The advance into Austria, the outpost against the Magyars in the tenth century and later against the Turks, proceeded mainly along the Danube valley which, like the side valleys was cleared for cultivation in the lower part and for pasturage on the upper slopes. The fortification of the frontier was, even at an early time, a very systematic work. As early as the first quarter of the tenth century King Henry I established fortified places against invading enemies. The following is an interesting description of how he proceeded.

It should not be kept secret with what circumspection King Henry, after he had obtained a peace for nine years from the Hungarians, set about to strengthen the defenses of his homeland and to subdue the alien aggressors. . . . He began with selecting every ninth man of the peasantry who was capable of bearing arms (*milites agrarii*) and installing him in a fortified place (*urbs*). There he had to find and prepare lodgings for his eight other comrades and their kin and to store a third of the harvest. The other eight also had to sow and to mow and to harvest for the ninth and put everything in a safe place. The *Thing*, all their meetings and feasts were to be celebrated according to his will in these places. They worked hard day and night to learn in peace what would be needed against the enemy in times of trouble. Apart from these fortified camps there was no defense or wall.[17]

In later centuries this process was accompanied by a lively mining activity and by the development of towns on the basis of original mining camps, especially in the Sudetes, the Erzge-

16. Helmold. *Cronica Slavorum.* In B. Schmeidler (ed.). *Scriptores Rerum Germanicarum*, Vol. I. 1937, p. 174. (Author's translation)

17. Widukindi. ". . . *rerum gest. Saxonicarum Libri III.*" In P. Hirsch (ed.). *Scriptores rerum Germanicarum.* 1935. (Author's translation)

birge, Slovakia, Styria, Carinthia, and further east in Bosnia and Serbia. Later in the eighteenth century, under Maria Theresa, a determined colonization of the eastern borderlands set in. The Banat and the Bacska, especially, were settled with soldier-settlers, whose presence was expected to strengthen the political and economic security of these parts.

However, this early movement could not go on indefinitely. Gradually it came to a standstill and in some parts it retreated. It had reached its peak around A.D. 1300, and was followed by a period of stagnation. In virtually all parts of central Europe there were regions that were neglected, fields that were abandoned, and villages that were deserted. In south and west Germany the acreage of these abandoned lands, the *Wüstungen*, has been estimated as one half of the area previously under the plow, and for Germany as a whole as about 25 per cent.[18] The reasons for these drawbacks are not quite clear. Wars, pestilences, economic fluctuations, and population decline have been advanced as causes. All may have played a part, but the explanation may be even simpler: No movement, and most certainly no movement carried on with such tremendous energy and on so large a scale, can go on for too long a time. Moreover, the frontiers of expansion in relation to the number of available settlers had been reached, and apart from this, settled conditions in the older lands had been consolidated. The people were, therefore, less attracted by adventures into the unknown and insecure regions of the moving frontier.

The next phase was one of the rape of the forests, not one of clearing for settlement—at least in general. There is no need to dwell on this aspect of the interaction of man and environment. Suffice it to say that with the discovery of new lands overseas the need of timber for ship-building rose fantastically; the Portuguese, Spanish, English, and Dutch navies were the main users. This continued until the first ironclad ships were built in the nineteenth century. The lasting and most creative results of the great conquest of the woodlands was the new structure of settlement that emerged from this centuries-long activity. The losses in abandoned villages and stagnating towns are minute in comparison with the grand achievements of an effort that laid the foundations of a structure of settlement for generations.

The forces that caused the great west-east movements are not well known. There are hardly any original sources available to shed light on this important development. It is, however, very probable that the political and social conditions in

Stagnation and Retreat

Urbanization and Rural Settlement

18. Darby. *Op. cit.*, p. 198.

the regions between the lower Rhine, the Maas, and the coast contributed toward this conquest of unsettled lands. The growing urbanization was accompanied by a growth of population. Industrial activities brought into being a fluctuating class of artisans, craftsmen, and workers who were politically and economically unstable. At the same time, an unaccustomed money economy began to take root, and a more rational mentality spread to all strata of society. Attachment to the soil and to the lord of the manor, to a town or a territory weakened, and the hitherto sharp frontiers between town and country began to lose their significance. Even those who lived outside the town walls, especially the craftsmen and traders, felt like townspeople. Moreover, a crusade against the Slavs was a welcome means of distracting the attention of the people from the disasters nearer home that war and nature had brought about. The enterprising spirit of a wealthy and audacious citizenry and the ever-stirring warlike spirit of the nobility searched and found in the East a new outlet for their energies.[19]

It was only natural that the colonization proceeded simultaneously in the rural and urban field. The foundation of new towns was primarily the work of the kings, whereas very often villages owed their origins to individual and private initiative and also to the nobles and the monasteries. The kings had a direct interest; they granted far-reaching new privileges to the merchants and traders, especially in central Germany, or confirmed the old ones. In the long run, this was a remunerative process, soon imitated by the lower ranks of the feudal hierarchy. Thus, political ends were reconciled with economic needs and rural settlement; power, markets, and colonization were on a par. This was clearly expressed in the transformation of the old trading centers: The streets widened into the market which they enclosed like a village common. Soon the merchants' houses began to line these thoroughfares, and churches were erected. Later, new streets were added, either parallel to the old ones or crossing them, and in this manner the first precursors either of the gridiron or of irregular plans came into being. Gradually the old parts of these towns merged with the new quarters.

Something similar happened in the countryside. The scattered settlements of the clearings grew together into a common *Gemarkung,* and the field systems were adapted to the new economic and social conditions. The larger villages, the *Kirchdörfer,* received their church and other public buildings. The success of the colonization was assured by the cooperation of town and country. It has been estimated that before A.D. 1200 about 100 towns were founded on colonial lands; 400 in the first half of the thirteenth century and almost the same number

19. K. H. Quirin. *Die Deutsche Ostsiedlung im Mittelalter.* 1954, pp. 24, 25.

in the second half. By the fourteenth century this number had decreased by about 100, and by the fifteenth century it was less than 100.[20] How intimately village and town were interrelated is proved by the fact that in numerous cases the same regular layout was used in the colonial rural and urban communities. This was, however, nothing unusual. In virtually all cases, in all parts of the world where colonial settlements were founded, ground-plans were regular, an unquestionable sign that one will was behind this enterprise, a will that imposed its intentions with military rigidity upon the physical structure of these outposts.

The colonization of the East is not comparable to one mighty stream. Rather it was a slow trickle of innumerable rivulets in all directions. It was a movement that sprang up here and there and that gained a footing sometimes in the most unexpected places. It left large tracts untouched; it receded sometimes only to reappear in another place; it was composed of a multitude of totally different directions, each of different scope and intensity. Only the main direction remained unaffected, the movement toward the East.

20. K. H. Quirin. *Op. cit.*, p. 34.

THROUGHOUT her history, Germany, as the heartland of Europe, has been the battlefield for contending ideas and varying forces that converged on her from the surrounding countries or arose within her own territory and then spread outward. The foreground of the political scene has been dominated by mighty rulers and innumerable princelings who carried on their great or petty contests for power under the cloak of opposing ideologies. But underneath these noisy and often blatantly cynical contests the life of the masses went on in all its immense variety and strength. The ravages of war, pestilence, and internal strife have destroyed much, retarded developments and exterminated innumerable people. But what has survived belongs to the great achievements of humanity, equal to the supreme creations of any other country. German art, architecture, and city planning have made a contribution toward the cultural life of mankind without which the world would be a poor place to live in. German thoughts and ideas have fructified many other countries. It is against this background of lasting values that the more ephemeral goings-on in the political field should be viewed. A survey of historical changes is therefore indispensable for understanding the manifold forces that have shaped the physical, social, and economic structure of Germany's cities, towns, and villages. Such a survey, however, has to be restricted only to those facts that have a direct bearing on the history of city development.

The course of German history is very involved. Her territory was never clearly delimited by nature—as is the case, for instance, in Spain or Great Britain or Japan. Her frontiers were, and still are, open to all sides, except perhaps in the south where the Alps form a barrier (although this is pierced by numerous passes through which ideas and men have traveled in both directions).

In Caesar's time the Rhine was Germany's effective western frontier. Under Augustus, however, the Roman frontier was moved beyond the Rhine, although with varying success. In the year 12 B.C. Drusus occupied an area corresponding roughly to the present Netherlands, and a canal, the *Fossa Drusiana,* was built connecting the Rhine and the *Lacus Flevus,* partially corresponding to the Zuider Zee. Drusus advanced toward the Weser and crossed it, and a Roman garrison was stationed in the regions between the Rhine and the Elbe. After the annihilation of three legions under Varus in the year A.D. 9 in the Teutoburger Wald, attempts were made by Germanicus Caesar to restore Roman power; but in the end this proved unsuccessful. Along the greater part of its course the Rhine remained the frontier of the Roman Empire. A Roman army was stationed

CHAPTER 2

Historical Background

Roman Period

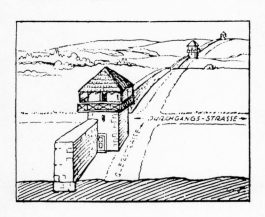

17. Reconstruction of the Roman *limes. Above:* moat with stockade of the *limes* in Upper Germany. *Below: limes* between Lorch (Württemberg) and the Danube, the so-called "Devil's Wall."

Charlemagne and the Early Middle Ages

on this river with two headquarters, one at Mainz in Upper Germany and another one near Xanten in Lower Germany. This gave origin to a number of towns that were to play an important role in German history. Among them were Trier (Augusta Trevirorum), Köln (Colonia Agrippinensis), Bonn (Bonna), Worms (Borbetomagus), Speyer (Noviomagus), Strasbourg (Argentoratum), and Augsburg (Augusta Vindelicorum).

Later the frontier of Upper Germany was moved forward beyond the Rhine, and a fortified *Pfahlgraben,* a palisaded ditch, was erected to protect it. It began at a point between Bonn and Coblenz and led to Miltenberg on the Main, turned southward to Lorch in Württemberg, and then eastward to the Danube. The final line was fixed, probably under Hadrian, and in parts advanced still further. This consisted of numerous blockhouses and forts in the rear, interconnected by a stone wall that began where the earthworks stopped. The stone fortifications reached the Danube at Hienheim near Regensburg, which at first was a frontier post and later became a legionary fortress surrounded by fields that supplied food for the garrison. This region of Germany enclosed by the Roman *limes* developed a culture that up to the present day has retained many characteristics different from the rest of Germany.

During the following centuries the German tribes beyond the frontier, driven on by peoples advancing from the East, began to move forward. The Franks, Alemanni, and Suevians, and the Burgundians and Vandals attacked the Rhine frontier while the Ostrogoths and Visigoths marched against the lower Danube. All these tribes strove forward and engaged in constant battles with hostile forces in the rear and enemies in the front who tried to stem their advance. By the end of the sixth century the whole basin of the Elbe was occupied by the Slavs, with the exception of the Saxon territory that stretched in the north to the Danish frontier near the Eider. The subjugation of the Frisians who dwelt in the region of the North Sea coast was begun in A.D. 689 by Pippin of Heristal and finally completed by the Emperor Charlemagne. Charlemagne conquered the Saxons in the last third of the eighth century; his empire then extended to the borders of Denmark.

When Charlemagne began the consolidation and unification of Germany he was faced with two unreconciled forces: the Christian hierarchy of the Church and the still pagan spirit of the people, for the Christianization of preceding centuries had not found a ready response among the masses. Charlemagne's great achievement was not merely the unification of his realm under the banner of Christianity, but a coalescence of the still living ideas and habits of antiquity with the new forces that Christianity had brought to the fore. This is evident, on the one hand, by the presence at his court of eminent scholars educated in the tradition of Rome and Greece, by his own study of Latin and Greek, by his building the cathedral at Aix-la-Chapelle in an antique-Byzantine style; and, on the other hand, by his unifying reform of the script, by his establishment of cathedral schools for languages, by his interest in sermons in the native tongue, by his preservation of old rights and privileges of the people, and by his collection of the national epics. His person and his deeds symbolized the great synthesis on which the Occidental world has rested up to the present time.

The Emperor introduced a Frankish system of government —Frankish officials helped reduce the antagonism between the tribes—and Christianity, which spread as the most powerful force over the whole of central and western Europe, began to create a more or less homogeneous culture. Charlemagne furthered this development by granting land privileges to the clergy and by founding monasteries, schools, and bishoprics. The tribal rulers had vanished and their territories were now ruled by counts.

By the Treaty of Verdun in 843 Germany was more clearly defined as a region than it had been before. The Germans had their own ruler, Louis, whose realm included most of the lands east of the Rhine, with districts around Mainz, Worms, and Speyer on the left bank. Another treaty, also of great importance to the formation of Germany, was concluded between Charles the Bald and Louis the German at Mersen, Holland in 870. It added to the German Dominion all the lands to the west of the Elbe and the Bohemian mountains and, in the west, on the left bank of the Rhine, a territory comprising the present Alsace and Lorraine. This realm contained the five archbishoprics of Mainz, Trier, Cologne, Salzburg, and Bremen.

Feudalism grew during these times. The dukes who had been elected by the different regions acquired extensive domains from which they made large grants to their followers. The power of the dukes, strengthened by the landed aristocracy, increased until by the beginning of the tenth century the royal authority had been reduced to a minimum.

Henry the Fowler ruled in the first part of the tenth century and contributed much toward the defense of Germany against the Magyars. Hardly any towns or fortified places existed outside the region once under Roman influence. It was therefore imperative to strengthen those outer regions. This Henry did by founding fortresses and walled towns. His efforts were primarily devoted to northern and eastern Germany and met with great success. Under his son and successor, Otto the Great, the consolidation of Germany progressed, and with it feudalism.

But because of Otto's energetic leadership all feudal lords, even the highest vassals, recognized him as their superior. He founded the bishoprics of Schleswig, Ripen, and Aarhus for the Danes; and for the Slavs he founded those of Brandenburg and Havelberg, among others, and later the archbishopric of Magdeburg, including the sees of Meissen, Zeitz, and Merseburg.

But the feudal lords did not acquiesce in the over-riding authority of any king or emperor. The struggle between them and the Crown went on throughout the Middle Ages, just as the contest between emperor and pope continued for several centuries. Under Henry III, who ascended the throne in 1039, the Dukes of Swabia, Bavaria, and Carinthia evaded his direct overlordship. Others followed; and although they did not sever the bonds abruptly and completely, on the whole they undermined the power of the Crown and erected a barrier between ruler and people. Henry was crowned Emperor by Pope Clemens II and helped to extend the influence of the Church over western Europe. He initiated an era that although of the utmost importance to the papacy was of doubtful gain to Germany. Under his reign the towns prospered and commerce and trade expanded, particularly along the Rhine and the Weser.

The self-consciousness of the Occident as an intellectual and spiritual entity was kindled by the monasteries, especially by the Cluniac monks. This was an aristocratic organization: Abbots and many monks belonged to the Burgundian aristocracy, and all Cluniac monasteries were subordinated by a rigid discipline to the mother-monastery—like a spiritual army ready to march in the name of Christianity. This religious force joined with the temporal aristocracy, and each exerted a profound influence upon the other. Just as the monks became an aristocratic and hierarchical power, so the feudal lords absorbed the spirit of the militant monasteries. They withdrew gradually from active participation in economic life and turned to intellectual and spiritual interests when they were not engaged in war or feuds. The feudal lords were rulers not only of the temporal but also of the religious organizations at this time; consequently, they also ruled the monasteries, which had to supply soldiers while their abbots and many of their monks and nuns were members of the lay-aristocracy. Feudalism and monkdom were bound together by innumerable ties. In this sense the movement that spread from Cluny was one of the most potent forces in forming the medieval world.

The lay-aristocracy of the late tenth and the early eleventh centuries bowed to the ideas of the Truce of God (the *Treuga Dei*), first observed in 1031, and to the conception of a Public Peace (the *Landfrieden*). At first this was accepted only in

France, in small territories, and for certain weekdays. Then it gained momentum and spread to Germany. The military activities of the Knights diminished, and soon conferring knighthood became only a religious ritual by which the knight vowed to observe the spiritual tenets of Christianity, as well as absolute self-sacrifice for the highest aims, protection of the helpless and weak, unconditional sincerity, and generous Christian magnanimity. A new Christian type was born who had to find other fields for his military prowess now that his sword could no longer be used at home. He became the active exponent of the Christian-militant expansion of the Occident and rallied to the banner of the Crusades.[1]

Frederick I, called Barbarossa and one of Germany's greatest rulers, was crowned at Aix-la-Chapelle in 1152. He conquered the Slavic lands to the east of the Elbe, which had been insufficiently subjected—one of his main tasks and one at which he succeeded. But that was not his only achievement. His peaceful conquest, the penetration of these regions by cultural means and their opening for trade and commerce, was an even greater success. He founded new towns and helped those that already existed. He established new bishoprics and revived others. He settled colonists between the Elbe and the Oder and restored internal order in the West by using existing laws and issuing new orders against offenders of the peace and by ruthlessly suppressing the robber barons. Under these conditions the towns flourished, and their inhabitants were devoted to the Emperor who granted them extensive privileges.

Frederick II, crowned at Aix-la-Chapelle in 1215, was Germany's most interesting and most magnificent sovereign. He possessed six crowns, those of the Empire, Germany, Sicily, Lombardy, Burgundy, and Jerusalem. His reign was remarkable in many respects, but it was of special importance because he conceded to the Church that he would not take part in episcopal elections, not erect new toll centers or mints on the lands of the spiritual lords, and not allow the building of towns in their territories. By these concessions he made the prelates actual sovereigns and an alien body in the Empire. After a decade they were given full rights of jurisdiction over their lands and were referred to as *domini terrae;* this raised them virtually to the status of independent sovereigns and, at the same time, restricted the freedom of the towns in their lands. In 1235 the Emperor held a diet at Mainz, which was attended by many princes. This was an event of great importance to Germany, because the great "land peace" (*Landfrieden*) was proclaimed, whereby private war was declared illegal except when justice could not be obtained otherwise, a chief justiciar was appointed

The High Middle Ages

1. A. Weber, *Kulturgeschichte als Kultursoziologie*. 1935, pp. 252 ff.

for the whole Empire, tolls and mints erected after a certain date were abolished, and other measures for the maintenance of law and order set in motion.

Frederick II's successors ruled with constantly decreasing authority, and the border countries became practically independent. At the same time, the offices, territories, and private fiefs of the princes were made hereditary. This meant that they ceased to be at the disposal of the emperors and could be passed on within the same princely family. This resulted in Germany's being split up into innumerable principalities.

The period from 1254 to the crowning of Rudolf of Habsburg in 1273 was called the Great Interregnum. It was a period of trouble, disunity, and disorganization. The emperor's authority had been destroyed, and the multitude of small and large feudal domains had become independent states. The western part of Germany was a chaos of tiny territories; only east of the Elbe and Saale, in the lands conquered from the Slavs, were the territorial units larger, comprising Saxony, Bohemia, and Austria. But in contrast to these petty rivalries and endless local wars the arts flourished, the towns prospered, and trade and commerce experienced a great upsurge. From the trading centers of Italy, Venice, Milan, and Genoa, routes led over the Alpine passes into the industrious towns of South Germany— to Augsburg, Regensburg, and Nürnberg; down the Rhine into the wealthy towns of Ghent, Bruges, and Ypres in Flanders; and into the Hanse towns of the North, which were all linked together by trade-routes extending to Flanders, the North Sea coast, and the Baltic. The towns of the Hanseatic League numbered about seventy. The League controlled the whole trade of the North and had factories in Novgorod, London, and Bergen.

Urban Society

Small market towns were dotted over the country at a distance of 4 to 15 miles from each other. A network of roads connected them with the villages and manors interspersed between them. This web of urban and rural settlements grew wider toward the East, while it narrowed in the South and West especially, and particularly in the Rhineland. The average population, even in the larger cities of the Rhine basin, hardly exceeded 30 thousand. Within these urban aggregates, which were still in the process of formation yet powerful and attractive enough to be great factors of political and economic renewal, the first European movement toward freedom developed. This was a ground swell in a sea of religious and intellectual agitation, moving slowly at first, but gradually increasing in intensity and extent. It grew out of the tensions between the new freedom that town life promised and the thralldom that lay heavily on the countryside. It found succor in the growing strength of the guilds, in the weakening influence of the urban patricians, and in the steadily increasing financial and commercial activities of the towns. At the same time, a poor class of workers began to penetrate into the urban structure.

Gradually the towns assumed the lead in the intellectual life of the nation. The masses of the artisans and craftsmen began to reshape their own democratic culture on the basis of the inheritance from the Church and the aristocracy. But the more the new classes gained through self-examination and insight, the more their original self-assurance gave way to a critical attitude, not only toward individual conditions and people but generally toward life as a whole. The old values began to crumble and the old authorities to lose their hold over the mind of the masses. It was a period of revolutionary upsurge on a broad front; not merely because of the fading away of a knightly world or because of the rise of a well-organized and prosperous bourgeoisie. The urban society of this time, with all its contradictions of piety, propriety, and boisterous liberty, was perhaps not fully aware of its own part in this fool's paradise. "The world is full of folly. Who can remain free of it?" was a saying of the time. The meaning of life was at stake, and toward the end of the period this uncertainty, this diffidence, found its symbolic expression in the dance of death. These serial representations of the fate that awaits all men, the humble and the mighty, the poor and the rich, appeared in many parts of Europe, and were the mirror of a pitiless self-reflection and confusion.

But this disintegration and distrust were embraced and partly hidden by a deepening awareness of Christianity, by an intellectual scholasticism and an emotional mysticism that found their supreme embodiment in Gothic cathedrals with their unsurpassable sculptures and the translucent beauty of their stained-glass windows. These cathedrals were the final victory of unsubstantial space over the solidity of matter, the absorption of reality into transcendental unsubstantiality. They symbolized a renunciation of daily life, yet expressed the whole plexus of its manifold forces.

The reign of Maximilian I is generally regarded as the end of the Middle Ages. He has been called the "Last Knight." He resisted the French attempt to sever those provinces of his realm that had belonged to the Burgundian dominion. The old feudal structure was waning and the Crown had no effective influence on the princes who instituted local diets in their territories. Mercenaries replaced the feudal obligation to military service, a development which made the princes and their vassals even

The Renaissance

77

more independent of the Crown. New ideas were stirring, and men began to emerge from the narrow world which the unquestioning belief of the Middle Ages, the spiritual dictatorship of a corrupt Church, and feudal ties had woven around them. The Renaissance was dawning, and the mind of man awakened from a slumber that had prevented new adventures of ideas and had enclosed his mind in the narrow confines of an outworn and hollow routine. In sharp contrast to the political scene with its innumerable smaller and larger territorial units, ideas, aspirations, goods, and artistic impulses were more easily diffused and accepted as the unifying bond of a common culture. The cities expanded; their closely knit social structure weakened; and their economic influence spread over larger areas. The burgher of the Middle Ages, hitherto protected and bounded by the shells of family, guilds, confraternities, and the visible *enceinte* of the walls of his town, began to break out of these confines—in spirit and in fact. A new world opened before him, baffling at first, but soon accepted as an outlet for his changed attitude to life. These liberating forces found their greatest ally in the Reformation. On All Saints' Day, 1517, an obscure Augustinian friar, Martin Luther, nailed to the doors of the church in Wittenberg the theses against the misuse of the papal power by selling indulgences. The Middle Ages had come to an end.

18. Silver mining at Leberthal (Vosges) in sixteenth-century Germany.

78

19. Selling and making shoes, from Hans Sachs's *Book of Trades*, 1568. Woodcut by Jost Amman.

The revolutionary forces that had grown during the centuries and had shaken the religious and feudal hierarchies broke through when the spiritual and social constellation was ripe for a new departure. At the beginning of the sixteenth century there was only one country where these forces could be successful. This country was Germany. Stirred up from the bottom but not yet consolidated by a uniting authority like England and France, the revolutionary elements found an outlet in the Reformation. Since the invention of printing the masses had had a voice, and this voice made itself felt; after Copernicus and the empirical studies of Regiomontanus and Behaim, the veil that the era of faith, the Middle Ages, had woven around men's minds began to disintegrate and a new conception of the universe emerged. The self-confidence of the artisans and craftsmen led them to new methods of working; they improved their tools and the handling of their products; wind and water were used more and more as power; the clock and the compass

20. *Merchant.* Woodcut by Hans
Weiditz, 1519-20.

were invented; and many other improvements were made.
Luther himself was a son of the people. He came from a mining
region in Saxony, where the urban economy rested on a broad
base of restless workers and miners. These men had never really
been absorbed into the civilizing trends that, stemming from
Antiquity, had created a strong coherence of tradition.

The new religion fell on fertile soil. It corresponded with
the democratic sentiments of the masses and gave expression and
meaning to the individual person's free will and self-salvation,
without the intercession of priests. It fanned the flames of a
revolution embracing the whole of life; and yet it remained
unfinished like so many other incipient movements in German
history. It helped to unchain the Peasants' Wars and the radi-
calism of the Anabaptists, both ending in defeat. It was the
source of the Religious Wars in the following century, which
weakened Germany more than any other event. But it opened
the doors to the Renaissance and, beyond it, to the Scientific
Revolution.

Charles V, who followed Maximilian after the latter's death
in 1519, ruled Spain, Naples, Sicily and Sardinia, the Netherlands, Burgundy, Austria, and the New World. During his reign,
internal wars and revolts in Germany went on, and the Peasants'
War (the *Bauernkrieg*) broke out. This was a spontaneous re-

bellion of oppressed people, brought about by ruthless exploitation exercised by princes and other great landowners, but also by economic changes. Free migration and resettlement of the peasants were obstructed, although in many districts the holdings had become so small by repeated subdivisions that a peasant family could not live on them. A large-scale revolt began in 1522. Smaller outbreaks had occurred before this date, but they had been of a more local character. The banner of the peasants was the *Bundschuh,* a clog upon a pole, and under this sign the revolt was joined by many knights who had grievances of their own resulting from the loss of their feudal rights and the introduction of Roman law, and by adventurers and workers from the towns. The peasants demanded social, economic, and religious redress, and appealed to the Biblical prophesies as promises of a new life that would be free of oppression and bring prosperity. Some of their moderate claims were granted by the more prudent lords and prelates. But the revolt spread, and involved the Rhineland and Thuringia. The war ended in 1525 with a disastrous defeat of the peasants. The princes took cruel vengeance, especially because the rebels had committed reckless crimes against life and property. Luther supported the winning side after he had first taken up a more mediatory position; he had actually encouraged the reprisals *against* the rebels by publishing a pamphlet, "On the Murderous Peasant Hordes."

Protestantism spread, and the antagonism between the adherents of the new creed and the Catholics grew. At the diet held at Augsburg in 1555, agreement was reached that Catholics and Lutherans, although not Calvinists, should have the same rights; but this did not put an end to religious strife or bring freedom and toleration in religious matters. The State remained supreme and the doctrine *cuius regio eius religio* was accepted. The stage was set for the religious wars of the future.

21. *Carpenters.* German woodcut of the early sixteenth century.

The Thirty Years' War

In 1618 the Thirty Years' War broke out, affecting all parts of Germany. It was concluded by the Treaty of Westphalia, which changed the map of Europe. France received Metz, Verdun, Toul and the Austrian territory of Alsace; Sweden gained Western Pomerania, Stettin, Verden, and Bremen; Hanover, Saxony and Brandenburg increased their territories; and Switzerland and Holland became *de facto* independent sovereign states.

Germany was in a disastrous condition. The population had decreased by 10 to 20 million. The rural districts, especially, had suffered grievously. Large numbers of peasants had left the land and migrated to the cities; numerous villages had been abandoned; and agriculture had almost ceased to exist, owing partly to the death of farmers or to their enrollment as soldiers and partly because the stock had been killed and houses destroyed. The peasants had no money to rebuild their houses and restore their fields. They were at the mercy of the great landowners who imposed hard dues and unfavorable terms of tenure and provided capital only on very harsh conditions. The decrease in population led to a reduced demand and consumption of agricultural products and consequently to low prices and a greatly restricted area of land under the plow. The plight of the big landowners was hardly less. They had to raise mortgages at a high rate of interest, but were assisted by the states which declared moratoria or remitted the interests. Industry and commerce suffered equally, and foreign goods swamped the market; the factory system began to throw out of work many handicraft workers whose disintegrating guilds could no longer provide economic security. Moreover, the mouths of Germany's important rivers, the trade arteries of the country, were under foreign rule. The Dutch occupied the Rhine; the Swedes and Danes, the Weser, the Elbe, and the Oder; and the Poles, the Vistula.

The towns were impoverished, and many faced ruin because of the enormous levies they had to pay to save them from invaders. The mineral resources that had been a major contribution to the wealth of Germany were exhausted or had lost much of their value through the increasing import of metals, especially silver, from the New World. Material interests were paramount, and intellectual life had almost come to a standstill. French influence, spreading to the courts of the princes, filtered down to the wealthy citizens and to the middle classes. Germany had reached the nadir of its culture and prosperity.

The political and administrative structure of Germany was split up into many territories, the number of which has been estimated at about 1800, and which included tiny domains of Free Knights of the Empire (*Reichsfreie Ritter*), dependent directly on the Emperor. Apart from these units there were about fifty imperial cities (*Reichsfreie Staedte*) with a total population of about 750 thousand inhabitants; a few ancient commercial towns like Bremen, Hamburg, Augsburg, Nürnberg, Ulm, Brandenburg, and Frankfurt am Main; and numerous small country towns that also relied on old privileges and did not belong to the territory of a prince. These free cities, governed by patrician families, seldom had any progressive economic and intellectual life. The population of the 63 ecclesiastical territories was about 3 million. These territories were governed by bishops or abbots and the cathedral chapter and, on the whole, were badly administered more in the interests of the leading families of the ecclesiastical rulers and the nobles who were members of the chapters than in the interests of the citizens. The temporal principalities and countships amounted to almost two hundred. All their petty rulers were eager to maintain splendid courts with many courtiers, empty demonstrations that made the introduction of new taxes necessary to maintain this costly ostentation. Then there were the large principalities, first among them the lands of the Habsburgs consisting of the Kingdoms of Bohemia, Austria, Styria, Carinthia, Carniola, Tirol, and certain territories in southern Germany. Finally, there were the territories of the Hohenzollern mainly composed of the lands from the Elbe and the Harz Mountains to the Vistula, separated East Prussia, and some districts on the Rhine and in Westphalia. Other territories belonged to the House of Wettin that ruled Saxony, the House of Wittelsbach that owned Bavaria, the House of Guelf of Hanover, and the territories of the Duchy of Württemberg, the Margravate of Baden and the House of Hesse. The powers of the diets of these lands were gradually, but systematically, reduced by the princes who, in the course of the seventeenth and eighteenth centuries, became absolute rulers.

The century following the end of the Thirty Years' War was a dismal period for Germany. New wars broke out; notably wars with the France of Louis XIV and with the Turks who had advanced toward Vienna; the War of the Polish Succession, fought mainly in Italy and the upper Rhineland; the Silesian Wars between Frederick the Great and Maria Theresa; the Seven Years' War, ending in 1763; and the War of the Bavarian Succession, concluded in 1779. It was a politically sterile period, and one which saw the consolidation of Prussia and forced upon Austria the recognition of the fact that Prussia was there to stay. But culturally Germany began to revive, and soon the arts and architecture flourished again.

The Baroque and Rococo, the styles of passion and grace,

The Baroque and Rococo Periods

of pomp and delicacy, of a new feeling of space and of matter in violent motion, dominated the artistic scene. Some of the most beautiful and entrancing palaces and churches and many residential and ecclesiastical buildings were erected. The time of Germany's great geniuses in music and poetry—of Bach, Haydn, Mozart, and Beethoven, and of Lessing, Schiller, and Goethe—was approaching, and German philosophy began to make its eminent contribution to the development of ideas and reasoning. It was an ironic coincidence that Germany's political weakness was compensated for by her ideal and intellectual greatness, making this epoch an outstanding one in the history of the country and driving home the lesson that a state need not be powerful to be great.

The Age of Napoleon and Revolutionary Ferment

The age of Napoleon saw a further humiliation of Germany and particularly of Prussia. Only the victory of the War of Liberation, won after the disastrous defeat of the Napoleonic armies in Russia, changed the situation. The Holy Roman Empire of the German Nation had come to an end in 1804, after having lasted for almost a thousand years, and the map of Europe was changed once more by the Congress of Vienna which sat from 1814 to 1815. Austria was deprived of all her western possessions and of Poland, with the exception of Galicia, while she recovered parts of northern Italy. Prussia received West Prussia, Posen, and Upper Pomerania in the East and, in the West, Westphalia and the Rhine Province. Bavaria was given more or less its present extension. After the Congress, Germany consisted of 39 states that included the free cities of Hamburg, Bremen, and Lübeck.

The German people had to pay a high price for the peace. Prussia, especially, was to live through a period of darkest reaction, and the obedient subject of the sovereign state became the docile representative of the following decades. The courageous and well-meant attempts of the ministers Stein and Hardenberg in Prussia to introduce reforms which would awaken the people's active interest in public affairs were doomed as soon as the national emergency after Napoleon's great defeat of Prussia at Jena and Auerstedt had lost its depressing impact. Once the danger was over, the reforms lapsed and were forgotten. But in spite of the masses' philistine complacence the spark of liberty had kindled a faint flame of hope and intensity that finally flared up in the Revolution of 1848 and led to the German Constitution one year later. The old reactionary ministries were overthrown in many German states, and it seemed as if a new era were dawning. But the German Parliament at Frankfurt was not equal to its task although it was animated by a liberal spirit of progress, humanity, and enterprise. By shady manipulations the people were robbed of the fruits of their initial success mainly because the masses remained indifferent philistines.

Prussia, and with it Germany, reached the height of power in modern times in 1871 when, on January 18, William I was proclaimed German Emperor at Versailles after the victorious war against France. Germany now comprised a territory of some 200 thousand square miles with a population of 41 million people. After the war against Denmark, she had acquired the Duchies of Schleswig and Holstein. In 1871 she was still mainly agricultural, but the Industrial Revolution made rapid progress and the so-called *Gründerjahre* after 1871 were a period of industrial consolidation and expansion. As in the France of Napoleon III, the slogan *enrichez-vous* was all-powerful, and many fortunes were made. A wealthy middle class grew up, and the industrial workers, though unorganized, began to influence political life, while the rural population remained followers of the landed aristocracy. As the cities and towns grew, their citizens played an increasing role in party politics. But they made no contributions to an artistic renewal. It was a time of general decline in the arts and of adulation of material progress and technological advance; city planning in this period was shallow, pompous, elective, and without genuine value. This artistic decline reached its lowest ebb under William II, but began to give way to a revival of art and architecture just before World War I, after which Germany ceased to be a great power. The turning point in her history had been reached.

But once again, in the 1920's when Germany was powerless, new forces began to emerge, and German architecture and town planning revived. New ideas were born and found enthusiastic support among the young generation, which provided some of the best architects and planners of this time. The enormous material prosperity that the country had experienced during the peaceful period from 1871 to 1914 had disappeared. The national wealth had been dissipated by inflation, and intellectual life had to be recreated. Today Germany's fate is still in the balance, and in spite of "the economic miracle" after World War II, it is an obvious fact that this material recovery is not being accompanied by a corresponding renewal of the arts and city life. The destructive bombing of many of the historic cities was too great to be followed by a creative rebuilding. However, it seems that some efforts have been made to make use of the progressive ideas that took shape while Germany was cut off from the world at large. But so far no genuinely new and inspiring language of form has been found. The wounds that were inflicted by the National Socialist regime were too deep, and what has been built or planned still carries the stamp either of a clumsy and crude pomposity or of a timid modernism.

Triumph and Decline

EVERY FORM of gregariousness postulates and creates a characteristic form of economy. Village life brings men together in a more immediate and personal way than town life, not because the village is generally smaller, but because the thinking and feeling of the villagers are more strongly related to subconscious sentiments and spontaneous reactions than are the more abstract ways of thinking of urban society. It is not that the cooperative will is alive in the village in unspoiled purity: peasants harm and hate each other just as much as townspeople. They cooperate no more than the people in towns, but their natural and unavoidable companionship and association and the herd instinct are stronger in the village and are dependent on more subjectively felt aspirations and reactions. The peasant is primarily attached to his family, more lastingly than to his community or to the state. These are basic human qualities that explain the great and fundamental similarity of the peasants in all countries as well as their generally conservative attitude.

In the village the identity of the work creates a natural assimilation that nobody, however hard he may work individually, can evade, and which unites all members of the community, whereas in the town it is the awareness of rational expediency and of the complicated interaction of innumerable technical forces that holds the urban society together. The peasant waits for the gifts of nature; he is powerless to influence the natural rhythm; he can do no more than help to improve the quality, and increase the quantity, of her gifts. In principle his work is restricted to the producing of raw materials, and thus he remains nearer to nature. The periodicity that nature imposes forces him into a periodicity of life that all his fellow peasants have to share. It drives him irresistibly into a community that he does not create himself. The rhythm of industrial work that is dependent on the will of men is alien to him. It is significant that the peasant has never been the original creator and bearer of a nonmagical religion. His piety has grown out of and has rested on the adoration of fertility and on his identification with the land. The peasant waits; the townsman commands. The peasant grows into his community; the townsman organizes his society. The village is a community of men who are basically similar; the town is an organized association of vastly different types. The scale of the village is the individual house; the scale of the town is the block. The streets of the village connect the houses; those of the town connect the various districts.

As in all other countries the biological family was the core of rural organization in Germany. It was mostly identical with

Rural Settlement

the house or the farmstead and presupposed a certain stage of agricultural development. A family farm with its main dwelling and outbuildings may have grown out of a larger group, such as a clan or a voluntary association, based on neighborly cooperation. But the opposite may also have been possible: Several farms may have grown together into a larger unit. In the first case, a compact village would have been loosened up by a thinning-out and subsequent dissociation of farmsteads that were previously part of the village proper. In the second case, individual and isolated farms would have been absorbed into a compact village. A rural community was a neighborhood unit, and as such it was also a working unit because certain economic functions were common to all its members, and certain parts of the land served a common purpose. Thus, regulations for the cultivation of the fields and other activities had to be observed, such as the *Flurzwang*—the need to plow, sow, and harvest at the same time—or the use of the common forest, of the *Allmende,* the common lands for the pasture, and of the common hunting grounds. Of course, all this influenced very decisively the structure and development of the rural settlement, at times to the disadvantage of the village, at others to its advantage, depending upon the community's ability to adapt itself to the various needs and conditions of the village or to a larger political unit. A frictionless organization was essential because occasionally pastures, meadows, forests, and water belonged to different villages. The actual layout of individual villages was not necessarily influenced by these commonly owned lands, but the plan of the settlement as a whole—that is, of the village and the fields —was almost always subject to the particular structure of this wider area. On the other hand, the way in which the land was acquired was of considerable importance: if it was through peaceful acquisition, it was mostly the individual households that took over the land and organized the common work; if the gain had been made in war or by illegal measures, it was mostly a political unit that owned the land as a common property and regulated the work. Both developments considerably influenced the layout of the village and the fields.

The conditions were different if a clan controlled the common activities. In contrast to the individual peasant household, cooperation between clan members was not continuous nor necessarily based on common ownership. Moreover, up to a certain degree the clan was the opposite of the house community, for it accepted those who, for one reason or another, had dissociated themselves from the narrower group. The clan comprised several house communities, but it could also be a disintegrating factor that received only certain members of individual households. The sphere of influence of the neighborhood household community and the clan could be either identical, antagonistic, or merely physically separated. Whatever pattern this relationship took, however, affected the inheritance of the villagers, and therefore the density and form of the village; the influence of these social factors on the physical structure of the village and the field system should not be underestimated. Whether the land was subdivided or kept together, or whether second sons built their own farmsteads in the same village as their fathers or somewhere else, was of vital importance.

A rural settlement consisted of the village and the surrounding country as far as the latter belonged to the immediate functions of the settlement as a whole. Meadows, fields, pasturelands, forests, and water were means of production, just as roads and footpaths were means of communication. Size, form, and structure of the village and field system were decided according to such natural conditions of the land as situation on a plain or in the mountains, on a plateau or in a valley, on fertile or poor soil, on water resources or on dry land. But German settlers, like those in all other regions of the world, have always successfully tried to adapt their settlements to difficult and even adverse conditions and above all to the social and economic needs that ultimately were the formative elements of their society. Wherever the challenge of nature and of the social and economic organization were similar, the response was similar.

In all parts of Germany villages were laid out either as linear or as clustered settlements. The linear villages were mostly connected with cultivation and were situated along streets, in narrow valleys, on terraces, along rivers, and as particularly regular villages on embanked rivers. A certain modification of this type sometimes developed in valleys that were wider at the entrance than at the end. In such a case the village layout was often adapted to the shape of the valley and interspersed with single homesteads. Clustered villages, on the other hand, were not as restricted to cultivation as the linear types. Often they also grew up in pastoral districts. They were both regular and irregular, sometimes focused on a center—an open space to be used for cattle or a market—sometimes with no definite orientation or shape. But all had in common an actual plan that was intimately connected with the particular pattern of the field system surrounding it.

In general, gregariousness, the need for protection and mutual aid, and certain geographical factors were favorable to compact villages, whereas a dispersion of individual farms was, among other reasons, the result of a strongly developed sense of possession, of a will to power, of only small and dispersed fields of good land, of large tracts of land available for settlement, or of a broken country. All these factors usually overlapped, but sometimes not fully so; and sometimes they were not at all operative. Generally speaking two principles opposed each other: the principle of an equal share for all and that of the monopoly of individual persons; and this antagonism was bound to produce the gravest conflicts. Often, the words Tiberius Gracchus spoke to the Romans were also valid for Germany: "Men of Rome, you are called the lords of the world yet have no right to a square foot of its soil."

During the Middle Ages agriculture spread over Europe from west to east. As early as the thirteenth century in the northwest, it had reached a sufficient state of development that was fairly reliable as a basis of food supply. This was possible because the rural settlement had attained a certain stability, and cultivation and village community were systematically interrelated. However, eastern Europe was at this time still far behind these achievements, and the inequality between East and Northwest had far-reaching consequences for Europe as a whole. On the one hand, famines depleted the population and weakened the efficiency of agriculture; and on the other, migrations undermined the safety of the countryside and the productivity of agriculture.

The economy, especially that of the early Middle Ages, was very sensitive to disturbances and violent fluctuations, the more so as trade in grain was still in its infancy. Men lived on what they produced themselves and the reserves of money and food were meager. They could hardly rely on reserves put aside in better times by individuals, monasteries, territorial rulers, or towns; for what available stores existed were totally inadequate as soon as serious difficulties arose. Moreover, men could not rely on the economic help of the religious orders that had played so important a role as pioneers in the colonization of new lands, for they were beginning to turn more and more to ecclesiastical activities. At first the Benedictines had devoted only three hours to devotional exercises and seven to work, and the Cluniacs and Cistercians had done the same; but now their economic guidance was diminishing; and, in any case, it would not have been sufficient to counter successfully the recurrent famines, which spread sometimes rapidly over large parts of the country. People believed that they were caused by supernatural influences announced by an eclipse of the sun or the appearance of a comet. Thus, a fatalistic mood developed, and efficient counter-measures were made almost impossible. The real causes were, of course, long winters, inundations, and such commercial hostilities as prohibition of exports from other regions, wars, and feuds. These famines often lasted for two or three years; but even longer periods were reported, although these latter may actually have been times of rising prices resulting from the preceding famines.

Apparently, famines had a tendency to spread over such continuous and homogeneous economic regions as Bohemia, Bavaria, and Swabia. For example, a general famine was said to have occurred in 1315-1317, affecting, if the report is correct, the whole region from Breslau in Silesia to Doornik in Belgium, and extending from the Baltic to the Alps.[1] Of these general famines there were four in the ninth century, two in the eleventh century, five in the twelfth century, and one in the thirteenth century. During the thirteenth century these more widespread famines decreased, and a shift from west to east is discernible.

The famines helped to keep the migrations moving, although they did not cause them, and in this way contributed to the spread of colonization and to the foundation of new villages. In the twelfth century, central Europe was considerably overpopulated in relation to the economic capacity and productivity of agriculture at the time—that is to say, to the then occupied and cultivated area. This was a factor which favored the trend of population toward the east. The lower Rhine Basin, especially, furnished considerable contingents of Dutch and Flemish settlers. This exodus, and the mortality from famines and epidemics reduced the population, making it easier for the rest to procure the necessary means for their livelihood and sufficient space for their own settlement. This loosening-up also caused the reduction of famines, the establishment of numerous colonial settlements in the East, and the growing stability of rural conditions in the West.

In the course of the following centuries the center of population shifted more and more from west to east—now, not only through the spread of rural populations, but also as the result of the concentration of large numbers of people in the towns. In 1939 the center of population was to the north of Vienna, whereas around 1720 it was still to the east of Munich. For Europe this shift was quite considerable—although compared with the United States, where it moved about 562 miles from east to west within 100 years, it was insignificant.[2]

During the Middle Ages, which was one of the greatest periods of colonization, the foundations were laid for the structure of settlement as we know it today. In its turn, the early medieval structure had been influenced by the development that went on

Table 1. Shift in Famines According to Century and Country

COUNTRY	Ninth	Eleventh	Twelfth	Thirteenth
Belgium	3	4	9	2
Middle Rhine	7	3	6	2
West Germany	3-4	8	6	5
Bavaria	5	4	4	7
Saxony		4	9	4
Bohemia		1	1	4
Austria		1	3	7

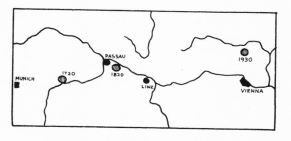

22. Shifting center of population.

1. F. Curschmann. *Hungersnöte im Mittelalter.* Leipziger Studien aus dem Gebiet der Geschichte. 1900. Also for the following, *passim.*
2. After J. Haliczer. "The Population of Europe, 1720, 1820, 1930." In *Geography.* 1934, pp. 262-273.

during the prehistoric period. The remarkable unevenness of more-or-less well-populated and cultivated districts with almost prehistoric settlements was manifest by the alternation of empty areas. This contrast was even more evident in the disparity between the old and the new settled regions. All this had a profound effect, not only on the distribution of the woodland, but also upon the structure of settlement, the field system, and the agrarian and municipal organization. In the neolithic period and during the Bronze Age, people moved into the hitherto empty spaces of central Europe; for only now were they able to cultivate the land by plow agriculture and animal husbandry. At first the people occupied only districts that were relatively accessible—that is, the more open and, above all, the drier steppe regions. Here they spread their settlements during the following centuries, using an extensive and manureless cultivation as far as this type of agriculture permitted and avoiding the damper areas.[3]

The Middle Ages changed the face of central Europe to an enormous degree. They transformed the natural landscape into a man-made one and revolutionized the structure of settlement from an almost exclusively rural pattern to a strongly urbanized one. Today, the occupation of new land in Europe has come to an end with the exception of negligible parts; we have come a long way from the early and isolated hamlets and villages—which, like islands, occupied the clearings in the forests—to the continuity of the present cultural landscape. The most diverse, often even antagonistic tendencies, combined during the Middle Ages and later to extend the *oikumene* of Europe and create the rural structure that was to last almost to the nineteenth century. The increase of population and the lust for power and property of the lords temporal and spiritual influenced equally the spreading occupation of the country: Forests and marshes were pushed back, the basis of food supply was widened, and with it came into being the central European village and its diverse field systems. It was in the development of a grand organization on a grand scale that the manifold ethnological, social, and geographical influences crossed but were, in the end, balanced by the common sense with which the peasants adapted themselves to nature and at the same time dominated her.

What was central Europe like after the fall of Rome? There were about 40 million people living in western Europe in the third century: roughly 30 million in Italy, Gaul, and Spain; and 10 million in Britain, Scandinavia, and those regions of Germany east of the Rhine. It is likely that the material culture of Europe at the time of Charlemagne was not too different

3. R. Gradmann. *Vorgeschichtliche Landwirtschaft und Besiedlung.* Geographische Zeitschrift. 1936.

throughout the Empire. It was a rural civilization; towns played no significant part. True, there were different types of houses and cultivation: for example, in the region of the Elbe men used the *Hakenpflug* (hook-shaped plow) for the square fields, and built round villages; whereas at the mouth of the Rhine the long intermixed fields were tilled with the wheel plow and clustered villages were preponderant.[4] And in western France, in the Alps, and on the Weser the population lived mainly on single farmsteads; whereas to the south of the Alps they lived in compact and townlike villages.

However, these distinctions were only differences of degree, not of principle. What is essential is the fact that neither in the previously Roman territories—in Roman Gaul most of the places were small villages with their *Mark,* the *pagus*—nor in the as yet unconquered lands did an urban civilization exist. The region of the Rhine was without towns. *"Per quos tractus"* [between Mainz and Cologne] *nec civitas ulla visitur nec castellum nisi quod apud Confluentes. . . . Rigomagum oppidum est et una prope ipsam Coloniam turris.*[5] This was the case as early as the fourth century; in A.D. 406 Mainz and Worms were destroyed, the Roman towns on the eastern bank of the Rhine and at its mouth having already perished during the preceding century.

Even more important than the general lack of towns was the economic fact that inside the town walls, as far as they were still standing, there lived, at the time of Charlemagne, the same people as outside: namely peasants. "There is not any reason to suppose that the population in the bishops' sees or the fortified places differed from that in the countryside."[6] The old towns were in ruins, and their buildings were used as stone quarries for new churches and monasteries. It is significant that the term *Mark* was applied to town and country alike, alongside the expression *suburbium,* meaning merely "near the town." Thus, such terms as *Marca Wormacia* or *Marca Bingiorum* for the areas both outside and inside Worms and Bingen were not uncommon. As late as A.D. 845, Strasbourg, the old Argentoratum, was still partly uninhabited and in ruins. And an Arabian traveler in the tenth century reported that only a section of Mainz was inhabited, while the rest was given over to agriculture.[7] It was much the same in the Roman settlements on the Danube, including Vindobona (Vienna), where villages often grew up among the ruins of the towns; and much the same, also, in France and Italy. The urban centers had ceased to fulfill their specific economic, commercial, and administrative functions.

4. W. Sombart. *Der moderne Kapitalismus,* Vol. 1. 1926, pp. 40 ff.

5. "Throughout these areas there is not a city to be seen, not a fortified place, except that at the Confluence . . . there is the town Rigomagus and one tower near Cologne itself." Ammianus Marcellinus. 16.3. Quoted after Sombart. I. 41.

6. S. Rietschel. *Die Civitas auf deutschem Boden bis zum Ausgang der Karolingerzeit.* 1894, p. 85.

7. G. Jacob. *Ein arabischer Berichterstatter aus dem 10. Jahrhundert.* 1890, p. 13.

The Goths and Langobards ravaged the countryside and razed the towns. Of their rulers there were reports such as, *"ad solum usque destruxit"* or *"expugnavit et diruit"* or *"muros civitatibus subscriptis usque ad fundamentum distruens vicos has civitates nominare praecepit."*[8] An agricultural population lived in the towns during other periods as well—this fact, in itself, being nothing unusual—but for different reasons. The towns were rural towns (*Ackerbürgerstaedte*), where, in addition to purely urban pursuits, at least a portion of the food supply had to be produced by the citizens themselves. Such towns cannot be compared to the ruralized towns of the early Middle Ages or with the estates of the wealthy people outside the walls; for in the latter cases, these persons were not all peasants, agriculture being for them merely a sideline of their activities.

From this waste and destruction two types of rural settlement gradually began to develop: the village and the manor—that is, the peasant farmstead and the estate of the feudal lord. The more the seminomadic stockbreeding agriculture gave way to a sedentary, though extensive, cultivation, the more both categories of settlement revealed their basic character.

The village economic and social structure, based on certain kinship ties, was primarily devoted to cultivation. As far as possible, the individual groups of settlers received equal pieces of land corresponding to their capacity for work and consumption. Areas for common use, like pastures and so forth, were then added. This was true for the Slav communes as well as for the Celtic clans, the Germanic associations, and the Romance community. All had the same principles in common: village self-sufficiency; mutual aid among its individual members; and almost complete isolation of one village from another because, at least in the early period, connecting roads did not exist. Interaction was reciprocal: Roads were missing because production and consumption took place in the same spot; this was because there was no overland trade. Only the different structure of the manors worked toward the development of roads. Certain activities in the village, such as milling and forging, were collective, for they were too large or too complicated for one family.

The attitude of the feudal family of the manor differed from that of the peasant community inasmuch as the position of the head of the manorial family was stronger, and consequently the voluntary, collective spirit of the peasants dependent on him was weaker. This led to a gradually increasing discipline and organization of the whole manor economy. The relationship

8. "He razed it" or "he took it by storm and destroyed it" or "after writing off the cities he demolished their walls to the very foundations and directed that these cities should be called villages." *Chronicles of Fredegarius Scholasticus*, 71; cf. Paulus Diaconus, IV, 23, 24, 28, 46.

between the manor and the households of its peasants rested above all on a large number of duties and payments of the latter—that is, on tributes in kind and on personal services. Thus, an intimate amalgamation of village and manor came into being, in which the lord of the manor was in the fortunate position of the rich man whose consumption and production were guaranteed by the work of others. How did the large estates of the Middle Ages develop? The basic precondition was ownership of land by the king (during the Carolingian period), and later the existence of imperial estates. These enormous areas were divided among the settlers who had to pay a rent if their allotted land was wooded. Six reasons for the formation of the large estates during the Middle Ages have been advanced:[9]

1. Acquisition of large pieces of *Mark* land by the princes at the time of occupation, that is, before the Folk Migrations.
2. Occupation during the Folk Migrations of the land by the kings, who handed it over to their followers.
3. Free donation of land by landowners to important ecclesiastical and secular persons.
4. Growing separation of land formerly part of the *Mark* and *Allmende*.
5. Easy acquisition of land by purchase and mortgage according to early popular laws.
6. Illegal, erroneous, or forcible acquisition of land remaining undisputed and becoming legal by prescription.

All the men of the manor belonged to one social class, whether ecclesiastical or temporal: They were wealthy and powerful enough to make their wishes come true and not to work themselves and were therefore free for other activities, such as religious service and war. Because of such characteristics, royal, feudal, and ecclesiastical estates developed as nodal points for the network of rural settlement. These men played a leading part in the colonization of the East. They comprised a smaller or larger number of pure consumers who were completely divorced from the actual production. Often the land of the manor was dispersed over the area of several villages; and, according to the importance of the lord of the manor, there existed a group of retainers apart from the usual contingent of peasants, laborers, artisans, and craftsmen. This changed only gradually when the lords began to clear their own forests and found their own villages. In such cases, a village community would be formed in which the manor became a voluntary member. The usual procedure was as follows: A *Bifang** was marked out, and on it a *Salhof* (or *curia,* a manor) was built, the surrounding country

9. Sombart. *Op. cit.,* Vol. I, p. 60.
* *Bifang* or *pourpris* meant the marking out of large parts of a forest for clearing.

being reclaimed and developed by the villeins. Thus the area of cultivation increased, more manorial farmsteads were laid out on which the peasants of the manor were settled. The *Bifang* also gave the feudals who laid claim to it the right to dispose of the land surrounding it.

The agricultural production of the manor took place mainly on the farms of the peasants who had to deliver a part of their produce to the lord, either directly or indirectly through the *villicus*. The foodstuffs and other raw materials produced on the individual farms were processed on the manorial court, the center of the manor around which were grouped numerous peasant farmsteads, and then delivered to the king according to previous arrangements. At the same time, the manor worked for its own agricultural needs on its own soil (the *Salland*) and with its own workers who lived within the precincts of the manor unless they had small farms of their own. The manorial economy was intimately interwoven with the economy of the village; it was subject to a community-regulated cultivation (the *Flurzwang* of the village) if its fields were dispersed among the fields of the peasants, as was the case in Carolingian times; and both manorial and village herds used the same pastures.

Two tasks had to be accomplished: An organization had to be built up to provide collection and distribution centers for the dispersed property, and village and manor economy had to be adjusted to each other. The demand for industrial products on a manor was considerable. Apart from agriculture proper, other activities like weaving, dyeing, tanning, building, toolmaking, and forging went on; wheelrights and coopers, are only a few of the many trades that these industries required. A list of the activities that went on at the manor of the monastery of Fulda, of which an extract follows, is of interest in this connection. It is said that the works of the villeins consisted of

. . . plowing, errands, services on the manor, smiths' works, the catching of bees; pigs, he-goats, sheep, flour and fishing-nets all to be delivered. Five women have to weave shirts out of the flax supplied by the manor. Official land is given only to the keeper of the forest, the shoemaker, the cup-bearer, and to one man who owns half of a *hufe* [a hide] and is liable to service on the manor.

From another place inside the manorial domain of Fulda it was reported that

. . . seventy-one villeins deliver *"sicut est consuetudo in Thuringia"* woollen goods and blankets. Thirty women weave up the manorial flax and owe three days of service to the manor.

From still another place

. . . comes linen from sixty peasants held in serfdom who had to produce linen from their own flax; goat skins, eggs, flax, oats, salt, beer, and taxes in money are to be received in another place.[10]

Other villages had to supply beer and timber for the brewery as well as a weekly delivery of fish.[11] From other parts of the country came wine, cheese, honey, tablecloths and towels, wrought iron work, metal ornaments, sickles, axes, hatchets, dishes and kettles. The sphere of influence of a manor economy was in no way inferior to the great variety of its industrial organization. In early times it had already become a fairly complicated social and economic organism.

By the end of the Carolingian period the principle of the manor economy had been perfected, and in the following centuries the number of manors increased until this development came to an end in the twelfth century. The dissolution of the old "villication organization," so called after the *capitulare de villis* of Charlemagne in the twelfth and thirteenth centuries, marked an important turning point in the agrarian history of the Middle Ages. The *villici,* the bailiffs, became independent and separated their farms from the manor, while the lords of the manor preferred to lease the peasants' farms to those who had worked them, renouncing their claim to personal and other services and to taxes. This was a sort of liberation of the peasants, although only a very qualified one.

In general the variety of the rural settlements was not great. This held good for villages and field systems alike. A healthy and empirical rationalization was the basis for the layout of the fields. The land was divided and arranged according to the principles of the best usefulness to the peasants and of the most efficient connection with the structure of the village. These goals were reached so far as technical possibilities permitted and social and economic needs of the Middle Ages demanded. But the old systems lost their efficacy and became obsolete as soon as the conditions changed.

The most common use of the land was based on its division into three categories: arable land, meadowland, and wasteland. These three divisions formed the *Flur,* the common area of the village. The arable land supplied the villagers with the raw materials for food and drink, usually bread and beer. The meadows served as pastures, and supplied the winterfeeding, usually hay. The importance of the meadows was much greater during the Middle Ages and immediately afterward than today.[12] It has been estimated that during the fifteenth century the price for meadowland was five times higher than it was for arable land

10. R. Eberstadt. *Der Ursprung des Zunftwesens.* 1915, pp. 270-271. (Author's translation)

11. *Ibid.*

12. W. G. East. *An Historical Geography of Europe.* 1956, p. 99.

during the nineteenth century. The conclusion to be drawn is that the need for winter fodder and its scarcity must have been exceptional. This fact produced, in many cases, an interesting effect on the siting of the villages. Good meadows were mostly restricted to the richer and alluvial soils right on the rivers and lakes, one reason why villages were often situated on the banks of streams. This assured not only an adequate water supply, but also the hay for winter. The great importance of the meadows would often lead to siting villages at right angles to the river—that is, with their narrower sides to the river—in order to keep the banks as free as possible for the meadows. Meadows and wasteland were part of the *Allmende* (common land), to which also belonged roads and open spaces in the village. The arable land, the fields, was individual property, but its cultivation was subject to the *Flurzwang* (community-regulated work). The wasteland was by no means what its name implies: it comprised the woodland, sandy heath, peat moor, ill-drained fen, or coastal marsh, and usually extended over a very considerable area. It supplied vital products such as meat and fowl, fuel from timber and peat, timber for building, reeds, and fish, and served as rough pastures as well. These three categories of soil guaranteed self-sufficiency for the village, and were to become in later times the basis of the surplus economy that served the towns.

It was above all the open-field system that spread over large regions of Europe, from England and France to Germany and beyond as far as the Vistula, interrupted by certain regional variations conditioned mainly by geographical factors such as marshland or mountainous country. With the open-field system was connected, in most cases, the nucleated village in which the houses, surrounded by small gardens, stood closely together, and where the meadows bordered on the river while the fields were situated on higher ground amid the wasteland.

This general arrangement was mostly combined with the division of the arable land according to the quality of the soil. This so-called *Gewann-Flurteilung,* composed of plots of land, aimed at giving to each peasant household in the village an equal share in the different soils according to quality, lie of the land, and surface area. Each peasant household received, therefore, a narrow strip in different parts of the land in *Gemengelage*—that is, the individual property was intermingled with the shares of the other peasants. This principle tried to combine social equality with rational cultivation of the land as far as this was possible. However, it resulted in a technical irrationality and a grave complication of the work for each individual peasant, who was forced to till his fields at the same time and by the same methods as the rest and was therefore subject to the *Flurzwang*. Moreover, since there were no roads and paths, he could not reach his own fields without crossing those of the other peasants. This was a serious drawback and had a direct bearing on the layout of the village: the houses could not be built on the fields because each peasant's property was dispersed over a wide area. Consequently, they had to be erected where they were as central as possible to all these scattered plots—that is, in a compact village.

This field system was combined with an annual rotation of crops: one third of the fields remained fallow while the other two thirds were under the plow. This principle corresponded to the primitive possibilities of the time that were dictated by the natural conditions and that had to be accepted as hard facts. The three-field system came into use from about the eighth century onwards and spread over large parts of western and central Europe. It could be applied only if the arable land and the meadows had been marked out beforehand and after cultivation of the fields had been given prominence. In the Alps and other mountainous regions, cattle breeding and alternation of pasture with field use, so-called *Feldgrass-Wirtschaft*, continued for a long time. The three-field system lasted for over one thousand years, contributing essentially toward the conservatism of the village.

Around the year A.D. 700 the population of western and central Europe had reached its lowest level. It increased, however, until by the end of the eleventh century the estimate of about 35 million might be correct. By the end of the thirteenth century the population had increased to about 50 million. In Roman times, the highest density of population had been around the Mediterranean, but by A.D. 1300 new centers had developed in Brabant, Flanders, and the Parisian basin (Table 2).

Especially from 900 to 1300 civilization spread over Europe from west to east, and with it the population grew and trade and clearing of woodlands increased. The agents of this colonial penetration were above all the Germans and the Church of Rome. They advanced into regions inhabited by Slavic peoples, who were mainly cattle breeders but who had given up a nomadic way of life. They lived in fortified settlements that often had the characteristic form of a circular or ring-fence village (a *Rundling*), or any other layout that permitted them to assemble the animals in a central open space surrounded by the houses. Trade and commerce among the Slavs had hardly developed, and cultivation was of minor importance. Therefore, to the German traders they delivered only those products which they could supply from their animal husbandry or hunt-

Table 2. Population Around A.D. 1300. *

British Isles	4 million
France	14 million
Provence Dauphiné Lyon	1 million
Spain and Portugal	6 million
Italy	11 million
Germany including The Netherlands	15 million
Denmark	1 million
Sweden	600 thousand
Norway	300 thousand
Total	52,900,000 million

* After Carr Saunders, *World Population* (1936).

99

ing—furs, hides, honey, wax, fish, and amber. The Franks, who played an important role in the advance eastward, were also still predominantly engaged in pastoral activities apart from a primitive cultivation—if one is to judge from their folk laws which refer more to the former than to the latter.

This colonization produced two types of settlements, one with nonagrarian functions and one with a purely agrarian character. The nonagrarian foundations, the ecclesiastical, military, and administrative centers, sometimes grew into towns just as did some of the settlements based on the mineral deposits of the Harz Mountains and the Erzgebirge. Purely agrarian settlements consisted of individual farms, compact or loosened-up villages, and hamlets. The houses of the hamlets were often separated by meadows and gardens, and the fields, though in *Gemengelage,* were not always combined in *Gewanne.* These hamlets had their origin mostly in small clearings of the forest.

All this proceeded rather unsystematically. To mention a few aspects of this haphazard development: The distribution of the medieval markets did not result from the creation of nodal points in a rational network of roads, although traffic did exert a certain influence upon the situation and potential growth of the markets. Narrow and local interests were most likely more important. However, slowly and gradually the really useful centers gained the upper hand, and the markets which had originated because of purely local needs stagnated. It was similar with the churches, which were often built in the depth of the forest by a feudal lord. These foundations served not so much the religious needs of the people as the financial needs of the lord, who, as principal churchwarden, expected a profit from his investment; for if a village should develop around the church, he would receive tithes from the settlers.

During the eighth and ninth centuries the river valleys to the east of the Rhine and to the north of Mainz were settled. This was the origin of such monasteries as Fulda and Hersfeld, of bishop-towns such as Erfurt, Fritzlar, Freising, and of military stations against the Slavs along the line of the Elbe, the Saale, and the Bohemian forest such as Magdeburg, Forchheim, Lorch, and Regensburg. At first, all these places resembled villages more than towns. But in the tenth century this wide net of older nodal points began to fill up, and at the same time the advance to the East proceeded. Merseburg, Meissen, and Leipzig marked the subsequent stages of this movement. Sites where rivers crossed were generally preferred. Existing Slavic settlements were often taken over. Brandenburg, Breslau, Gnesen, and Posen followed; on the Danish frontier places such as Oldenburg, Bremen, and Hamburg were founded, and in the North,

Schwerin and Wismar as stations against the Slavs. Vienna, the Roman Vindobona, began again to function as a center of traffic and commerce. It became a *civitas* in A.D. 1137. The colonization extended to Styria and Carinthia.

The village of the Franks was part of a larger area, of the so-called *Mark,* which often comprised several villages that shared the *Allmende.* Forest and pasture, natural resources, and the nearer parts of the *Mark* belonged to the village. Neither the boundaries of the *Mark* nor those of the land belonging to the village proper were fixed. How did this situation arise? There are several possibilities: New villages were separated from the old village and so shared automatically in the original *Allmende;* or villages were founded by outsiders but within the same *Mark;* or several villages were laid out simultaneously. It is also possible that in the course of time the land of the village was no longer a sufficient basis of food supply; in this case parts of the *Allmende* were turned over to cultivation thus reducing its extent. This happened, for instance, in the Hohenstaufen period from the middle of the twelfth to the middle of the thirteenth centuries.

The oldest known working unit was the *Hufe,* the hide. The underlying idea was to give to a family a sufficient amount of land on which they and their hired hands could live. The allotted land was divided into *Morgen* (the equivalent of about 2 acres), a *Morgen* being a piece of arable land that could be plowed during the morning—hence its name—of one day or in the course of one day with a pair of oxen. A hide comprised as a rule 30, more rarely 60, *Morgen* of arable land together with the land for the house and the garden, all the dwellings, and the use of the *Allmende.* It was, therefore, not so much a definite unit of measurement as a general term of ownership and property rights.

Two antagonistic principles were at work when a village was founded and *Gewanne* were laid out: social and economic. The social principle of the equality of property, expressed in the distribution of equally valuable pieces of land, scattered the land of one owner over a wide area. In keeping with this principle the land had to be redistributed when the village grew and new peasants joined the community. Therefore, the economic principle had to be subordinated to these social tenets, although the peasant's not being able to work his field in one continuous process as one contiguous unit was highly uneconomical. The formalistic-legal principle and the idea of a community of peasants gained the upper hand.

It was different if the decision were up to a single person—the lord of the manor; then the idea of an independent community became secondary and his interests prevailed. His interests were above all economic; he regarded the whole collective of peasants as a profitable entity, and did not pay too much attention to their communal ideas. A feudal lord could therefore easily apply purely utilitarian and economic principles when distributing the land among his peasants. This is one reason why villages founded by the will of a single person developed ground plans and field systems that were generally different from those of an autonomous peasant community.

The idea of the hide did not originate in connection with the division of the land into *Gewanne* but exclusively from the need to guarantee a peasant family's food supply. It may be suggested that in the early Middle Ages the hides were fairly large because cultivation was still more or less extensive and land was sufficiently available. However, one of the decisive factors of the agrarian structure was not so much the size of the hide, but the distinction between the land of the peasants and the land of the *Kätner* (the lower-class agriculturists). The *Kätner* had no fields of their own on the *Flur,* only gardens by their houses or on the fields, or, only land that was left over between the *Gewanne,* that was formerly common, or that could be cleared or reclaimed from the pastures. *Kätner* land was a casual conglomeration of small plots.

During the early, and even later, development of agriculture the peasant farm remained the basic unit of the agrarian structure. Political and social influences absorbed it into higher forms of the economic organization. Where small estates had been founded during the tribal period and large estates of the Franks had risen, there developed the specific economy of the free peasants and the manor during the Middle Ages. Changes, if there were any at all, did not result from economic or technical factors but from political and social transformations. The economy remained constant; therefore, the working unit remained constant too. What was changing was the social dependence of the peasants, although this did not affect the structural layout of the village. It was for this reason that the agrarian history of Germany up to the height of the Middle Ages was a history of political and social fluctuations, not of a developing technique, a growing economy or village planning.

When, in the twelfth, thirteenth, and fourteenth centuries, the colonization of the East gained momentum, an increasing mixture of Germanic and Slavic forms of settlement set in. By the twelfth century, the clearing of the forests on a large scale had more or less come to an end in old Germany but had not yet done so in the colonial territories. The number of places for settlement that existed in the old Germany of the thirteenth century hardly increased at all until the nineteenth century. On the contrary, many were abandoned. More arable land was gained chiefly by extending the *Flur* of the existing villages. New villages were laid out or old ones developed by special officials (*locatores*) who were rather like general contractors—"developers" who delivered the settlements ready-made from the clearing to the settlers. The *locator* generally received a larger estate in his new settlement, about four to six hides, and was granted the right to keep a tavern among other privileges.

Settlements were established in clearings beside the existing Slavic villages or on abandoned villages, or else the old Slavic villages were interspersed with German settlements. The great majority were villages, very rarely hamlets or single farmsteads. They consisted mostly of two rows of houses lined up on an elongated, square, or slightly curved open space, or along a street as street-villages. In the valleys of the Central Uplands the farms were more loosely grouped. The dike and marsh villages in the colonial country were similar. The land of the compact villages was divided into a few *Gewanne* and further subdivided into strips, sometimes adjoining the farmstead, in which case the arable land, the meadows, and the forest would be situated one behind the other. Street villages in clearings had their land laid out in long strips behind each farmstead, in so-called *Waldhufen,* which stretched up to the margin of the forest; on marshland the same principle was applied, and the strips were called *Marschhufen.* New units of measurement were used in this process: the king's hide among the Franks comprising about 59 acres, and the Flemish hide about 42 acres.[13] The feudal lords who came with the princes received so-called knights' hides which were five to eight times larger than the ordinary hides of the common people. From this name derived later the term *Rittergut* (estate of a knight). Just as their houses were built together in the same village, so the knights' hides were intermixed with those of the peasants. The knights were the peasants' neighbors, not their lords. However, this more companionable state did not last long; gradually the old spirit of arrogance and superiority emerged and the knights claimed their rights as lords as they had done in the mother country.

The history of rural property proceeded on three lines. The first developed out of the old peasants' organizations based on the hide of the large estates of the Franks, the first economic organization resting on the principle of self-sufficiency. After its dissolution, the hide of the peasants continued in southern Germany as an economic unit, and became a source of income for the landlords who were themselves not engaged in agriculture. In the course of the centuries the intensively worked

13. W. Wittich. *Epochen deutscher Agrargeschichte. Grundriss der Sozial-Oekonomik,* VII. 1922, *passim.*

Table 3. *Population around 1600* *

	Area in sq. mi.	Popu-lation	Population density per sq. mi.
Italy	114,000	13,000,000	114
Spain and Portugal	225,000	10,000,000	44.5
France	182,000	16,000,000	93.4
England and Wales	57,900	4,500,000	780
Scotland and Ireland	61,800	2,000,000	32.5
Netherlands	9,670	3,000,000	311
Denmark	15,450	600,000	38.8
Sweden, Norway, Finland	416,000	1,400,000	3.37
Poland and Prussia	81,000	3,000,000	370
Germany	278,000	20,000,000	72.0
Total	1,420,000	73,500,000	51.7

* The average density is 50 per sq. mi. (After Carr Saunders.)

holdings of the small peasants grew out of this hide-economy. The second line began in the Northwest; there, the big landowners divided their estates into small units which they rented to the peasants. The rent was paid in kind, that is in corn, and sold on the markets, a combination of natural and money economy. The peasant remained unfree although he was free to cultivate his fields. It was not until the state intervened that the peasant was able to dispose of his own land and regulate his inheritance. The third line concerned the estates of the big landowners which finally developed into large-scale economic units on a capitalistic basis.

The line of the Elbe, the Saale, the Thuringian Forest, and the Fichtelgebirge was roughly the structural divide of the settlement of central Europe. To the west of this line the structure of settlement rested on Germanic influences existing in those regions, and on Frankish elements introduced from outside Germany; other influences, above all those of Roman origin, were also absorbed into the pattern of settlement. To the east of this line the structure of settlement may be called secondary: It had Germanic and Frankish characteristics and spread over the existing and thin Slavic layer of settlement. It remained secondary because the combined Germanic and Frankish conquest had at its disposal colonial methods and an agrarian organization incomparably higher than those of the Slavs. Two conclusions often drawn from this difference should be avoided: The first, that to the west of the dividing line the compact or nucleated village predominated, is incorrect; the second is that ethnological differences determined the various forms of settlement, that is, of the single farm, the street village, the compact village, the ring-fence village, and so forth. The actual reasons lie much deeper. They should be sought, first, in the different relationship of the community to the system of cultivation and of the fields and, second, in the different ideas about what was more important, the social equality of the village members or the economic rationalism of the village economy. These problems were not at all conditioned by ethnological factors.

The pedigree of the village (Figure 23) and Table 3 should be evaluated against the background of Europe's increasing population, which, in the course of 300 years—from about 1300 to 1600—rose by 32 per cent.

The village pedigree gives a general survey of rural settlement in western and central Europe and in a few adjoining countries. It shows that three groups can be distinguished, each having different origins but all leading to the same form of a regular, ribbonlike village. As has been repeatedly stated, the layout of the village alone is meaningless; only the plan of the village and the plan of the field system taken together can explain the functional structure of the settlement as a whole. Time was essential as a formative power. A slow development was often accompanied by a greater adaptation to the existing conditions, especially in the past, while a fast development often led to a ruthless disregard of men and nature. However this may be, there was always a regulating power which imposed a definite and functional system upon the settlement. Even in what were apparently the most unsystematic medieval villages in the clearings, the organizing instinct of the community or of individual personalities could be discerned. Slowly growing settlements were less subject to the stylistic influences of the time than were those founded by territorial princes. In these latter cases every transformation or expansion was detrimental to the original conception, and almost invariably spoiled the essence of the plan. But if a settlement grew up slowly over a longer period of time a systematic development was easier—at least before the modern time of unlimited possibilities.

A compact village may have grown together by an agglomeration of farmsteads with their land, not merely of single houses with gardens, either because a large area was available or because the village had only a small number of inhabitants. The layout of these fairly old villages was not developed in a functional relation to a road system. The picture was different in a nucleated village where the dwellings, with their outhouses and

23. Pedigree of the German village.

1. Terp villages are situated on small hills off the coast sufficiently high above the tide.
2. Villages in marshy areas.
3. Villages built around a common.
4. Slavonic villages where fishermen live together.

24. Ströbeck, in the Harz Mountains—a clustered village.

gardens, were arranged in close interdependence with the roads. The seemingly unsystematic arrangement of the individual farmsteads in these nucleated villages may have been an economic necessity because it was essential to have an interior open space where men and animals could assemble. However, in such cases the village was more compact and less loosened-up than where the farmsteads were haphazardly situated on a gradually developing network of roads. Different again was a compact village whose layout was related to only a few roads which were the main axes of a larger network. These "road-oriented" clustered villages would sometimes originate from a simple, compact settlement, as described above, where the original nucleus was preserved. A great variety of compact villages can be distinguished, all of which can be traced back to a road network, or to a specific relation to squares and open spaces, or to the arrangement of the farmsteads as primary elements. A certain classification is possible according to the pattern of the roads, that is, according to whether they radiated from a center, led in several directions without starting at the same point, or were without any clear direction at all. In general, the first two types were more common on even terrain, while the last was more characteristic of difficult and undulating country. All three had their fields mixed up in *Gewanne,* and the problem was how best to correlate the arrangement of the houses with gardens and the field pattern.

Clustered villages which had grown together from a loose agglomeration of smaller villages were especially characteristic in mountainous regions and, in particular, of the lower Rhine and the Westphalian lands. The compact villages of this region had their origins in prehistoric settlements.[14] The increase of arable land that was divided in *Gewanne* and the growing density of the village itself proceeded mostly under the leadership of a lord of the manor in connection with the extension of the clearings over the forest-clad hilly and mountainous land. In this case single farms were younger and outside the unity of a clan or a community: they separated from the group and became economically independent. The structure of the *Flur* decided the different types of settlement. Where *Eschflur* existed, the villages were more open and loose, but where the *Esch* was transformed into a *Gewannflur* the villages grew more compact. Where, apart from an *Eschflur*, *Kämpen* were laid out, the villages were dispersed and the farmsteads were scattered over the land. If only *Kämpen*, without the concentrating effect of the *Esch*, existed, the dispersal of the individual farms was greatest. An *Esch* was a modified *Gewannflur*, but the individual *Eschen* of one village did not form a continuous *Flur;* they were isolated from each other by wasteland. The long-settled peasants had mostly their plots in long strips in the various *Eschen* near the village, although they were not always equally allotted to the individual *Eschen*. *Flurzwang* was introduced for sowing, plowing, and harvesting. In this part of Germany

we find small ecologically conditioned localities that rise slightly above the ground. These were used as the oldest plots of ploughable land and have apparently determined the location of settlements since prehistoric times. They were called *"Esch"* and were owned only by peasants in possession of the full rights of their estate. These fully righted peasants (*Erben*) joined for working the *Esch* into so-called *"Eschgenossenschaften"* from which the social substratum was excluded. In its most extreme form, the *Esch* was managed in a one-field system, which, year after year, served for the production of rye. This *Esch* pattern was surrounded by extensive areas of low-lying lands, heath, or bogs (*Markungen*), where pasturing was the normal activity. In the outfield small plots for minor crops might alternate with long years of heath or bogs.[15]

A *Kämp* was a younger form in comparison with the very old *Esch*. A *Kämp* was owned by only one peasant and was always surrounded by ditches, hedges or fences. The *Esch* remained open. A *Kämp* was a small, compact field of about 300 by 900 feet and was sometimes isolated from other *Kämpen*, but also in some cases grouped together with them. Its working was

14. R. Martiny. *Hof und Dorf in Altwestphalen.* 1926, *passim.*
15. G. Pfeiffer. "The Quality of Peasant Living in Central Europe." In Thomas (ed.), *Op. cit.,* pp. 258-259.

not dependent on communal regulations and it was owned by the upper and lower classes of the peasantry alike. The conversion of the old *Eschflur* to the larger *Gewannflur* needed more hands and therefore new houses, which had to be located between the already existing farmsteads of the village, thereby making it more compact. If *Eschen* and *Kämpen* existed side by side, the old *Eschen* exerted a concentrating influence, preventing a dispersion of the *Kämpen* with their houses over too large an area. These latter were then grouped loosely and fairly closely around the *Esch*. This type of settlement was a perfect example of a layout that, while apparently irregular and unsystematic, was in reality extremely organic and functional. These loose villages were small and had a population of only 100 to 300 inhabitants.

These villages could be classified in three groups: the loosened-up and scattered settlements; the more coherent open villages; and the compact villages which increased in density by the later addition of the houses of small peasants. For this type the roads were the primary structural elements, for the smaller farmsteads were located on the roads while the larger ones were situated at a certain distance. Thus radial, netlike, and other forms developed and the compact settlements were gradually transformed into a sort of street village. However, in a perfectly compact village all farmsteads were situated directly on the roads. On the other hand, the scattered villages in their most typical form consisted of large farms, and in this case the roads were secondary and dependent on the dispersed arrangement of the farms—they were mere access roads. Roads were completely lacking in the older villages of this type, a fact that was still verifiable in the eighteenth century; only footpaths connected the individual farms with each other or with a main road.

The colonial penetration of central and eastern Europe was intimately connected with the spread of the street village. The Franks were the principal agents of this advance from the West into the regions that had been subjugated by Charlemagne. After the division of the Empire into Neustria and Austrasia, the nuclei of France and the later Germany respectively, the eastern Franks had settled in the Rhineland while the western Franks occupied Roman Gaul. Wherever Frankish influence was at work, the street village was the characteristic form of settlement, be it in northeastern France, in the Rhineland, along the Main, in the Central Uplands of Germany, in Saxony, in the region of the Danube near Vienna, in Moravia, or in the east German colonial lands. This does not mean that the street village was the ethnological form of the Frankish race specifically. Rather, the street village was particularly suited to colonial

penetration, the essence of which was to move on, to create certain fixed points for protection and for further advance. The conquerors occupied the new lands, but they did not spread over large areas the way natives in their own land did. They needed lines of advance, military roads, and strong points in a hostile country, and they proceeded in exactly the same way the French pioneers did many centuries later in North America under similar conditions. The overriding task of the Franks was to organize their advance and to organize it quickly and efficiently in order to produce lasting results. They had no time to develop a complicated social structure. Military considerations were decisive. Natives, on the other hand, could let their social structure grow slowly into family or clan collectives or on the basis of elective affinity. Thus, ruthless organization was pitted against organic evolution.

The Frankish organization had to absorb a tempestuous and spontaneous outburst and direct it into productive channels. Colonization meant for them movement, not a stand-still; and this movement marched forward along the roads that were to become the framework of the structure of settlement. Along these lines their settlements were laid out on these roads, and gradually they grew into permanent villages. No complacent spirit of rest guided them—one that could have created restful places with gregarious and peaceful people or spacious villages with many streets and open spaces like the villages in northwest Germany with their complicated social features. Theirs was a spirit of a dynamic forward-pressing conquest over ever-lengthening lines of communication. Their houses had to be built close together in order to reduce the length of the streets which

25. Street village of Finkenstein, Silesia, Poland.

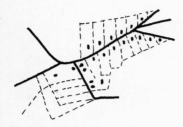

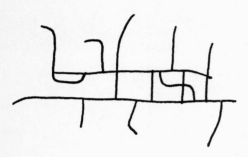

26. Villages of Gellep (*above*) and Kerpen (*below*).

they adjoined and to afford mutual protection. This explains their relatively compact and distinct form which stood out clearly from the surrounding countryside.

The street village with its streamlined form embodies this spirit exactly. It absorbed the motion; it did not stop it. Therefore, the street was the line of orientation in these villages. These villages were distinctly characteristic of the Franks not for peculiar racial reasons, but resulting exclusively from the fact that the Franks were the leading agents and exponents of this colonization. Originally the Franks had been acquainted with the single farmstead, to which they adhered in the basin of the lower Rhine, and with the clustered village. But in the course of their advance they abandoned isolated farms in favor of the compact village, above all for reasons of protection. One of these old villages was Gellep, the old Gelduba, mentioned by Tacitus —another was Kerpen near Bergheim. In the case of each, orientation in direct relation to the street was obvious, although it was modified by the general tendency of these villages toward a compact settlement with *Gewannflur*.

The *lex Salica,* which was promulgated after Clovis' conquest of northeastern France in A.D. 486, contained directives for the regulation of the agrarian conditions and, in this connection, mentioned villages whose fields were not intermixed, but separate and without pastures. These villages were probably manorial foundations; their economic system was hardly known to the Germanic tribes but found a ready appeal among the Franks. Although their form still resembled an irregular, clustered village, a certain tendency toward a more regular and systematic layout was unmistakable. This was especially the case where a number of single farmsteads were arranged along an existing road or where sidestreets were loosening up the village.

More obvious were, of course, the street villages located in mountain valleys. These types were a preparatory stage; they were laid out on several streets, a form often found in northeastern France. In the second half of the fifth century these villages were mostly manorial settlements which were fortified and which had been founded by feudal lords when they had received land as a fief from the Merovingian kings. Such places were laid out under the *Gewann* system and sometimes had common pastures. They were gradually incorporated in the great road systems of the Franks, which can be traced back, at least partly, to the Romans, who had a strong sense for the importance of axial order as a formative element of planning. These villages of northern France were mostly situated near old Roman forts, and this alone reveals the strategic nature of their foundations. On the other hand, the clustered villages filled the meshes between the lines of the traffic network, while manorial villages were almost without exception situated on the roads. This can be deduced from the structure of the *Blockflur*.

Apart from these clustered villages based on streets and roads there were others with a much clearer and simpler arrangement. In almost all these cases Roman influences had been at work. The original Roman system of settlement probably consisted of single farms connected in one way or another with the road, which may have fulfilled the function of an internal field way. Similar plans still exist today in Alsace—for example, in the Wassenwald near Zabern. In numerous cases the Franks settled—in the regions within the limits of the *limes* this held good for the basins of the Rhine and the Moselle—in Roman *villae*, with their well cultivated lands following each other at distances of only about half a mile, thus making the valleys appear rather densely settled. However, the Roman military camps introduced a more rigid scheme that became the starting point for the Frankish settlement. Outside the Roman camp was the so-called *vicus canaborum* (*canaba* meaning a "wooden booth"), a camp village for traders, settlers, and innkeepers who had their temporary quarters in this "suburb." The main street, the *via praetoria*, was crossed at right angles by the secondary street, the *via principalis*, and sometimes by another side street, the *via quintana*. It was most likely that the Franks used these camps as prototypes for their fortified villages, especially when decisions on how new villages were to be founded began to pass from the folk community to the individual person of a feudal lord. When the latter stage had been reached, the camp was replaced by a manor that the leader of the colonists built for himself and which often became the origin of a castle. A street village in front of the manor replaced the *vicus canaborum*. The adaptation of military prototypes for a semi-military purpose—that is, for colonial conquest and colonial settlement—was obvious. This explained why, in many street villages, the manor was situated at one end—for example, in the street villages to the east of the Elbe and in numerous villages of the Rhineland.

Roman influence was also evident in other respects as, for instance, in Lorraine: The houses were built close together, an arrangement common to many places in the Roman lands north of the Alps, which can still be observed. Two reasons were operative: The Roman system of settlement used the roads as bases for the layout of the villages; consequently the houses were built together as closely as possible. As spatial elements of village and city planning, the streets needed a clear and definite limitation if they were to be more than nondescript "interspaces";

27. Villages of Heeren, near Unna, Westphalia (*above*), and Haussömmern, East Germany (*below*).

111

obviously an almost contiguous row of houses fulfilled this purpose better than houses with wide open gaps between them. Further, even in its simplest form street building was expensive. Consequently, the length of the street was reduced as far as possible by a close proximity of the houses.

The fact that the Germans did not know rational principles of settlement seems to have impressed Tacitus as unusual. In *Germania*, 16, he especially mentions that the Germans lived in separate homesteads. This remark has been mostly misinterpreted as meaning that they lived on isolated farms. In reality, the houses did not touch each other, a layout which to the Roman Tacitus was unknown. Max Weber mentions, in his *Römische Agrargeschichte* (1891), the Italian example and remarks that the settlement of Italy was not a patrimonial-autocratic procedure under the leadership of a ruling family, but the work of rigidly and administratively organized associations of equally important families. He concludes:

An essential difference from the Germanic principles of settlement seems to exist: the political conditions of the regions of Italy which were settled at the time of the immigration and the higher technique of the immigrants were the cause that in contrast with the Germanic villages those of Italy were at least partly fortified places. Thereby an indelible semi-urban character was impressed upon the settlement from the very beginning. These villages tend to become agricultural towns, a development which implanted in the whole agrarian structure the tendency to be susceptible at an early stage to modern economic prnciples. This element determined later the character of the Roman colonization.

This conclusion is no doubt correct and helps to explain the close arrangement of the houses in the formerly Roman regions. In the course of time the Romans' immense colonial tasks imparted to their colonization an almost modern rationalization and a high standard of efficiency. They used methods that could easily be organized and mastered anywhere by those who had to apply them. The street village was therefore the obvious form of settlement. It made possible the solution of the social problem by association and of the economic problem by a combination of house and fields, as far as this was feasible. At the same time the village was related without any difficulty to the road system. When the street village was taken over by the German colonization of the East it gradually degenerated into a stereotyped, routine pattern; it was revived by the influence of the Slavic settlements.

The Roman roads were the prerequisite of the later "Roman" street villages since no Roman camp could be established without good access roads. Thus the road also became the axis for the Frankish settlements, and the street village became the principal type of colonial development. This axial principle had, on the other hand, certain disadvantages. The longitudinal extension was practically unlimited. But as the village grew, so did its problems of defense. It became increasingly difficult to defend the parts farthest away from the manor, which was always situated at one end of the village. This was one reason why a certain concentration became necessary. If a larger number of farms had to be accommodated, the solution was to build villages with several streets. Examples were Genneville, St. Aubin, d'Arguency, and Knielingen in the Palatinate. In these cases the village was fairly compact; each house was directly accessible from the roads, and all houses were equally protected by the manor which sometimes became a fortified castle. This was somewhat similar to the situation of the castles of the *Daimyos* in Japan, which were surrounded by villages that also profited from the protection of the lord and his castle; such villages formed a sort of "forecourt" to the castle. With the inclusion of people without landed property, such a combination could lead to a disintegration of the purely agrarian character of the settlement. The houses would then grow closer together and crowd around the castle which militarily dominated the land and became a source of consumption for the industrial products of the village. In connection with this structural transformation the one-sided, longitudinal extension of the village often gave way to a certain centralization—a form similar to that of the small country-towns which were focused on the church or on a central market square. Moreover, it was not unusual for the ecclesiastical or secular lords to deliberately attract a market to their villages.

Special types of street-villages, or more generally of ribbon-villages laid out in the course of the colonization, were the *Marschhufen* and the *Waldhufen* villages, marsh villages and forest villages, respectively. Preferably, they occupied the border between the marsh and the *Geest*, the coastal upland in the Dithmarschen, Oldenburg, and in Holland. Situation on the *Geest* was preferred because the danger of floods made it impossible to live on the marsh and also because the fields were laid out on the higher *Geest* and the pastures on the lower marsh.

In front of the *Marschhufen* villages, *Warft* villages were established. A knoll occupied by these small settlements would rise to 15 or 20 feet over the normal water-level, and may have originally been crowned by one house only. But as more houses were gradually added, the knoll was enlarged, and a church would be built. Floods destroyed these settlements repeatedly, but again and again the settlers returned and built their houses on these precarious hills. These knoll villages date back to very old times before dikes were built. They belong to the more ancient form of the struggle between man and sea, long before it was known that a major flood occurred almost every ten years and that an unusually dangerous tide would spread its devastating power every 15 years over the man-made settlements. It took several centuries for this periodicity to be discovered.

The space of these knoll villages was very restricted. The houses were crowded together. Rain water had to be collected for drinking in *Soth* (small tanks in the ground) or carried in from the mainland. But when dike building began, the picture changed. Only a few houses stood on few of these small *Warften,* three lines of villages thus following one behind the other: the *Geest* villages, the dune villages on the dunes with names ending in "don" or "den," and in front of both, the *Warft* villages.

When the coastal population began to build dikes systematically and to reinforce them efficiently, a new belt of marshland formed, and another piece of land was wrested from the sea. *Warft* villages ceased to be established because the dikes protected the new land. The houses stood singly on the *Kögen*

28. *Wurten* village of Rysum, north of Emden.

114

29. **Wurten** village of Manslagt, northwest of Emden.

—that is, the land between the dikes—or else the villages extended along the dikes, therefore often having place names ending with *Deich* or dike. Locks and drainage channels were the *raison d'être* of small hamlets and harbors from which the settlements spread further out over the land. Thus five types of settlement developed: *Geest* villages on the raised embankments along the *Geest* and on tongues of land where even small towns sometimes grew up; long dune villages; compact *Warft* villages; long dike villages; single homesteads on the outlying land near the sea and on the foreshore; and small groups of houses on the roads leading through this area.

The houses of the genuine *Marschhufen* villages were lined up at the inner slope of the dike along the road. The *Hufen*, the hides, extended as long strips, one beside the other, inland behind the houses. This type of village, which directly com-

30. *Marschhufen* village of Loppersum, near Emden.

31. *Marschhufen* village, west of Hamburg.

32. *Waldhufen* village, East Germany.

33. *Waldhufen* village,
eastern Thuringia.

bined house and field, developed from the eleventh century
onward. Today, many of these villages are situated at a distance
from the sea because, in the course of the centuries, the area
of the reclaimed land was extended by new and advanced dikes.
Orchards were interspersed between the homesteads on the land
that had gradually risen and been improved. These villages
were laid out on the top of the dikes on only one side of the
road. In general, marshes along rivers were more densely settled than those on the coast and had more cultivation and horti-
culture, whereas the sea marshes had more animal husbandry.
At the beginning of the sixteenth century large peasant holdings—on the *Geest* of Bremen, for example—had mostly four

117

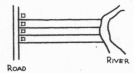

34. Village between river and road.

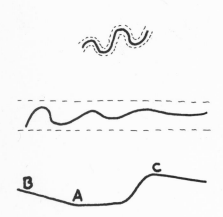

35. Patterns of riverside settlement.

hides—120 *Morgen* (77.5 acres)—an area that could be worked with four horses. The smaller holdings had only two hides, worked with two horses. The fields were scattered over the *Geest* in *Gewanne*; in other words, they were intermixed. The only difference of the fields in marshland was the varying length of their extension from the dike; the width was more or less the same. The channels for drainage were the natural boundaries between them. The large peasant holdings in the marsh consisted of from 80 to 400 *Morgen* (52 to 260 acres) and the smaller holdings from 40 to 80 *Morgen* (26 to 52 acres). Large estates were unknown in these regions because their cultivation from one end, the head of the dike, was unfavorable, the more so as it had to be carried through in a relatively short time. These villages extended over long distances on the dikes and often merged into each other without a break. The old *Warften*, the small knolls, are today mostly deserted or, in a few cases, occupied by a church.[16]

Waldhufen villages, forest villages, were mostly laid out from the bottom of the valley upward. The houses were lined up on both sides of a river or a street, and the fields covered the slopes in long strips from the valley to the edge of the forest; this was not parceled out among the peasants, but preserved as a whole. The quality of the soil was irrelevant for the division of the land, but the size of the hides varied between 120 and 150 *Morgen* (79 to 110 acres). These forest villages could be extended almost ad libitum: there were villages in the Erzgebirge and the Sudetic region which spread over 6 to 7 miles. Size and layout depended on the course of the river or the shape of the valley. If both were identical the settlement plans were different from those where this was not the case. In the former instance, the available space was restricted if the meander of the river and the valley were narrow; in the second instance, the settlement could develop more freely. An additional factor was the relief. If the slope was steep, the settlements would be situated on terraces as narrow street-villages. The case was entirely different if they occupied higher terraces, such as at C of the sketch; then the lowest terrace in the valley at A would be the main site, especially if the bends of the meander were large. On the other hand, if the flatter side of the valley at B offered more space, villages with several parallel streets forming an elongated rectangle could be laid out. Especially frequent were T-shaped villages where side-valleys opened into the main valley.[17]

These different types of villages were all intimately connected with the advance of the colonization and with the local

16. K. Bode. *Agrarverfassung und Agrarvererbung in Marsch und Geest.* Abhandlungen des Staatswissenschaftlichen Seminars, Jena. 1910.

17. B. Dietrich. *Der Siedlungsraum in eingesenkten Mäandertälern.* Schlesische Gesellschaft für vaterländische Kultur. 1917.

topographical conditions. In this connection, it should be pointed out as particularly important that colonial villages had often to fulfill defensive functions because, it is generally assumed, the towns were the sole and the earliest forerunners of the fortresses. If a village was situated in a vulnerable position, the inhabitants fortified it. Street villages lent themselves especially well for this purpose, and even more so did ring-fence villages, which were natural village fortresses par excellence. However, virtually all types of villages existed side by side, not only in the colonial regions, but in Germany proper. There were clustered villages in Alsace that, legally, were directly dependent on the emperor, so-called *Reichsdörfer;* or manorial villages which were mostly street villages dependent on a manor; or, in the Rhineland, clustered and street villages alternating with each other. In Bavaria, street villages with the houses turning their eaves to the street were preponderant.

A vast region of about 115,830 square miles had been opened up by the colonization beyond the line of the Elbe and the Saale and added to Germany. This movement advanced toward the east in three large curves; in the southeast almost to the Adriatic Sea; in the regions of the Oder to the northern Carpathians; and in the region of the Baltic Sea to the Kurische Haff. On the whole, the street village remained the main agent of this penetration. Its form, however, got more and more stereotyped and rigid. The houses began to be built in close and systematic relation to squares and streets, for the street gave the village not only its characteristically long form, but also the circular or square open space in the center, that became the

36. *Anger* village of Heiligensee, Brandenburg.

indispensable prerequisite for the layout. The more the penetration proceeded eastward, the more the street village grew in width and in coherence, and, often, merged into the *Anger* village.

The systematization of the village in the East was accompanied by a corresponding systematization of the town. The eastern towns came into being during the twelfth and thirteenth centuries, about 700 years after the fall of the Roman Empire. The Roman camp had hardly any direct influence on their layout, and the Slavic towns like Moscow were also too remote to serve as prototypes. The assumption cannot be ruled out that the colonial street-village may have been the link between the Roman camp, whose streets crossed each other at right angles, and the colonial towns of the Middle Ages. However, the spirit dominating the colonization was certainly much more important: It was a spirit of organization, determined to create as soon as possible distinct and definite conditions in the new regions. Thus, the layout of the villages was dominated by one main street and one or two side streets, and the layout of the towns, above all, by the square, the *forum,* and the market (the *praetorium*). This is not surprising, for these simple street-patterns were used in all parts of the world where settlement and conquest went hand in hand. They still exist in the Latin American towns founded by the Spaniards, in China, in Greek colonies, and in native villages of Africa.

The eastern lands of central Europe had been occupied in precolonial times by the original Slavic inhabitants. These people had extended their living space by pushing the forest back and laying out their fields in the clearings, although they hardly went as far as to remove the tree stumps. But this latter is by no means a negative criterion of these early times, for as late as the nineteenth century this method was not unknown in East Prussia; and even during the twentieth century it could be found in Lithuania and southeast Europe.[18] The Slavs' single farmsteads and community villages had spread far beyond the naturally open regions. The invading colonists were therefore faced with a rudimentary structure of settlement that had spread, though thinly, over large areas. Only gradually had these widely dispersed settlements grown together into village communities, for the extended family- or clan-system of the Slavs when they were advancing from the East made it more difficult to develop village communities on the basis of elective affinities. The extended-family organization was transferred by the western Slavs to Germany, and as late as the thirteenth century, land was held in common by the clan—in Mecklenburg, for instance. Even during the seventeenth cen-

18. H. Wilhelmy. *Völkische and koloniale Siedlungsformen der Slaven.* Geographische Zeitschrift. 1936. 3. p. 88. See also for the following.

tury, vestiges of this custom were lingering on, although only as mere formalities.

The extended family was a decisive factor in the Slavs' early settlements on single farms. Only gradually did groups of farms grow together into hamlets and thus originate the Slavic clustered villages.

On the coherence of the families depended the duration of the compact block system of the fields, which were parceled out only when the families disintegrated. In this way there developed a field-pattern that outwardly resembled a German *Flur* (intermixed fields owned by different peasants), but which, in reality, was the exact opposite: Within one block, which became subdivided in the course of time, the fields belonged mainly to consanguineous families; further subdivisions evolved from family rights that had arisen out of former divisions through repeated inheritances and similar conditions; and the land was not equally shared according to its quality. The essential point is that when these villages had to be extended, clustered villages with subdivided block-patterns of land, and not street villages, developed from the Slavic single farms and hamlets. The street village was introduced from outside; and from the combination of western and eastern types of settlement, a mixture of elongated street and compact and centralized villages evolved, as, for instance, the *Anger* village with its village green in its manifold forms.

Arable land first occupied only a small area because cattle-breeding prevailed. The hook-shaped plow, a light plow that could easily be moved in all directions, broke the soil only superficially. When the yields decreased, a new piece of land was cultivated. This shifting agriculture caused the origin of small plots that were irregularly distributed over the land. When conditions finally became settled, field boundaries were marked out. These early settlements were often situated near running water, with no consideration of the field system, because agriculture still had to take second place to collecting, hunting, fishing, and breeding and domesticating animals. In this way, a haphazard distribution of settlement spread over the country, consisting of small hamlets—as the oldest type of village—often with an interior enclosed space where the animals could be assembled. Since defensive needs played an important role, these villages were often fairly compact, either in the shape of a ring-fence or a contracted *Anger* village.

A ring-fence village was a more or less circular settlement around a central open space with only one entrance. A detailed topographical investigation has shown that these villages were preferably sited on diluvial elevations, or on other formations

37. Ring-fence village
of Werbellin, Brandenburg.

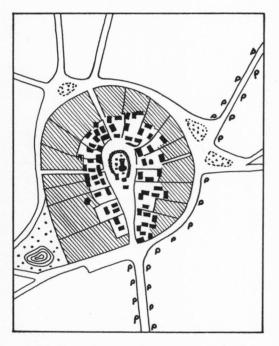

38. Ring-fence village of Brügge,
Brandenburg.

that were accessible from one side only. This would support the assumption that the defense needs turned the natural features, the shape and situation of the villages, to the advantage of the inhabitants. The fields of the ring-fence settlements were laid out either in block or radial patterns, the latter more often on plains than in undulating country and also more frequently when these circular villages had been established in clearings during the colonial period. Ring-fence villages were a very rational type of settlement; considerable and systematic planning and execution were needed to arrive at this simple, yet functional, plan. The narrow arrangement of the houses expressed a strong social awareness and coherence and produced an impressive architectural formation. Ring-fence villages could not be extended; they were, therefore, extremely conservative.

The advancing colonization was accompanied by a reallocation of the fields through extension and combination of unclaimed Slavic plots. This in its turn promoted the introduction of the three-field system. The irregular block fields were replaced by long and parallel strips, and the heavy, iron plow displaced the light, hook-shaped plow. The main principles were extending the food supply and greater systematization. Equal distribution in *Gewanne* was still unimportant in these early times. The area of arable land was often increased by extending the strips of the fields from the low-lying ground to the diluvial uplands. This explains why the older and lower parts were clearly distinguishable from the systematically laid out upper portions, a visible symbol of two different layers of civilization. Smaller settlements were often combined, and quite a few of these disappeared in this process. The Slavic settlements were transformed, but the western forms of colonization were also undergoing a modification. To the not yet very distinct forms of the hamlet, the circular settlements, and the one-entry villages were added combined forms—new street- and square-patterns and clear, ring-fence settlements with *Gewanne*. This period of inception was fundamental to the structure of German settlement in the East; everything that followed was of secondary importance. The early settlements were loosely dotted over the country or in small groups. The density grew only when the colonization turned into a steady mass movement in the later Middle Ages and when *locatores* began settling peasants systematically. The high point of density was reached in the twelfth and thirteenth centuries. During the fourteenth and fifteenth centuries a gradual standstill set in.

Apart from the organized colonists, other larger, though less homogeneous, groups arrived and occupied the less favorable, marshy and wooded parts of the country. They laid out their settlements as *Marschhufen* villages, following the Dutch examples, and, in the intermediate zone between eastern Thuringia and Saxony, arranged their fields in *Gewanne*. These strips of the *Gewanne* in wooded and hilly regions extended over the undulating terrain and cut through forests and meadows. This grouping in *Gelänge* (lengthwise) made it possible to connect the house and the fields and to combine the whole property in a contiguous stretch. At the beginning, these attempts were timid and tentative and led only to a certain loosening up in the region between the old and the new settlements. A distinct and unscattered pattern of fields and houses existed only in the villages in river valleys, marshes, and bogs. The community principle had only secondary importance. Houses were widely separated, and the unity of the street and the coherence of the village decreased. The unifying influence of the *Flurzwang* had come to an end.

After the great waves of the main colonization had come to a rest, a postmedieval amelioration set in, principally affecting the following three regions:

1. Systematic marsh villages, established on the alluvial soils of the basin of the Vistula, where refugees from Holland settled during the sixteenth century. The precarious situation of these settlements demanded the building of dikes and drainage channels. These works were nothing unusual to the settlers and could best be combined with *Marschhufen* villages. At first, the pioneers could only rent the land individually, not own it as hereditary property. But the common work on the dikes nevertheless created a strong community feeling.

2. Climatically unfavorable regions—for instance, the rocky wilderness of still unexplored mountains—where, even here, land was scarce. Purely agricultural settlement of small numbers of peasants was impossible; a combination of several types of economy was, therefore, the best solution—combining, for example,

forest clearing, mining, and minor cultivation, sometimes complemented by home industries. This poor and mixed economic basis resulted in "stunted," forest-line villages, having some elements of genuine *Waldhufen* villages but which were too small to yield more than one third or one half of the food supply of a full farm. This was characteristic of the post-colonial period, which was more industrially conditioned than the first, almost purely agrarian, epoch.

3. A few isolated clearings of the woods were still possible in the higher parts of the mountains, especially in the Alps in connection with the search for metals, but less in the Central Uplands. These settlements grew relatively fast into hamlets or street villages. Houses and fields were almost always combined, although they were small and were distributed in block form all over the land. These postcolonial settlements had in common the fact that, owing to the lack of easy and good situations, they had to use more difficult terrain and so evolve a physical and economic structure suitable to these specific conditions.

In the course of the centuries the population of Europe, especially of western Europe, increased, and the density of rural settlement grew. Everywhere towns sprang up and the pressure of population became stronger. National states came into existence and took the initiative away from individual persons or groups—from feudal lords, the Church, or tribes. The state became the agent of a systematic colonization and the territorial prince, the exponent of this enterprise. Colonization lost its spontaneity and became a means of national policy, used and misused by the state administration. The Thirty Years' War had left behind an enormous devastation. In a report to the Great Elector of Brandenburg, it was said, "The fields have turned into forests." Dikes were falling to pieces, villages were abandoned, and peasants emigrated. It was during this period that large estates were originated, concentrated in the hands of the unemployed knights, officers, and similar professions. Pestilence and famine reduced the population.

Colonization by foreigners was therefore a welcome, and even necessary, solution because the natural increase of the native population was insufficient. However, this colonization was different from what it had been before. The princes were interested in an influx not only of peasants but also of craftsmen and artisans who were available among the refugees from religious persecution. These people settled, above all, in towns. It was a difficult problem that the municipalities had to solve. Frederick the Great remarked when asked to settle groups of his subjects, "Take some from our own country but families from abroad must take part or the families of the countryside

39. Village of Schöneberg, near
Berlin, Brandenburg.

will not increase." The newcomers were a problematic gain, although in general they brought with them a higher civilization. From 1640 to 1740, about 100 thousand colonists were settled by the Prussian administration alone, especially in East Prussia and in the Kurmark. Between 1740 and 1786 their number rose to 300 thousand, and about 900 new colonial villages were established. At this time, the population of Prussia increased considerably. After the death of Frederick the Great a recession began, and between 1816 and 1865 a large portion of the peasants' land was absorbed into the large estates. This was not surprising, for the numerous laws, by-laws, and regulations issued in the interest of the peasants remained more or less on paper, and the repeated emphasis on the need to settle new people among the old stock who would give them a fresh impulse proved to be a rather mixed blessing. Two observations were characteristic: In *"Circulare wegen Urbarmachung überflüssiger Waldungen in Ober-Schlesien rechts der Oder"*—Circulars concerning the clearing of superfluous woods in upper Silesia to the right of the Oder—it was said that

. . . attention should be paid to settle preferably industrious German people in the new villages and establishments in order to cultivate the better the reclaimed fields and by their presence to stimulate the lazy, indigenous Polish nation to greater efforts and more industry.

The basic idea was correct; new opportunities should be created, above all, for new settlers without restricting those of the already established peasants. This was one reason for reclaiming woodlands and wastelands. However, after the death of Frederick the Great, independent voices were raised; they were so numerous and so obviously justified that one is almost inclined to regard the new settlements of Frederick the Great as, at least partly, fake villages. In 1787, a certain Hoyms wrote:

In my most humble opinion the first duty of the leader of a State consists in his care to increase the number of men as far as possible, to guarantee continuously their livelihood, and to settle them in such a manner that they can be most useful to the State. Both these demands have not been fulfilled by the settlement of foreign colonists in compact villages. They have the habit of making use

125

of the benefits of the State and then running away, and for this they cannot be blamed; for owing to the disproportionately great number of foreigners they have often been assigned to places where they had difficulty in earning their living. In other places they would have robbed the old inhabitants of their food and the fruits of their industry.[19]

Colonization was not directed only toward the East but also toward the Southeast, thus the term *Peuplierung* was coined. The Prussian administration approached the problem from three sides. As the first step, the gap caused by wars within the villages had to be filled, so free farms were given to new colonists. This produced a higher density within the existing structure of settlement. Thereupon, as the second step, existing villages had to be enlarged without disadvantage to the available food supply. As in most cases, the arable land could not be extended, only small farms could be laid out, and only cottagers with small plots of land could be settled on older soils—rarely was this possible for full peasants with more than 20 *Morgen* (13 acres). What little expansion there was, was made possible by a minor external extension of the villages without much internal rearrangement of the fields. However, the old medieval layout was not compatible with the stereotyped plans of the state's colonization, for after the Middle Ages, hardly anything changed until about 1750. Finally, as the third step, new settlements were founded—that is, the density of the settlement structure for the country as a whole was increased. For instance, in 1773, a declaration was issued "according to which in suitable places of Silesia new villages were to be built.[20] Thus, in northern Upper Silesia alone 100 new villages were established. Altogether, 12 thousand families in 200 new colonies were settled in Silesia during this period.

This method was especially applied to the cultivation of the so-called *Brüche* (the marshy parts) of the Oder, the Warthe, and the Neisse. The settlements were mostly marsh villages, but such new forms as checkerboard plans were also used. There were so-called *Luch* villages, which extended on the edge of the valleys where they were protected against flooding; on one side, the parallel strips of the fields sloped down to the low-lying land, and on the other, they were limited by the street. In the East, numerous forest colonies came into being because timber was still rather valueless.

The peasants' community bonds weakened, not being compatible with the growing individualism; *Gewanne* lost their purpose; a separation of the individual plots began, and the dispersion of property came to an end; fields were regrouped

19. This and the preceding quotation from H. Schlenger. *Friederizianische Siedlungen rechts der Oder bis 1800.* In Beihefte zum geschichtlichen Atlas von Schlesien. Heft 1, 1933.
20. G. Schmoller. *Die Preussische Kolonisation des 17. und 18. Jahrhunderts.* Schriften des Vereins für Sozialpolitik. 1886.

in elongated plots, accessible by field paths if a direct combination of house and land in short pieces was not possible; and the *Flurzwang* ceased to exist. These aims could be reached in two ways: the government could influence the landlords to use their manorial rights in the interest of colonization; or it could use its own land for this purpose. Against the landlords' strong opposition, formerly peasant-owned land was restored and the exact size was laid down. Frederick the Great decreed: "For each farm, not less than eight Magdeburg *Morgen* of fields, meadows and garden, but not more than twenty," and for each new village, at least six such farms. At this time, the distances between villages were still so great that new places could be founded on the boundaries between the village *Marken*. The colonists received, apart from the land, cattle, tools, and seeds.[21]

A remark about the ideal village in the *Encyklopädie der bürgerlichen Baukunst* by Stieglitz, published at the end of the eighteenth century, is of interest:

The villages should be laid out in such a manner that the homesteads are built in two opposite rows and somewhat separated from each other with houses for cottagers and crofters between them and that a continuous street runs through the whole village. Behind the houses should be the gardens and the fields and all the other land of each peasant who would, therefore, be in a better position to manage his farm and to get immediate help from his neighbor in case of fire, burglary or any other misfortune.

21. G. Schmoller. *Ibid.*

40. Village of Kup, formerly Carlsruhe, Silesia.

This was the ideal form. In reality, many different types of street and other villages were founded.[22] For instance, an attempt was made to reserve the village street for the inner traffic and to direct the through-traffic to a main road, a solution that led logically to a compact layout still further strengthened by separating the house from the fields or by having smaller fields with separate access paths. However, street villages with the same kind of separation were also established—for example, Klein Cyste. The village of Süsserode in Silesia was laid out by a secretary to the Forestry Commission who, acting as surveyor, marked out the plots for the houses and the fields. It consisted of a double row of eight houses on each side, surrounding a rectangular *Anger* (a central open space), and of 66 Morgen (45 acres) of cleared arable land for about 70 persons. The fields varied in size according to the topographical conditions. In another case, a one-sided street village of 15 houses was built, the houses with the fields behind being situated on one side and the sheds and barns on the other. Especially interesting were the radial villages like Jedlitze, Marienau, and Carlsruhe (Kup), all in Silesia. Kup was actually a hunting lodge in a deer park surrounded by small houses. It was shaped as a regular hexagon with twelve houses on each street, sector-like gardens behind them, and four streets in the northern half leading out. The center was occupied by a public building.

When villages were enlarged, the new settlers were separated from the old ones by being placed in a new quarter. In 1776, Frederick the Great wrote a letter demanding that

Whole villages and colonies shall be established at once among the vulgar and rude people who live by themselves, do their work and earn their livelihood in isolation; then the population of this country will see better and be aware of how the others manage and work.

In general, the villages consisted of 40 or 50 families on the plains and in fertile country, of whom about 16 were peasants and the rest cottagers, gardeners, and craftsmen. In mountainous regions, the number of peasants decreased to about eight.

Apart from the purely agricultural villages, colonies for people engaged in home-industries were founded near the towns. The amount of land allotted to these people varied according to their profession and hours of work. Spinners in the Oder- and Warthebruch received, for instance, 4 to 12 *Morgen* (3 to 8 acres) of arable land; nearer to a town, only ½ to 2 *Morgen* of garden land, for example, in Zinna and Nowawes near Potsdam, colonies founded with 200 and 400 families respec-

22. W. Kuhn. *Kleinsiedlungen aus Friederizianischer Zeit.* 1918.

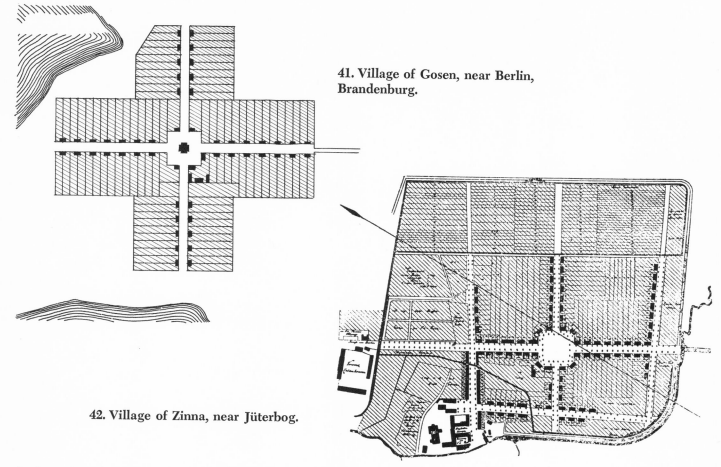

41. Village of Gosen, near Berlin, Brandenburg.

42. Village of Zinna, near Jüterbog.

tively. Their houses were crowded together and had only a narrow frontage.

Four categories of colonies can be distinguished:

1. Mining colonies based on the work of the colonists, who acted as part-time peasants and part-time craftsmen, or as workers such as charcoal burners or woodcutters. On an average, 30 to 40 plots were laid out in a linear arrangement.

2. Forest colonies for woodcutters, generally consisting of about six houses with small gardens or small fields.

3. Agricultural colonies, consisting mainly of agriculturists, with perhaps a blacksmith, a shoemaker, and a few other professional people.

4. Colonies of craftsmen and weavers consisting of a varying number of houses—in Silesia, for instance, from 6 to 20. Of public buildings there were mostly a school, a bakehouse, and similar institutions. The situation of the villages depended on their specific needs—water for industry, and communications for the transport of goods, although byways were preferred. However, unfavorable situations were common, especially during the first years after the establishment of the colonies, because new land had to be opened up or reclaimed, and clearings of the

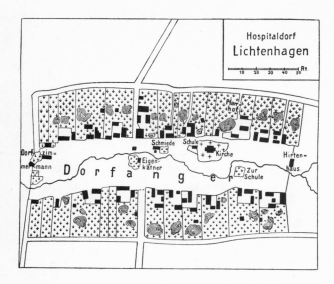

43. Germanic *Anger* village of Lichtenhagen.

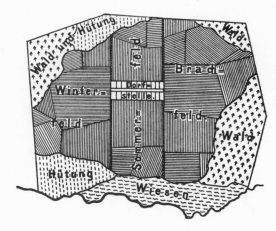

44. Field system of a Germanic village.

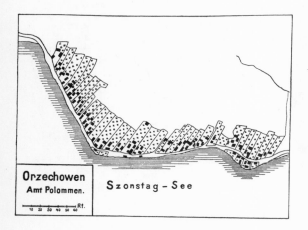

45. Masurian lakeside village of Orzechowen, Poland.

woodlands had to be made carefully since the forests were by this time considered precious.

All the different streams of development merged in the northeastern province of East Prussia. Here, in a relatively small area, the Slavic and central European influences met. The circular *Anger* villages of the original Prussian inhabitants alternated with elongated *Anger* villages, with settlements of the Lithuanians and Masurians, or with manorial foundations. At the beginning of the nineteenth century, a veritable pattern-book of settlement types had been composed.[23] The long and rectangular *Anger* village developed mostly on wooded land, generally having a double line of houses. The actual area of the village had sometimes the considerable width of about 2000 feet and was occupied by 12 to 24 houses which were separated by gardens. A long *Anger,* the village common, extended about 500 to 1000 feet between both rows of houses and was accompanied on either side by roads running between the *Anger* and the houses. In the course of time, the *Anger* was often used for the erection of public buildings—the church, the inn, the bakehouse, the smithy, and similar institutions. The buildings were surrounded by small gardens, spoiling the spatial unity of the common. If the *Anger* remained as an open space, it was used for the animals and called *Kotla,* its ponds and brooks serving as watering-places for cattle; in this way two functions were combined: cultivation, carried on by the village, and animal husbandry, centered on the *Kotla.*

These villages were closed at both ends, from each of which branched off three roads, one as an extension of the *Anger,* and the other two at right angles connecting the neighboring

23. R. Stein. *Die Umwandlung der Agrarverfassung Ostpreussens durch die Reform des neunzehnten Jahrhunderts.* Schriften des Königlichen Institutes für Ostdeutsche Wirtschaft an der Universität Königsberg. 1918. Heft V.

places; altogether they formed a T. The fences behind the houses ran mostly in a straight and uninterrupted line over the whole length of the village and along a footpath at the outer boundary of the village proper that led to the fields. The fields were distributed in tiny plots over the village land. They were grouped in sometimes as many as eight *Gewanne* because, in the course of the centuries, many new pieces had been added by the clearing of the woods, in which each peasant received a share. The size of all the fields together varied between 40 and 80 hides. Although these villages seemed to resemble the street villages of the Slavs, in reality they were quite different.

When the Masurian street village was situated on the shore of a lake, it had, of course, only one row of houses. The street would run along the shore, followed by the houses and, behind them, the fields. The essential difference between this and the *Anger* villages was that no street village, not even one with two rows of houses, had an *Anger,* and that the dwellings were lined up along the street. The reason was that cultivation was more important than animal husbandry, which was rather poor. The houses stood close together, sometimes even without gardens. The straight line gave way to a greater irregularity; the village street and the fences behind the house plots were less systematically laid out. About 20 to 30 farmsteads formed a village with up to 8 hides, which were distributed in a manner similarly to those of the *Anger* village.

The villages of the original Prussian inhabitants developed slowly in the course of time. The Teutonic Order, the agent of the colonization, desisted from the use of force against the personally free peasants. The rigid colonial system was therefore missing. The villages were mostly laid out in an approximately circular form with a fairly large *Anger* for the cattle and only one exit to the pastures, the so-called *Palwe.* The area of the fields was small. These villages were mostly situated away from the roads. During the eighteenth century the fields were gradu-

46. Old Prussian horseshoe village of Sollecken.

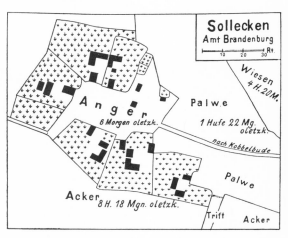

47. Masurian street village of Giesen.

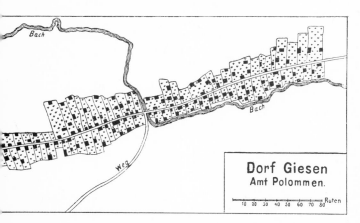

48. Old Prussian *Anger* village of Schmiedehnen, with fields.

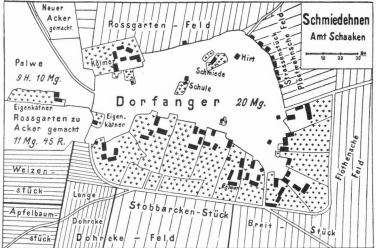

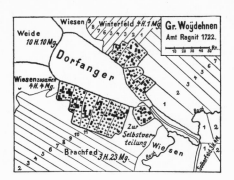

49. Lithuanian horseshoe village of Gross Woydehnen.

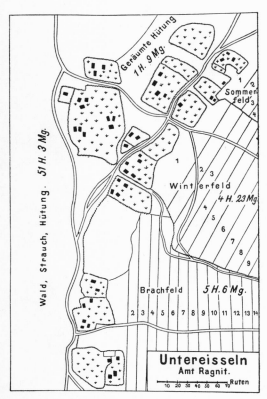

50. Lithuanian dispersed village of Untereisseln.

ally enlarged by the reclamation of new land and by bringing parts of the *Palwe* under the plow.

The oldest type of Lithuanian settlement was probably a semicircular village, resembling a horseshoe, which was specifically adapted to animal husbandry. It is likely that at first, the houses were relatively loosely grouped around the central open space. However, concentration became greater under the influence of the authorities, only to be loosened up again in the eighteenth century. At that time, each peasant received a compact piece of land, in the middle of which he could erect his house. The fields covered only 10 to 20 hides. Often the village was not centrally situated amidst its fields, the narrow ends of which would adjoin it at one side only, the rest expanding wedgelike outward. Social and economic equality characterized the Masurian and Lithuanian villages, although less outspokenly than in the Germanic settlements. The *Allmende* and community regulated cultivation were common to all types.

The manorial villages varied according to the origin of the peasants; however, the manor was always situated at one end of the village street.

The colonization of the East had not come to an end in the time of Frederick the Great. A Prussian Commission was active in the former Province of Poznan until shortly before World War I. The villages built by this commission for purely political reasons were dull and stereotyped. Everything was rigidly prepared by disingenuous bureaucrats who simply took patterns out of their pigeonholes, whether for a church, a dwelling, an inn, or any other building. It was the sordid end to a grandiose movement which led from a dynamic, collective, and enthusiastic advance to the desiccated and feeble activities of a few filing clerks.

After World War I, almost all settlements of eastern Germany became Polish. In 1919, a strong interior colonization began in Germany, which aimed at self-sufficiency for the settlers and at a better food situation for Germany. Large estates were

132

divided and the land was given to individual peasants. Between 1919 and 1930, more than 1,730,000 acres were assigned for this purpose, and more than 48 thousand farms were formed, of which about 34 per cent had fewer than 5 acres and 43 per cent over 25 acres. This was perhaps the first time that interior colonization in Germany was undertaken, not for military or political reasons, but for social and economic ones. A certain rationalization in the layout of villages and field systems was distinguishable, although no new types were developed. Dispersed settlements for the large farmers and street villages for the small peasants and agricultural workers were predominant. The tendency was to create many new and independent farms that would sell their produce in the open market and which could be run as family enterprises.

Central Europe, with its great political, social, and economic fluctuations, is a particularly instructive field for studying the essential conditions and variations of the rural structure of settlement. Certain functions that could be shown in this connection are of a general significance, above all the intimate and mutual relationship between the plan of a village and its field system. So-called "chance" developments did not exist, and the idea of an unsystematic village is incorrect because it arises out of the misconception that the layout of a village could exist in isolation and was not part and parcel of the larger functional unit of the plan of settlement as a whole consisting of the village and the fields as an indivisible entity.

It is a long way from the ancient association to the village community with its communal land and communal work in the fields, to the self-sufficiency organized by the manor, to the colonization regulated by the state, and finally to the present individualization of work and ownership. Along this way, practically all types of villages have played their appropriate roles, and all sorts of social organizations have been tried out. Today, the community spirit of the village has disappeared as a formative factor. If it lingers on at all, it is only in the sphere of the subconscious, for otherwise, it has been overshadowed by the individual interests of the individual peasant.

Yet it is not dead. The environment and the rhythm of growing and decaying that nature imposes on those who work on the land, create a strong bond among the peasants that cannot be ignored. The common life of the village draws its vital forces from the gifts of nature equally bestowed on all and also from the inevitability of obedience to this rhythm shared by all members of a village. Between these poles move a passive acceptance of a certain monotony and the easy overestimation of the importance and directness of even minor events.

THE social class representative of the early Middle Ages was made up of peasants. However, their importance as principal members of the social structure declined in the course of development, and the townspeople emerged as the leading group. The dualism between towns- and countrypeople lasted for many centuries, in spite of the former's attempts to extend and to strengthen their influence over the surrounding country and in spite of the inescapable mutual dependence and complementary nature of their economies. When towns and cities began to cut out from the countryside their own living space as a distinct unit, they took the first step in establishing economic domination over the rural population; they formed small, economically autonomous islands in the vast sea of agricultural lands. The more the power of the state and its capacity to organize its territory increased, the more the homogeneity of these small units dissolved and the more the state took over numerous functions; thus, not every town had to defend its own domain. But a few towns were developed as fortresses that could protect larger areas, while others became seats of certain administrative functions of the state or of industries. The sphere of influence of the towns grew, especially when communications improved and traffic increased. A differentiation of the urban centers set in, and the autonomous and intimate unity between the towns and their hinterland disintegrated. The towns drew together, and the countryside sank to the level of a more or less passive space between them.

Rural settlements dominated the scene until agriculture had reached enough stability and efficiency to deliver a sufficient surplus to concentrations of consumers. It was at this point that the great period of urban development was initiated, and a new way of life spread its spiritual and economic tentacles over the country. After an era of great influence, the political power of the towns declined. But their social and economic importance grew.

After the interlude lasting from the fall of the Roman Empire until the renewal of city life—a period during which peasants and agricultural colonists played the leading roles—the burgher, the agent of a rational urban economy, advanced his claim based on reason and necessity and also on moral and religious grounds. The peasant not only submitted to these aspirations but went over to the townsmen, for he felt that "town air sets people free," liberating them from servitude and feudal bonds. However, in the course of time, the more the moral and religious links between the members of the urban guilds weakened, the more the economic profit motive gained the upper hand; and with this change, the conditions for the dominant

Urban Settlement

position of a new category of persons were called into play. The official, the agent of the new society, took over and began to organize the life and work of the obedient subjects of the emerging national state; in other words, he began to hem in organic growth and to replace it by organized expediency. He deprived the towns of their privileges and restrained the territorial claims of the feudal hierarchy. It was a long process that moved so slowly and imperceptibly that the official hardly realized that he himself was being dethroned and his master, the state, represented by the industrial and commercial leaders, was being made the "nightwatchman of the private interests."

Roman Settlement

After the steam roller of the Folk Migrations had leveled the visible remnants of the Roman Empire, urban life, as far as it had existed at all, was almost at a standstill. The Roman organization that had held the administration together had disappeared, the country had been given over to agriculture, and the distinction between urban consumers and agrarian producers had been reduced to a minimum. The self-sufficient economies of the manor and of small and scattered groups of peasants were able to supply the basic needs of the population. An immense opportunity for a new beginning lay before central Europe.

No German towns had existed in Germany during Roman times; the camps laid out by the Roman conquerors were, above all, military institutions and were situated in the western part of the country, mostly in the valley of the Rhine. Tacitus' statement, *"Nullas Germanorum populis urbes habitari est"* (Germania, 16) confirms the fact that not only town life but compact settlements in any form were unknown to the Germanic tribes. Farmsteads were separated by considerable open spaces: *"suam quisque domum spatio circumdat"* (Germania, 16). However, there did exist strong points that served as refuges in times of danger. The German word *Burg,* translated by the Romans as *oppidum,* comes from *bergen,* meaning "to protect" or "to enclose." The *Burgen* were often either placed on hills, a situation that strengthened their defensive position, or else protected by rivers. The Altenburg in Hesse, for instance, was an *oppidum.* Other river *oppida* were Asciburgium, at the confluence of the Ruhr and the Rhine; the *oppidum* Batavorum, at the mouth of the Rhine; and the *oppidum* Ubiorum, later the nucleus of Cologne and one of the very few permanent settlements—most of the other *oppida* being used only temporarily in times of war. These *Burgen* were not the beginnings of the medieval towns, at least not directly, although a few had been founded on sites later occupied by towns. But the continuity between the two was only a topographical one that assumed no particular significance until some of the sites of the old Germanic *Burgen* were used in Carolingian times for the erection of royal castles. The contribution of the Germanic people to the development of cities was nil, for the *Burg* cannot be considered a formative element that they, themselves, originated.

Military necessities were the prime mover of the Roman settlement. The frontiers had to be secured; thus, camps were established. Civic reasons played hardly any part, although a few places had to fulfill functions that were not of a purely military nature. A Roman trading settlement had been established before 49 B.C. not far from Basle; and somewhat later, Colonia Raurica, which had been a Celtic *oppidum,* was founded by the Romans—Augustus named it Augusta, and later it was known as Augst. Camps were established on the Danube and the Rhine—for example, Carnuntum, near Hainburg to the east of Vienna; Vindobona (Vienna); Augusta Vindelicorum (Augsburg); Vindonissa (Windisch), in Switzerland; and Vetera (Xanten). Strong points were established at Mogontiacum (Mainz), Koblenz, Antunnacum (Andernach), and Basle.

It was different at Cologne and Trier. After conquering the tribes who had inhabited this region, Caesar transferred the land in the vicinity of the present Cologne to the Ubians. Within their territory, the *oppidum* Ubiorum was founded about 12 B.C. on one of the terraces that was safe from floods. At first, this was a sort of suburb with certain characteristics of a Roman town, though it had not yet been organized as a *municipium.* Under Tiberius, the *oppidum* Ubiorum became strongly fortified, and was peopled by numerous Roman veterans. In A.D. 50, it was made a *Colonia Juris Italici* with the name of Colonia Claudia Agrippina, and about twenty years later it was surrounded by walls and towers. The veterans were the leading class of this early urban society. Laid out on the Roman checkerboard plan close to an old strong point, it became a wealthy town owing to a considerable trade in cloth and wine, an affluence that led

51. Blockhouses on the Danubian *limes* at the time of Marcus Aurelius. Relief from the Marcus Aurelius column in Rome.

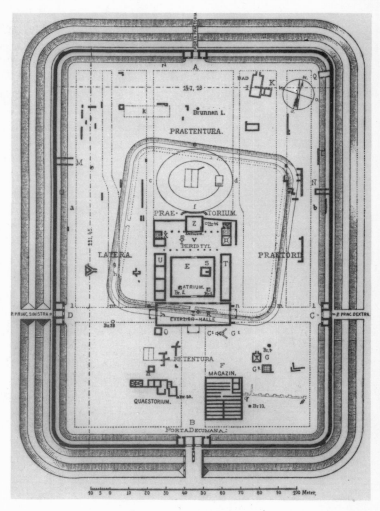

52. The Saalburg *castrum*.

53. Roman Trier about A.D. 300.
Scale—1:30,000.

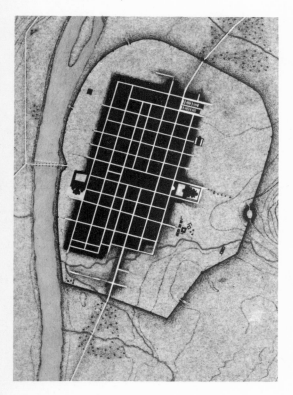

to the creation of many splendid public buildings. Trier developed similarly in the territory of the Treveri. It was founded by Augustus in the years 16–13 B.C. with the name Augusta Treverorum.

Numerous other places were founded and followed a similar development, although mostly on a smaller scale. In connection with these settlements, traffic and commercial centers developed on unprotected sites but in favorable locations; and, independently, resorts were established where mineral springs promised a successful therapy—for example, Aachen, Baden-Baden, and Wiesbaden. In A.D. 179, Marcus Aurelius established Castra Regina (Regensburg) on the site of the Celtic settlement of Radasbona at the confluence of the Regen and the Danube; and under Septimius Severus, Vindobona and Carnuntum were elevated to *coloniae*. During his reign from A.D. 284–305, Diocletian fortified many places, especially Trier, which, in 286, was made an imperial residence. But Roman rule began to weaken, and the time of the foundation of towns came gradually to an end in the fifth century.

The *raison d'être* of Cologne and Trier was not purely military, although the settlements of veterans introduced a military element. However, quite a few camps assumed a more civic character by adding a nonmilitary population to their garrison. There were, for example, Sumelocenna (Rottenburg), which became the most important town of the Roman province on the right bank of the Rhine due to an influx of people engaged in peaceful pursuits, and Andernach on the Rhine. But they were exceptional. A military and a civic settlement existed side by side in Wimpfen and Heddernheim, where the nonmilitary settlement grew up in the immediate vicinity of the camp as in Rottweil on the other bank of the Neckar.

The first Roman settlers, even in fortified places, used wood and earth, locally and easily available raw materials, for buildings. But soon stone was introduced, not only for fortifications, but also for public buildings. The fortified enclosures and the camps were laid out in squares or rectangles, forms that were then transferred to the towns. This system was rigidly adhered to, provided the relief, or other physical conditions, did not

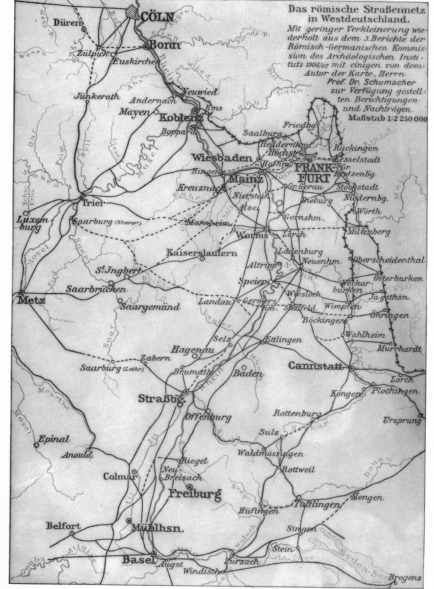

54. Roman roads in western Germany.

139

make deviations necessary. Streets crossed each other at right angles, and the blocks were also mostly rectangular. The principal streets, the *decumanus* and the *cardo,* formed the main cross of the layout, the *decumanus* running straight from the *porta decumana* to the *porta praetoria.* All towns had a *via principalis,* the highway leading out to the open country. This plan can still be distinguished in many towns of Roman origin—for example, Cologne, Trier, and Augsburg. The town's economic center was the *forum,* usually a rectangular space situated at the intersection of the main streets and surrounded by such public buildings as the *basilica* for the law courts, shops, or the *curia,* the meetinghouse of the town council. Not all towns had walls; and even such important places as Mainz, Trier, Strasbourg, and Worms were walled in only fairly late—that is, in the third to the fifth centuries. But because the walls had a religious meaning for the Romans—the foundation of a town was accompanied by a sacred ritual in which a plow traced the course of the walls and was then carried over the place where the gates were to be erected—they were most anxious to have their towns enclosed as soon as possible.

It may be assumed that in many cases the Roman towns had been preceded by settlements of traders and craftsmen, which had grown up next to, and under the protection of, the military camps in situations favorable for traffic and trade. The *canabae* of the traders gradually grew together into a *vicus* that usually extended along the highway on both sides. It was by no means a village but, instead, a trading suburb and often the nucleus of a future Roman town.

Economically, the Rhineland was far more advanced than the Danube region because here numerous soldiers, whose needs gave rise to commercial activities on a relatively large scale, had to be concentrated in defense of the frontier. Cologne and Mainz were the main trading centers. Trier manufactured cloth, porcelain (*Terra sigillata*), pottery wares, glass for windows, and mosaics; and in the surrounding countryside, vineyards were cultivated. Cologne became famous for its glass, Mainz for its artisans and its porcelain. The porcelain industry spread over the entire Rhineland; forty places have been identified where porcelain was produced. Brickworks were established in many places, mostly run by the legionaries. Metalworks were founded in the valley of the Maas. This activity attracted numerous merchants and traders, among whom the Jews were prominent, who developed a lively trade with other countries and within the Rhineland itself. The arts flourished, and social life reached a high level of civilization.

Although certain links between Roman principles of city

planning and those of the following period were preserved, the essence of medieval city development evolved from an entirely new and independent concept of the layout and function of urban settlement. The Roman organization of urban life was dead. To the Germanic tribes, walled-in places were symbols of servitude and were incompatible with their ideas of tribal living and self-sufficing agriculture. Even in Merovingian times they disdained any form of compact and townlike settlements and left their villages unfortified. The tribal chiefs built their farmsteads outside, not within, the *Volksburgen,* or *Fluchtburgen,* and never protected them by walls or fences; and in the tenth century, when Henry I wanted to safeguard the country against invasions, he did not fortify the existing settlements but used temporary meeting-places, transforming them into *Burgen.* Under these conditions, Antiquity's legacy of ideal and material achievements in city building was of no interest to the Germans, and either it frittered away over the centuries or else was completely forgotten. The way was free for the new ideas and forms that grew out of the social and economic conditions of the following period. Roman traditions lived on in architecture, but city building had to begin afresh to develop its own forms and methods and express them in a new language of form.

The barbarian invasions destroyed the Roman civilization. Economically, the towns suffered through pillage, fire, and outright destruction. Many towns perished forever, and only unimportant settlements developed later on or near their sites. The political and economic functions that the destroyed towns had fulfilled were taken over by other settlements, but not until the Middle Ages. In general, the historical continuity of urban development was interrupted. There were a few exceptions—such as at Frankfurt, Trier, Cologne, Mainz, Worms, and Speyer— but though a certain continuity was preserved where the old site had been retained and remnants of the Roman walls and buildings had survived, the Roman town as an administrative and cultural entity ceased to exist. Large open spaces that had been occupied by houses were now used for cultivation, and the inhabitants became, in many cases, part-time agriculturists. However, it would be wrong to assume that the towns of the Merovingian period had sunk to the level of agrarian settlements. They remained centers of trade and commerce, although on a greatly reduced scale; and a certain technical tradition of the arts and crafts was preserved.

Because connection with the Baltic trade was still difficult, it was not until the end of the Carolingian period that commercial activities began to revive energetically along the great river

The Middle Ages

valleys of the Danube and the Rhine and, to a lesser degree, in the region of the Elbe. In general, the revival of the urban structure as a productive factor of the national economy was still in its infancy. The municipal administration of the Romans and, with it, local self-government were dead. In their place, officials of the king or emperor, counts or bishops ruled the towns. Their sway was not restricted to the towns where they had their residence but extended over the country of which the town was the center. These officials lived in a fortified castle (*palatium*), which was often installed in surviving Roman buildings. The bishops built their own castles near the principal church. The officials represented the king and ruled the towns in which they resided, but legally their castles belonged to the king.

Just as in Roman times a *vicus* of traders and craftsmen had grown up outside the camp or the fort, trading settlements developed around the seats of the bishops, also called *vici*, which were important elements in the reviving trade and commerce. During the Merovingian period, the cultural and political center had still been in the Mediterranean region. Under the Carolingians it shifted to the North to the lands between the Seine and the Rhine. In this revival of trade under Charlemagne, the needs of the Church played a leading role. Bishops and monasteries required for ecclesiastical and secular purposes precious fabrics and garments, objects of art, works of artisans and craftsmen, books, oriental spices, building materials, windows for churches, bells, and innumerable other products. Therefore, it was not unusual for the erection of churches and monasteries to lead not only to the establishment of new trading settlements but also to the foundation of other ecclesiastical institutions on important roads or at points favorable for traffic.

The foundations for the new towns of the Middle Ages were laid by Charlemagne. During his reign, numerous fortified castles were built, which were to become the nuclei of towns. These castles were known as *Königsburgen*, royal fortified castles,

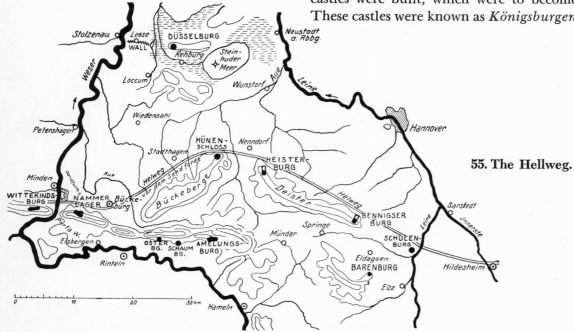

55. The Hellweg.

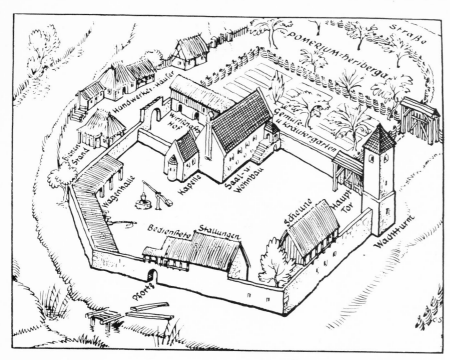

56. A ninth-century *Königshof*.

57. A twelfth-century *Kaiserpfalz*, re-built from a *Königshof*. Based on a 1614 drawing of the Pfalz Hagenau in Alsace.

and coexisted with those of the bishops as the precursors of the new urban network that was to cover Germany in the following centuries. They were built along the rivers, frontiers, and highways that extended from the west toward the northeast.

The most important highway was the Hellweg; it led from Cologne to Dortmund, Soest, Paderborn, and then either to Hameln and Hildesheim or to Corvey, Gandersheim, Goslar, Halberstadt, and finally to Madgeburg. Another road ran from Dortmund to Münster, Osnabrück, Bremen, Stade, and Itzehoe to Hedeby, or via Herford, Minden, and Verden to Hamburg. All these places had fortified castles; in some cases, old Saxon manors were used. Like the old Germanic *Burgen,* they were fortified with earthen walls and wooden stockades, just as the new monasteries and castles of the bishops had, at the beginning, to be content with the same primitive protections. It was particularly characteristic that to the west of the Weser these residences were square and rectangular—that is, their form was based on Roman prototypes—but that further to the east they were laid out in a manner similar to the Slavic ring-fence villages. The castles of the bishops occupied the greater part of these *Königshöfe.* The castles protected the trading settlements that grew up in their immediate vicinity. This development can be found in many parts of the world—for example, in Japan, India, the Middle East, and the Near East.

A distinction should be made between merchants' and traders' settlements. The former provided the merchant with permanent quarters where he could spend the winter and from which he could set out on his yearly trading missions. This type of settlement was predominant in the western part of Germany and perhaps also in the region of the Danube. The traders' settlements were more common to the land between the Weser and the Elbe, and served as depots where the traveling merchants could store their goods under the protection of a royal official. Depots were established on frontiers and functioned as sorts of *entrepôts* for the exchange of goods.

At first, merchants' settlements occupied only a small space. Situations on rivers were preferred because the goods could easily be loaded or unloaded. This led to settlements along the banks of rivers—for example, Mainz, Worms, Regensburg, and Passau. The crossing points of rivers were also favored sites. Merchants during the Carolingian period did not supply the

58. Lenzen on the Elbe, Brandenburg. A medieval settlement at the foot of a hill crowned by a *Burg*, which is either Carolingian or Wendish, thirteenth century.

town where they lived with regularly required goods. The necessities of daily life were provided by the individual households themselves or, on a larger scale, by the manors. Merchants supplied salt, spices, metal, weapons, amber, silk, wax, honey, and furs, and also slaves—most of which were used by the upper classes of the ecclesiastical and temporal hierarchy and by the royal court. An independent transport trade did not exist; therefore, the merchant had to visit the places of production and, at his own risk, bring the goods to the places of consumption. These merchants traveled and traded over relatively long distances, staying at home only during the winter.

We should pause for reflection. It is fairly easy to assemble an imposing array of factual evidence that bears upon the development of the medieval towns. But this would hardly explain why the towns were what they were, how they grew up, and where they stagnated. The essence of the medieval towns cannot be understood without insight into the tensions, aspirations, and ideas that operated in the deeper layers of men's minds, at times driving them to seemingly contradictory actions and at times urging them to act in unison with their fellow burghers.

The Carolingian Renaissance created the first conditions for the great development of urban culture in Germany. This period was still overshadowed by the tradition of Antiquity, although this influence paled before the ever-growing spiritual and political power of the Church. Only slowly did rural and urban thinking begin to move apart. The monastic orders—the Benedictines, the Cluniacensians, and the Premonstratensians—first settled in the countryside, not in the old Roman towns. An upheaval, a clash of two eras, embraced all classes of the population, and from it the cities and towns of the Middle Ages emerged as standard-bearers for a new civilization and a new mentality.

The burgher was the exponent of this revolution of environment. He spent his life in the narrow-wide world of the town he had created against the peasants and feudal lords. He could do this successfully only because he was completely absorbed into his town, which he limited deliberately in space and in social stratification. He derived his most creative powers from this limitation and experienced his town as the center on which everything was focused. In this respect he repeated the attitude of the citizen of the Greek *polis*. His picture of the universe was still that of Aristotle: The earth rested in the center of the universe, which was itself conceived as a gigantic globe. But the self-assurance of the Greeks, their positive attitude toward life, had given way to a deep diffidence. The Church tried to sublimate this anxiety by the consolations that an unquestioning faith would offer, but it could not bridge the dissonance between the realities of life, which it regarded as phantasmagoria of the devil, and the unconditional claims of faith. It could not respond to the demands of reason and of intellect, which marched on indefatigably and without concern.

The medieval burgher was a man of limitations, just as his town and its social structure were limited. He was deeply embedded in the tremendous transformation that was shaping a new life and a new mental attitude. But these new goals were impaired by the doubt the Church had imposed when it demanded self-examination and, in the case of failure, offered only an abundance of torment. Extraordinary tensions existed between the positive *élan vital* of the young peoples of Europe and the negativism of the ascetic severity of the Church. Sin and grace, inner renewal, and intensity of faith were like retarding fetters, and undermined the essential and unconscious forces that could have made a breakthrough to a liberated attitude toward life. All this was reflected in the towns of the Middle Ages: Limitations as well as tensions found their visible expression. Medieval man was faced with problems that demanded from him ultimate decisions the more he tried to penetrate their secrets and the bewildering discord between faith and life. His instinctive impulses, this accumulation of explosive urges, were tamed only with great effort. They made him search for support among others, with whom he could ease his responsibility by uniting his own, individual will with the collective will of the group, with whom he would feel enclosed and sheltered by his town. He needed the visible limitation of the walls as the expression of this urge. He needed the human scale—for the medieval town was a town of the pedestrian. Within this outer protecting shell, he needed the inner shells of the guilds and the family. He needed the Church; but he placed beside the church his administrative buildings, his town hall, and his guild halls. The burgher of the Middle Ages was a revolutionary. He built his own world against a different spiritual attitude and against other people who had come upon the stage before him. His tensions impelled him to move on, to shed the rhythm of the countryside imposed by nature, and to escape the servile dependence upon his former master. From a spiritually and materially unfree being, he matured into a free man, but not yet into an individualist. He became a group-individualist.

Under the guidance of the universal Church a new social structure developed, which gave rise to numerous urban agglomerations. When agriculture had reached a sufficient exten-

146

sion and efficiency, and when the food supply from the surrounding countryside was more or less reliable, urbanization gained momentum, although for a considerable time it moved only slowly and irregularly. For many decades, the towns north of the Alps still had numerous open spaces that served as fields for cultivation or as gardens, and the inhabitants owned arable land outside the walls. To a certain degree, therefore, the towns were at first still self-supporting. The people who came to the towns formed a socially stratified group that was not yet one community but, instead, several communities within the society of the town, consisting of religious fraternities, guilds, associations, and their families. The inhabitant of the Greek *polis* has been described as a *zoon politicon,* who came to the city in order to share with others in the political and civic life. The inhabitant of the medieval town was a *zoon economicon,* whose activities were economically conditioned. Out of this fact developed the social structure of the town.

The towns of northern Europe differed in origin and subsequent development from those of the South. In the North, which was less urbanized, the social, political, and economic position of the landed feudal lords rested on the servitude of the peasants —that is, on their lack of freedom. From the very first, the new urban centers originated as a contrast to the countryside, whether they developed on Roman sites or around a fortified castle or as a trading settlement. The attraction of the towns can hardly be overestimated. Quite a few of the so-called *Wüstungen*—that is, deserted villages or small places—were directly caused by this attraction that drove the inhabitants from these decaying settlements to the towns, especially if the soil were not too fertile. The towns became rallying points for all antifeudal tendencies, even though they first grew under the guidance of a feudal lord. On the other hand, the South, especially Italy, was much more strongly urbanized. The feudal lords who came in the wake of the Folk Migrations settled in the towns even at a time when the natural economy was still the main form of urban production. The more the towns began to recover, the more they became the residences of the nobles and their retainers who played an essential and active role in the developing corporate life of the towns. Over the centuries, the influence of the aristocracy gradually diminished, and the countryside became dependent on the municipal administration. In many cases the peasants had helped the feudal lords to extend their tyranny over the towns. But after the burghers' victory, feudal property was sold to wealthy citizens and the peasants were "liberated," although they remained excluded from any political power. The economic policy of the towns was dictated by purely urban considerations; either the general consumers' interests prevailed or later, after the rise of the guilds, the influence of these producers was decisive. In the North, the feudal lords maintained their power over the countryside longer than in the South where the peasant had exchanged feudal lords for urban masters at an earlier date.

The spirit that spurred the growth of the German towns was also the agent of a functional transformation leading to a new social and economic structure. Above all, this spirit consisted in the longing for freedom, the yearning for a more active life than in the country, and the will to use the trade learned in the narrow confines of the home industry or manor economy in wider and more liberated surroundings; attached to this was the longing for greater security, which the unprotected countryside could not offer, and for new bonds based on common and elected interests to supplant the old ties of blood and the narrowness of family seclusion. The growing importance of the town was, to a high degree, the direct result of a balanced social structure, for this alone empowered the towns to fulfill their task efficiently and with foresight. The number of inhabitants was moderate, and the composition of their population was perfectly adapted to their purpose and mission of initiating a new economy.

The two professional classes that had not existed before in a similarly organized and outspoken form were the craftsmen and the merchants. It was not only their appearance as such but the new mental attitude of the period that gave these two groups their extraordinary impetus. Both demanded a right to work, and this new right demanded a new professional honor that had not existed before. The individual person took part in these achievements only as a member of his profession, which, as a corporate body, dictated his attitude and succeeded in realizing his and his group's demands. The craftsmen and the merchants gave the towns their character against the opposition of the peasants and the feudal lords. They needed the peasants to supply food to the towns and to buy their goods, but they had to get rid of the nobles if they wanted to be masters in their own houses. Thus, the peasants were forced to give up, or at least to reduce, their own home industry, to buy their industrial requirements in the town, and to sell their agricultural products only to "their" town. In this way, autonomous economic units came into being, and production, consumption, and trade were monopolized. The towns enforced their will by road mileage and storage statutes—that is, by the so-called market law—and sometimes they built granaries to store the grain: it was an enforcement that made use of certain transport and storage privileges. Essentially it was the same method used by the famous (or infamous) Navigation Act—this Act created a monopoly by decreeing that goods should be imported or exported only in English vessels. As early as Richard II's reign, it was ordered that "none of the King's subjects should bring in or carry out any merchandise but in English ships."

At the same time, the fight against the feudal lords went on. They were forced out of the towns, but this was not enough; their power over the countryside had to be broken. The burghers insisted that the castles of the lords within the towns disappear; they achieved this by force and extorted or bought special privileges, according to which castles could not even be erected within a certain distance from the town. This was also why not even the emperors, to say nothing of the nobility, had a legal right to take up their quarters in a town. Protection against both the feudal barons and the peasants and the fact that shelter had to be given to the latter in times of unrest demanded the self-protection of the towns, which could best be provided by walls. The burghers needed and had walls against their enemies, whereas the barons had their fortified castles and defended the rural settlements that grew up around them without walls. It was the difference in spirit that created these different forms; those classes or persons whose life was devoted to warlike activities merely fulfilled their essential purpose in life when they were fighting—for example, the Spartans, the lords of the Swiss castles, or the *daimyos* of Japan. But the peaceful burghers needed the auxiliary means of the walls.

After a certain stability had been reached, the towns eliminated everything that was economically and socially alien to them and used everything that was needed and in their interest. Their structure was so organized that they could live and let live. Everyone could earn his living. The social and economic differences were relatively insignificant owing to the small size of the towns and the intimate ties that bound the individual citizen to his professional group. Like the *polis,* the medieval town did not grow beyond a certain limit, although numerous towns were enlarged; on the other hand, the urban population was often reduced by epidemics, pestilences, famines, wars, and the high death rate, thus counterbalancing the influx of new people. When the trades were full, no new members were admitted. Last but not least, the feudal lords made immigration difficult because they did not want to lose their *adscripti glebae.* As in Greece, this restriction of the growth of the towns often resulted in new foundations.

The internal balance of the urban social structure was possible only as long as the state was weak. It lacked the administrative organization that could have held together a large territory, and at whose nodal points urban agglomerations could have developed as administrative centers of the state. Moreover, with a few exceptions, permanent royal residences did not exist; the kings were still itinerant rulers. This was not contradicted by the Church's request that its bishops reside in a town with good communications and not in a place of "moderate size." The medieval state was only strong when the ruler was strong. Because this was rare, the German Empire split up into innumerable small territories, and the political power of the towns increased. Compared with France, the German evolution was entirely different. The French kings began with a small, compact sphere of influence and extended their sway over other regions hardly beyond the Ile-de-France—one reason why France was, and still is, not nearly so fragmentary as Germany and why her towns had more modest political ambitions.

The German towns, on the other hand, had strong political ambitions. They wanted to dominate the surrounding country. In reality, however, this goal was only very seldom reached, for the opposing forces were too strong. The feudal lords retained considerable influence, even though they had to give up peasants or sell their privileges to the towns. Fundamentally, they acted against their own interests when, for the protection of their territory, they founded new towns; for these towns had to be filled with defenders. Because the defenders were anxious to exchange the countryside's lack of freedom for the freedom of the towns, they did not come voluntarily and had to be granted privileges.

The following is a condensed and selected summary of Max Weber's remarks on this point:

The specific political and economic quality of the medieval towns explains also their attitude to the extra-mural classes. This is, however, different in different towns. They have all in common the contrast of the economic organization to the nonurban political, professional, and seigniorial structures: market versus *oikos*. This contrast should not be viewed simply as an economic "fight" between the political lord, that is the lord of the manor, and the town. Such a fight existed, of course, whenever the town received people who were politically and manorially dependent and whom the lord wanted to retain; or when the town accepted them as "external" burghers into the association of the citizens without their actually moving to the towns. For the towns of the north this latter was soon made impossible by the princes and the king. However, the economic development of the towns as such has nowhere been opposed in principle but only their political independence. And it was natural that the feudal members of the warrior class, the king at their head, regarded the development of autonomous fortresses within their political sphere of influence with the greatest distrust. In the same way, the dissolving tendency which the market economy of the town could exert upon the manorial and, indirectly, upon the feudal organization and which, as a matter of fact, it did exert with varying success, did not necessarily operate in the form of a "fight" of the towns against the other interests. On the contrary, in a very large measure a community of interests prevailed. To political and manorial lords taxes which they could levy were more welcome. But it was the town which gave to the subjects of the lords a local market for their products and, therefore, the possibility to pay in money instead of in kind or by compulsory service; in the same way, it gave the lords the possibility to make money out of the sale of their natural products in the local market or abroad the more capital was attracted to commerce instead of consuming them *in natura*. Moreover, the more the local and interlocal traffic developed, the more money could the political and manorial lords gain from all sorts of tributes which would accrue from this traffic. The foundation of a town was, therefore, from the founder's point of view a commercial enterprise as a welcome source of cash income. This specifically medieval, north-European mode of founding new towns is, as a matter of fact, a "profit" business in strongest contrast to the foundation of fortresses which is represented by the *polis* of Antiquity.[1]

The rural people formed their own community organizations, which were subordinate to the feudal and ecclesiastical lords of the manors, and had their own jurisdiction. They were not absorbed into the towns as a social group, although the urban centers remained magnets for the individual peasants. Thus, the contrast between town and country continued to grow and, in the Peasants' Wars, led to the demand by the radical groups of peasants to destroy the towns, a demand that arose not from an acute hatred but from the unconscious aversion of countrypeople against what were for them artificial formations created in opposition to nature. The townspeople, on the other hand, regarded the dull and monotonous narrowness of the countryside as something they had left behind; they were happy in their freedom and looked down upon the thraldom of the peasants, who experienced the town as antagonistic to their open country, as something alien and unnatural that had been cut out of the wide spaces of the land and was rigidly limited as a space *sui generis*. For them, the town was a negation, a denial of the natural conditions of life as they understood them. The unfathomable mystique, so deeply interwoven with nature, could flourish in the countryside, whereas in the towns discoveries were made, people were realistic, and such strange things as the printing press were invented. Town versus

1. M. Weber. *Grundriss der Sozialökonomik.* 1925, pp. 580-587.

country—yet very real and material economic interests enforced an uneasy cooperation. The countrypeople realized, however reluctantly, that the towns were indispensable and complementary to their economy, that they offered protection and refuge in war, that they were their natural centers for traffic and trade and for the market; but they also sensed that a new spirit, which made them uncomfortable, was emanating from the towns, a spirit that disintegrated their natural and simple economy and replaced it by the circulation of money.

Their success assured the towns that they were on the right path and that, despite their small number of inhabitants, they were superior to the country. They knew the causes of their success, and because they knew them, they built their social structure systematically on these foundations. Man as an individual being had more worth here than in the country; he was a voluntary and free individual member of urban society. This spirit of freedom made the towns of the Middle Ages strong and, at the same time, rational. They were places of organized and clearly specified work, which developed on a religio-ethical basis. Their growth was an integral part of the rhythmic change in which the population tended, at certain times, to spread over a large area and at other times to concentrate in limited spaces or along definite lines. The population of the countryside, on the other hand, decreased or increased only slowly. This was the case during the Middle Ages: after the occupation of the land had come to a halt in the thirteenth century, the rural population remained relatively stable and evenly distributed over the open and cleared forest regions until the fifteenth century. Then the urban population began to increase more rapidly, and the number of urban agglomerations grew. Their desirable goal was not a maximum but an optimum population.

During the Middle Ages the towns were fairly isolated from each other because traffic was still underdeveloped. This isolation heightened the sense of safety that the walls of the towns offered. But feeling really sheltered was only possible within a space that was limited, easily accessible in all parts, and that could be experienced directly. The extensions of the towns were therefore small. Towns of a medium size covered on an average an area of not more than 124 acres, and small towns only 10 to 25 acres. The latter, especially, had a very high density of population and buildings because they were not wealthy enough to extend their area. The few exceptions were Cologne, which had grown by the second half of the sixteenth century to about 37 thousand inhabitants and an area of almost 990 acres, and Lübeck, Strasbourg, and Nürnberg, all having more than 250 acres. In the small towns, whose radii were hardly more than half a mile, the wall remained a reality and an ever-present experience as a symbolic idea for the inhabitants who, except in the few larger cities, numbered mostly only a few hundred. This held good especially during the early period. But it should not be forgotten that the medieval towns were "garden cities," with large open spaces for gardens and fields and squares. Yet the walls were a portentous symbol: If they remained, the town stagnated, for then the past was stronger than the new life to which the increasing power of the state was opening the door; if the walls disappeared, the way was free for new tasks, for a new social structure, for a greater material and spiritual mobility, but also for the unforeseeable hazards of an unknown and dangerous future.

If Roman sites were used, the size of the first German towns, built during the Carolingian period, was determined by the circumference of the Roman walls. This was the case in Cologne, Regensburg, Mainz, Worms, and Metz. The area enclosed by the old walls was mostly too large, and the built-up area covered only a part of the original Roman town. The towns of the early Middle Ages needed only a small space for the castle and the *vicus:* Dorestad, the main trading center for the Frisians occupied no more than 30 acres, 5 for the castle and 25 for the *vicus.* Bishop-towns were larger because the bishops' castles and the churches alone needed more space: Speyer occupied 15 acres, and Minden and Münster about 17 acres each. In general, the castle-*vicus* settlements during the eighth to tenth centuries covered on the average from 22 to 37 acres.

From the eleventh century onward, the urban areas increased considerably, especially those of the old Roman towns. To illustrate, Regensburg occupied the *castra regina* with 62 acres and the *pagus mercatorum* with the parish of St. Emmerau, 89 acres, which were fortified in A.D. 917 and walled in at about A.D. 1100; and Cologne consisted of the suburb of St. Martin with 62 acres that were added to the 237 acres of the Roman area. On a smaller scale, other towns, such as Bremen, Hildesheim, Halberstadt, and Naumburg, showed the same tendency to enlarge their areas. This development continued in all regions of central Europe from the twelfth century onward. Cologne grew from 296 acres in 1106 to 585 acres; in 1180 the building of the walls that were to enclose an area of about 990 acres was begun. This size was sufficient until the nineteenth century. Goslar reached its maximum size of 185 acres as early as 1108. Other places showed a similar growth—for example, Soest and Dortmund, Osnabrück and Augsburg, Strasbourg, and Hamburg.

Many towns reached their largest extension in the thirteenth century. Either they grew by adding new settlement units to the old nuclei—which often retained their original character as individual parishes with their guilds and certain religious functions, as sort of neighborhood units (for example, Osnabrück)—or else grew together from a number of independent towns—at Danzig and Braunschweig from five towns; at Hildesheim, Kassel, and Königsberg from three; and in numerous other places from two. Braunschweig was the oldest and most famous example; in the twelfth century three new settlements, the Altstadt, the Hagenstadt, and the Neustadt, developed not far from the old nucleus of the castle and the *vicus*. These three settlements became towns, and in the first half of the thirteenth century each received its own town council; the two old settlements of the actual nucleus were elevated to towns after 1300. It was not unusual for the individual town units to be separated by wooden barriers, especially at night, even when they were close to each other and had a common wall. In contrast to the old nucleus, the newer parts of the towns were often laid out regularly, and could easily be distinguished by their more systematic plan because they were the work of the lord of the town and, as such, were planned as a whole by the will of one person.

In numerous cases, towns grew by incorporating suburbs that were not towns in a legal sense. This happened where a settlement existed outside the walls, such as a trading, industrial, mining, rural, or ecclesiastical agglomeration—that is, a village, church, market, or mining community subject to the temporal or spiritual lords of the town. Many such extramural settlements existed outside the German towns of the Middle Ages. They came into being along the main roads leading to and from the towns. Memmingen in Bavaria may be a representative example: all three of its suburbs were situated on the main roads; the oldest in the east on the road to Augsburg, the southern suburb on the road leading south, and the third suburb on the road to Ulm. Situations on rivers frequently produced suburbs on the other banks—for example, Cologne with Deutz, Regensburg, Frankfurt, and Würzburg. In other cases, the area for the extension of the town had to be reclaimed, and the new settlements would then form an independent suburb within the urban territory. For example, in 1196, a swampy meadow outside the walls of Hildesheim was given to some settlers from Flanders who made it habitable by draining it and building a dam. This suburb developed and became a town in 1232. Towns on rivers and on the sea tended to expand along the banks or the shores and, to a lesser degree, inland, where their extension remained more or less stationary. Other places grew by adding concentric rings around the nucleus, thus expanding fairly symmetrically in all directions—for example, Soest, Nördlingen, and Münster. Internal "extensions" were carried out where open spaces had made an early settlement difficult, as on sandy tracts or swamps. But the fields, vineyards, and orchards that had existed within the towns at the beginning of the Middle Ages were also gradually built up, just as the open and unused land between urban nuclei—that is, between the old and the new town units—was eventually developed.

The early Middle Ages was a period of great migrations. The population was fluctuating. The twelfth century saw, above all, the stabilization of urban freedom; and the thirteenth century, the organic development of the guild system that had resulted from these movements of population. The migrations proceeded from the country to the towns and, at the same time, spread over large regions, advancing the colonization and opening up new lands. The groups that flocked to the towns consisted of landless proletarians and of craftsmen and artisans from other urban places. The feudal lords abandoned their fortified castles in the towns and withdrew more and more from taking an active interest in their own economies to passively receiving taxes. They became capitalists, whereas the peasants changed from bondsmen, who had to perform compulsory services, to suppliers for the next town, which enabled them to pay taxes in money to their lords. The feudal classes were, in this way, progressively eliminated from the new economy, which became the exclusive prerogative of the enterprising urban bourgeoisie. Still another reservoir supplied the increasing population of the towns: in general, from the ninth to the twelfth centuries and later, the population grew as the result of natural increase; this excess population swelled the number of those who had migrated from the country to the towns.

The migrations to the towns originated in neighboring districts. It has been established that for Frankfurt during the fourteenth century, for instance, 46.7 per cent of the new citizens came from a distance of 2 miles, 39.3 per cent from 2 to 10 miles, and 14 per cent from over 10 miles. The figures for the fifteenth century were 23.1 per cent, 52.7 per cent, and 24.2 per cent respectively.[2] The radius of immigration increased in the later part of the fourteenth century. This proved the growing attraction of the town and also the widening of opportunities and the improvement of communications. The proportion of people who came from other towns and villages to the more attractive places can also be illustrated by the example of Frankfurt: In the fourteenth century, 28.2 per cent emigrated from towns and 71.8 per cent from villages; the figures for the fifteenth century were 43.9 per cent and 56.1 per cent, respectively.[3] This

2. K. Bücher. *Die Entstehung der Volkswirtschaft.* 1926, p. 461.
3. *Ibid.,* p. 456.

may be taken as proof that in the early period, the rural population wanted to escape from their servitude and that later the feudal lords took certain countermeasures that rendered the loss of their serfs more difficult. Further, when the trades that could be supported by the relatively limited urban market were full, an embargo on immigration closed them against the influx from the country, while the exchange of workers between the towns continued.

Apart from the fluctuating group of male and female servants and laborers who made up the urban proletariat, the core of the population consisted of the burghers and those who stayed only temporarily in the towns. These outsiders were not numerous, for nobody who was not a burgher was tolerated in the urban community for a long time. In the larger towns, the core of the social structure was composed of patricians, guild members, and the clergy. These latter remained legally outside the urban corporations, but they were hardly a burden on the urban economy because their income was secured by prebends and pious bequests. It was different in the case of the monastic orders. The Church had followed the general trend and complemented their settlements in the country by monasteries of the mendicant friars in the towns, particularly of the Dominicans and Franciscans. Through these monastic orders, the Church accommodated itself to the changing circumstances, trying to preserve its universal influence and to penetrate into all classes of society.

The social structure of the medieval towns did not consist, like present-day society, of human atoms held together by the identical social and economic interests of their class; instead, it was built up of small groups in which the individual burgher was embedded, above all, economically but also, generally, with his whole private life. Families, guilds, ecclesiastical orders, and religious fraternities embraced him. The family sheltered not only his immediate kinsfolk but often also his more distant relatives, even journeymen and apprentices. It was not one of these ties but the complex of all of them that made up the fabric of life in the medieval town. In addition, the forces calling these ties into being were the same that had determined the development and form of the towns and the activities of the population. The Church was one of the greatest patrons of architecture and the building of churches attracted large numbers of craftsmen and artisans to the towns. Religious reverence was the moral basis of the guilds, which imbued their members with a high and mutual responsibility. The weakening of this basis was the beginning of the end of the very idea of the guilds and their original purpose; they became purely economic organizations.

A fully developed medieval town was a brotherhood not unlike the Greek *polis:* There the god of the *polis* and here the saint of the town united the citizens. In contrast to all preceding religions, Christianity dissolved the still existing remnants of clan consanguinity with their aura of magic and taboo. This was one of the most important reasons why the Church was supremely essential for the origin and development of the medieval towns. Under the guidance of the Church, elective affinities developed in place of consanguineous bonds. This was in striking contrast with the East—with India, China, Japan, the Islamic countries, and old Russia—where, because the extended family and the clan were preserved, an urban community as a covenant between individuals that disrupted the coherence of the family could not take root or, if at all, only in a very modified form. The *confraternitates* were, therefore, indispensable for the growth of the towns and in some cases, may have even preceded the political and professional associations.

The towns were economic units limited by their productive capacity. Their extension was, thus, organically restricted by the facts that the greatest part of the production was consumed in their own economy, that the communications covered only short distances, and that work place and living place were under the same roof. This last almost automatically excluded decentralizing tendencies and furthered concentration. Traffic was technically inefficient, and its capacity was, therefore, particularly dependent on the expenses involved. The sphere of influence that could be covered by the urban production—that is, the sale of goods—was the greater the longer the distances were from which agricultural products could be brought to the towns; for the urban products could be exchanged for provisions within the same limits in which the food supply was delivered; and the urban trades could develop in the same ratio. The more this interdependent interchange widened, the more the expansive forces of the towns were mobilized; this in its turn led to an increase of population and, consequently to the spatial extension of the towns.

The starting points of the economic cycle, market and organized trade, were mutually exclusive. The market was the place of exchange where consumers and producers met at certain intervals. This personal contact was not necessary if traders took care of the exchange. Traders did not contribute toward the growth of the town; and wholesale trade remained for quite a time exclusively in the hands of trading merchants, or was conducted at the fairs. The importance of the fairs was independent of the importance of the town where they were held; size and importance of these places were not, at least in the early

Middle Ages, influenced by the fairs, for there, only goods were traded that were not produced in the narrower territory of the towns, such as spices, dried and salted fish, furs, brocades and fine fabrics, jewelry, fruit from the South, wines, and salt. In general, the rarer and more precious goods were supplied by long distance trade, and the simpler and more common goods were produced locally by individual craftsmen or at home. Production and consumption of the goods for daily use remained fairly constant and, in any case, did not develop on a scale large enough to disrupt the economic or social structure and, as a consequence, demand the enlargement of the town.

Further, a large number of medieval towns came into being as places of refuge for the countrypeople living in the vicinity; they served as the protecting *"Burg."* This function originated the *"Burgrecht,"* and the status of *"Bürger,"* *burgensis,* for those who enjoyed this protection and explained why, at the beginning, the burghers were still, to a certain degree, bound to the agrarian structure—that is, to the lord of the castle and the manor economy. In the course of time this connection disappeared and the distinction between the urban consumers and the rural producers became clear-cut and permanent. Simultaneously, the previously military and protective union—the *burgenses* had to perform services as soldiers or watchmen—changed to a territorial partnership on an economic basis. The *"Burgrecht"* implied not only the right of protection but also the freedom of the market and free trade. At first, "market" meant simply the square where goods were exchanged; later this was transferred to the town as a whole, which acted as a market for the surrounding country; and the "truce of the market," which was valid only for the duration and area of the market square, became the "truce of the town" and safeguarded its own jurisdiction. This increased the social contrast between peasants and burghers, and, since every contrast was tantamount to the existence of limiting barriers, this legally privileged position of the towns operated also against their expansion.

An urban territory in central Europe—that is, town and country—covered on an average an area of about 4 German square miles. But in the eastern parts of Germany, in Silesia, Brandenburg, Mecklenburg, and Pomerania, it often included a much larger area with several villages and even more often with from 40 to 300 arable *Hufen* of its own. This tended to ease the urban finances and enable the burghers to acquire land. This combined land unit of town and country was called the *Weichbild,* the area of a town's jurisdiction.[4] Within this area, the peasants could travel to and from the town on the same day and exchange food and raw materials for industrial goods. What

4. J. H. Clapham and Eileen Power. *The Cambridge Economic History of Europe,* Vol. I. 1941, p. 87.

could possibly be produced in the town had to be produced by its own economy. This was one of the most significant principles guaranteed to the trades: to sell by exclusive right in the urban market and to admit foreign products only if they were not produced in the town. If the trades were not complete, the town council remedied this by inducing foreign masters to settle in the town. The individual trades were housed in the same streets or grouped together in the market square because the protection of the producers, that is, of the craftsmen, involved also certain duties. The public and controllable and open competition was expected to guarantee the quality of the goods and reasonable prices; this was easier if the same goods could conveniently be compared. On the other hand, the urban consumers had an exclusive right to buy and had to be assured that enough goods were always available. Consequently, imports and the sale of goods outside the walls were forbidden, and middlemen were excluded. These economic measures established around the towns and their territories an invisible but firm girdle, whose centralizing effect was reinforced by the use of different coins, weights, and measures in the individual urban territories.

The urban economy was a continuation of the manor economy. However, this does not mean that the former developed directly out of the latter; rather one stage followed the other inasmuch as the economy was specialized in general and in detail. In the manor economy, all sorts of work were carried out simultaneously and in the same place. Then agricultural and industrial activities moved apart, and the latter were split up into numerous branches; the laborer of the manor was replaced by the craftsman who worked for money and owned his own tools, materials, and workshop. Here the development came to a halt for the time being. The regulations of the guilds systematically restricted the number of journeymen whom one master was allowed to employ, the intention being to prevent the rise of capitalists. And for the same reason the guild members looked askance at every attempt of the merchants to gain influence over the production by the infiltration of capital. The merchants could buy all goods, but not the labor of others. If conditions demanded a subdivision of the work, the existing guilds were split up into subguilds but without a concentration of different trades in the same workshop. In general, worker and work remained intimately connected from beginning to end, and no outsider could dispose of the means of production. This personal relationship between work and worker was one of the creative factors of the Middle Ages that prevented the falling apart of personal and functional life and was the cause of the great achievements of the arts and crafts during this period. It helped

159

to retain the human touch and the human scale that pervaded the towns, and, above all, it made the rise of a class of specialists, of experts for only a fraction of the products, impossible. Medieval man was not fragmentary; he was a full human being in spite of all his shortcomings and failures. Life and work were one, and the towns were an integrated entity, not chaotic mixtures of antagonistic forces as our cities are.

To sum up the complicated course of economic development and, by implication, of the growth of the towns of the Middle Ages: The urban economic development had its origin in the village. Every village formed a more or less self-contained and self-supporting economic unit. Consequently, industry was dispersed over the whole country. Every unit comprised all branches of industry as far as they were already specialized, and each craftsman produced only for his own small group. These early home industries were situated in the center of the area for which they worked—that is, in the village, which was surrounded by the "means of production," the fields, and the pastures.

In the same fashion, the manor comprised all industries needed for its existence. The lord of the manor had to change his residence within his domain in order to consume the goods produced in the different parts of his territory. It was a complex organization that gradually grew from a system centralized on the manor to a decentralized structure with submanors and numerous villages.

Like both the other types, the urban economy was self-supporting, closed, and diversified. The industries were concentrated in the towns, which were the centers of their territory and, as such were surrounded by a purely agricultural district. As far as possible, the rural home industries were suppressed by the towns in the interest of their own production. Within the

59. Rostock. Engraving by Matthaeus Merian, about 1650.

60. Nuremberg, from the southeast, 1493.

town, the industries were grouped according to their categories. Commerce was concentrated in the market, mostly in the center of town, and the various trades in the same streets or quarters.

The economy of the state, the next stage, dissolved the self-contained economic units of the towns and integrated them with the still surviving home industries and the state-owned and state-run establishments. This was the period of mercantilism.

By the end of the twelfth century, about 50 towns existed in the German Empire of which 30 were bishop- and monastery-towns; 10 were new foundations; and 10 were of an older origin, belonging to the King—Aachen, Dortmund, Frankfurt, and Goslar—or to the archbishops of Cologne, Mainz, and Magdeburg—Soest, Erfurt, and Halle. By the thirteenth century, the number of towns had reached 500. Hardly any of these new towns had originated as trading settlements of the old style except those on the Baltic Sea, such as Lübeck, Stettin, Danzig, Rostock, and Wismar, which served the trade with the Scandinavian countries and Russia. It was characteristic that these new trading towns grew up almost exclusively at the frontiers of the Empire because the distant trade with foreign countries increased at this time. But the great majority of the new towns within Germany were founded for different reasons. An ever-decreasing percentage was situated on important traffic arteries, that is, on rivers and roads. The most common preceding settlements on which new towns grew up were fortified castles, which had only stockades and earth walls. Examples were, among others, Quedlinburg, Nordhausen, Duderstadt, Aschersleben, Donauwörth, and Tübingen.

In the twelfth century the interests of the feudal lords in the foundation of new towns had mainly been economic. This changed when the state developed into a territorial and more homogeneous unit covering large and contiguous territories. The foundation of towns became an instrument of territorial policy. Emperor Frederick Barbarossa initiated this trend by building numerous fortified castles, which he garrisoned with imperial vassals. Other princes and feudals followed, including the archbishops and bishops, and by the end of the twelfth century— as the result of this policy—numerous new towns had come into being that had grown up around the fortified castles and which had gradually increased in size, functions, and importance. Some of these new places became centers for certain administrative tasks; others became residence-like places especially for the ecclesiastical lords, who were more inclined to establish a permanent residence than the restless feudal lords.

The placement of fortified castles within the towns varied greatly. In the older places, they mostly occupied the center of the town, while in the newer foundations, they were located at the periphery on a site that offered favorable conditions for defense. Consequently, hills were preferred, and when these were not available, protection by water was sought—for example, in Brandenburg, Breslau, Hanover, and Tangermünde. In the later Middle Ages, the castles often formed part of the fortifications of the towns.

Villages were in many cases incorporated into the towns, especially in the later period. This means, not that these towns developed topographically from villages, but that villages in the immediate vicinity of the towns were included within the urban area. Examples were Stendal, Dortmund, Helmstedt, and Halberstadt.

The Physical Structure of the Towns

The social and economic changes transformed the physical structure of the town. At first, spaciousness of layout and a certain agricultural activity of the burghers prevailed. Numerous townsmen had at least a garden, or cultivated small fields outside the walls. A market square was rare in the early period, and did not exist even later in towns that had developed from older settlements. Trade was still in its infancy, and the burghers produced a part of their agricultural and horticultural products themselves. The exchange between town and country was not yet sufficient for a special market square, that would have swallowed up valuable space that could better be used for other purposes. It was therefore necessary to gain land by other means: In Cologne during the twelfth century, an arm of the Rhine was drained, and a market laid out on the reclaimed land; a small river was covered in Rotterdam; a river bed was dammed up in Amsterdam. If there was a market square at all in the older places, it was small. On the other hand, in the new settlements, especially to the east of the Elbe, the market squares were large, sometimes almost 5 acres, where cattle markets and annual fairs were held. When, in the course of time, the trades increased and the importance of the cattle market decreased, buildings for the regular weekly markets were erected in these large squares, as well as stalls, that later developed into dwelling houses, the weighhouse, and administrative and other structures. If the remaining space became too small, a *Neumarkt* (a new market) was laid out.

This development is particularly important because it reduces to its true value the theory according to which the origin of the towns was inseparable from the development of the market. In reality, the early markets were often held outside the walls or in neighboring villages, or market squares had to be created artificially and at a later time. Many factors worked together in the development and foundation of the medieval towns—the need for defense, the longing for freedom, the growth of the trades and handicrafts, political considerations and religious requirements, commerce and trade, favorable sites on roads, rivers, lakes, and coasts, and numerous others—and only the sum total of all can offer a sensible explanation for the intricate interaction of these innumerable and often seemingly contradictory forces that were instrumental in developing the towns of the Middle Ages.

In general, the Middle Ages knew open spaces only for practical purposes, such as market squares and cemeteries. Pageantry and ostentatious compositions for display were hardly reconcilable with the rational layout of the towns. The numerous small widenings of streets fulfilled a practical function: They served for the water supply. At certain intervals, where the streets widened, water fountains were erected. The irregularity of many medieval towns has been explained as the result of a deliberate romanticism. This is just as wrong as many other superficial judgments on the Middle Ages in general, as, for instance, the following:

The Pack-donkey meanders along, meditates a little in his scatter-brained and distracted fashion, he zigzags in order to avoid the larger stones, or to ease the climb, or to gain a little shade; he takes the line of least resistance. . . . The Pack-Donkey's Way is responsible for the plan of every continental city.[5]

5. Le Corbusier. *The City of Tomorrow.* 1947, p. 23.

But man, proud man, used his intelligence and therefore created the straight line; he should thus admire the "rectilinear cities of America." In reality, the plan of the medieval towns was rational, purposeful, and systematic. What appeared to be unsystematic was the intricate network of the streets. But this again was the consequence of attaching a greater importance to the houses than to the streets. The houses were the primary element of the town, and as such determined the layout in general and in detail. The streets were of secondary importance. This was only logical, for in a town where the pedestrians set the scale there was no need for straight and wide thoroughfares. The main function of the streets was to give access to the houses and to retain the human scale of the narrow and low buildings that accompanied them. Motion was not the essence of the street pattern, and there was no need to be in a hurry.

It may be assumed that the market street preceded the market square. This is corroborated by the fact that among the towns of southwest Germany belonging mainly to the twelfth century, plans based on market streets, or on a cross of market streets, were more numerous than those with a market square. As time and colonization advanced toward the East and toward northern Germany, the towns with market squares were more usual. This was the case in the thirteenth century. The original form of industrial settlement was a narrow street flanked by the houses of the tradespeople. When commerce and industry increased, this market street was widened and sometimes further enlarged by adding parts of adjoining cemeteries. The first place of this type mentioned in old documents was Radolfzell on Lake Constance. Its Privilege of the year 1100 is still extant. It said that the bishop of Reichenau separated a piece of land from the *Allmende* of his manor "which could be sufficient for a market settlement."[6] The plan shows a wide market street with a cemetery adjoining it. Freiburg im Breisgau, dating back to 1120, developed a similar layout: A wide market street ran through the town in the main direction of the traffic. Being a larger place, Freiburg had a more complicated plan: The main street was crossed by other streets and two squares were laid out. Other towns with similar streets were Lippstadt, Westphalia (1168); and Neumarkt, Oberpfalz, Bavaria, on the road from Regensburg to Nürnberg. The layout of most of these smaller, and many of the larger, towns had its origin in the combination of wide market street and adjoining cemetery—for example, Bruchsal, Baden (1200); and the new part of Braunschweig (at the end of the thirteenth century).

If the market street was crossed by a side street, as often happened in settlements placed at the crossing of roads, the second

6. R. Heiligenthal. *Deutscher Städtebau.* 1921, p. 14.

street was also used as a market street. In these cases, the cross of the market streets became the nucleus of the town plan as, for instance, in Villingen, Baden (1130), with a cemetery at the crossing of the two streets. The same principle of wide streets was applied at Dinkelsbühl, Bavaria; at Bernburg on the Saale; and at Brandenburg, Mark Brandenburg. The plan of Isny, Württemberg (1171), was similar to Villingen: The square at the crossing of the streets was originally not occupied by the church because the market square was at first located in the church village outside the town. Munich, Rothenburg, and Nördlingen had the same plan, the last being developed to a starlike layout because more streets were radiating to a greater number of gates. In all these places the market streets remained reserved for the market in spite of the existence of a central square.

Gradually, the market streets disappeared and were replaced by the central market square. Finally, they were hardly distinguishable from the other side streets. The market square usually had the dimensions of one building block. Examples are Hamm, Westphalia (1225); Sorau, Silesia (beginning of the thirteenth century); Dresden, Saxony (about 1200); and Breslau, Silesia (1242). Depending on the proportion of the building blocks, the shape of the market square was either rectangular or square.

The fortifications of the towns enclosed, especially in the more important cases, not only the narrower area of the towns proper but also the urban territory, the old town *Mark,* and often an even wider circuit. These outer fortifications consisted

61. *Surrender of a Town.* German woodcut, 1514-1516.

165

of the so-called *Landwehr*, an earthen fieldwork with a moat sometimes reinforced by bastions and watchtowers. Where these outer fortifications were less elaborate, at least a lookout was provided from which a guard could keep watch and inform the garrison by visible signals. In larger cities, this post was the origin of an extensive intelligence service.[7] When the traveler had passed the turnpike of the *Landwehr*, he would be impressed by the extension of the fortifications that surrounded even a small town. The walls rose 25 to 30 feet, and were crowned by numerous towers and turrets, especially at the gates. Behind them rose the spires of the churches and the roofs of the higher buildings. It was a silhouette that symbolized the pride and the wealth of the town, lively and harmonious, forceful and aggressive

However, even in the fourteenth century, many towns had to be content with much simpler fortifications. These consisted of stockades, a moat, and earthworks. But everywhere the burghers and the lords were anxious to surround their towns with strong fortifications of stone. Money was collected from the inhabitants; the monasteries of the towns made contributions; and slowly the new fortifications began to take shape, a work that often lasted for generations. On the old earthworks arches were erected to support the new walls. At the same time the moat was deepened and widened and a glacis added. Gates, mostly at the main roads, interrupted the walls. They were regarded as the most vulnerable parts of the fortifications and, therefore, were made especially strong with towers, sometimes with a second inner gate, and always with a drawbridge, a portcullis, and a heavy door reinforced with iron. It was the duty of the burghers to patrol the walls at night, especially the footpath along their inner side. But soon this proved unsatisfactory, for it needed the acquisition of expensive land, and the guards could observe little or nothing of what was going on outside. Consequently, either the passage for the guards was transferred to the top of the walls, which were made thick enough to carry it behind the battlements, or else a wooden passage on supports was constructed on the level of the battlements. At about every 120 feet the walls were crowned by saddle towers or by half towers, which were open to the town and vaulted in their lower part. Here an arsenal of catapults, darts, arrows, and other weapons was kept. Stairs led from these vaulted chambers to the top of the walls, over which the defenders assigned to the different sections of the fortifications could reach the battlements.

The development of many towns was intimately connected with the consecutive stages of their fortifications. Roman walls, walls around the castle and the market settlement, and finally

62. Dinkelsbühl. Fortifications at the Wörnitz Gate.

7. K. Lamprecht. *Deutsche Geschichte*, Vol. IV, p. 211.

walls around the town followed one another. In some cases, a small glacis, an external slope, was preserved between the wall and the moat—for example, in Strasbourg, where the *Bischofsrecht,* the law of the bishop, decreed that "the distance between the wall and the end of the rampart shall be sixty feet wide and the wall itself shall occupy thirty feet." It seems that this space between wall and moat was later either leased—for instance, at Stralsund—to ropemakers or as a market, or that the moat was used for pisciculture, as in Dortmund.

The number of gates was another indication of the history of the towns. They were above all situated on the main roads and had a decisive influence on the layout of the streets. Towns with only one gate were extremely rare. Two-gate towns were traversed by one main street, which they closed at either end. These places represented the simplest type and remained, during the Middle Ages, small towns—for example, Bitterfeld, Hörde, and Itzehoe. Three-gate towns existed when one arm of the street cross did not lead to a gate; they were incompletely developed modifications of the four-gate type, such as Rottweil and Offenburg or the circular Hannöversch-Münden. Much more numerous were the towns with four gates. Some dated back to Roman camps—for example, Cologne, Strasbourg, and Regensburg; others were new foundations. The reason four gates were very common is that four streets led to the four points of the compass, as in Villingen. Five gates were less frequent for obvious reasons: Each new gate diminished the safety of the town, was an additional financial burden, and increased the military duties of the burghers. Therefore, a fifth gate was built only when traffic demands required it and when it promised economic advantages. This was the case in a number of new foundations —Lippstadt, Neuss, Saalfeld, Oppeln—or the result of a complex development—Freiberg, Pasewalk, and Wismar. Six-gate towns were also the outcome of a complicated process, mostly of a combination of several nuclei of settlement—for example, at Meissen or Halle, where castles grew together with markets or old and new towns had coalesced or similar transformations had taken place. In the late Middle Ages, only a few of the more important towns, such as Aachen, Trier, Konstanz, and Cologne, had more than six gates. This was the case especially in the bishop towns: Naumburg had nine gates; Hamburg, ten; Hildesheim, sixteen; Madgeburg, seventeen.

After the twelfth century, both fortifications and layout in the new foundations were designed at the same time, and formed, therefore, a technical unit. The layout was subordinated to the fortifications. The walls were adapted to the relief, whereas the streets divided the urban area into the most favorable build-

63. Dinkelsbühl. The Nördlinger Gate, seen from the town.

167

ing blocks without much consideration for the irregularities of the terrain. This explains why the right angle, the most favorable shape for the building blocks, was only very rarely sacrificed for a better adaptation of the streets to an undulating terrain, and why, in many small towns in narrow valleys, stretching along a main street parallel to the valley, the side streets led over the shortest, that is the steepest, way to the higher parts. It was characteristic that traffic very rarely determined the layout of the streets, for movement was less important than the good situation of the houses or the most suitable form for the building blocks. It is therefore erroneous to assume that the inner layout of medieval towns was adapted to the relief of the terrain. The fortifications were, but not the interior of the towns. It was only through the fortifications that the layout was indirectly influenced by the terrain as, for example, where a town was placed on a hill so that the walls followed the contours in a circle; as a result, the streets formed concentric rings parallel to the walls, whereas the radial side streets were often rather cumbersome.

The medieval towns were not consciously planned according to aesthetic principles. We do not possess one single document in which it is shown that a city council paid attention to the layout of the town as a whole or even to building blocks as aesthetically conceived entities. If there were any references at all to considerations of beauty and deliberate embellishment, they concerned details, individual houses or groups of houses. Defense and a favorable division of the urban terrain remained the primary objectives of the layout.

What gave the towns their unrivaled unity and harmony? The answer is simple: The voluntary and instinctive union of the individual and general will and the merging of personal consciousness and group consciousness created a language of form and a social responsibility that guaranteed an inescapable framework of cultural certainty and made deviation from aesthetic norms impossible. In other words, medieval culture was a complex and all-embracing oneness that endowed every work of art with the same spirit. It enabled the individual craftsman and artisan to execute his work in contemporary forms of a high quality—the result of an unconscious assurance and stylistic lucidity. Consequently, without any deliberate adaptation, the individual buildings merged into one grand harmonious whole. They formed a unity of spontaneity by the sheer fact of their existence. The towns of the Middle Ages were the result of this spontaneous harmony. As Pascal said centuries later, "Diversity which does not merge into unity is negation. Unity which does not depend on diversity is tyranny." Individual buildings, not a deliberate plan, held the medieval towns together. Their layouts, in spite of their seemingly unsystematic appearance, were the most systematic achievements in the whole history of city planning. The individual buildings, not the streets, were the primary units that produced the organic structure of the towns. Apart from the common language of form, the necessary use of indigenous building material, because of insufficient transport, and restriction to the small variety of dwelling types that the economic conditions had developed contributed toward the aesthetic harmony. The very recognition of the primacy of the houses produced the distinctive functionalism that was one of the main characteristics of towns during the Middle Ages, although this is not apparent to a superficial observer. There was a marked difference between the main streets and those that opened up the remaining space between them. There were short blind alleys, closes, all kinds of streets, and small squares that efficiently served the community's purposes. Traffic and residential streets were clearly distinguished as the result of this profoundly practical approach. The medieval towns were the last example of a functional balance between houses and streets. Subsequently, the beginning of the end set in; the "Cult of the Street" began.

The typical medieval dwelling was a small, narrow house owned by those who lived in it. The rooms were arranged one behind the other; they were not yet lined up along a corridor. The windows were small. Place of work and living space were under the same roof. The whole was a perfect "dwelling machine," functional, spacious, and intimate. Medieval houses did not develop from peasants' dwellings but grew up independently, out of the common archetype, the one-room house. This can still be seen in the small houses that have been preserved from the later Middle Ages and in the relation of families to houses and rooms. For instance, in Fürth, Bavaria, in A.D. 1604, 343 families lived in 368 rooms, which were distributed in 140 houses; that is, only half of all dwellings had more than two rooms.[8]

The smallest type of house was the terrace house, about 15 feet wide, with one or two rooms on the ground floor and mostly no rooms in the attic. These dwellings often belonged to a monastery or to a patrician family, and were rented to the poorer workers. They formed groups of four or more dwellings all under the same roof. The best known example of this type was the Fuggerei in Augsburg. Here Jacob Fugger, a member of the wealthy family of merchants and bankers, erected two-storied houses in 1519 for his weavers. There was a self-contained

Houses and Streets

**64. Ulrich Fugger,
by Hans Maler zu Schwaz.**

8. After Heiligenthal. *Op. cit.,* p. 31.

flat on each floor, consisting of two rooms and a kitchen. The upper story had a separate entrance. But this was not the first private development. At the end of the fourteenth century, to name only one other example, a settlement of a similar type was built at Ghent, in Belgium.

The houses of the craftsmen always had two stories. The original one-room unit on the ground floor was preserved as a workshop, whereas the living rooms occupied the second floor. Because the lots were usually very narrow, the houses developed in depth. Stairs led from the workshop to a small hall on the upper floor, where there was a hearth and a narrow window that gave only a dim light to this part of the house. The hall opened to one room at the front and another one in the rear. Toward the courtyard, a small space was partitioned off to store material.

The houses of the merchants also originated as one-room dwellings. Even in the fifteenth century, the ground floor often consisted of only one large hall and one or several small rooms. If the hall extended through all the stories up to the tie beams of the roof, as was the custom in northern Germany, a mezzanine floor with several living rooms was added above the small rooms, which were partitioned off from the hall on the ground floor. A hatch connected the hall with the roof, making both available as storerooms. In southern Germany, often the entire upper story was used for living rooms, and the connection between the hall and the roof was effected by an outside crane. The different kinds of goods that had to be stored influenced the layout of the houses; for example, Nürnberg's trade with the South consisted of many commodities that could be stored in the roof. This led, therefore, to high roofs with several storerooms. The trade of Cologne, on the other hand, consisted mainly of products that had to be stored in cellars, such as wine and fish; consequently, the roofs were of less importance than in Nürnberg, and played a minor role in the appearance of the houses.

The houses turned either their gables or their eaves to the street independent of what their neighbors did. Only very rarely were the building blocks completely closed by continuous block fronts. It was a semi-open development that characterized the medieval towns. Everywhere, greater or smaller gaps between the dwellings permitted a view over the backs of the houses to the higher buildings in the next street, to the churches, to the castle, and to the fortifications as the outermost limit of the burghers' limited world. The age of the perspective view, of the planned vista, was still far off. Intimacy and proximity reigned, and variety and casual surprises created a manifoldness of effects that could hardly be surpassed. Unity in diversity resulted even when the general layout was stereotyped and dull. Restrictions of height were unknown, nor were they needed since the general sense of conformity made reticence a natural law. Moreover, more than two stories were useful only for larger commercial houses, a possibility that was rare. The four- or five-storied buildings at the market square remained within the limits of a modest height because their stories were low. Where the ground floors of the buildings were opened by arcades, these were used by tradespeople and craftsmen for exhibiting and selling their goods.

Despite the enclosing effect of the surrounding buildings, the squares were very rarely homogeneous creations of space. One of the few exceptions was the Prinzipalmarkt at Münster, Westphalia, with its continuous arcades and the repeated motif of the gables; here, the individual houses formed a closed wall of the market space. But in general, it was contrast, rather than similarity, that created the beauty and architectural accents. The individual buildings lining the streets or surrounding the square were spatial elements. They created space in depth; they were projecting and receding parts of the configuration as a whole, not integral components of a deliberately planned pattern as in a perspective view or in a square with homogeneous buildings on all sides. What bound them together was the harmony of style and, above all, their scale and their contrast to the larger buildings—the churches, the town hall, and other public edifices. It was a space produced by echelonlike effects and by the contrasting values of the mass of low houses to the towering accents of the public buildings. The difference in height between the low dwellings and the monumental buildings was so great that this alone subdued the variety and heterogeneity of the dwellings and reduced them to a basis on which the important buildings rose. This contrast, with its unifying effect, was the greatest factor in medieval city planning. The destruction of this contrasting harmony by widening the streets and squares around the cathedrals in many German towns was left to the vandalism of the nineteenth century, which sacrificed the contrast of scale to a misunderstood beauty, to considerations of traffic, and to "bigness." These remodelers failed to comprehend that the vigor of the scale rested on the proximity of the low houses crowding tightly around the cathedrals and on the vertical accents of the churches overpowering the horizontal lines of the massed houses.

Green, open spaces for the public did not exist in the medieval towns. In strong contrast to the residential towns of the eighteenth century, which developed their layout from the landscape architecture of this period, the towns of the Middle Ages had no greenery. Nature, being an essentially antagonistic force, was not admitted to the urban scene; private gardens consisted merely of a few flower beds cut out of a pavement of stone. Not until the seventeenth century was this rigid exclusion of nature broken; not until the *enceinte* of the fortifications disappeared did the relationship between man and nature alter and a new spirit introduced itself into city planning. This development reached its final and decisive perfection in Bath. Then modern city planning began.

The visitor from the suburbs or the outer districts near the fortifications was struck, in approaching the center of town, by the narrow and tortuous streets and lanes that were laid out without any apparent system. Regulations regarding width existed only for the principal streets, which were supervised by representatives of the king or feudal lord. These men decided how far the entrances to cellars and any other parts of the houses could project into the streets and generally dealt with any disturbance in traffic. To enforce their regulations, a representative on horseback was sent through the streets with a lance held sideways across his saddle, and fines were imposed on the owners of any house that his lance touched. But improving the streets was not the concern of the authorities, at least not at the beginning. Most streets remained unpaved.

There was a marked difference between the old towns of western Germany and the colonial towns of the East. In many cases, the western towns rose on the rubble of ancient towns, sometimes on Roman ruins. These sites easily absorbed in their porous soil the refuse of the new towns. It was different in the East; here the new settlements grew up on virgin soil, and at least a minimum of sewerage was needed. To a certain degree, this was provided by the pavements of the streets, however primitive this may have been. But in general, the streets were extremely dirty. Nobody went out without wooden-soled overshoes; even the saints depicted in paintings by the earlier German masters were apt to wear some sort of protection over their shoes. The custom of long-pointed shoes may have been caused partly by the assumption that a longer sole would prevent sinking too deeply into the dirt of the street. The gutters were mostly in the middle of the roads, thus making them still less passable. Watering places for animals were dispersed all over the town, and draw wells spilled their water unchecked into the streets. Sweepings, remains of food, even dead animals were thrown out of the houses; this habit assumed such proportions that some cities resorted to the institution of communal dumping places. In addition to all these unpleasant features, there were numerous vacant lots and dilapidated houses that also served as dumping grounds for all sorts of rubbish. Brooks and rivulets running through the town were not usually walled in or covered.

During the early part of the Middle Ages, most houses were simple wooden buildings with shingle or straw roofs, which gave ample nourishment to frequent fires. Detached, individual houses persisted throughout almost the whole of the Middle Ages. The result was that on the larger plots, several smaller houses were built in addition to the main building. These smaller houses were often covered by one roof, and it is said that up to 20 houses were sometimes combined in this way. The house was not only the family's living place; it also contained under the same roof, if inhabited by a craftsman or merchant, storerooms, a workshop, and a salesroom. The interior was sparsely furnished, and only very rarely was the cold floor covered with carpets or mats. The rooms received little light through the small windows, and a glass substitute in the panes reduced its intensity to a pale indifference.[9]

Against the background of the historical, geographical, social, and economic forces that have been described on the foregoing pages, against this background of a seemingly contradictory manifoldness, there stand out certain imponderables and certain facts of a great and lasting significance. The imponderables are space and scale, and the facts resulting from the specific character of the former are embodied in the streets, squares, houses, and other buildings that make up the urban configuration in general and in detail.

Space. City planning is architecture on a larger scale. But because city planning is hampered by the weight of practical obstacles, it cannot move forward at the same pace as architecture. Thus, spatial ideas during the Middle Ages were not as clearly visible or as far advanced in the urban picture as they are in individual contemporary buildings; this was true especially for churches. Consequently, the urban space was still at rest when space consciousness had begun to press matter apart in the medieval cathedrals, to separate matter into functional elements and to evolve a succession and juxtaposition of space units and space relations where movement and countermovement of space, where upsurge and expansion, reduced matter to a functional minimum. The urban space was lagging behind this tempestuous development, and the social space created by it was far removed from the transcendental uplift of the Gothic cathedrals. The world of forms remained a realistic one, within which man moved and lived his daily life. Neither urban nor social space had much in common with the architectural space of the cathedrals and the religious space it enfolded. They

Space and Scale of the Medieval Town

9. This description has made use of the graphic account that K. Lamprecht gives of medieval life in *Deutsche Geschichte.* IV, pp. 223 ff.

65. *Adoration of the Magi,* by Stephan Lochner. Altarpiece in the Cathedral of Cologne.

stood at the two opposite ends of medieval emotions and excitability; one expressed the life-asserting demands of ordinary existence and the other, the ultimately life-denying demands of the Church and religion. The young and vigorous peoples to whom Christianity had been brought and who had to unlearn their old rites and customs were not prepared to forego their *élan vital,* their unsophisticated acceptance of life, and the physical pleasures this world, the flesh and the devil, could offer. It was a paradox, an inner dissonance, a situation full of explosive and contrasting potentialities. This antagonism ran through the whole of the Middle Ages and found its vehement expression in the grotesque and refreshingly vulgar representations on capitals, in the gargoyles, and in other parts of the medieval churches; at the same time, the most ethereal sculptures and the most dematerialized structures created an atmosphere of transcendence and spiritual absorption. The robust enjoyment of life and appreciation of brute matter that could be experienced in the narrow reality of the urban and social space competed with the religious hysteria that flowed from the immaterial space of the churches which accompanied the way to the altar along the nave and the way up to God into the vaults, sustained and intensified by the unending polyphony of lines and surfaces.

Yet the realistic space of the urban environment and the transcendental space of the cathedrals were not mutually exclusive of each other. They were merely two different aspects arising from the same source, the complex nature of man. With equal power, each emanated from his longing for confinement, for proximity, for sheltering narrowness in his daily life, and for the human scale of his urban environment where he could live out his natural impulses and his elementary social aspirations; and each responded to his longing for absorption into the immaterial infinity of the heavenly spaces where his self-conquest and his piety would be rewarded. Both these longings were ever-present in the soul of medieval man, and each found its outlet in its own language of space; the one in the earthly space of his town, and the other in the transcendental space of his church. Is this the same complementary contrast as between a Gothic painting—for instance, Stephan Lochner's altarpiece in the cathedral of Cologne—and an obscene sculpture on a capital or an inextricable ribbon ornament? The figures in Stephan Lochner's painting are almost self-contained entities held together by the golden background and related to each other by certain movements in detail—an outstretched hand, an inclination of the head, a turn of the body—rather than by an all-embracing, deliberate and premeditated composition in general. On the other hand, the figurative scene on a capital or the intertwined lines of a ribbon ornament produce an involved language of lines, an unending stream, a fantastic linear excitement; yet these labyrinthine and convoluted coils, curls, and spirals, this primordial and dark chaos of lines, were born out of the same craving for a dematerialization of the solid stone, for a metaphysical escape from reality, as the Gothic churches with their mathematics of stone raising man from earthly narrowness to celestial ecstasy. What all these various trends of representation had in common was that they evolved as surface representations without spatial depth—that is, without perspective. But the particularly interesting conclusion suggested by these seemingly discordant trends is that they were all present in both the urban space and in the architectural space of the churches. The answer to the question raised above is, therefore, a paradox: The spatial concept hidden in the more popular and earthly sculptures and ornaments corresponded to the urban space and to the space consciousness latent in the religious paintings and

66. Clasp of Prince Uffila, A.D. 700.

67. Capital in the Abbey of St. Benoît-sur-Loire, depicting the temptation of St. Benedict.

the architectural forms of the churches; in either case, all were operative. And this was only natural, for man did not consist of two separate beings, one for his ordinary daily life and one for his religious and exalted existence. It is in this sense that the "complementary contrast" on which this argument is based should be appreciated, for only then can the particular character of the medieval space be understood and its formative influence upon the towns comprehended.

In the preperspective Middle Ages, space was composite and finite, bounded by the physical entities of individual houses, each of which retained its own, and more or less isolated, identity. "Not immediately, but by a very complex and difficult process of thought [man] arrives at the idea of abstract space—and it is this idea which clears the way for man not only to a new field of knowledge but to an entirely new direction of his cultural life."[10] Before assessing the stage of development the Middle Ages had reached in this "process of thought," we should recognize that

the progressive awareness of spatial relations, both in the human race and the child, takes place on two quite distinct levels, which the psychologists distinguish at the *perceptual* or *sensorimotor* level, and the *representational* or *intellectual* level. There is a *sense* of space, and an *idea* of space, and they have quite distinct origins. It is commonly assumed that representational space is merely a registering of perceptual space, but in reality . . . the sensorimotor awareness of spatial relations is a separate and genetically earlier stage of development. From the very beginnings of existence this sensational awareness is linked with the progress of both perception and motor activity, and undergoes considerable development before speech and image representation make their simultaneous appearance. Then, on the basis of this symbolic activity and of intuitive thought generally, a representational structurization of space becomes possible. This method of space construction proceeds quite independently on the intellectual level, giving rise to those systems of perspective which, at a later stage of human development, were to play such havoc with the sensory foundations of art.[11]

In accordance with this excellent definition, the Middle Ages possessed a sense of space but not yet an *idea* of space. This means that spatial relations existed; but they were simply there, not deliberately created. They existed by the sheer juxtaposition of houses and their connection with the streets or squares. It was a pure topographical distribution, not a consciously-thought-out or -experienced space creation, which resulted in a plurality of viewpoints each related to a single object; or there were as many viewpoints as there were objects, that is, buildings. This preperspective space was the main characteristic of the medieval

10. E. Cassirer. *An Essay on Man: An Introduction to a Philosophy of Culture.* 1953, p. 65.
11. H. Read. *Icon and Idea.* 1955, pp. 59-60.

towns. It offered casual views between the coulisselike buildings, and radiated the specific unity that had been achieved by unconscious effort, by the spontaneous union of the individual and the general language of form that common culture and social awareness had made a natural property of all members of the community. To revert once more to the comparison between the religious paintings and the ribbon ornaments: like the figures in Stephan Lochner's altarpiece, the houses were individual entities; and the town, like the entire painting, was a sum of many small pictures or of many separate details. But the town as a whole had the same unexpected qualities as a ribbon ornament: the tortuous streets and lanes, the casual and short views, the contrasting lines and surfaces, the mysterious appearance and disappearance of single parts, and the suggestive intersections of buildings and streets. All this flowed from a marvelous and spontaneous sense of space, but in spite of the great variety of its bodily manifestation, it remained a space at rest bounded by solid matter. On the other hand, in the architectural space of the cathedrals the revolt against matter had already achieved quite different results; here space was in motion, and matter was gradually reduced to a functional minimum.

The use man made of his sense, or of his idea, of space was always, and is still today, intimately connected with his picture of the universe. During the Middle Ages, this was the universe of Aristotle, which was finite and in which both space and matter ended at the sphere of the stars. It was conceived as a "full universe or plenum," implying a *horror vacui,* nature's abhorrence of a vacuum.[12] It was "self-contained and self-sufficient, leaving nothing outside itself." The earth was the center of a system that consisted of a series of concentric spheres; matter was continuous, and the circular movement of the stars and planets was perfect because the circle was the perfect figure and represented the changeless, eternal order of the universe. This system dominated medieval cosmological ideas until Copernicus and, above all, Giordano Bruno burst the shells that had limited the free view of humanity.

How were these ideas reflected in medieval city planning? It was still a "primitive space" that was enfolded in the urban scene.

Primitive space . . . is more nearly a life space: the space in a room, or in a house, or in a community. It has a "top" and a "bottom," and "east" and "west" (or "front" and "back"—many primitive words for direction derive from words for parts of the body and reflect the intrinsic differences of these parts). Each position is a position "for" some object or "where" some charac-

12. T. S. Kuhn. *The Copernican Revolution.* 1957, p. 86. See also for the following.

teristic activity occurs. Each region and direction of space is characteristically different from every other, and the differences determine the behavior of bodies in each region. Primitive space is the active dynamic space of everyday life; distinct regions have distinct characteristics.[13]

This is, in scientific language, an accurate description of the urban space of the Middle Ages—"an everyday life space," finite and articulated by a continuum of matter with the earth as the center. Such a conception excluded even the faintest idea of a perspective view, whereas the Copernican notion of the heliocentric universe moved man and the earth to the periphery, from where the sun could be seen *only as through* a perspective view.

However, the Aristotelian system was to medieval man more than an astronomical conception. It was a symbol and a reality; it was the universe that Dante made the enfolding shell for his *Divine Comedy*.

[It] mirrors both man's hope and his fate. Both physically and spiritually man occupies [as Dante saw it] a crucial intermediate position in this universe filled, as it is, by a hierarchical chain of substances that stretches from the inert clay of the center to the pure spirit of the Empyrean. . . . Man lives in squalor and uncertainty, and he is very close to Hell. But his central location is strategic, for he is everywhere under the eye of God. Both man's double nature and his intermediate position enforce the choice from which the drama of Christianity is compounded. He may follow his corporeal, earthly nature down to its natural place at the corrupt center, or he may follow his soul upward through the successively more spiritual spheres until he reaches God.[14]

This is the direct equivalent of the coexistence of the religious space and the urban space, of the devotion of the religious paintings and the vulgar animalism of the sculptured capitals and the emotional and searching excitement of the ribbon ornaments. This theme of human ambivalence, of the oscillation between sin and salvation and of the "complementary contrast" between man's daily and religious life, was lifted and adapted in the *Divine Comedy* to the essence of the medieval scheme of the universe. These ideas were to medieval man a reality, and they were reflected in all his works, in his architecture and in his towns. They explain why there could be no *idea* of space but only a *sense* of space; why this space was still "primitive," or "concrete"; and why space was not yet the formative element in city planning that it was to become after the Copernican Revolution. These imponderables should be ever-present in the minds of those who try to appreciate the essence, the grandeur, and the beauty of the towns of the Middle Ages.

13. *Ibid.*, p. 96.
14. *Ibid.*, p. 111.

Scale. Within the finite space enclosed symbolically by the protecting shells of the family, the guilds, the fraternities, and the concentric spheres of the universe, and physically by the town walls, man set the scale. Just as the earth was the center of the universe, man was the center of his own narrow world. It was on this central position and on the fact of his own littleness that the scale of the town as a whole and of all its parts was focused. This limitation was not only a physical asset but also a moral assertion, for Aristotle's conclusion that "evil is a form of the unlimited, and good of the limited"[15] was still a powerful, latent idea that, although unapparent to the masses, shaped their minds and actions. It was a human, pedestrian scale, which pervaded the urban scene. In brief, with its aggregate of bodily accents, it was the perfect, complementary counterpart to the space continuum. Space and scale were not things in themselves, and space was not yet a formative building "material." Scale depends upon proportions, upon the relationship between different bodies.

No purely medieval towns are extant; with a few exceptions the old houses were replaced in the Renaissance and in the following centuries. Only the Romanesque and Gothic churches and a few civic buildings, when they have been preserved in their original settings, can give us an idea of the medieval scale.

15. *Nichomachean Ethics.* Loeb Classical Library, No. 73, II, VI, 14.

68. Market square in Rothenburg, by Friedrich Herlin, 1466. From the altar in the Church of St. Jacob.

It is, therefore, almost impossible to adduce existing examples of medieval towns. We have to make the best of old paintings, even though they do not reproduce the actual situation at the height of the Middle Ages. A picture of the market place at Rothenburg may be a fairly representative example. Painted by Friedrich Herlin in 1466 on the altarpiece of the church of St. Jacob, it shows the square before the new town hall was built. The striking feature that is immediately evident is the total lack of coordination among the buildings. It is a casual agglomeration of individual architectural units; yet the whole is homogeneous and, in its irregularity, harmonious. It is not a balanced composition in the sense of the Renaissance when everything was subordinated to a definite idea. But although this uniting idea is missing, the market place is held together by the larger scale of the public buildings, in particular by the old town hall and the consistent scale of such details as windows, doors, and gables. The walls of the square are not continuous or uniform; they consist of separate architectural bodies interrupted by the streets that run into this central square. The scale is small, and its smallness is emphasized by the similar proportions that relate each building to all the others. It is a loose juxtaposition correlated by the instinctive certainty of the contemporary style and by the human scale.

This unerring medieval sense of scale was even more evident in the relation of the churches and the surrounding space. The Romanesque cathedrals were the vessels into which streamed the enthusiasm of religious devotion and the sensibility of the

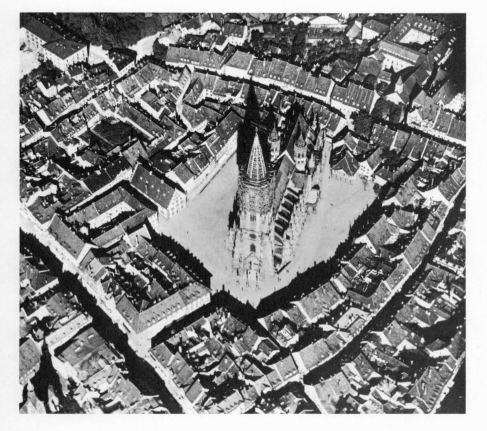

69. Cathedral square in Freiburg.

70. *Opposite:* **Ulm. Cathedral soaring above the low houses of the burghers.**

180

artistic genius. These buildings were still earthbound, still nearer to fortified castles than to transcendental places of worship. Their masses were planted firmly on the ground, and the open space around them was deliberately not too narrow. Compared with Gothic cathedrals, the distance between the Romanesque church and the surrounding buildings was generally wider, since it needed more room for its weighty mass. The houses and the distance between them and the church provided the necessary scale to set off the proportions of the main building. The strong verticality of the Gothic cathedrals, on the other hand, required a relatively narrow open space; they needed the contrast of the burghers' low houses whose small scale, the closer they huddled together in the immediate vicinity, increased the imposing height of the cathedrals. The ideal situation of a Gothic church was determined by the human scale, not by an imaginary vista or a beautiful square. The more the worshipers, on their way to church, were brought up against it suddenly without a gradual approach, the more they felt their own insignificance and smallness, and the more immediate and absorbing was the power of the vertical movement.

Just as there was only a sense, not an idea, of space, so there was merely a sense, not an idea, of scale. This scale was not symmetrical or adapted to a definite rhythm, nor was it exact. It was a composite of several scales harmonized by the sensual appeal to the people who moved within the urban space. This asymmetrical scale, emphasized by a syncopic rhythm of suspension and resolution, created an immediateness, a contrast of volumes, and a coherence of receding and projecting elements that could easily be experienced by the inhabitants. It was a daily-life scale and a daily-life rhythm everybody knew from his own home. There was something casual about it, like the casual arrangement of furniture and of the many objects for daily use. In other words, it was natural and spontaneous, not unusual or calculated. It sprang from the same trend that made the ribbon ornaments an unending labyrinth without beginning or end where all parts were of the same value and recoiling in themselves—a multiform repetition. And it was also equivalent to the naturalistic foliage slung around the capitals of the Gothic cathedrals. If we compare this realistic spontaneity with the way in which the Renaissance and the Baroque period solved the same problems, the picture is quite different: Symmetry and one dominant rhythm then become the essence of almost all architectural compositions; there is a definite beginning and end, a predetermined and unitary scale, a subordination of all parts to one leading idea, one point of view that determines the scale and the rhythmic movement toward it, and a deliberate repression of the spontaneous and natural. Multiformity and parity gave way to an intentional unity and gradation. The known intimacy of daily life disappeared and was enhanced by a grand scheme of the unusual and the spectacular.

The inner tensions that made medieval man a revolutionary being drove him to the outermost confines of his limited conception of the universe. These tensions undermined his unquestioning belief and disintegrated the shells within which his daily life proceeded. The year 1543 was a year of destiny for him, for in this year, Copernicus published his *De Revolutionibus Orbium Caelestium,* which formulated clearly what had been unconsciously in the minds of many.

[My] misgivings and actual protests have been overcome by my friends . . . [one of whom] often urged and even importuned me to publish this work which I had kept in store not for nine years only, but to a fourth period of nine years. . . . They urged that I should not, on account of my fears, refuse any longer to contribute the fruits of my labors to the common advantage of those interested in mathematics.

These words were contained in the letter Copernicus wrote to The Most Holy Lord, Pope Paul III.[16] They were symbolic of the beginning of the Renaissance.

The earth was removed from the center of the universe; the Aristotelian conception of the universe was swept away; man could no longer see it as if from its center; and he was moved, with the earth itself, to the periphery of the universe. The change was a revolutionary one, which had made itself felt long before the publication of *De Revolutionibus* and which had already begun to transform the whole of life, the arts, and the towns. Nevertheless, when the book was published, it was forbidden, and Luther, in a strange partnership with the Catholic Church, declared its conclusions null and void. In one of his "Table Talks" in 1539, even before the book's official publication, Luther condemned it by saying,

People gave ear to an upstart astrologer who strove to show that the earth revolves, not the heavens or the firmament, the sun and the moon. . . . This fool wishes to reverse the entire science of astronomy; but the sacred Scriptures tell us [Josh. 10:13] that Joshua commanded the sun to stand still, and not the earth. [And in 1610 Rome stated:] To assert that the sun stands immovably in the center of the universe is absurd, philosophically wrong, and a formal heresy, since it is in flagrant contradiction to the Holy Scriptures. To assert that the earth is not fixed in the center of the universe, that it is not immovable but even revolves each day

16. The quotations are from Kuhn. *Op. cit.,* pp. 137 ff.

on its own axis, is absurd, philosophically wrong, and at least an incorrect belief.·

If the great ones of this world chose to adhere to such a conviction, it was hardly possible to expect the simple citizen to be less traditional. Small wonder then that, quite apart from the very tardy development of the art of city planning itself, the towns and their inhabitants changed but slowly. Yet the tensions latent in the masses had produced the creative atmosphere for the Copernican Revolution, for its originator did nothing but absorb and systematize the stirring forces of his time that could be sensed but which had not yet found their articulate expression.

Not until February 17, 1600 was the way toward the modern age entirely cleared. On this day, Giordano Bruno was burned at the stake in the Campo di Fiori at Florence. He was the first to assert that the sphere of the fixed stars is not the limit of the universe, that the universe has no limits but is infinite, and that there is no point absolutely at rest. In *Cena de le Ceneri* he stated:

The world is infinite. Therefore there is no body that can be said to be in the centre of the world or at the frontier thereof or between two of its frontiers. Bodies can only be said to have certain relations to other bodies or to frontiers that are chosen arbitrarily.

Giordano Bruno only expressed the general feeling that life in a narrow sphere is unbearable and that a free and wider view is essential. The shell-like limitations were bursting; the expanding influence of the towns and the breaking-up of the guilds and of their coercive unification were being publicly, though not officially, justified. Only now did the development of the medieval town really come to an end; only now were its burghers losing their revolutionary urge and exchanging it for an unproductive parochialism. At this hour, modern man was born, and with his birth came a new attitude toward life, that of the Renaissance and the Baroque. But with the new development spread the influence of the state, and the free burgher became an obedient subject. The simple limitation of the town came to an end and gave way to a complicated system of defense which would more efficiently withstand the new technique of the far-reaching firearms. The perspective view, the outlook over a wide area, became the accepted principle of city planning.

Renaissance man differed essentially from his medieval predecessor; but even though his world was widening, he remained limited in his views. The Renaissance was a transitional period, a prelude, not yet an absolutely fresh beginning. Very slowly the *credo quia absurdum* spirit began to fade. Only the Baroque unveiled a freer view, although still gropingly. Nevertheless, the shell-like limitations of human existence were disintegrating, although the anthropocentric and geocentric conceptions of pre-Copernican times dissolved but slowly; for they had penetrated the deepest layers of human existence. Central Europe was faced with a double problem: in contrast to southern Europe, where the ideas of Antiquity were more strongly alive, and in consonance with its Faustian urge for restless inquiry and its insurgent quest for ever-new insights, it concentrated its powers not only on penetrating and understanding the secrets of nature but, at the same time, on preparing the technical machinery for the exploitation of the possibilities the new knowledge offered. The North was, as always, less rational than the South; it was thus characteristic that most of the schemes for the "Ideal Town" emanated from Italy, not Germany.

Because the Reformation had undermined the universal claim of the Catholic Church, individual responsibility replaced unquestioning belief. All this created a problematic situation that drove men to search for new outlets, to loosen the old bonds, and to unravel anew the relationship between God and environment. These extraordinary tensions led to scientific investigations, which in turn had important results. The invention of printing, the laws of Kepler, the medical works of Paracelsus are but a few examples. Common to all was the religious character of their search for truths. Knowledge of, and insight into, nature was identical with a living *Weltanschauung*. An uninterrupted line connected this speculative spirit of the Renaissance with the mystical ecstasy and the transcendental dynamism of the Middle Ages at one end and, at the other, with the urge toward infinity of the Baroque; whereas the South, especially Italy, lived in the shadow of Antiquity, even during the Middle Ages. In the north was the Gothic cathedral with its negation and dissolution of matter and its dynamic space relations; in the south was a church like San Miniato at Florence, with its solid walls and space at rest, repeating the spirit of the Pantheon.

The climate of the age was extraordinarily conducive to the Copernican Revolution. It explains why the time was ripe for this great breakthrough into the outer spaces of the universe. The voyages and explorations had widened the outlook and made man aware that behind the narrow world of his everyday life there were other worlds waiting to be conquered and other questions to be solved. Half a century before the birth of Copernicus the Portuguese had voyaged along the African coast; three decades later Columbus discovered the New World; Magellan had circumnavigated the globe. This outburst of far-flung activities demanded better maps and techniques, which in turn required a more correct knowledge of astronomy. The discovery of new lands convinced men that ancient geographers had handed down to posterity a totally inadequate picture of the world and that their teachings were not the last word. The calendar reform, in which Copernicus took an active part, was carried through under the official auspices of the Church. All these innovations created an atmosphere favorable for the Copernican Revolution. Humanism also played a decisive role in this development, although it was opposed to Aristotle and to traditional university learning.

The humanists did not, however, succeed in stopping science. During the Renaissance a dominant humanistic tradition outside the universities existed side by side with a continuing scientific tradition within the university walls. In consequence, the first scientific effect of the humanists' dogmatic anti-Aristotelianism was to facilitate for others a break with the root concepts of Aristotle's science. A second but more important effect was the surprising fertilization of science by the strong otherworldly strain that characterized humanist thought. . . . The otherworldliness of humanism derived from a well-defined philosophical tradition . . . [which,] unlike the Aristotelian, discovered reality in a changeless world of spirit rather than in the transient affairs of every day life. Plato, who is the tradition's ultimate source, often seems to dismiss the objects of this world as mere imperfect shadows of an eternal world of ideal objects or "forms" existing outside of space and time. His followers, the so-called Neoplatonists emphasized this tendency in their master's thought to the exclusion of all others. . . . [The God of Aristotle] had been conceived as an architect who displayed His perfection in the neatness and order of His creation. . . . [He] was well suited to the finite Aristotelian cosmos, but the God of the Neoplatonists was not so easily bounded. If God's perfection is measured by the extent and multiplicity of his procreation, a larger and more populous universe must connote a more perfect Deity. To many Neoplatonists the finitude of Aristotle's universe was, therefore, incompatible with God's perfection. . . . During the Renaissance this revived emphasis on God's infinite creativity may have been a significant element in the climate of opinion that bred Copernicus' innovation.[17]

However, in spite of his revolutionary ideal, Copernicus remained in some respects a traditionalist. His universe was still finite, terminating in the sphere of the fixed stars; and within it, the heavenly bodies moved in circles with a uniform velocity. This conservatism was highly characteristic of and equivalent to the ideas still at work in all artistic creations of the Renaissance, including city planning. Space was still at rest; the individual spatial elements of a Renaissance town were still bounded by the limitations of the periphery and still

17. Kuhn. *Op. cit.*, pp. 126, 127, 131.

focused on a center, a square, a church, or any other spectacular feature. It was still a side-by-side plan, not yet a flowing-together as in the Baroque. Like Aristotle, who held that "evil is a form of the unlimited, and good of the limited," Copernicus used moral principles as arguments to prove the correctness of his system. He said in the eighth chapter of *De Revolutionibus:*

We conceive immobility to be nobler and more divine than change and inconsistency, which latter is thus more appropriate to Earth than to the Universe. Would it not then seem absurd to ascribe motion to that which contains or locates, and not rather to that contained and located, namely the Earth?

Here we have the astronomical counterpart to the still fixed periphery of the towns. And in the tenth chapter, Copernicus went on to say,

We find . . . an admirable symmetry in the Universe, and a clear bond of harmony in the motion and magnitude of the Spheres such as can be discovered in no other wise.

Symmetry and harmony were the principal tenets of Renaissance aesthetics, and their application could be felt in all plans of Renaissance towns—in the general layout, in the street system, in the shape of squares and houses, and in the distinct and static aggregation of all forms of Renaissance art.

Looking back from the vantage point of the present, we can see that the ideas of Copernicus were an intermediary step toward modern ideas of the universe and, as such, the perfect expression of the notions that guided the city planning of this period and of the Renaissance in general; for this was an intermediate period between the Middle Ages and the upheaval of the Scientific Revolution of the Baroque. The cosmology of Descartes was a typical product of this insurgent period. He regarded matter as uniform and the infinite universe as devoid of empty space. His universe was full but divided in an endless variety. It was a universe without any vacuum, where the movement of any part of matter resulted in the movement of all matter. Descartes believed that the motion of the countless solid particles that filled his universe proceeded in vortexes. These ideas were exactly the same as those of the Baroque architects and city planners: infinity through the continuous movement of uniform matter—in other words, infinity through matter in motion. The infinity of the sky painted on the inside of cupolas and ceilings; the convulsion of matter that resulted in a profusion of coalescing forms and diffuse outlines; the *horror vacui,* that is, the horror of plain surfaces; the excited sequences of squares; the perspective view of the streets—all were bound together by the longing for infinity. Newton put the seal on this long line of development when he conceived a universe independent of the spiritual order. God was the prime mover of a wonderfully and smoothly working universe; but He was "pensioned off," and watched the harmonious operation of His creation as an onlooker. The complex of all these revolutionary ideas, which had piled up since the end of the Middle Ages, struck at the heart of medieval theology and disintegrated the social structure. In the human sphere, this reevaluation of man's relationship to God and to his fellow men had far-reaching repercussions. Small and integrated groups were superseded by the rationally conceived state, a transformation made possible only because the individual beings hitherto embedded in the all-pervading group consciousness became aware that they were alone in this world and that the former intimate relations with other members of their group were dissolving. To these isolated individuals, this world appeared as a limitless expanse, as something that was moving away from instead of enfolding them. The tensions that this new attitude toward life engendered were expressed in a changed conception of space—that is to say, in thinking and planning on a larger scale. Men responded to the new spaciousness without desiring to be lost in it. In the Middle Ages the pedestrian had set the scale of the town. Now it was the carriage that, although used only by the rich, was a factor of importance because the upper classes exerted a decisive influence upon the life of the town and its architecture. Everything became restless. The streets ceased to invite a leisurely stroll; the perspective vista and the monotony of the long rows of more or less identical houses radiated a motive power that concentrated the attention almost exclusively on the view at the end of the streets and induced a steady movement forward. The width of the streets was in many cases quite disproportionate to their actual purpose. The desire to line the streets with an uninterrupted block front led to the erection of façades, behind which the rooms were arranged independently of the external appearance of the house, and even to the absurd idea of closing an interspace between two houses merely by a front wall crowned by the principal cornice.

The imponderables that the revolutions of Copernicus and his successors had ushered into the world of everyday life were accompanied by changes in the social and economic field. As already stated, northern Europe remained captive to an atmosphere of irrationality for a longer time than the South. The feudal lords in the North took part in the newly developing economy only to a minor degree. Social controversies occupied a relatively important place. A new morality of work and profession developed, leading finally to a work-centered existence and paving the way to the almost blind submission to the alleged requirements of present-day techniques and science. The towns began to lose their narrow limitations, and the expansion of the urban area increased. Their sphere of economic influence grew and with it their interdependence, stimulated by trading over larger distances and by the strengthening and extension of the League of Cities. Urban emulation in material and intellectual fields had far-reaching effects. The universities lost their inherent character, and urban society, hitherto held together by the guilds, was rent by class conflicts. The town that was experienced directly and the burgher who knew his place in the urban society were superseded by the symbol of the invisible state and by its obedient subjects. These new bonds were forged by the now fully-developed money economy, by the increasing specialization of work, and by the princes, who were idols of the power of the state and arbiters between town and country and between the towns competing with one another. For a considerable time, the material and ideal culture of the towns remained high, but their political influence decreased; the economic links with the surrounding country loosened; commercial and financial transactions were conducted on an international scale, and the social contrasts increased. The way led from the collective responsibility of the guilds to the meaningless and indirect responsibility of the modern corporations, from the organic integration of trades and crafts and the all-embracing faith to the lifeless organization of industry and to the fission between "mathematics and mysticism," between reason and emotion.

The Renaissance opened up a view to a new world. It gave a new meaning to the town walls, a transformation that was clearly revealed by the improved technique of the firearms during the Baroque period. With the Renaissance, a new development set in: The military engineer fixed the *enceinte* first, and only then did he design within it the plan of the town, adapting it to this surrounding belt. The beginning of this period coincided with a new theory of city planning, which demonstrated its main principles in the design of "Ideal Towns," a movement particularly characteristic of Italy. The growth of many urban communities, that despite their walled-in existence, had just begun to breathe more freely was now restricted by a new limitation: Fortifications had become too complicated and too expensive, so that expanding a town was not so simple as before. A few places, however, took over the protection of others, so that the walls of these latter became unnecessary. But the fortress towns were hemmed in by their *enceintes;* their buildings grew in height, and they lost their last remaining open space.

Together with the walls, the meaning and layout of the streets were changing. The streets assumed primary importance, and the blocks of houses were fitted in between them without much consideration for the basic requirements of the houses themselves. A perspective view was desired, and for this, thoroughfares were needed. The web of the streets was the main element of the plan. The periphery became more significant. But aesthetically, everything was still at rest; it had not yet been drawn into the vortex so typical of the Baroque.

The town burgher, the group-individual, changed into the loyal citizen of the state or the subject of a prince. These new trends emerged slowly and were manifest at first in a decay of old ideas and institutions rather than in a determined acceptance of new conceptions. The unquestioning, faithful reliance on the religious doctrines of the Church of Rome did not quickly fall to pieces. The anthropocentric notion of the universe had penetrated too deeply into the life and mind of humanity, and furthermore, continuing to live within narrow limitations was so much more convenient than facing the problems of the newly gained infinity. People sensed the new but did not dare to take the decisive step. The eternal child in man longed to preserve the protecting shells of the celestial globe; and he felt safest in its center. But the new possibilities proved more powerful and forced a reevaluation of the familiar situation.

At first, only a few dared to think freely and to acknowledge the new reality. Others fell in with the altered course more instinctively. This vanguard consisted of the spiritual and social elite, of the great discoverers and inventors, and of the more enlightened princes. Prince and state were identical: *L'état c'est moi.* But the prince of the Baroque was not like the despot of Antiquity; he was not prince and God in one, but merely the apex of the social pyramid. His palace was not the center of the town; it was the beginning and the end of the perspective view. Karlsruhe and Mannheim are the best known examples. In Karlsruhe the palace was planned and built first, and the town, with its 32 radial streets converging on the palace, was added later only as an appendage to it—the perspective view as the symbol of political power. Mannheim, founded in 1606 where the confluence of the Rhine and Neckar provided a good and protected site, was first a fortress consisting of the prince's residence, an octagonal fortification surrounded by an *enceinte,* and a small and regular town that was also enclosed. The location of the residence was still in the medieval tradition, which made it advisable to build it at the periphery and to separate it by a wall from the town. When the fortress had to be dismantled after a war was lost with France in 1689, the residence was rebuilt according to entirely different principles; a direct contact with the town was established, and seven of the thirteen parallel streets of the town led directly to the palace. The town was now architecturally dominated by the residence and symbolically by the prince.

The decline of the Church meant the rise of the state and, with it, of capitalism and nationalism. The medieval towns' extraordinary and swift development had already come to an end long ago. But the establishment of new towns was rare; in most cases, existing places were merely extended. The old vigorous rights of the guilds and of the towns stiffened into rigid paragraphs, and the burghers lost their independence and revolutionary *élan*. The feudal lords became courtiers or officials or landed squires, while the peasants' status deteriorated more and more. Some towns became centers of the new state administration. Traffic and commerce increased in spite of territorial taxes and tolls. The powers of the Middle Ages—the nobility, the towns, the territories, and the various corporations—realized that the new problems had to be solved by a different and greater corporate body that was guided by an organized administration, itself supported by an efficient militarism. This collectively responsible administration depersonalized the life of the citizens, while it raised the central figure of the prince to unattainable heights. All this meant, on the one hand, specialization of the population and the towns, and, on the other, an increasing unification of the economy. This centralization aimed at a closed state economy. It is one of the major ironies of history that at that same hour in which the birth of internationalism, the discovery of new lands, and the immense possibilities of a free expansion were seen, the seeds of modern nationalism were sown and the internal divisions which the states had just begun to overcome were reborn on a larger scale. The dawn of a world-wide view was destroyed by the petty policies of rival cabinets, which resembled the attitudes of *parvenus* who were more interested in quantity than quality. All sorts of central organizations were founded: national mercantile marines, national posts, national newspapers, national industries, national commercial enterprises, and many others. The absolute national state established its own industrial enterprises in order to stimulate industry by its example. The princes took an active interest in this development and were, so to speak, the first entrepreneurs of their nation, for they alone commanded sufficient financial resources, or at least could exert sufficient pressure to make these ventures a paying concern.

The state's centralizing tendencies gradually replaced the equal status of numerous towns by hierarchical inequality—that is to say, a restricted number of towns took the lead and became more and more important, their population increasing more quickly than in other places. With this development a certain specialization of the towns set in; there were fortress towns, commercial towns, industrial towns, and so on. The towns where regular fairs were held followed a similar course. The more the mobility of trade and commerce increased, the more the local markets of the Middle Ages and the Renaissance declined. The direct contact between the traders and the consumers was progressively replaced by indirect supply. In the course of time, a few places gained the lead as general or specialized fairs. For the duration of the fairs, temporary buildings were erected in the squares of these towns. Permanent buildings were the exception. During the seventeenth and eighteenth centuries, each of the larger states may have had about a dozen of these markets, among which a few international fairs were particularly important. In Germany these towns were Leipzig, Frankfurt am Main, and Frankfurt an der Oder.

When the merchants began to invest capital in the industries of their home country, mass production, though still on a small scale, developed and with it, a class of laborers who contributed to the increase of population in those towns where factories or industries were established. The influence of the guilds decreased, and the autonomous marketing area of the towns was absorbed into the larger territory of the state. Interlocal organizations of entrepreneurs were founded—one of the oldest was the Calver Zeughandelscompagnie of 1650 in Württemberg, the company for trade in textiles—and specialized associations of traders and manufacturers were formed, such as, for instance, relatively large enterprises for printing and paper manufacture soon after the invention of the printing press. All this exerted a considerable influence upon the towns; those remaining outside this development declined more and more, and those taking part in it flourished. This transformation went on although the direct exchange of goods between the towns and the surrounding country still remained the basis of the economy. But the restrictions were removed, and the peasant could sell his produce and buy what he needed in the open market.

In the wake of the religious persecutions and as a result of the more liberal general attitude, a new migration, although less extensive than the great redistribution of population of the Middle Ages, accompanied these changes. The princes were the principal agents of this movement: either they called new settlers into the country and assigned them to certain towns, or they furthered the migrations within their territories to the towns by offering building sites and building materials free of charge. The labor policy of this period had a similar effect; it resulted in what has been called the competition of the states for the skilled worker. The technique of work was still intimately connected with and dependent upon the person of the worker; the technical skill he had learned through long experience in his trade could not yet be transferred easily or automatically to other workers. Therefore, the state followed the same policy as had the towns during the Middle Ages; it tried to increase the influx of skilled workers and to prevent their departure. The task of the state was different merely in so far as it had to attract not only craftsmen and workers but also entrepreneurs. Germany settled weavers and other workers in new places founded especially for this purpose. But the influx of skilled workers into Germany needed particular inducements. Southern Europe and France, with their longer and more coherent tradition, were in a much better position, although this changed after the Reformation. The North had missed, as it were, the full impact of the Renaissance and so lost the direct and early contact with the new technical methods of work. To make up for this delay it invited skilled foreign workers for whom room had to be found in the towns. It is characteristic that the West and the South of Germany—that is, the Catholic regions—suffered much less from this lack of skilled labor. However, the influence of this early "industrialization" on the growth of the towns should not be overestimated; fundamentally they remained small or medium-sized places. During this period, the urbanizing power of consumption was still greater than that of production.

The relationship of the towns to the country was also changing. At the end of the Middle Ages there were about 3 thousand towns within the Holy Roman Empire including small market towns, the sphere of influence of the latter places hardly exceeding that of a larger village of today. In Germany proper, the influence of a town in the Southwest covered an area of about 40 to 50 square miles; in the central and northeastern parts, about 60 to 85 square miles; and in the East, where the distances between the towns were much greater, 100 to 170 square miles. On an average, a town was the center for 30 to 40 hamlets and villages. On the whole, this relation was healthy because it was the result of a functional interdependence. During the seventeenth and eighteenth centuries, the sum total of the towns remained more or less the same, but a certain number of the rural settlements became "townless"; they lost their center of orientation while the towns were no longer exclusively dependent on "their" restricted territory. New "central places" grew up, and their sphere of influence included not only villages and hamlets but also other towns. This meant that the previous principle according to which the number of inhabitants of a definite region was directly related to its size, that is, to its potential food supply and industrial capacity, was no longer valid.

Moreover, the distinction between the primary and secondary agents of city development was increasing. The primary agents were those who were able to use and to attract the productive capacity of the urban sphere of influence by their own power—that is, who by any activity, or by their own money, could live and let live; for example:

a king who levies taxes; a landed noble to whom rent is paid; a merchant who makes a profit in trading with foreigners; a craftsman, an industrialist who sell their industrial products abroad; a worker whose works are sold outside the walls; a physician who has patients in the country; a student whose parents live in another place and who lives on the allowance from his parents; etc.[18]

The secondary agents were those who "filled" the towns but who could not live by their own unaided efforts and had to rely on the primary agents; for example:

the shoemaker who made the shoes for the king; the singer who entertained him with his songs; the owner of a restaurant where the landed nobles ate; the jeweller from whom the merchant buys the jewellery for his mistress; the manager of a theatre which the craftsman visits; the bookseller who delivers the books to our writer; the barber who shaves our physician; the landlady from whom our student rents his room, etc.[19]

This secondary category of the agents of city development was increasing at an accelerated pace during the seventeenth and eighteenth centuries, and contributed considerably to the transformation of the social and economic structure of the towns and to their changing importance in status and influence. The distinction between the "town-founding" and the "town-filling" agents was clearly understood by their contemporaries, owing perhaps to the simpler conditions, which could be unraveled and interpreted more easily than our own complex situation.

If people assert that the trades which are commonly assigned to the guilds have greatly increased since this time, this is out of the question. For as these depend only on the local consumption and the number of inhabitants, it is obvious that all who are occupied in this way can never form a populous and flourishing

18. W. Sombart. *Der Moderne Kapitalismus. Die Vorkapitalistische Wirtschaft,* Vol. I, No. 1, p. 131.
    19. *Ibid.,* p. 132.

town but should be considered, on the contrary, as a necessary consequence of the useful inhabitants of a flourishing town.[20]

The definition of a town of the eighteenth century may also be of interest in this connection, although its rather old-fashioned and involved wording may be somewhat baffling. In his *Staatswirtschaft*, Volume 1, Section 477, published in 1758, Johann Heinrich Gottlob von Justi wrote:

A town is an association of societies, families and individual persons who live together in a safe place under the supervision and direction of a collegium of the police that is called a town council or of other authoritative persons who are entrusted with the administration of the police institutions in order to pursue with so much greater success, effect and unity those trades and provision merchants' activities which are required directly as necessaries of life and for the comfort and convenience of the country as well as for the communication of the entire profession of victuallers of the country. . . . [A town shall be guarded in such a way] that the entry is possible only at a few places which have been explicitly marked for this purpose and which are called gates or doors because the administration of the police which is the principal means of this final purpose of a town cannot be carried out in any other form.

During the Middle Ages and the Renaissance the leading cities were very unevenly distributed; only the smaller places and middle towns north of the Alps formed a comparatively regular network. The greatest urban concentration had developed along the Rhine and especially in Flanders. This extraordinary conurbation was caused, at least partly, by the fact that here in the West, the vast open spaces for the spread of colonization that had been offered by the East were missing; there, agrarian colonization had been an important factor in keeping the urban population low. The region of the Rhine delta was the given gateway for trade with England, and the Baltic countries, including Russia. In the West, the sphere of influence of these towns reached as far as the Seine and the Rhône, in the East, to Westphalia; and in the South, to Franconia, Swabia, and Switzerland. It was only at the end of the fourteenth century that another urban agglomeration developed in Austria and Bohemia. Local, interlocal, and international interests and connections were intimately interacting, and led to the organized cooperation of towns in the form of federations or leagues, to the growing importance of a few cities, and to the merchant guilds gradually weakening the craftsmen guilds. Cooperation among wealthy merchants of individual towns increased, and local interests were brushed aside more and more.

20. *Het Welvaren van Leiden.* Handschrift uit het Jaar, 1659.

At the same time, the methods of production grew more complicated, thereby disintegrating the restrictions the guilds and the towns had imposed. The trades began to re-migrate to the country because they could pay less in wages in the villages, and the peasant with his cottage economy was again integrated into the cycle of production. The state tried to reconcile its mercantilistic policy with this transformation of the urban economy and with the relationship between the population figures and the food supply. The original structure remained practically unaltered almost up to the French Revolution and changed only when the new capitalistic principles, the monopolies and class privileges, and the slowly forming large industrial enterprises made this absolutely inevitable. But the autonomous economic policy of the towns came to an end, and the wealthy citizens took part in the new economic policy of the state. They established their enterprises in cities that offered the best geographical and economic conditions and expected protection from the state, not from the towns. However, the tendency to restrict the growth of the towns was still alive. In place of the instinctive certainty that had kept the social and economic structure and the size of the medieval towns in a sound balance, the Renaissance opened a new chapter in city planning with the theory of the "Ideal Town": instead of the organic limitations of the Middle Ages, theoretically conceived and organized restrictions were operative from the very beginning.

In numerous cases, the reruralization of industry resulted in a local subdivision of industries if parts of production and manufacture remained in the town. This created new bonds between town and country, although of a different nature, no longer caused exclusively by a division of work between industry and agriculture but by a complementary cooperation within rural and urban industries. At the same time, a certain territorial concentration and specialization of industries began to take shape, superseding those of the towns on their old and smaller scale: iron and textiles concentrated in Westphalia and Silesia, respectively. The factories were not large, and did therefore not contribute appreciably toward the growth of the towns. Moreover, where special conditions did not exist, the purchasing power was moderate and the number of consumers small. Production was, relatively speaking, no cheaper than today, perhaps even slightly more expensive. Further, a large portion of the goods were still made at home, for example, wine, beer, candles, and the greater part of the clothing and tools; and apart from this home production, hired labor was employed in certain cases, and home-raised raw material was given to people who processed it. Under these conditions, the industrial enterprises could not have been large. For instance, only 600 to 700 journeymen were employed by 1498 independent masters in Frankfurt am Main[21]; and this number did not increase materially in the next centuries. In Heidelberg there were 240 independent workshops: 123 with one journeyman; 55 with two; 24 with three; 6 with four; and one with five, these last being masons.[22] A printing house in Lörrach had 200 in 1745. The Berliner Porzellan Manufactur employed 400 workers in 1798; Meissen, only 26 in 1719 and 378 in 1750. These few figures are admittedly insufficient to give a comprehensive picture of the situation, but they are nevertheless representative of the general type of industrial production. Only during and after the Industrial Revolution did cities and towns begin to grow faster and on a larger scale. Before this time, their internal social and economic structure was transformed not so much in size, but rather by a change and a selection in their relative importance.

City planning became an instrument of state policy, a tendency favored by the new legal and administrative ideas and forms quite apart from the changing way of life in general. Since the state was omnipotent, it had not only the right but the duty to be an active agent in city planning. The conditions were propitious: the theory of city planning, widely discussed in speech and writing, demanded a systematic expression and procedure. This was perfectly natural in order to meet the requirements of the changing technique of defense, the desire for display, and the idea of perspective. Pageantry has always been connected with systematic preparation; it has never been the spontaneous demonstration it pretended to be. And an impressive perspective view can be achieved only through straight and wide streets, through correspondingly laid out squares, and through viewpoints systematically distributed within them or at their ends—that is, by methodical planning, not by unregulated growth.

Thus, various factors combined to make city planning an element of state policy, which, if applied efficiently, contributed to the prestige of the prince. Apart from the erection of palaces, which were mostly too pretentious, numerous other means were used: Special consideration was given to the layout of homogeneous squares surrounded on all sides by uniformly designed buildings, to wide and uninterrupted streets, to the extension of towns in accordance with definite plans under the supervision of the state or by private contractors who were commissioned by the state authorities, and to the allocation of building plots

21. K. Bücher. "Die Bevölkerung von Frankfurt a.M. im 14. und 15. Jahrhundert." *Socialstatistische Studien* (XIX, 736 S.), 1, Band, 1886.
22. F. Eulenburg. "Zur Bevölkerungs- und Vermögensstatistik des 15. Jahrhunderts." In *Zeitschrift für Sozial und Wirtschaftsgeschichte,* III, p. 457.

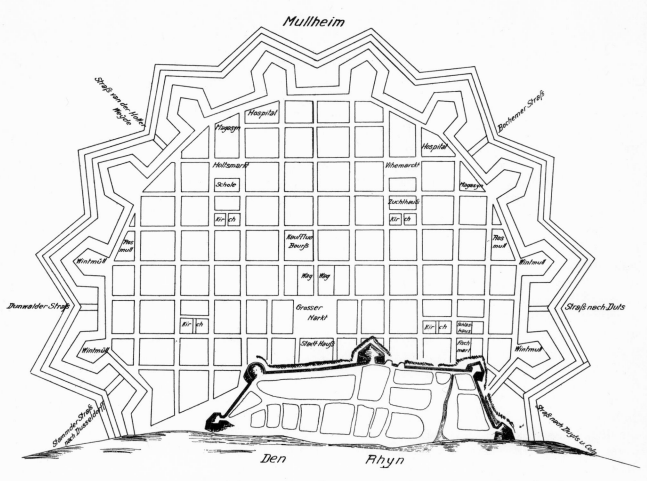

71. Design for the rebuilding of Mülheim on the Rhine, after a plan printed in Amsterdam in 1612.

72. An Ideal Town, by Joseph Furttenbach the Younger, from *Gewerb-Statt Gebäw*, 1650.

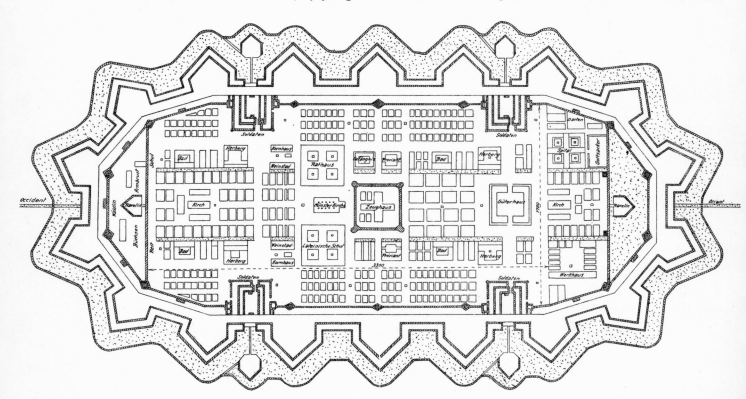

with the obligation to erect houses conforming to a single pattern. Everything was liable to regimentation. The bylaws of the time did not leave much liberty in detail or in general. Mannheim, at the beginning of the eighteenth century, was typical: among other things may be noted the fixed orientation and height of the buildings, the height and number of stories, the depth of the buildings, the shape of the roofs, the situation and size of the front doors and windows, and the prohibition of all external decoration in order "to make the whole street appear one house."

The Thirty Years' War had destroyed numerous buildings and whole towns, the rebuilding of which was one of the princes' main tasks. Not only new buildings had to be erected but the whole atmosphere of the towns had to be filled with a new life, for trade and commerce and cultural activities had suffered grievously. The mercantilistic policy of this period rested, above all, on the revival of the trades and industries; and this was primarily connected with the towns and their well-being. Therefore, privileges, immunities, and subsidies were granted in order to attract tradespeople to the towns. The obsolete municipal laws were reformed and adapted to the law of the land.

Consciously and unconsciously the new idea of the universe was being expressed in the conception and actual plan of the towns. A system of streets and squares was laid out, developing from the periphery inward within a wide and comprehensive spatial scheme. And this periphery itself, the fortifications with their bastions and their projecting and receding lines, was a symbol of the new and aggressive spirit. It enforced a clear arrangement of every part of the urban organization within the town as a whole; it assigned a definite place and form to all squares, streets, districts, military establishments, and even to the individual public buildings and the dwellings. Abstract and geometrical patterns played an ever-increasing role in this transformation. Whether the streets were laid out radially or on a gridiron plan, they had in common a central square, which, however, was now nothing more than a meeting point of the streets running to the important parts of the fortifications. For Germany, Joseph Furttenbach the Younger showed in his plan for an Ideal Town how these new ideas should be applied in practice: now the arsenal was the center, and the church, the former focus, was removed to the side. This was the theory; the reality was, of course, quite different. If the residence of a prince was the starting point of the plan, the perspective view toward the palace was the backbone of the layout. Apart from Karlsruhe and Mannheim, Erlangen, Karlshafen an der Weser, and Ludwigslust in Mecklenburg, were representative

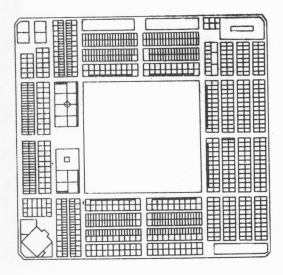

73. An Ideal Town, designed by Albrecht Dürer.

variations of the same idea. The motif of focusing the town on a palace was not entirely new. In 1527, Albrecht Dürer had designed a plan for a residence town in the shape of a square surrounded by arcades; in the center stood the palace, while the public buildings occupied the corners of the plan. It is likely that aesthetic considerations influenced Dürer's choice of the center for the palace, for the practice and custom of his time had preferred to make it part of the fortification.

"The wider and more straight a street the more beautiful it is." These laconic words appeared in I. F. Penther's *Lexicon architectonicum,* published in 1744, under the heading "Street." They expressed perfectly the ideas of the time that were to exert an almost devastating effect, for they led to a blind "Cult of the Street" and a disregard for the quality of the houses that could not have been foreseen by the early propagandists of these principles. Straight, wide streets were recommended for reasons of defense and ostentation, but also because they helped to dominate the town more easily: the better every part could be overlooked, the more efficiently could troops be used in case of internal insurrections.

The increasing concentration of capital and the greater mobility of money as a means of exchange led to speculation in urban sites. As a consequence of this development, the poorer quarters became separated from those of the rich; the former were more densely built up than the latter. The poorer classes were restricted to the older and less healthy districts or were housed in new dwellings erected for speculation. However, parallel with these trends, especially in Germany, ran a land policy systematically directed by the state and conducted with the aim of eliminating as far as possible the ill effects of *laissez faire.* During the seventeenth and eighteenth centuries, new towns were built, and existing ones were extended on public land owned by the state or the prince or by the towns themselves. The towns were empowered to acquire private land under favorable conditions, in many cases for not more than its agricultural value. The intention was to influence the parceling-out and the price of the land and, beyond this, to control permanently the land and price policy of the towns by the state. Thus, the common law of Prussia decreed: "The number of dwelling houses shall be preserved and without special permission several of them shall not be combined into one." But these few well-meaning intentions did not alter the fact that great disadvantages were accepted without any understanding: the distinction between residential and traffic streets, which had dominated medieval city planning, was given up in favor of a uniform system of equally important streets, thus for a long time depriving European city planning of one of its most valuable elements. The state administration regulated the layout of the streets and the size and shape of the building sites; it stereotyped and reduced everything to a dull uniformity.

The new social and economic order had a far-reaching effect upon the relationship among the places in which men lived, worked, and sold. The market square lost its importance: It was used principally for buying and selling food. Shops made their appearance. "Shops" had existed before this time, but they were fairly primitive and usually consisted of only one room adjoining the workshop in the craftsman's house—if there was a separate room at all. The medieval "shopkeeper" would have some goods in stock or put a few of his products in the window. There were also market halls for single commodities such as cloth, furs, shoes, bread, and grain. Now sale and production, home and workshop, retail and wholesale trade separated. The mixed retail shop gradually disappeared from the larger towns, at first retreating to the provincial places, then to the villages, and finally selling only cheap goods for daily use.

These changes considerably influenced the structure of the towns and the houses. Life was divided between the dwelling place and the office and workshop; and although the distances were still short, some time had to be spent on the daily journey to and from the place of work. Family life and business life fell apart. The need for communications grew. In general, one walked for short distances, since only a small number of carriages were in use, and they were far beyond the means of the average tradespeople. Nevertheless, the restful, stationary life of the Middle Ages, with its tranquil confinement within the circles of the family, the guild, the church, and the town walls was broken up, and its pace accelerated. Personal life and working life lost their mutual balance; work became the center around which everything else rotated until it swallowed up the whole of man's thinking and feeling, his loyalty and interests; it dictated the cycle of his daily life, until fragmentary man, the "expert," the finished and dangerous product of our own time, resulted, functional life having gained an absolute ascendancy.

The new town house was wider than the medieval house; it usually had five, instead of three, windows on each floor and turned its eaves, instead of its gable, to the streets. Italian influences played their part: The castles of the feudal lords of the Middle Ages gave place to the town houses of the nobles. These changes responded to the desire for ostentation, for these wider houses, which were used especially in the main streets, appeared more important than they actually were. The individual house was now a subordinate part of a complete block

201

front. The Baroque preferred to arrange the rooms along a corridor and to specialize them for different purposes. Such houses were eminently suited for division into several units. They ushered in the era of the flat that could be rented. Living accommodation of this kind was needed especially for the growing number of officials and military personnel. Smaller and narrower houses were built for craftsmen and the lower middle class. However, the size and the shape of the building blocks were dependent not on the size and shape of the houses erected on them but exclusively on the pattern of the streets.

The growing importance of gardens and parks as an element of city planning began during the Renaissance and the Baroque. Verdure penetrated the towns. The idea of a pleasure garden as separated from and contrasted with, the garden for practical purposes was not unknown to the Middle Ages, although in reality the kitchen garden of the fortified castles or the rare and small gardens of the town houses were the main, and for the most part, the only medieval contribution in this respect. Up to the end of the sixteenth century, the essential features of medieval gardens were preserved: The actual layout, not a spatial conception, was the purpose of the formative principle; the individual parts were arranged as more or less unconnected entities, not forming an integrated whole; their mutual relationship was just as independent as the coordination of the garden and the house; and each part of the garden was a sep-

*Gardens, Parks,
and Urban Design*

74. Railed and "chessboard" garden of 1470.

Martius, Aprilis, Maius, sunt tempora ueris ·   VER Puerili compar   Vere Venus gaudet florentibus aurea sertis ·

75. *Spring,* **by Pieter Brueghel the Elder. Engraving by Petrus a Merica, 1570.**

arate section. This corresponded to the general practice of the Middle Ages, to the loose or unrelated juxtaposition of individual houses, and to the subordination of the streets to the buildings. Even when the physical separation of garden and house was avoided, an architectural composition that would relate them in one spatial arrangement was missing. The building was not, in the early decades of the Renaissance, the dominating motif on which the garden was focused. This was especially evident if a palace was situated on a hill; in this case the garden was laid out at the foot of the slope. But even on level terrain the garden was often independent of the main building, as, for instance, in the Residence of Munich. This practice continued until late in the seventeenth century when a theory of the ideal garden as one integrated whole had already been worked out.

In general, however, the natural conditions of the terrain

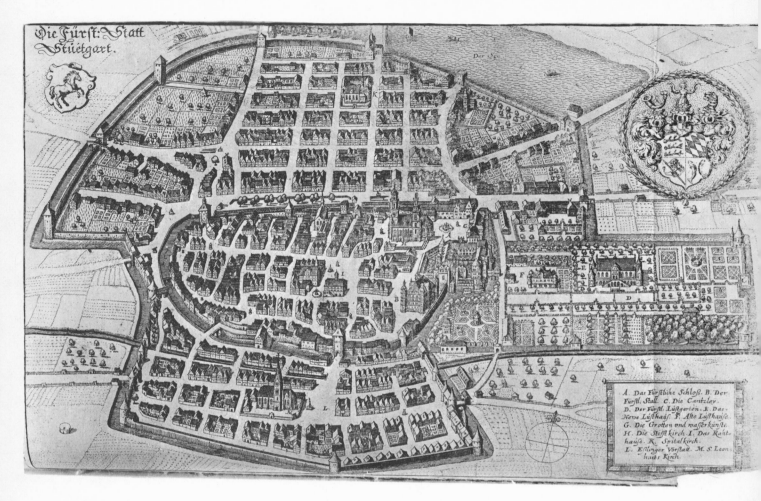

A. Das Fürstliche Schloß. B. Der
Fürstl. Stall. C. Die Cantzley.
D. Der Fürstl. Lustgarten. E. Das
Newe Lusthauß. F. Alte Lusthauße.
G. Die Grotten vnd wasserkünste.
H. Die Stifftkirch. I. Das Raht-
hauße. K. Spitalkirch.
L. Eßlinger Vorstatt. M. S. Leon-
hards Kirch.

76. Stuttgart. Engraving by Matthaeus Merian, 1643. *Topographia Sueviae. . . .*

were respected; the will to remodel it was not yet strong enough. Like the rooms of the dwellings, the individual elements of the garden remained for a long time without intrinsic relations among themselves and to the buildings: the actual purpose and the utility principle decided their shape and situation as self-contained units. The pleasure gardens at Stuttgart and Coethen in Anhalt were laid out in this older style. The latter, especially, was devoid of any of the new ideas that had been theoretically formulated by the more progressive contemporaries: eight gardens, different in size and shape, were grouped around the moat and separated one from the other by walls or arbored walks.

At the beginning of the seventeenth century, the tendency to combine the individual parts in one garden grew stronger; the whole complex was united in an elongated rectangle, the longer axis of which corresponded to the axis of the house. The gardens at the town houses of the patricians may have introduced this principle; the oblong shape of the terrain, which resulted from the division of the urban building plots, may also have contributed to this development. The central axis was not yet conceived as a perspective view; it was often interrupted by hedges or arbored walks. It simply connected the individual parts and did not yet introduce motion as a spatial link. The transformation of the Residence Garden at Munich is a representative example of the changing ideas. The plan of 1613 shows the separation of garden and palace; a covered passage over the moat was the only connection. The rectangular parterre was surrounded by an arbored walk. The main entrance led to a small garden with trees; at the other end of the parterre followed a kitchen garden consisting of six beds, a fish pond, and, as a *point de vue,* a gazebo (a *Lusthaus*) covering the whole width of the enclosing wall. By the end of the seventeenth century, the garden had undergone a considerable transformation: the arbored walks had disappeared; the parterre, not

77. Cöthen. Engraving by Matthaeus Merian, 1650. *Topographia Superioris Saxoniae. . . .*

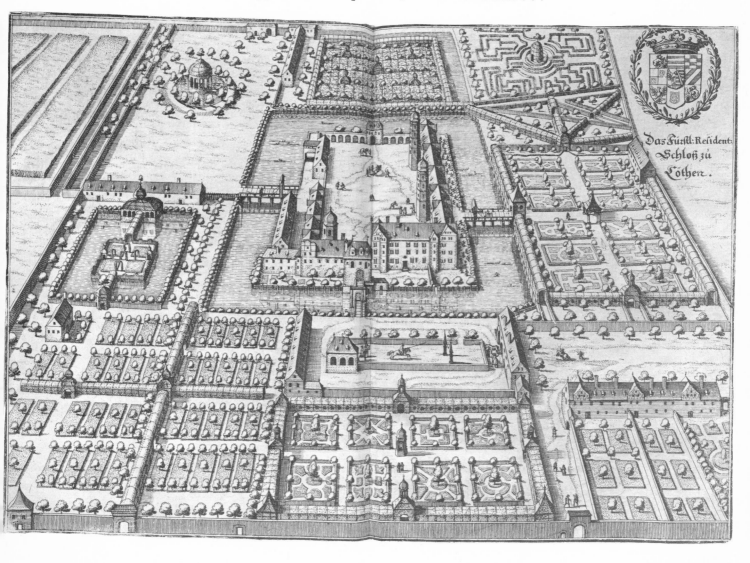

Das Fürstl: Residentz Schloß zu Cöthen.

focused on a central feature as before, was divided into four large square compartments, each of which had its own distinctive character as a herb and flower garden, or as a labyrinth, or as a garden with trees, or as a boxtree parterre surrounded by tall espaliers and accessible only through gates. A perspective led from the central pavilion through the kitchen garden, now consisting of only two parts, to the small house in the fish pond, and finally to the *Lusthaus,* the summer pavilion, at the enclosing wall.

The Baroque gardens were a replica of the house; they repeated on a larger scale its interior organization, responding to the new spaciousness and the new systematic coordination of the hitherto arbitrary sequence of individual elements. Halls, passages, and rooms corresponded to large parterres, alleys, niches, and spaces enclosed by bushes and hedges. A central alley continuing the axis of the building and traversing the whole length of the garden, diagonal alleys and paths, and alleys running parallel along the borders of the whole complex helped to accentuate the unity and to indicate an idea of the size and character of the general layout. The simple juxtaposition gave way to a deliberate contrast of the open parterre and the compact mass of the groves and bushes or the vertical

78. Schlaccowerdt, Saxony. Engraving by Matthaeus Merian, 1650. *Topographia Bohemiae....*

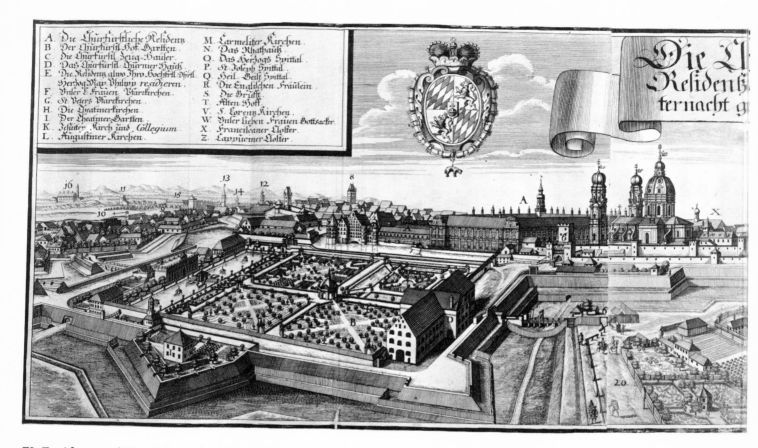

79. Residence of the Elector of Bavaria in Munich. From Michael Wening, *Beschreibung des Churfürstentums . . . Ober- und Niederbayerns.*

accents of trees. Contrast of spatial elements and volumes instead of geometrical juxtaposition was the aim of the landscape architects: the main building was surrounded by the open spaces of the parterre—contrast between surface and volume; within the parterre itself only low yew bushes or small trees were used —emphasis by repetition of a similar dimension; groups of bushes were placed to arrest the view and to incite curiosity— increase of spaciousness by the subdivision of the distant view. The number of units that made up the parterre was gradually reduced. Instead of the narrow footpaths between the beds, wide promenades opened a free and easy view over the large surface of the parterre. Here, unhindered by bushes and hedges, the courtly ladies could display their elegant and voluminous robes with ease and nonchalance. Finally, the parterre was laid out as one unit and the oblong replaced the square; motion and definite direction took the place of rest and self-contained balance, a characteristic solution of Baroque architecture and city planning.

80. The so-called "Perspectiv" or "The End of the World" of the Palace Gardens at Schwetzingen, creating the illusion of a wide open landscape.

The desire for unity and spaciousness found its consummation in the perspective view. On level terrain, this was achieved by long alleys or canals; in hilly country, by stairs or cascades and by subdividing the view with fountains, sculptures, or *ronds-points,* thus creating a perspective sequence and making the garden appear larger than it really was. The logical consequence of this development was the elimination of the separation between the garden and open country. The perspective view within the garden was no longer sufficient. The first step in extending the view was the erection of a belvedere at the end of the garden, through whose windows the countryside beyond the wall could be seen. Later, the walls were interrupted by openwork gates through which a view over a wider landscape was possible. Finally, the gate and the walls disappeared, and only a ditch separated the man-made garden from nature. The last frontier had fallen, a revolution that would have been impossible in the Middle Ages and even in the Renaissance. As in architecture and city planning, it was left to the Baroque to demolish limitations and to make the yearning for infinity a reality. This led so far that painted perspectives had to serve as substitutes for nature. This was nothing new in itself; it had been used, for example, in ancient Pompeii and during the Renaissance in connection with architecture. But the Baroque applied it in order to make man-made nature, that is, the garden, appear part of the open landscape, as in the Garden of the Residence at Passau or in Schwetzingen, where at the end of a dark passage a brightly lit landscape appeared in an artificial opening of a rock.

The most important terrace garden of the Renaissance, the *hortus palatinus* of the castle at Heidelberg, was influenced by Italian prototypes. It was laid out in the years 1614–1619 by Salomon de Caus. Each terrace was treated as an independent unit without any relation to the composition as a whole, and more with an eye to variety than to unity. But the use made of the terrain showed an extraordinary understanding of the great opportunities offered by the steep slope. It was a mere appendage of the castle, still medieval in conception and execution despite the French training of de Caus and Italian influences.

Gardens of the plain hardly existed in the seventeenth century. Even when the terrain was flat, artificial differences were created. However, apart from this general trend, there were two types of gardens that marked the approaching end of a creative development and the beginning of drawing-board garden designs. The one was characterized by the most rigid regularity: the palace was situated in the center, and a perfectly symmetrical

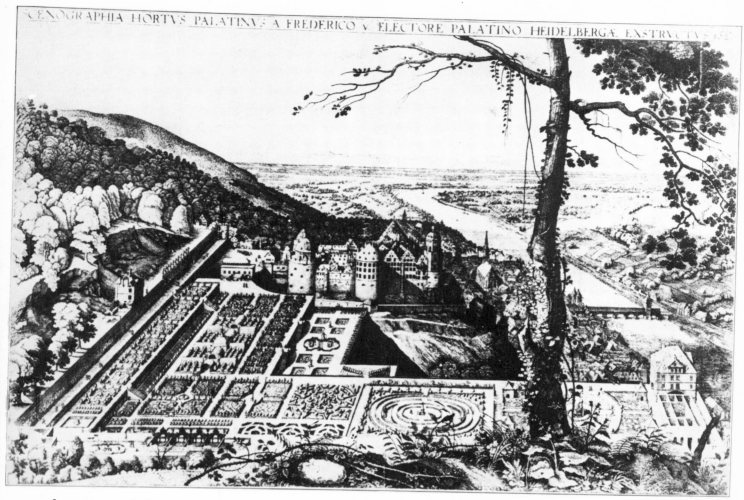

garden surrounded it on all sides—for example, the Grosse Garten in Dresden and the Hunting Lodge of Marquardsburg, near Bamberg. The result was driest monotony and a lack of spatial interrelation. The other type, almost the exact opposite of the former, abandoned dull rigidity for an abundance of details, asymmetrical arrangements, and involved groupings. The *villa suburbana,* the Favorite at Mainz, built by the Elector of Mainz at the beginning of the eighteenth century, was partly influenced by the second type of garden design—that is, partly by the German Rococo, and partly by French examples. The garden extended along the river on a terrain that sloped gently down to the banks. The peculiarity of the site may explain the unusual layout: the entry from the town on the narrow northern side was arranged sideways to the main axis and was accompanied by a long promenade, both running parallel to the river and leading to the parterre, which occupied the central position of

81. Heidelberg. Hortus Palatinus. Engraving by Matthaeus Merian, 1620.

209

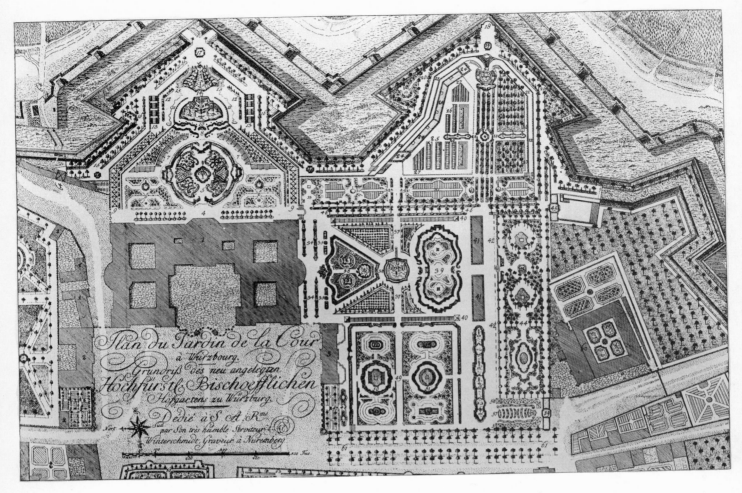

82. Würzburg. Gardens of the Residence of the Prince Bishop.

83. Favorite at Mainz, 1726.

84. Garden of a townhouse. Engraving by Josephus Furttenbach, from *Architectura universalis*,
Ulm, 1635.

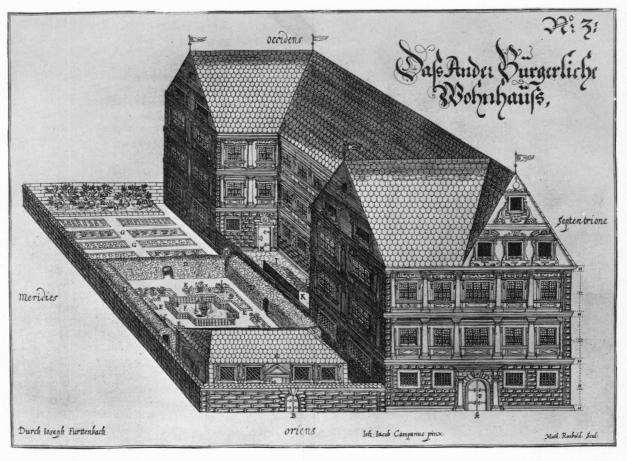

85. Another design for a townhouse garden by Josephus Furttenbach, from *Architectura recreationis*, Augsburg, 1640.

the garden at a right angle to the river. Then followed the amphitheater of the orangery. The small palace, the actual *raison d'être* of the ensemble, occupied a corner of the site, unconnected with the gardens. The Favorite was destroyed in 1793. The palace garden of Veitshöchheim, near Würzburg, represented a similar type.

Town gardens were laid out behind, or beside, the house. They were small, and the Middle Ages regarded them more as a *hortus conclusus* than as a flower garden in our sense. However, they were the starting point of the subsequent development. When the Renaissance princes, stimulated by the examples of Italian contemporaries, began to add gardens to their castles, the patricians followed suit. Their terrace houses on the oblong plots made the layout of a long garden behind the houses inevitable. Garden and house were often separated by a courtyard that was closed against the garden by a wall, a hedge, a pergola, or a balustrade—an echo of the medieval isolation of garden and house. If the terrain was too small, only one or two square beds around a tree or a fountain served as a substitute for a larger garden. Mostly situated at the long side of the house, the gardens designed by Furttenbach were distinguished for their adaptation to the site and for the perfect balance between their small dimensions and the use of various features in detail: about two-thirds of the whole area were occupied by the flower garden; the parterre, grouped around a fish pond, was surrounded on three sides by arbored walks and on the fourth, by a balustrade or pavilion. By the middle of the seventeenth century, the practice of subdividing the house garden into several small parts began to disappear; and hedges, pergolas, and arbored walks were discarded in favor of a larger scale and a better relationship with the house. Germany was relatively slow to adopt the French principles, which D'Argenville clearly expressed by the words, *"de faire du grand dans du petit,"* and *"il vaut mieux n'avoir que deux ou trois pièces un peu grandes qu'une douzaine de petites qui sont de vrais colifichets."*[23] This was a typical Baroque thesis, which made sham solutions a blessing in disguise and tried to reconcile hollow and ambitious emotions with the limited possibilities of reality. German garden design, on the other hand, clung for a considerable time to the mistake of trying to reproduce *en miniature* a large garden in a small area. The tendency *" de faire du grand dans du petit,"* to create the illusion of greatness, was, however, too attractive even for German landscape architects. The house garden at Nürnberg, published in Volkamer's *Nürnbergische Hesperides* (1708-1714), showed a de-

23. Antoine-Joseph Dezallier d'Argenville. *La Théorie et la Pratique du Jardinage.* 1709.

86. House garden of I. M. Vutter. Engraving by Johann Christoph Volkamer, *Nürnbergische Hesperides*, 1708.

sign that hid the walls behind tall hedges in order to avoid the impression of a solid limitation or, at least, to give scope to speculation and fantasy, deluding the spectator into the belief that behind the verdure of the hedges the garden might extend still further.

During the seventeenth century, arbored walks went out of fashion, and were replaced by open alleys. But again Germany hesitated to adopt these new ideas. Where covered walks were laid out, instead of the delicate vaults of latticework covered with the foliage of creepers and supple plants, rows of trees formed a solid roof, while between their bare trunks air and light streamed in from all sides. In general, however, the alleys were open, for the Baroque preferred the unlimited sky to the narrow confinement, especially over longer distances. "The widest alleys are the noblest," stipulated Claude Mollet.[24] This dictum

87. *Bosquet* in the gardens of Prince Eugene of Savoy in Vienna. Engraving by S. Kleiner, about 1730.

88. *Opposite:* Pleasure garden, designed by Josephus Furttenbach, from *Architectura recreationis,* 1640.

sounded the same demand that I. F. Penther was to repeat a century later in the *Lexicon Architectonicum* referring to the streets: "The wider and more straight a street, the more beautiful it is." Only in the eighteenth century did the covered walks reappear—in Würzburg and Veitshöchheim, for example—and with them was revived the fondness for a smaller scale and a greater intimacy. This went together with the capricious predilection for *"verdures extraordinaires,"* as D'Argenville called the green sculptures that were cut out of box, beech, and other trees in the forms of pyramids, cones, obelisks, animals, and human figures. The end of the architectural garden was approaching, and the passion for variety put an end to symmetry and unity.

This love of the unexpected, of the search for the unknown, and of the intricate that cannot be taken in at a single glance

214

24. Claude Mollet. *Théâtre des Plans et Jardinage.* 1652

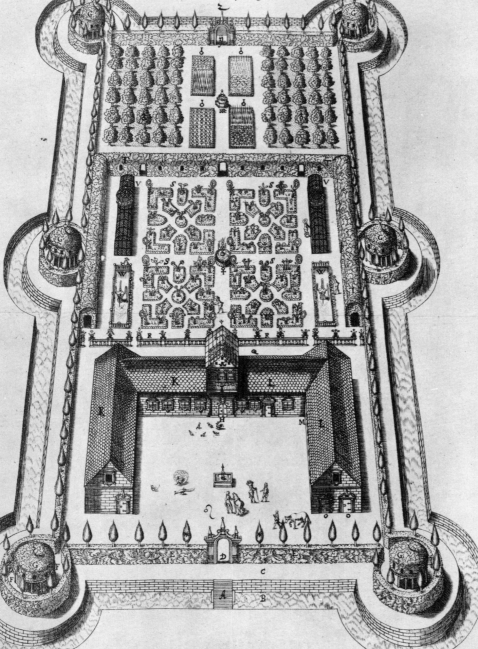

Der Erste Lustgarten,

Ioseph Furttenbach Inuentor.　　　Ioh: Iacob Campanus. pinxit.　　　M. R. Scu:

89. Design for a maze by Josephus Furttenbach, from *Architectura recreationis*, 1640.

90. Maze in the Cathedral of Rheims.

91. Reconstruction of the maze in the Cathedral of Chartres.

found playful expression in the labyrinth, the most purposeless misuse of human ingenuity and of the gifts of nature that even the Baroque could afford. In the domesticated landscape it was the equivalent of the mirror; by repetition it created illusion and a deceptive extension in depth. Its pocket infinity held out possibilities of adventurous exploration: to stand still was impossible; to move on was imperative. All this had a particularly strong appeal to the men of the Baroque, for it was symptomatic of the victory of space over matter and the eternal lure of infinity. For the Middle Ages the labyrinth was a symbol of the earthly pilgrimage, which was drawn on the floor of the churches —for example, in Chartres and Salzburg on a small scale, and in the cathedral of Reims, as a real way of prayer that covered an area of 35 feet in diameter. This labyrinth was designed in 1240, and in its twisting lanes those who had stayed behind could accompany in spirit the pilgrimage of their brothers to the Holy Sepulcher. The Renaissance revived its pagan origin. After the sixteenth century it was never missing in any of the larger gardens. At first, the square and the circle were the basis for the layout; but the Baroque discarded these forms as too simple and introduced the oval, which offered more and better opportunities for complicated patterns. In the second half of the eighteenth century, the Solitude at Stuttgart used this ground plan with concentric lanes.

Water afforded a welcome opportunity for the Baroque to introduce an element of genuine motion. The fountain was, in the Renaissance just as in the Middle Ages, the central point of the symmetrical garden. In the course of time the fountains, which had been relatively high, became lower and more compact; the distance between the basins was reduced, and the water flowing from larger spouts in broad streams gained in volume and agitation. Finally the lowest basin was sunk in the soil and enlarged in proportion to the parterre, while the height of the vertical body of the fountain diminished, a development characteristic of the tendency of the Baroque to prefer horizontality to verticality. The greater vertical accent of the cascades, which were another important feature of the gardens of this time, was counterbalanced by the vehement downward movement of great volumes of water. Grottoes, water tricks that unexpectedly poured water over the harmless visitors, and even water music produced by running water completed the arsenal of the garden requisites the Baroque employed in its search for richness, variety, pleasure, surprises—and for infinity.

At the end of the eighteenth century this picture changed under English influence. The garden was assimilated with nature, which was "corrected" only insofar as it seemed essential to soften its wild and unmodified originality and to gain a perspective view. But this idea itself had changed: The natural features were utilized, and silhouettes of large groups of trees, one behind the other, related the distant views, opening up between these groups to the general scheme in such a way that they were merely one, but not the dominating, element. This

92. *Wasserspiele*, water tricks, in the gardens of the Palace of Hellbrunn, near Salzburg, Austria.

subdivision of the distant view created the impression of depth through coulisses arranged *en échelon*. The architectural rigidity of the garden gave way to a more or less successful imitation of the natural landscape. This revolution had been prepared by several factors, the most important agent being the removal of the walls that enclosed the garden thus merging the man-made and natural landscape. Apart from these essential changes, which paved the way toward the Romantic Movement, the introduction of naturalistic features like grottoes and rustic details also played a part in initiating a new epoch of garden design. This was finally opened when the conventions of the Baroque society crumbled and the formative power of architecture and city planning declined. Then the garden became the playground of the painter, and the architect was dethroned as the practical and spiritual mentor. The parks were regarded as replicas of landscape painting in the heroic style, and the principles of painting were recommended as guides to the new landscape architecture. Colors, the different shades of green and the different hues of flowers, were consciously appreciated and were used to enliven the "picturesque untidiness" that had replaced the "cold symmetry." Fürst von Pückler-Muskau, the apostle of this style, declared:

Light and shade should be distributed everywhere usefully in the picture; [he meant the garden] thus the essentials of the arrangement as a whole will be successful, for lawn, water and fields not casting shadows themselves but only accepting them from other objects are the light of the gardener while trees, woods and buildings (also rocks when they can be used) should serve him as shadows.[25]

But there were also voices warning against this trend. Goethe declared that "Dilettantism and the toying with garden designs minimizes the exalted in Nature and neutralizes it by imitating it." And in another connection, he spoke of "the innumerable eccentricities of a restless and petty fantasy which had been strewn over the garden." Schiller, who tried to introduce a certain distinction between garden and park, remarked, "If the park is a contracted idealistic nature, as Pückler says, the garden is an extended home."[26]

But the sense of architectural order had not entirely disappeared. The compromising tendency of classicism allowed a certain degree of architectural organization near the main building: Pergolas, trimmed hedges, and symmetrical flower beds were interspersed between the irregular groupings of bushes and trees and the nondescript shapes of the grass areas; this was

25. Fürst von Pückler-Muskau. *Andeutungen über Landschaftsgärtnerei*. 1834, p. 36.
26. *Gartenkalender*. 1795.

believed to be a synthesis between the rigidity of the French garden taste and the asymmetrical liberty of the so-called English garden style.

The parallels between garden design and city planning are obvious. Apart from its own importance as an essential part of the history of urban development, the juxtaposition of both trends is particularly interesting; it brings out in strong relief the mutual fertilization and the most characteristic features of the successive stages of the growth and decline of both city planning and landscape architecture.

The immediate effect of the discovery of verdure as an element of city planning was felt when the princes began to develop their pleasure gardens, which, in the seventeenth century, were mostly situated outside the towns proper. Trees were not yet used in the layout of the streets and squares. It was not until the eighteenth century that a change took place.

In 1775, the architect Johann Peter Willebrand wrote: "It is an embellishment of the town, if such pleasure gardens exist for the amusement of the inhabitants as the Unter den Linden in Berlin; the Jungfernstieg in Hamburg; the gardens of Potsdam."[27] This was a great change, for hitherto, public open spaces had existed only for practical purposes as market squares or around the churches. The Romantic Movement fundamentally changed the relationship between nature and the general layout of the town. It made the revolt against rigidity and monotonous standardization a creative reality. In contrast to Karlsruhe, Bath was developed, and in this more liberated atmosphere, the medieval walls, the Renaissance *enceinte* of fortifications, and the deadening rigidity of the stereotyped patterns of the Baroque were now really and definitely done away with. The spread of the modern towns over the countryside had begun—although with devastating results.

It was left for the nineteenth century to squander the great legacy of the past, not by a deliberate denunciation of old forms, but by a fundamental misunderstanding of their functional significance. The sense and the idea of space were on the wane, and finally disappeared completely. The epoch of vulgarity was approaching, and states and cities and architects and city planners fell victims to a revival of empty and isolated features. They failed to understand the creative essence of the language of form in which the past centuries had expressed their ideal and practical needs and which could not be translated without great harm into the totally different atmosphere of the nineteenth century.

27. Quoted from A. E. Brinckmann. *Stadtbaukunst.* 1920, p. 89.

Residences, Cities, and Towns

The towns of the Middle Ages and the Renaissance had been self-contained units. The forces that had maintained their *élan vital* were centripetal, holding them together, stimulating their creative power, and making their limitations a source for group-consciousness and emulation by their citizens. When the walls fell and the inner bonds weakened, centrifugal forces gained the upper hand. But this led not to a new, voluntary discipline, but to regimentation and tutelage imposed by the princes and the rising state—and finally, chaos.

The Treaty of Westphalia, which ended the Thirty Years' War, recognized the three religious groups: Catholic, Lutheran, and Reformed Confessions. But it did not, and could not, prevent their adherents from exposure to oppression and hardship if they were subjects of a prince who held a different religious opinion. Thus a new wave of migrations set in, and Germany, which had lost a great number of its nationals and whose once fertile countryside had been devastated, became again a land of immigration. The loss was almost balanced by the influx of the Huguenots. After the revocation of the Edict of Nantes in 1685, almost 400 thousand industrious French citizens left the country. The great majority of these refugees came to Germany and settled mainly in Brandenburg, the Palatinate, Hesse, and Franconia. Other groups, such as the Waldensians, established themselves in Württemberg. The Hohenzollern deserve the main credit, for they helped the immigrants to begin a new life. They accepted not only the greatest number of the Huguenots but also fugitives from Salzburg and other countries. They also allowed the Mennonites to settle in Crefeld when this town fell to Prussia in 1702. The emigration from France was welcomed by the German princes, for it corresponded with the ideas of the mercantilistic period. People who had experience in industry and commerce as well as sufficient capital were urgently needed to take an active part in the revival of the German economy. Agents were sent to Holland where the immigrants had found their first refuge and to other parts near the French frontier. Their task was to convince the refugees of the benefits a settlement in Germany would offer them. But everywhere it was the territorial prince who took the initiative and called in new settlers; for the towns themselves, with a few exceptions, did nothing; the guilds were anxious about their professional secu-

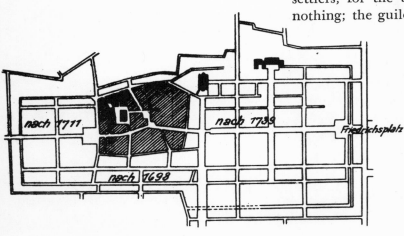

93. Crefeld. Extensions in the eighteenth century. An example of the growth of an industrial city in the mercantile period.

rity, and their influence was still strong enough to prevent their town councils from directly inviting these newcomers.

Crefeld, which was in a special position as a new member of the Prussian state, owed its growth to the influx of refugees. Between 1698 and 1739 three extensions of the town were carried out, increasing the area of this small medieval town ten times. Something similar happened in Brandenburg where the towns grew considerably. From 1685 to 1709 the population of Berlin rose from 18 thousand to 55 thousand people. King Frederick William I rebuilt 16 small towns, of which 9 were situated in Brandenburg and Pomerania. The means used in the task of rebuilding and settlement were somewhat the same as those used in the Middle Ages: Building plots that had become vacant were offered to people who were willing and capable of erecting a house, and subsidies for building materials and exemption from taxation were granted to them. The new attractions consisted in establishing financial institutions that would contribute up to nine-tenths of the building costs in cash, and in needy cases even more; in subsidizing the transport of building materials; and in exempting the new inhabitants from duties and giving them similar advantages. But the last word was the order that Frederick William I used in 1721 when he issued a decree forcing the owners of plots in the Friedrichstrasse in Berlin to declare their readiness to begin rebuilding their houses within a few days or face expropriation. The guiding agent of this policy was the state. The towns had to execute the order, as well as having the doubtful honor of paying for it. They had to build the roads and often to contribute land without any, or only a very minor, compensation. It was a national economy that the princes enforced. City planning was no longer an end in itself or an instrument to bring independent economic units into being. Its task was to create component elements of a total economy, within which they could exist only as parts of a greater whole.

The Dutch and the Huguenots brought the civilizations of their home countries to Germany. Dutch engineers planned Mülheim in the Rhineland in 1612. The large area within the fortifications was divided by streets crossing each other at right angles and leading to a street along the wall. The market square was situated at the crossing of the important east–west and north–south streets, the latter connecting Düsseldorf and Cologne. The town hall occupied a site on the axis of the central east–west street, which was flanked by the exchange and two weighhouses. Two smaller market squares, one for wood and the other for animals, were located symmetrically nearer to the fortifications, where the magazines, the hospitals, and the windmills

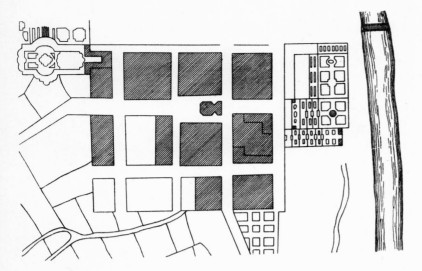

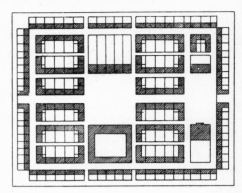

95. The New Town of Erlangen, founded by Huguenots.

94. Upper New Town of Kassel, founded by Huguenots. After a plan of 1757.

were erected. Four churches were distributed over the urban area. These were the requirements of a town at the beginning of the seventeenth century as seen by foreign city planners. In contrast to medieval plans, placing the exchange almost in the center of the layout was unusual; cemeteries were missing, thus special squares around the churches were unnecessary; a prison was needed because prisoners could not be kept in the towers of the walls as in the Middle Ages since the new fortifications had no towers. Another characteristic of Dutch influence was the axis that led to the main building and the symmetrical arrangement of the other squares and buildings in relation to this principal street.

The extensions of Crefeld were another example of Dutch influence. Dutch plans took as a starting point the streets and the building blocks, while French designs developed from the squares. The Dutch layout was widely adopted in the north of Germany, for example, in the Dorotheen- and in the northern Friedrichstadt in Berlin, and in Potsdam where even a *Gracht,* a Dutch canal, was introduced as the leading motif of a district.

An interesting example of the merging of Dutch and French influences was the plan for the Upper Neustadt of Cassel in the year 1688. The designer was Paul Dury, a Frenchman, born in Paris, who had worked for William of Orange in Maastricht. The plan was based on a rigid rectangular system with wide north–south streets and narrower east–west streets. The center was occupied by the French church whose access street widened into a squarelike forecourt.

All Huguenot towns were designed like the Upper Neustadt of Cassel: the houses had two stories in contrast to the height of the German houses which were more developed in width, with local stones at the corners, plain walls, somewhat more richly decorated doors, and balconies instead of the German oriels, and with Mansard roofs. The corner buildings were mostly three-storied. Town

222

hall and store were distinguished by richer forms. The whole had the character of bourgeois well-being, of a low flight of fantasy, of a comfortable middle class, and of a restful self-sufficiency.[28]

French influence was evident in the dominating position of the church and in its forecourt. The interrelationship between streets and squares was even more strongly emphasized in 1686 in the plan for Erlangen, which was probably designed by a Huguenot. French influence on German city planning became stronger only when both park and town began to develop as complementary elements of the total urban scene. The starlike layout that was derived from Vauban's fortifications was not adopted for the design of small towns in Germany. On the other hand, the eight- or ten-pointed star was used in the design of Versailles and for German residences. It is likely that this motif was introduced to France and Germany from Italy; for the arrangement of a principal street accompanied by two symmetrical and diagonal side streets all branching off from the same square was derived from the prototype of the Piazza del Popolo at Rome. Both these motifs have exerted a considerable influence on German city planning, especially in southern Germany where Italian architects worked at the beginning of the eighteenth century. The grouping of town, palace, and park at Ludwigsburg in Württemberg, probably designed by Donato Giuseppe Frisonis who was mentioned as architect in 1714, was never completed; but the plan was clearly of Italian origin. The market square with the two churches symmetrical to the main axis repeated the motif of the palace court where each wing of the palace contained a chapel.

Italian and French influences competed in South Germany, while Dutch and French infiltration prevailed in the North. When German city planning had reached a fairly independent stage, the main physical structure of the cities and towns had already been stabilized. Only details could be reorganized and expressed in the contemporary language of form. This is why individual streets or squares or buildings are more characteristic witnesses of the genius of the German Baroque than are whole towns. Places such as Karlsruhe or Potsdam, Mannheim or Ludwigsburg, Würzburg or Dresden, Ludwigslust or Munich, were essentially less German than Rothenburg, Dinkelsbühl, Nördlingen, and many other towns of the Middle Ages. But in spite of the great practical obstacles to rebuilding a town as a whole, there was a well-founded awareness of the principles that should guide the planning in general and in detail; there was a sincere effort to weld the individual achievements together and to subordinate them to a higher unity of style and archi-

28. C. Gurlitt. *Geschichte des Barockstieles in Deutschland.* 1889, p. 98.

tectural coherence; and there was an unfaltering consciousness of the need to express in a new language of form the manifold social and economic trends that exerted their revolutionary impact upon the life and the atmosphere of towns.

The soil for these changes had been prepared in the later Gothic period. Then, at the end of the thirteenth century, a new feeling of space began to take shape: hall churches with a unified interior space were built. These churches did not replace the three-aisled basilicas, but they were an indication, a precursor, of the feeling of a widening space and of the more horizontal proportions that were to be the characteristic elements of the Baroque. They sounded the concluding note of the Gothic and religious hysteria of the Middle Ages. Their interiors were more akin to a meeting hall than to the transcendental uplift of the Gothic basilicas; for the subordination of the individual to the community was gradually giving way to a coordination of individual members. The hall churches equalized the spatial tensions that had existed between the higher nave and the lower aisles. The individual space units were coordinated, no longer subordinated one to the other.

An uninterrupted line of continuous transformation ran from the Gothic to the Renaissance and finally to the Baroque

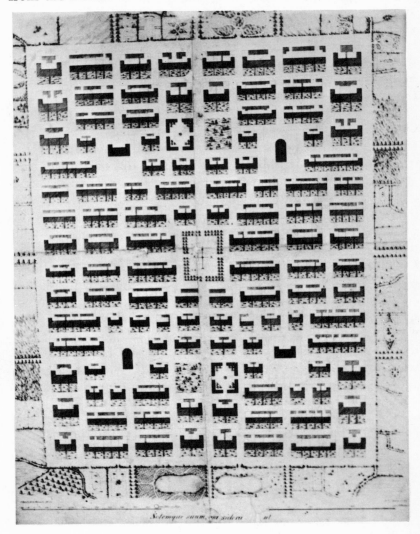

96. Plan of an Ideal City by Dr. B. C. Faust, 1824, with the inscription: "Zur Sonne nach Mittag sollen die Menschen leben." (People should live toward the sun, toward the South).

224

97. Design for a coastal town, with pier and stock exchange, by Friedrich Gilly.

98. Water color by Friedrich Gilly of the monument to Frederick the Great.

and Rococo. The typically German houses of the Renaissance, with their windows closely drawn together, expanding in height and width, and sometimes forming almost continuous strips, and the step gables with their scrolls and finials were witnesses that Germany had never lost the insurgent vitality and the dynamic tensions of the Gothic. The Renaissance was but an interlude until the Baroque opened the floodgates of excitement and the joy in the beauty of motion. This continuity of development, though latent at times, may partly explain why the German architects were less concerned with theory and why only a few attempts were made to work out an Ideal Town: there was less need for theoretical speculation and more reliance on the past and what it had to offer. This explains the relatively strong preoccupation with details of the town layout and the ready

225

acceptance of the foreign ideas that infiltrated from the West and the South. But when German art regained its creative power, when German architecture raised the jewels of the Baroque churches in Bavaria and Austria, then began the last great epoch of city planning before the sunset of the nineteenth century. The groping sense of space grew into an idea of space of a translucent clarity. Space as a creative and formative element of the urban configuration was rediscovered, and motion became the medium through which it was expressed. In this union of space and form, the streets and squares assumed a new significance in their relationship to the volume of the buildings.

This newly gained idea of space was lost in the nineteenth century. A general helplessness toward spatial problems was spreading. The streets became ends in themselves, and their organic relationship to the houses weakened. The surveyor took over from the architect; and the architects, cut loose from the reality of the emerging changes in the social and economic sphere, produced shallow, drawing-board schemes. Eclecticism became the daydream of this period after the faint flames of neoclassicism, which had produced at least a few though rather pale works, abated. The names that deserve to be mentioned are Klenze for Munich, Weinbrenner for Karlsruhe, Semper for Dresden, and Schinkel and Gilly for Berlin.

Friedrich Gilly is something of an exception. His work went beyond the mere adoption of eclectic form elements. His designs, such as the monument for Frederick the Great, were conceived, not in isolation, but as integrated parts of a complex relationship within the framework of a town as a whole. These problems occupied him for many years and finally induced him to prepare

99. Detail from Friedrich Gilly's monument to Frederick the Great.

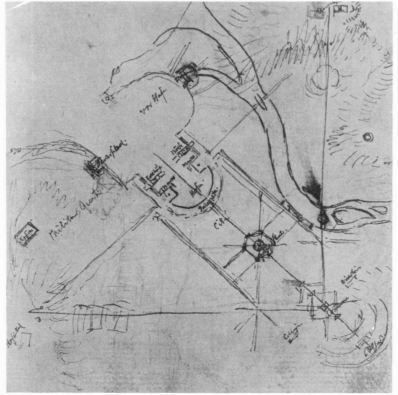

100. Design for a coastal town by Friedrich Gilly.

plans for an ideal city. His sketches for a town on the sea are rough drafts, a sort of practical exercise in city planning, a method he recommended during his last years to his like-minded professional friends. The town he designed was situated in a deep inlet at the mouth of a river opposite the barracks and defense installations of the military establishments. Near the harbor were the industrial and commercial quarters. The central axis of the symmetrical harbor continued as the main thoroughfare through the town, skirting the *Plazata* and leading, through a hexagonal square whose center was occupied by the "Greek Theatre," to the palace. On the hills outside the town were the hospital and the university. The design shows a perfect awareness of the demands of organic city planning and of the imperative need to adapt the physical layout to the topographical conditions.

Industry was concentrated in the cities, where a large reservoir of manpower was available, and this was the major factor of urban growth during the nineteenth century. The solution of this problem was completely misunderstood. The development schemes that were to meet this challenge of the growing need for houses and of the increasing traffic can broadly be grouped into two categories: the radial and the concentric layout. Paris stood for the first system and Vienna for the second. Both were failures. Haussmann's plan for Paris made no distinction between residential and traffic streets. It was merely a beautiful ornament and the prototype for many drawing-board schemes. Only a time in which a *parvenu* culture flourished could be enthusiastic about Haussmann's "grandiose" performance. It was an empty demonstration of ostentatiousness and profoundly antisocial. Instead of dispersing traffic, it concentrated it on a few *rondspoints,* and instead of helping to build houses for the growing masses, it produced embarrassing façades. The Ringstrasse of Vienna was the result of another fateful mistake: It preserved the old idea of an enclosing circle, making an organic extension impossible or at least problematical. Yet this pattern also was widely adopted in Germany, especially because the railway stations could be placed on this peripheral line of the circle. Gradually, however, the towns expanded beyond this ring; the whole system became more and more meaningless and in the end an obstacle to free development. The circular street followed the course of the old walls, which were leveled together with the moats. It used the medieval limitations as a starting point for modern extensions. It was a profound misreading of the situation and of the needs of the future—an outstanding failure that, like many other failures, found enthusiastic imitators.

The Nineteenth Century

These two so-called "solutions" were the last century's main contributions to city planning. More and more, national characteristics of cities and towns disappeared, until finally they merged into the hotchpotch of international atrocities.

How can this be explained? There are numerous reasons for this decay of artistic insight and formative power. Here it may be sufficient to stress the widening gulf between technique and architecture. Although painting experienced a renaissance from Goya to the French Impressionists, architecture was on the decline. The impact of the unlimited possibilities of science and technique had thrown architecture off balance. For the Romantic architects of this period, art was something that could be added later when the technical requirements of building were fulfilled. From this came the pattern-book ornaments and other details that were glued onto the buildings, and also the romanticism in planning that culminated in an imitation of medieval towns, as propagated by Camillo Sitte. The "founding years" after the war of 1870-1871 saw the greatest excesses of this misunderstood progress. They were the worthy precursor to the Wilhelminian era—although this period before World War I was also the turning point.[29]

A few figures show the extraordinary transformation that produced innumerable problems for city planning in Germany. Like all other countries, it failed to solve them. In 1830, Germany's population was 26.5 million, with a density of 145 people per square mile. By 1930, it had risen to a total of 63.2 million—by 140 per cent, of which 70 per cent lived in towns. In 1830, there were only 2 big cities within the frontiers of what, in 1930, was the German Empire: Berlin with 220 thousand inhabitants, and Hamburg with 112 thousand. By 1930, there were 52 cities within the same boundaries with a total population of over 20 million. In 1830, Munich had 66 thousand inhabitants; Cologne, 62 thousand; Leipzig, 41 thousand; Dresden, 56 thousand; Frankfurt, 43 thousand; and Stuttgart, 31 thousand. All the other cities had fewer than 30 thousand people, and many, not even 20 thousand. Altogether, only 1.5 million people lived in cities with more than 20 thousand inhabitants. But by 1930, this figure had risen to 27.2 million not including towns with fewer than 20 thousand inhabitants. In 1830, there were 164 middle towns and 19 big cities; by 1930 there were 693 and 181, respectively. In 1830, moderately large cities were relatively evenly distributed over the whole area of the country. Their function was to serve as traffic, supply, and administrative centers for the surrounding districts. Town and countryside were still fairly well balanced. Apart from these towns there were the commercial and industrial cities, which extended their

29. This period will be dealt with in the last volume as part of the international development.

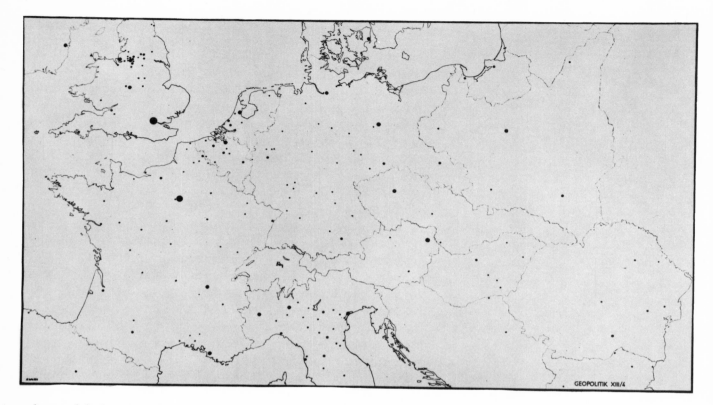

GEOPOLITIK XIII/4

101. Urbanization of Central Europe and adjacent countries in 1830.

sphere of influence over a wider hinterland, especially the sea-ports and those on the important arteries of the interior com-munications. But in general, the number of people whose life was cut loose from the immediate surroundings was still small. In contrast to other countries—for instance, France—the dis-tribution of cities and larger towns in Germany was more uneven. The natural landscape was more diversified, and the historical influences that had worked upon central Europe from all sides were more varied. The political fragmentation was considerably greater than in France and England. The growth of a city by ten or fifteen times was nothing unusual. New mining and industrial agglomerations developed within small areas out of villages.

In 1830, agriculture was still the main occupation. The Ruhr district had only 2 towns with more than 20 thousand inhabitants: Elberfeld and Barmen. Today, within the same area, more than a dozen cities, some with more than 500 thousand inhabitants, have grown together as large conurbations. Some-thing similar has happened on the Rhine, the lower Main and the Neckar, and along the Central Uplands. At the beginning of the nineteenth century, the Baltic ports were still more im-portant than those on the coast of the North Sea. But this changed the more industrialization increased and extended its influence over ever-widening areas. The population of Hamburg, which had suffered considerably in the Napoleonic Era, rose from 112 thousand in 1830 to 410 thousand in 1880, and to 1.2 million in 1930. During the same period, Bremen's population grew from 35 thousand to 325 thousand. Its development was less spectacular than that of Hamburg, but it gave rise to the foundation of Bremerhaven in 1830 as its outer port, to Geestemünde founded by Hanover, the largest fishing port of Germany, and to Wesermünde. On the other hand, Emden, which was connected with the Ruhr district by the Dortmund-Ems Kanal built from 1890 to 1899 and expected to stimulate its trade, stagnated after a short prosperity.

The concentration of industry in the cities and towns affected the countryside; its trades and rural industries declined. The ironworks of the Spessart, the Franconian Alb, and the Fichtelgebirge decayed; the nail makers of the Allgäu left their benches; the homespun linen of the Rhön disappeared from the market; and the weavers of Silesia were starving. The innumerable small trades that were carried on in almost every larger village had run their course: charcoal burning; potash boiling; glass manufacture; paper, oil, and tanning mills; clothmaking and pottery; wood carving; and many other manufactures were doomed to a slow but inevitable breakup. Road traffic came almost to a complete standstill when the railways had sufficiently developed. All this had a profound effect upon the rural population whose livelihood had depended on these trades and manufactures. The townsman dethroned the countryman as the central pillar of the German national economy.

The magnitude of these changes may explain, at least to a certain degree, why city planning of the last century did not rise to the occasion offered by the new and great problems of this period. The ideology of *laissez-faire* was too deeply rooted in the minds of the leading classes; and private competition and the "law" of supply and demand were regarded as the all-powerful agents that would automatically guarantee progress and prosperity. But on the reverse side of this optimism were the unhealthy tenement quarters for the masses, the over-flowing of the towns into the countryside, the senseless "Cult of the Street," and the bad housing conditions in all the cities and towns whose growth was the pride of the *nouveaux riches* and of facile politicians.

CITY SURVEY

The cities discussed in this section are arranged geographically, roughly from west to east, and according to Germany's division into *Länder*. The description of each individual city will necessarily differ considerably from the others in scope and character, selection of data, and visual documentation, depending, in each case, on its historical importance and its contribution toward the development of city-planning. Consequently, the survey should be viewed as a whole: All cities together form the framework within which the plexus of structural changes of growth or decline, of origin or stagnation of cities has been operative. Like a mosaic, each small piece is part of the whole, and only together do they represent the complete picture.

Emden, Lower Saxony. The whole area of the city is situated in the flat coastal marshes. All elevations are artificial: the *Warften* with their compact villages surrounding Emden, the old dikes, and the medieval walls. The soft soil has influenced the structure and style of the buildings in town and country: the light construction of the gabled houses with their double walls and their air space and the peasants' dwellings with their half-timbered work. Four stages of development may be distinguished:

102. First phase of Emden's development, 1000–1400.

1. *About 1000 to 1400.* The first historical record on "Amuthon," the later Emden, appears in the form of coins that were found during the years 1020–1051. At this time, the Emden *Warft* rose almost 9 feet above the marsh. Definite historical data are missing. There are possible Roman influences, and there may also have been Norman visits. The first dikes may have been built during the eleventh and twelfth centuries, at which time trade with Charlemagne's empire was possibly conducted. The *Warften* grew in height and size. The *Altstadt*, the old town, was founded together with a Franciscan monastery The first settlement was surrounded in the south by the Ems River and by several branches of its small tributary, the Ee (Ehe). Thus "Amuthon" was situated on an island that could easily be defended by deepening the river channels and by connecting moats and dams. *Aa* or *Ee* means in old Frisian "river" or "water"; and the mouths of these branches, and therefore the place between them, were called *"Mude";* hence the name "Amuthon," meaning "place between the mouths of the rivers." The situation was favorable for fishermen and peasants; it offered a protected site near their fishing grounds, meadows, and fields. Gradually, the large *Warft* and the smaller, secondary *Warften* grew together, and the settlements moved nearer to each other. It is doubtful whether the present *Warft* with the *Altstadt* has retained its original form and its old streets. In general, the older *Warft* settlements were circular, and the more recent ones oval; and the roads of the former were radial, while in the latter case they crossed each other. The earliest formation of the more recent *Warften* may date back to A.D. 500. It is possible that the Emden *Warft* belonged to this latter type, although there is no proof that the streets originally followed the corresponding pattern. It is more likely that in connection with the building of the church and the fortified castle around A.D. 1000, the original layout of the streets was changed.

103. Second phase of Emden's development, 1400–1550.

2. *About 1400 to 1550.* Emden took part in overseas trade. The *Altstadt* expanded, and its outlying parts were incorporated.

3. *About 1550 to 1700.* For the influx of artisans, craftsmen, traders, and religious

104. Third phase of Emden's development, 1550–1700.

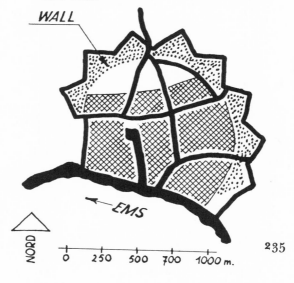

235

105. Fourth phase of Emden's development, 1700–1850.

WALL

NORD

106. Emden after 1576, showing the more densely built up old part with the town hall in the center, the canals, the main square, and the long, narrow building plots. Also shown is the later addition, which is very thinly and unequally settled. Both parts are surrounded by continuous fortifications.

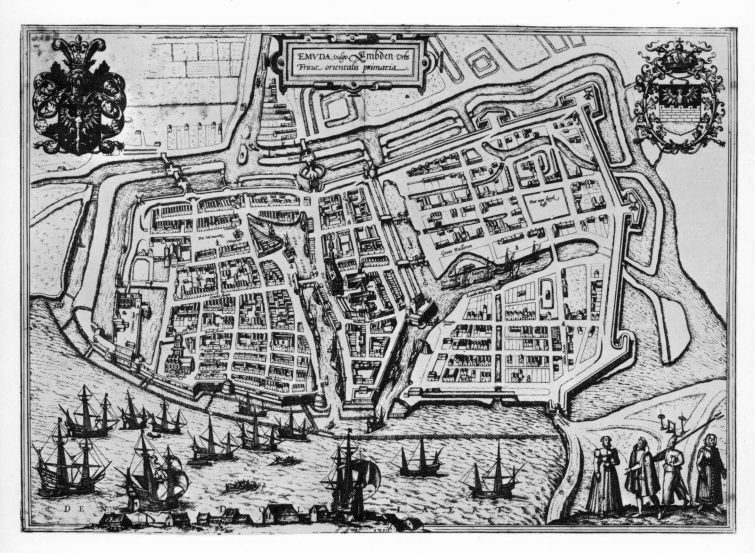

EMVDA, vulgo Embden vrbs Frisiæ orientalis primaria.

107. The center of Emden before its destruction in World War II, showing the town the hall, the narrow gabled houses, and the main canal.

refugees from the Netherlands, new dwellings, workshops, public buildings, and warehouses were needed. The area of the *Altstadt* was insufficient to accommodate the growing population. During the second half of the sixteenth century, the *Landmark* of the neighboring villages was incorporated; houses were built, streets and canals were laid out, and the fortifications were extended to enclose the new area and connect it with the *Altstadt*. On the long and narrow plots, resembling the Amsterdam layout with direct access to the water, the burghers built their houses with rich gables and portals, while the patrician families erected their more opulent town houses. Emden became one of the most beautiful towns in northern Germany.

The Dutch grew suspicious of this new rival. Their informants reported that in the three years from 1552 to 1555 on an area "half as large as the small town of Weesp (near Amsterdam) streets, lanes, closes with houses, workshops and offices were built; and that within this short time one hundred houses were erected." They told of the growing textile manufactures, of the great number of ships, the increasing development of trade and commerce with the West and the East, and of the herring fisheries. Large trading companies in London, Hamburg, Lübeck, Wesel, Cologne, Frankfurt, Strasbourg, Augsburg, Ulm, Nürnberg, and even Venice had their representatives, warehouses, or offices in Emden. However, this prosperity did not last. Gradually the refugees began to return to their homelands, and toward the end of this epoch the urban area became too large; the new fortifications, finished in 1615, were too

108. The Emden town hall and neighboring houses, a good example of unity of scale and unity in diversity.

generously conceived. The northern half of the city proper could no longer be filled with buildings. Nor was this all: The attempt to redivert the Ems into its old bed failed; the new course began to silt up again, and the sheet-piling wall that had been built at enormous cost and effort was destroyed by the river.

4. *About 1700 to 1850.* The failure to revive the former overseas trade resulted in stagnation. Although Emden had grown fourfold during the preceding period, the space that had been enclosed by the fortifications of 1615 remained only very thinly settled until the middle of the nineteenth century. The agricultural population used this space for fields or pastures. In 1601, the number of inhabitants had been about 30 thousand, but after the plague of 1665 it was reduced to 12 to 15 thousand. By 1749 it had decreased to 6894 persons. Emden suffered greatly during the Napoleonic period. It remained a small and insignificant town.

Bremen. The origin of Bremen is unknown. The word *Bremen* means "edge," and refers to the town's situation on the bank of a river, on the edge of a dune. The old landing place of the earliest settlement along the edge of the dunes of the Weser is clearly distinguishable in its long form. This point is the last place the Weser can be crossed fairly easily before it reaches the sea. It is likely that a ford, later a ferry, existed. This river crossing is reached by the tides, and thus became the meeting point of important roads where people would break their journey and buy and sell goods. The core of the first settlement probably lay near the present *Tiefer,* denoting in the early Middle Ages a district, not a street, and meaning "ferry at the Tie," the ancient meeting place. Between the dune and the Weser stood the huts of the ferrymen, craftsmen, traders, and fishermen. This was the Bremen that appeared on the stage of history toward the end of the eighth century.

As a bridge town alone, Bremen could not have attained its great importance had not a second factor played an even more significant role: the fact that it was the terminus for seagoing vessels and a center for river traffic on the smaller rivers of the Aller, Leine, Oker, Diemel, and Fulda—all of which could be used as waterways under the more small-scale conditions of the Middle Ages. Thus, overland and overseas traffic met, and Bremen became in the course of the centuries a transshipment point of the first order.

In 780, Charlemagne assigned Bremen and the surrounding territory to the Anglo-Saxon priest Willehad for his missionary activities. The first church was built on the Weser dunes and was consecrated in 789. The right to hold a market was granted in 965. The building of the first walls began in 1032, and about 100 years later, Dutch people, Hollanders, colonized the Bremen district, which is called Hollerland today. They irrigated the land and built dikes. Around 1200, walls and a moat enclosed the town in a semicircle. At

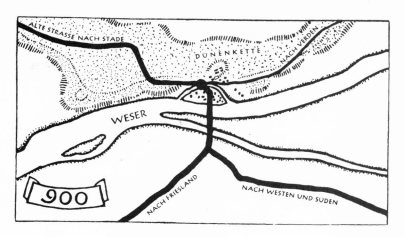

109. Bremen in 900.

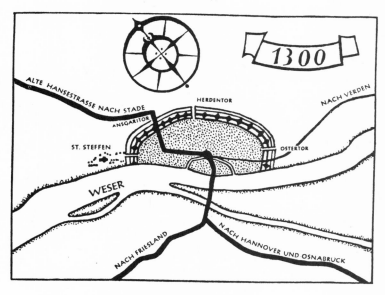

110. Bremen in 1300.

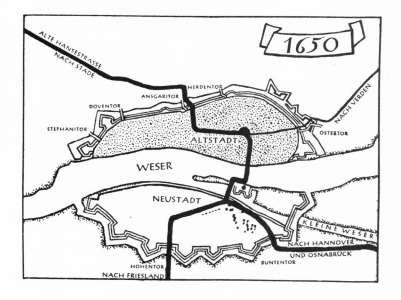

111. Bremen in 1650.

112. Plan of Bremen in 1730, by Georg Christian Kilian, showing the Vauban fortifications, the *Altstadt*, and the *Neustadt*. The old long landing place and the area around the church and the town hall, the original nuclei of the city, are clearly visible.

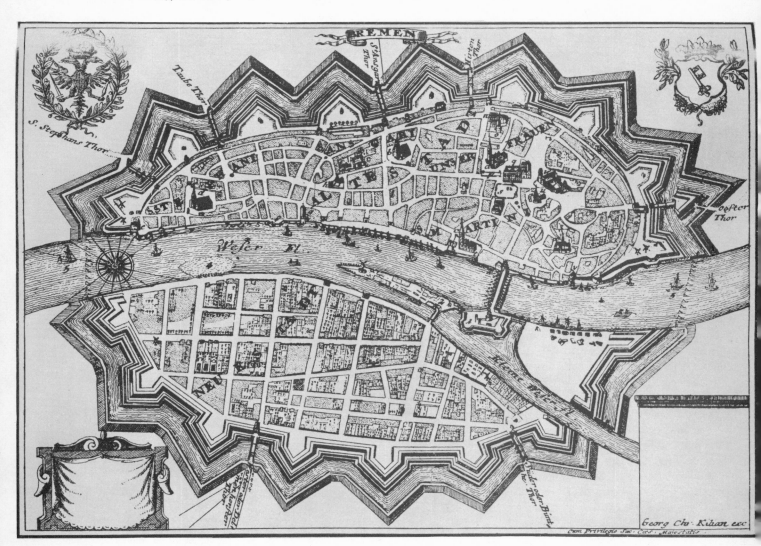

113. The *Braut*—fortifications at the bridge over the Weser—which were built in 1522–1531.

114. Bremen's market square, as it was in the middle of the seventeenth century (after a model), showing the town hall (*left*) and other public and private buildings. The composition is compact yet diversified. Note the contrast between the individual accents of the gables on the burghers' narrow houses and the larger units of the town hall, the church, and the Merchants' House opposite the town hall.

this time it covered with the commercial and industrial quarters, the landing place, and the episcopal district an area of about two thirds of the present *Altstadt*. In the first decades of the twelfth century, a settlement of fishermen and sailors grew up to the west of the town near St. Stephen. This settlement was incorporated into Bremen in 1302, but retained its own walls and gates until 1308.

Bremen joined the Hanse in 1358 and after a short time became one of its most influential members. Henceforth, the merchants determined the policy, development, and character of the city. Under their guidance and through their efforts the *Kaufmannstadt*, the city of the merchants, took shape with the Lange Strasse, as the main artery, which up to the present day has remained the seat of Bremen's great trading and commercial houses. The other professional classes could not compete with the merchant princes, although the craftsmen and artisans strengthened their position by the formation of guilds. They were, however, numerous and strong enough to add a new district of a distinct character to the existing quarters at the north of the Obernstrasse. Even today, the street names are a reminder of this period: the Knochenhauer Strasse, Pelzerstrasse, Hutfilterstrasse, and others. The inhabitants of this part were little people in comparison with the wealthy merchants, but welcome helpers

115. The *Altstadt*, with its green girdle (formerly the fortifications). The cathedral is in the center, and the old landing place is on the left.

116. The market square, with the town hall (1404–1409) and St. Petri Church (begun in 1043).

117. The Schütting, the old merchants' guild hall (1537–1538). This building was partly rebuilt after World War II.

118. Interior of the festival hall, on the second floor of the town hall, a symbolic expression of the city's greatness and wealth.

119. The Essighaus (1681), tall and narrow, with large windows typical of the Renaissance and a rich gable with scrolls and finials. This building adds a strong vertical accent in the narrow street.

and indispensable members of the community.

During the Thirty Years' War when the enemy threatened the northern part of Lower Saxony, the need for more comprehensive and more efficient fortifications became urgent. The town's defenses were particularly weak along the waterfront. Here the danger of an attack was greatest. It was therefore decided in 1623 to extend the fortifications to the other side of the Weser and to apply the most recent experiences of the contemporary technique of defense against the new and far-reaching firearms. One of the best military engineers, Johann van Valckenburg, was asked to design the new extension on the southern bank as a continuation of the *Altstadt's* fortifications. Thus the *Neustadt* came into being. Its internal layout was entirely subordinated to the peripheral *enceinte*. The streets crossed each other at right angles and ran directly to the bastions. A square—the *piazza d'armi* of the Italian theorists—was the center of the layout. The *Neustadt* was built not because space for settlement was scarce, but because the defense of the town demanded it. For centuries large, empty spaces

existed which, in the nineteenth century, were used by the older industries of Bremen as a welcome opportunity to erect factories, workshops, and warehouses. The previously long shape of the town, a semi-ellipse, became a full oval traversed by the Weser, a form which it retained for several centuries.

The foundation in 1673 of a trading settlement at the mouth of the Geeste north of Bremen, the *Karlsburg,* was one of the first steps to improve the situation of Bremen as a port for overseas trade, although it still took several centuries for this attempt to become a reality. By the middle of the eighteenth century, the Weser had been silted up to such a degree that no large vessel could reach the city: Loading and unloading had to take place about 26 miles downstream. It was not until 1824 that definite plans were made for a "Port of Bremen" at the mouth of the Weser. In 1827, the hitherto Hanoverian territory on the northern bank of the Geeste, where the ruins of the former *Karlsburg* were still standing, was transferred to Bremen; in the presence of the "whole population consisting of nineteen persons," the red and white flag of Bremen was hoisted. Work began immediately, following the plans of the Dutchman Van Ronzelen for the "Bremer Haven," and with it a decisive turning point in the history of Bremen was reached.

The fortifications of the city were dismantled in 1802, and it was resolved that "these as also the whole neighborhood of the town-moat should be transformed into pleasant gardens and terrace-like walks with shaded resting places." The landscape architect Altmann was entrusted with the design and execution of the plan. After the dissolution of the Holy Roman Empire of the German Nation in 1806, Bremen decided to call itself "Freie Hansestadt Bremen."

120. View over steep roofs into a narrow street with gabled houses.

121. Warehouses on the Weser. The Kornhaus (*center left*), built in 1590 and destroyed during World War II, served as a granary for the city.

Osnabrück, Westphalia. Osnabrück is situated in a parklike, hilly landscape traversed by the wide and swampy depression of the Hase, which narrows at this point to about 300 feet, thus making a crossing easy. Roads from many directions converge on this part of the basin. The area has been settled since the neolithic period and during the wars of Charlemagne against the Saxons became a strategic center of the first order, favored by the easy crossings through the Teutoburger Wald and over the Wiehengebirge. After a decisive victory over the Saxons, Charlemagne established a bishopric in 783 around which the town of Osnabrück developed. A dune on the southern bank of the Hase provided the necessary protection and a site for a *Königshof* which, together with the ecclesiastical group of buildings, dominated the roads and the river crossing. Since the seat of the bishop with the church in the center stood directly on the south–north axis, it was necessary to divert the main road in a wide bend to the west, a factor that was of considerable importance for the layout and further development of Osnabrück. This oldest part of the town, with the cathedral, the cathedral close, the cathedral school, and other buildings, was fortified. Walls enclosed this *Binnenburg* until late into the Middle Ages and isolated it from the rest of the town. The cathedral precincts are still clearly delineated by the lines of the Lohstrasse, Bierstrasse, and Herrenteichstrasse.

By the end of the ninth century, a craftsmen's and traders' settlement had grown up around this ecclesiastical district. The triangular form of the market square resulted from its situation on the place where the two main roads met. In about 1100, the *Binnenburg* and the *Butenburg*, the market settlement, were enclosed by one circumvallation. This second ring can still be followed from the Hasetor to the Neuer Graben. In the eleventh century, a *Neustadt* grew up in the south outside the walls around the collegiate church of St. John. This new city was fortified only by a moat and a fence, although it had its own constitution and administration. This twin town with two town halls was

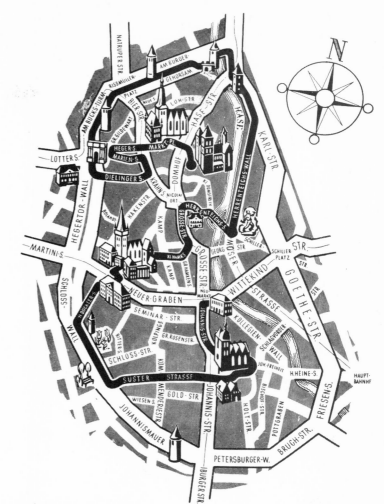

122. The *Altstadt* of Osnabrück.

unique in northern Germany. In 1306, both towns united into one community, but the *Neustadt* retained its independence. In contrast with the narrowness of the *Altstadt*, the *Neustadt* was spacious and its plots larger. The original character of a rural settlement was partly preserved. Even in the nineteenth century, the gardens behind the rows of houses were still used for the cultivation of rye. By this time the area which is shown in the plan of 1633 had been filled. The walls prevented an extension until the middle of the nineteenth century.

Around 1400 a *Landwehr* was built at a distance of about 2 miles from the town walls, with a circumference of about 20 miles. It consisted of two to three fences of felled trees, placed lengthwise one over the other. It was a defense more against robbers than against enemies.

247

In spite of its agricultural character, Osnabrück was during the Middle Ages and the Renaissance a town of craftsmen and traders. The daily market was held in the market square. The old town hall originally had three doors, two of which led to the stalls of the bakers and the butchers on the ground floor. The other trades had their booths in the market square, these were sometimes workshop, salesroom, and even living room in one. When, toward the end of the Middle Ages, the booths became insufficient, the bakers began to sell in their own houses, and the tailors and cloth-makers in the town hall or other buildings. The long-lasting economic prosperity that set in at the end of the Middle Ages owed its success, above all, to Osnabrück's most important native product—linen. The town derived a considerable income from this trade.

The conservatism of the population preserved the rural building type longer than in other towns of Lower Saxony and Westphalia. Apart from the general character of the houses with their gables projecting over the

123. The Ledenhof in Osnabrück.

248

124. Kleine Gildewart Street, with the town hall in the background. Note the large door of the first house.

125. Osnabrück's town hall
(*left*), with the choir of
St. Mary's.

street, many old dwellings had a large gate-way that led directly into the hall, the main room. This *Diele* served for all sorts of domestic and professional purposes, and was adjoined by small rooms on either side which received only indirect light from the main room. Stairways and galleries led to other rooms in the attic. Osnabrück is known as the town of the *Steinwerke,* buildings of natural stone, mostly the yellowish shell lime-stone found in the neighborhood. The *Steinwerke* preserved as late as the thirteenth century the old fortress character they had assumed before the fortification of the town. The outstanding example is the Ledenhof dating back to the fourteenth century. This *Wohnturm* is an excellent illustration of how these originally detached buildings grew together with the more ordinary houses that were later erected as adjoining parts.

Soest, Westphalia. Soest is the center of the *Soester Börde* and the *Hellweg,* the old highway that runs parallel to the Lippe River along the southern margin of the *Münsterische Bucht,* the lowland embayment around Münster. It was first mentioned in 836, although its origins date back to an earlier period, possibly to the beginning of the seventh century. It is probable that the first settlers selected the site because it offered a good water supply, and that they stayed there because a *Burg* on a hill provided protection for their settlement and for the *Hellweg.* Moreover, the soil was fertile and salt was available; grain and salt were the main commodities of the inhabitants and the principal basis of the town's prosperity in the following centuries. An Arab traveler who visited Soest early in the tenth century described it as a citadel where salt was mined. Its plan was cruciform with one gate each in the north, south, east, and west. During the twelfth and thirteenth centuries, the town enjoyed an almost American development. It expanded toward the southeast, and outside the western and northern gates a *vicus* grew up. In about 1180, Soest was surrounded by new walls, which are still standing today, and was divided into six parishes. Its layout resembled a wheel, its ten radial streets leading spokelike to the gates. But these streets were not straight; they were winding and crooked and interconnected by numerous narrow and short lanes.

Soest reached its greatest economic prosperity around 1200. At the end of the twelfth century, Hedeby as the terminal of the Baltic trade of Soest had been replaced by Lübeck, in whose foundation merchants of Soest had taken a prominent part. Via Lübeck, Soest traded with Visby and Gotland, with Novgorod and Riga, and became a leading member of the Hanseatic League. In the West, trading connections were established with Flanders and England. In the fourteenth century Soest severed its relations with the archbishop of Cologne and acquired a territory of its own, the so-called *Soester Börde* that included fifty-eight villages. By the middle of the thirteenth century, Soest had become the leader of the Westphalian towns. Long and bitter conflicts with Cologne filled the fifteenth century, ending with the victory of Soest. But this victory was the beginning of the city's decline because the political frontiers restricted its free enterprise. The Reformation was established in 1531. Soest suffered considerably during the Thirty Years' War, and at its end was powerless and impoverished. Gradually it lost its independence. One privilege after the other was abrogated, and finally Frederick the Great abolished the five-hundred-year-old constitution.

The nucleus of Soest was a peasant settlement. In the course of time it received market rights and became a town. Its physical layout was determined by two factors: its early peasant origin and its flourishing trade. Many houses were surrounded by cultivated fields. These ample estates rather than the streets

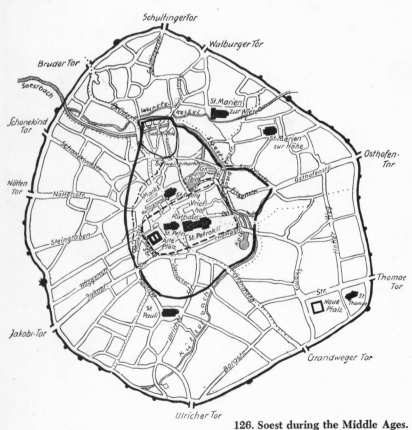

126. Soest during the Middle Ages.

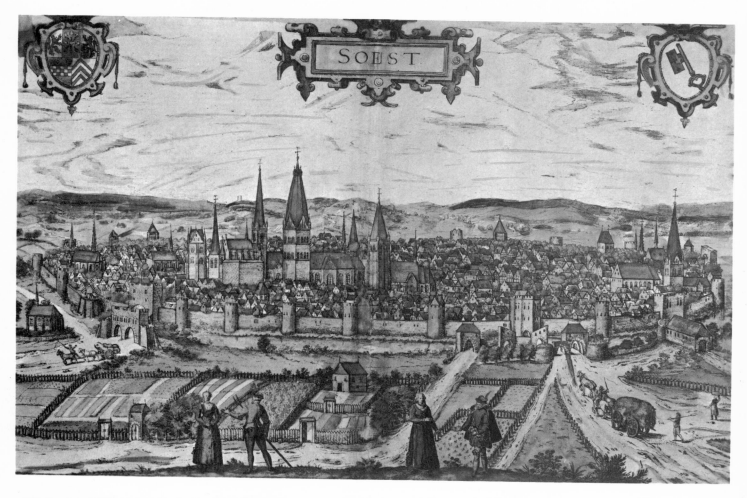

127. Soest in 1588. Engraving by Braun and Hogenberg, showing the characteristic skyline of the medieval town, dominated by church spires and enclosed by strong walls with numerous towers.

were the primary elements of the layout. It was as though they merely tolerated the roads that wound between them producing a veritable labyrinth—its plan was possibly the most irregular of all German towns. The hub of the wheel is the *Stadtburg*, the almost rectangular precincts that lie in the center with the town hall and the two principal churches. This rectangle covered an area of 510 by 840 yards and had four gates. Its larger part was reserved for ecclesiastical buildings: the bishops' castle; the Church of St. Peter with two cemeteries; and the Church and the Monastery of St. Patroclus, the cathedral. The rest was occupied by the burghers' houses and the

markets. The overcrowding of all streets and squares with booths and tradespeople gradually reached such dimensions that the highway (the *Hellweg*) with its heavy through traffic was diverted from the inner town, although this created but a passing relief. The area available for stalls and booths was so restricted that temporary sheds and huts had to be built against the outside of the walls where they could easily be burned down in case of war. When it became obvious that the inner town was utterly inadequate to house the ever-increasing population and its market activities, the market street was laid out outside the original area. It led from the

251

128. The Cathedral and the southern facade of St. Peter's (*left foreground*).

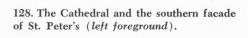

129. The Osthofentor, built in 1523–1526 by Master Porphyrius of Neukirchen (in Hesse). It combines the severe utilitarian character of the strong part of the fortifications with the lighter, more peaceful splendor that symbolizes the town's power and wealth and the scope of its civic ambitions.

castle to the new market square, and was lined on its west side by dwellings. A large part of the square was occupied by long rows of stalls and booths. A considerable extension of the town took place during the twelfth century: The fortifications with ten gates were rebuilt to enclose a fairly large area while retaining the old irregular street pattern. The new settlers came mostly from the rural neighborhood of the town, which now covered an area of 252 acres.

Soest developed from the Carolingian *Königshof,* and the castle of the bishops, the actual nucleus, became the market settlement of the tenth century and finally the town of the later Middle Ages, thus following the same subsequent stages of many other places.

130. In the Middle Ages, these half-timbered houses were inhabited by tanners, who used the water of the Loerbach (*left*) for tanning purposes.

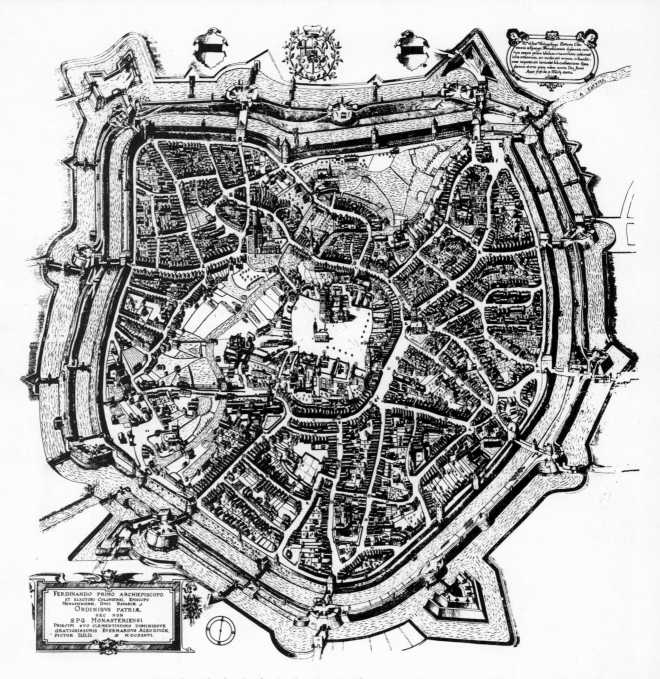

131. *Münster in 1632*, by Eberhard Alerdinck. The *Domburg* is in the center, surrounded by a continuous row of gabled houses built close together along a curved street that follows the line of the old walls. The market squares are part of this street to the east of the *Domburg*. With few exceptions, the irregular building blocks are densely built up. The almost circular fortifications have double walls, two moats, gate towers, and several bastions.

Münster, Westphalia. Münster is situated on the Aa in a lowland embayment in the midst of a landscape with dispersed settlements and isolated farms. It is probable that near the ford, there existed a Germanic sanctuary and later a Carolingian strong point or similar establishment. After 780, a church was erected with a convent, a monastery school, houses for the servants, and barns. This whole complex, called *honestum monasterium,* was protected by earthen walls, palisades, and a moat; four gates led to the main overland

254

132. The Prinzipalmarkt in Münster, one of the very few German squares with continuous arcades, before its destruction in World War II. The unity of the arcades gathers together the multiplicity of the individual houses, with their different gables, into one coherent whole.

133. The Lamberti Fountain, with the choir of St. Lamberti (*left*), some of the arcaded houses of the Prinzipalmarkt, and the corner of a house on one of the side streets.

255

roads. This *Domburg,* the fortified precincts of the bishop and the cathedral, rose between the crossing of the roads from Holland to Soest and Paderborn and from Cologne to Osnabrück and the Aa. It was a strategic point. This was the nucleus of Münster.

Toward the end of the tenth century, the *Domburg,* the *urbs,* was enlarged, and its rectangular form changed to an irregular circle. It attracted a steadily growing population, which settled outside the fortified area. This settlement, called *locus,* grew in the course of time. A church was built in 1040 and another one 50 years later, at about 1100. The economic center of this *locus* and the main building activity remained on the higher, and therefore more densely settled, right bank of the Aa. At the middle of the eleventh century the fortifications of the *Domburg* were abandoned, and new walls with ten gate-towers and moats enclosing *urbs* and *locus* were built. Their course followed the inner line of the present-day *Promenade.* The old principal road became the main artery of the town with the Prinzipalmarkt as the center, while narrow streets, lanes, and alleys formed an almost inextricable net covering the rest of the urban area. With a few exceptions, the 470 acres enclosed by the fortifications were completely built up.

In the late Middle Ages, the population numbered 8 thousand to 9 thousand inhabitants. After a rise to over 10,500 it fell to 5,800 as a result of internal feuds and the Black Death in 1669. But by 1795, it had reached 14 thousand. Münster's economic and cultural prosperity lasted throughout the Middle Ages, but declined in the seventeenth century. The town did not recover its original pre-eminent position which it had owed to its artisans, craftsmen, merchants, and painters.

Paderborn, Westphalia. Like Münster and Osnabrück, this was one of the stations on the *Hellweg,* the old road that began near Duisberg and led to Magdeburg where it met the Amber Route to the Baltic. The *Hellweg* ran through the nucleus of Paderborn, and was here joined by another road. This favorable situation was one of the factors guaranteeing the town's steady development. Charlemagne recognized the importance of the site and furthered the small settlement that grew up around the cathedral and the church of St. Mary. At this time, the place was still small, about 200 feet in diameter. But by 1200, after the devastating fires in 1000 and 1058, it had reached the extension of the present *Altstadt.* It has been walled in since the twelfth century. The nucleus with the church is clearly distinguishable, as is also part of the course of the old walls.

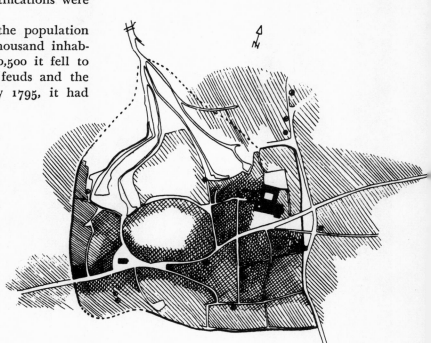

134. Paderborn about 900.

135. The fortresslike tower of the cathedral, the landmark of Paderborn.

136. Paderborn's high and narrow old houses, each with its own individuality.

137. Paderborn's town hall, begun in 1612.

257

138. Aachen in 1469, showing the original nucleus with the cathedral in the center.

Aachen (Aix-la-Chapelle), Rhineland. Its origins date back to Celtic times. During the Roman occupation it had a military bathing establishment and was famous for its hot sulphur springs. By the middle of the fifth century it fell, together with the Roman provinces, to the Franks. It became a *Königshof* (first mentioned in 765), and later the residence of Charlemagne, who built his fortified castle on the site of the present town hall. The chapel of the castle rises on the foundations of the Roman *thermae*. The castle with school and the clergy's living quarters, together with the market settlement that had grown up around this core formed the nucleus of the old inner town, which was walled in during the early Middle Ages. Its shape was a pentagon approximating a circle. The main street leading past the castle divided the *Altstadt* into two unequal parts. Population increase made an extension of the town necessary in the thirteenth century. The new fortifications with eleven gates begun in 1257 were completed in 1350. They were reinforced by bastions in the sixteenth century.

258

Düren, Rhineland. Düren is situated 19 miles east of Aachen on the right bank of the Rur. A short history of Düren was written in Latin on the back of the town plan, designed by Wenzel Hollar, to be found in the Amsterdam edition of 1657. A part of it reads in translation as follows: Düren, after Tacitus Marcodurum, a settlement of the Ubii came under Roman influence after their conquest of Gallia. Later, after their victory, it was occupied by the Franks and incorporated into Austrasia. At this time meetings of kings and princes repeatedly took place in the town. . . . In the year 1212 one began to surround it with walls. . . . Since this time the distinguished character of the streets, the trade of the burghers, certainly also its fortifications have increased its fame to such a degree that it is justifiably regarded as the apple of the eye of the towns of Jülich.

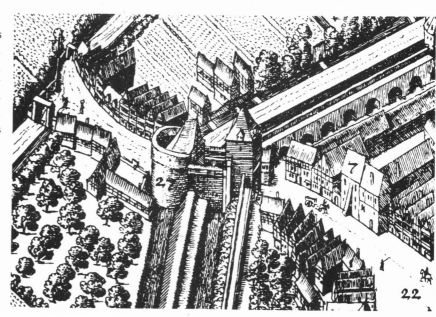

139. Sectional view of Wenzel Hollar's plan of Düren in 1634, showing the Holztor and part of the walls.

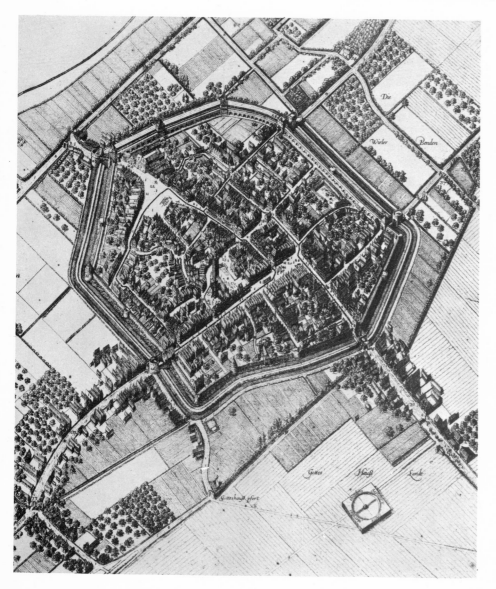

140. Hollar's plan of Düren. It shows the unsophisticated layout of streets crossing at right angles. The church occupies a site near the center. The building density is fairly high. The walls have five gates and a double moat.

259

Cologne, Rhineland. The city is set in the wide lowland embayment of the lower Rhine, which projects as a great triangle into the Rhenish *Schiefergebirge*. Through repeated changes of the relief and of the bed of the Rhine, terraces were formed. In the diluvium, the Rhine had spread its waters deltalike over the lowland embayment. This resulted in the considerable extension of the main terrace. In the course of time, this delta became narrower; and as the river bed cut deeper into the soil, deposits formed the middle terrace and later, the lower terrace. The present bed of the Rhine runs through the lower terrace. At its narrowest point Cologne was built.

The earliest settlement in the area of Cologne dates back to 50 B.C. After Caesar had exterminated the Eburones who had occupied the territory on the left bank of the Rhine between the northern edge of the Eifel and the present Krefeld, the Ubii living on the right bank moved into the abandoned region. The *civitas Ubiorum* received through Marcus Vipsanius Agrippa an urban colony, the *oppidum Ubiorum* which covered the area of the later Roman town founded in 12 B.C. It was planned from the very beginning for a great number of inhabitants and as a settlement for the Roman veterans The early gridiron layout was spacious, and was essentially preserved for the whole of the Roman occupation The first settlement was probably a street village extending on both sides of the present Hohestrasse. In A.D. 50 the *oppidum* was elevated to a *colonia* and a Roman town, which was soon surrounded by strong walls. For several centuries it was the seat of the administration of the province of the Lower Rhine, and received the name Colonia Claudia Augusta Agrippinensis. It was shaped like an irregular square, and covered about 240 acres.

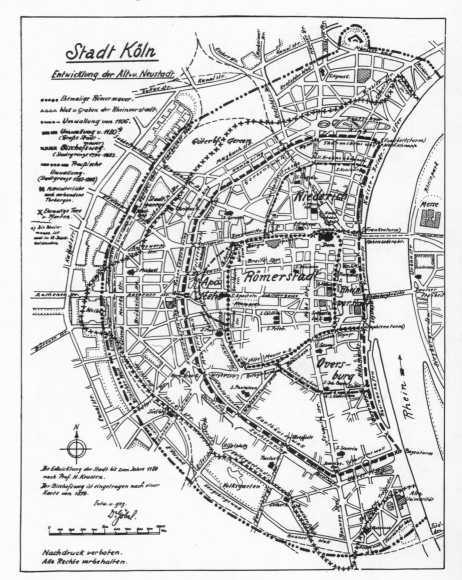

141. Development of Cologne.

The most important street, the present Hohestrasse, followed the course of the main south–north highway. Many of the east–west streets are of Roman origin. It is likely that the population of the Roman town was more numerous than within the same area during the most prosperous period of the Middle Ages. Apart from the solid public buildings, many light, wooden and half-timbered houses covered the greater part of the Roman town. There was little space left for gardens and fields. Farms and a few *villae* were dispersed over the countryside outside the walls.

Around A.D. 450, the town was occupied by the Franks who had settled within and partly outside the walls. They rebuilt the destroyed town and erected on the *Domhügel*, the cathedral hill, a *Königshof*, a royal castle, as the seat of the Ripuarian kings. The once flourishing military, administrative and trading center became a rural settlement. The walls were preserved but the whole western district seems to have been used as *Allmende*, commonly owned pastures, while the fields lay mainly outside the western gates. The population had been greatly reduced. In 881 Cologne was destroyed by the Normans. The changes in the Roman street pattern date back to this event and several fires. Around A.D. 1000 the old agrarian community had come to an end; the *Allmende* was divided up, and a new commercial life began to develop.

In the tenth century, the area between the eastern Roman walls and the Rhine, where a market settlement had grown up along the river bank, was included in the fortifications. This was the first extension of the Roman town (A.D. 980) after the area subject to flooding had been reclaimed. The Roman walls on the north and south sides were extended to the Rhine, not as walls but merely as earthworks with a moat. After a merchants' revolt against the archbishop, the burghers received the right to defend and to fortify their city, a right that had hitherto been the exclusive prerogative of the archbishop as lord of the town. In 1106, the suburbs, settled mainly by craftsmen, were surrounded by fortifications and included in the urban area that now covered 544 acres.

The last and greatest extension of Cologne was begun in 1180. It gave the town its form of a large semicircle with the Rhine as the base, a form that lasted for almost 700 years. The great rise of Cologne in the twelfth century, its commercial and political aspirations and activities, and its determination to defend itself in accordance with the best contemporary methods made the old fortifications obsolete. The city had become Germany's most important commercial center at the crossing of the south–north routes from the Mediterranean to northeast Europe with the west–east overland routes from London, Paris, and the northern countries to eastern Europe and the Danube region favored by the navigation on the Rhine as the main waterway of western Europe. Until late in the Middle Ages, Cologne was the greatest emporium of central European trade and commerce, the more so as at this time the Rhine was navigable for small sea-going vessels. The new fortifications with their strong walls, towers, and gates made Cologne an impregnable fortress. At first, the fortifications consisted only of a deep moat and earthworks. Stone walls were begun in 1200 and completed a few decades later. According to a description of 1526, the walls had 52 towers and 10 gates. The wall along the Rhine with many towers—22 were mentioned in 1470—was a work of the thirteenth century. The circumference of the semicircular walls was about 16,500 feet and along the Rhine 8400 feet.

Compared to the fortified area of 1106, the urban area enclosed by the walls had almost doubled to 991 acres and quadrupled compared to the Roman town. The new fortifications were the limit of the urban area proper, but not of Cologne's territorial sovereignty. The city became independent of the archbishop in 1288. The craftsmen, traders, and artisans, who had grown stronger in long and hard struggles with the patricians, forced the transformation of the aristocratic constitution into a democratic one dominated by the guilds which lasted until the French Revolution. Outside the walls there existed two legal spheres of influence: The *Burgbann,* for which the Council as the supreme

142. Cologne, by Anton Woensam, 1531.

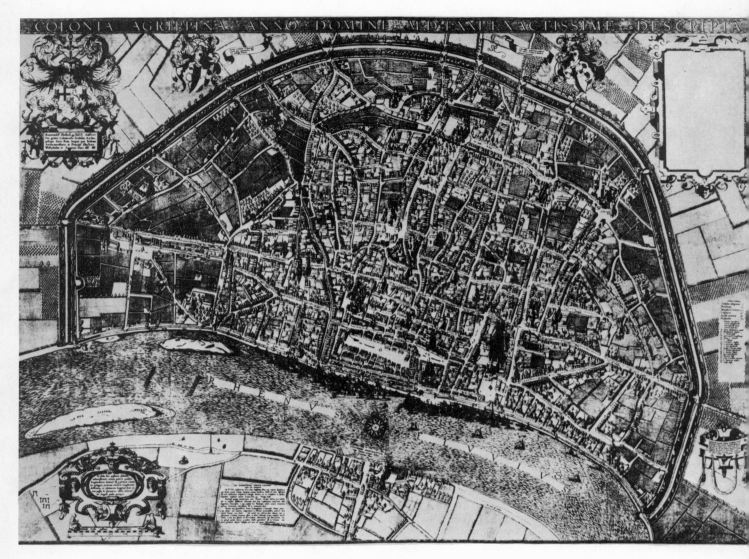

143. Engraving of Cologne in 1571 by Arnold Mercator.

authority of the city laid claim to the *ius territoriale,* and the *Bannmeile,* where it had certain sovereign rights. In the former case, the council administered the land register, the police, and the taxes and supervised the *Bauernbänke,* the associations of peasants who owned land in the outlying districts, as regards cultivation, protection of the fields, compensations, assessment of the land, maintenance of the roads, etc. In the latter case, the main object was to protect the urban trades against the competition of the rural craftsmen.

The structure of Cologne changed little from the end of the Middle Ages to the Napoleonic period. A comparison of Mercator's 1571 plan with a plan of 1815 based on a 1752 design shows that both had essentially the same open spaces in the outer districts between the walls and the old *enceinte* of 1106. In the earlier plan they consisted, apart from a few gardens, almost exclusively of vineyards. In the later plan the vineyards had decreased in favor of the gardens. The use of the open spaces had changed but not their extent.

264

A general view of the medieval city by Anton Woensam of Worms of 1531 shows the left bank of the Rhine with the houses, towers and churches rising behind the walls. The cathedral is unfinished. The whole is a compact mass of contrasting accents, of innumerable small and large units, physically held together by the walls and spiritually by the churches, Ships are loaded and unloaded; goods are stored or carried away on vehicles; vessels are built in a shipyard. It is a perfect picture of prosperity, enterprise, and civic pride.

In 1883, a new *enceinte* was built, for Cologne was one of Prussia's strongest and most important fortresses. This meant the incorporation of a few communities and a moderate extension of the city. On the right bank, Deutz, originally a Roman fort and a bridgehead for Cologne, was included in this process. When the inner fortifications were finally dismantled between 1881 and 1885, the limitations that had restricted the growth of Cologne and pressed its houses together within a relatively small area disappeared. The newly won area was converted into a boulevard, the *Ring*, nearly 4 miles long. Modern fortifications were built about half a mile farther out, and one thousand acres were added to the inner city.

Trier, Rhineland. This city stands where the valley of the Moselle widens between the Saar and the Ruwer. It is the central city for a large hinterland that extends on both sides of the Moselle and includes parts of the Eifel and the Hunsrück. This situation is an important asset because the scarcity of natural resources and the rather peripheral situation to favorable connections with more distant parts of Germany had a detrimental effect on the growth of the city. The regional, commercial, and industrial connections are, therefore, of particular importance.

Trier is one of Germany's oldest cities. The Roman town Augusta Treverorum was fortified by Augustus in about 14 B.C. and became a *colonia* in about A.D. 50. Diocletian made it the capital of Gaul and Constantine the Great selected it as his residence from 306 to 331. It was occupied in 455 by the Franks and became the seat of the Merovingian King Clovis.

The Roman city was laid out on the usual gridiron plan; it had fortified gates of which the Porta Nigra is still standing. It had an amphitheater, a basilica, *thermae,* and other public buildings of considerable quality. The

144. Engraving of Trier from the west by Matthaeus Merian, 1646.

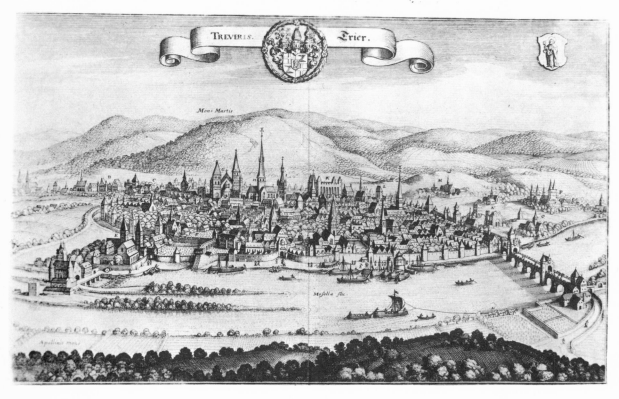

145. Plan of Trier in 1700. The old nucleus is still clearly visible, as is the original Roman layout. Large open spaces have been preserved in the outer districts.

146. Trier in 1746. The city's structure is still basically the same, although a few open spaces have been filled in.

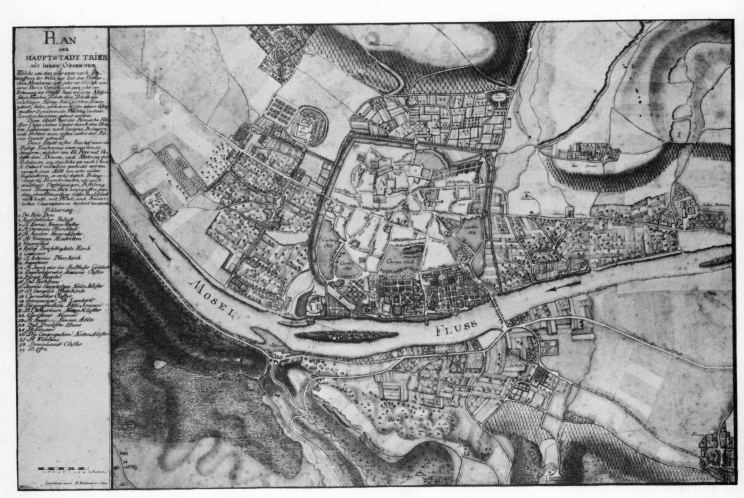

city suffered through repeated attacks by the Franks and most Roman buildings were destroyed.

Throughout the Middle Ages, Trier was a center of monastic learning and of the ecclesiastical domain of which the archbishops were the temporal and spiritual lords. In 1300 it had a population of about 8000.

147. Trier's Porta Nigra.

148. Trier today. The nucleus s surrounded by inorganic growth typical of the amorphous structure of a twentieth-century city.

Frankfurt am Main, Hesse. This city occupies a site beside an easy river crossing connecting North and South Germany. A moderately high ridge stretching from the Odenwald toward the Vogelsberg narrows at this point of the wide alluvial plain of the Main. Here the Romans built a bridge and a *castrum* on the present *Domhügel,* the cathedral hill. The name of *Frankenfurt,* Ford of the Franks, may have come into use around A.D. 500 when the Franks occupied the place, after dislodging the Alemanni. Later a *Pfalz,* a royal castle, was erected, and around it a market settlement developed. Although no definite data exist from which the actual site of the *Pfalz* can be deduced, it is most likely that it stood outside the area that was subject to flooding, that is on the *Römerberg.* The town was first mentioned in A.D. 793 by Einhard, Charlemagne's biographer, who reported that the Emperor spent the winter in the Villa Frankonsfurt. Frankfurt remained one of the residences of the Carolingian kings, *principalis sedes regni orientalis.*

The *Pfalz* with the royal hall, the chapel and other ecclesiastical buildings, and a hostel for accommodating the royal retinue had been walled in by the end of the tenth century. The precincts of the *Pfalz* and the market settlement that had grown up around it were surrounded by a semicircle of steep slopes. On its base line were situated the *Saalhof* and the Fahrgasse. The *Saalhof,* a *Wasserburg,* a fortified castle protected by moats, was probably founded by the German king Conrad III (1093–1152) on the bank of the Main immediately at the ford. North of the *Pfalz,* the Emperor Frederick I (1123–1190) founded a systematically laid-out town that surrounded the *Pfalz* and the settlement in a wide curve. The main east–west streets, the Schnurgasse and Töngesgasse, leading from the Fahrgasse to the *Kornmarkt* in the west, formed the framework that determined the layout. Narrow side streets connected both the main roads. A bridge was built, not over the ford at the *Saalhof,* but upstream as a continuation of

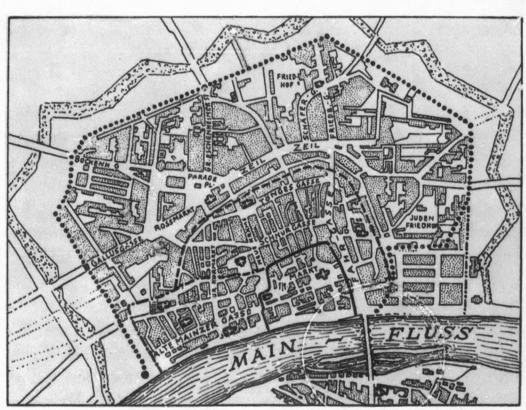

149. Development of Frankfurt.

the Fahrgasse. The town was fortified under the reign of Frederick I, the first emperor to be elected in Frankfurt. Finally, in 1356 Charles IV, in the Golden Bull, made it the city where the emperors were to be elected.

The *Altstadt,* including the old bridge and Alt Sachsenhausen on the other bank of the Main, surrounded the medieval nucleus up to the Grabenstrasse. The second ring, the *Neustadt,* was incorporated in 1333. The extension of the town created conditions that furthered trade and commerce and allowed for the settlement of numerous craftsmen, artisans, and traders. The town received the privilege of holding a second fair, in addition to the earlier one that had been granted at the beginning of the thirteenth century, and soon became one of the most important markets of the Occident. The extension of 1333 incorporated the residential quarters which had grown up along the highways outside the walls. A considerable area was added to the *Altstadt,* which was sufficient for many centuries. Even in the eighteenth century large open spaces were still available.

In 1475 a *Landwehr* with watchtowers was built. This protected Frankfurt's narrower sphere of influence outside the walls. The fortications around the town proper were modernized from 1632 to 1650. The old walls were preserved while the new bastions and ramparts were being built and partly finished during the Thirty Years' War.

Around 1400 Frankfurt had hardly more than 10 thousand inhabitants. Only during the fairs was this number exceeded by the great influx of visitors for whose temporary accommodation the burghers were well-pre-

150. Frankfurt in 1628. Engraving by Matthaeus Merian. The cathedral and the Römer are the two focal points of the densely built up *Altstadt.* The course of the old walls is clearly visible in the wide sweep of the curved street. The *Neustadt,* with numerous open spaces, extends beyond this line to the narrow walls, which have been partly modernized. Some of the house gardens show the typical Renaissance patterns of geometrical figures. Along the Main, continuous rows of houses replace the walls, which are strengthend by towers at the projecting corners. Between the houses and the river, an open space has been preserved for loading, unloading, and other activities connected with the river's traffic.

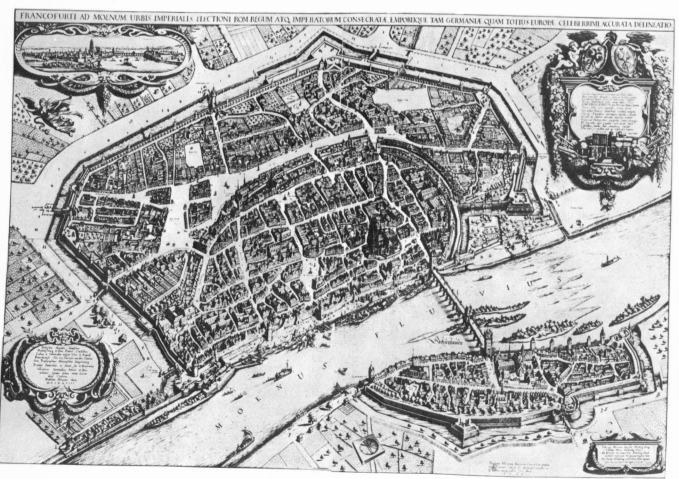

151. The Römer in 1830, by F. W. Delkeskamp. At that time, it was still a fairly homogeneous square, containing the town hall and the Church of St. Nicolas.

pared. The majority of the residents came from the immediate vicinity, from the region of the Wetterau. Immigration from the territories south of the Main was much less, but increased toward the end of the fourteenth century. Since 1554, almost 2 thousand Dutch people have settled in Frankfurt; they were refugees from religious persecutions. They were joined in the seventeenth century by numerous Huguenots expelled from France. These people stimulated trade and commerce and helped to introduce a more refined way of living and domestic culture. Around 1600, the population had increased to 19 thousand inhabitants, including a not inconsiderable number of Jews; by 1700, to 23 thousand; and by 1800, to 40 thousand. Then the pace quickened: In 1848 the population reached 58 thousand; in 1871, over 90 thousand; and in 1939, more than 550 thousand.

Hanau, Hesse. Hanau stands at the confluence of the Main and the Kinzig, which surrounds it in a wide bend. In the Hohenstaufen period (1138–1254), a *Wasserburg* was built on an island in the Kinzig which, together with a settlement grown up under its protection, was called Hagenowe. It received the right to hold a weekly market in 1303, and was fortified with walls, eight towers, and two gates. In 1528, the old fortifications were rebuilt. The walls were raised to 24 feet and strengthened by round, strong towers and a moat. They surrounded the *Altstadt* and the suburb that had grown up on the road to the bridge over the Kinzig. By the end of the sixteenth century, religious refugees from France and the Netherlands were settled on the large area that extended to the south of the *Altstadt* with the palace. The *Neustadt* is a typical Huguenot settlement; it has a central market square where

152. Hanau in 1636.

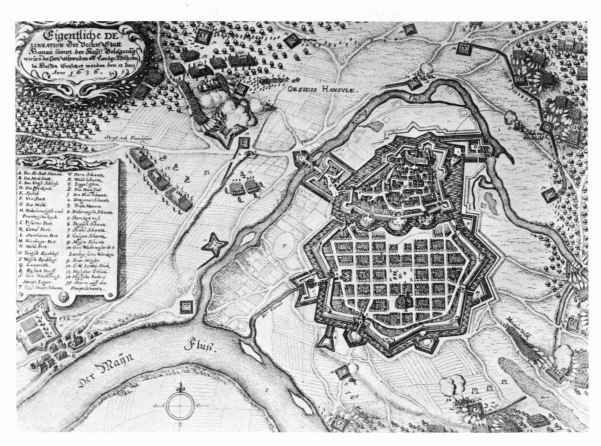

153. Engraving of Hanau by Matthaeus Merian.

the town hall occupies the center of one of its longer sides, the opposite side being opened up by a street with a view to the church. This church is surrounded by another square of the same dimensions. A third square connects the *Neustadt* with the *Altstadt.* This sequence of squares and the uninterrupted axis from the church to the palace show clearly foreign, especially French, influences. The new fortifications included the *Neustadt.* They consisted of five sides of an octagon with five gates, bastions, and a moat, and formed a continuous system with the ramparts of the *Altstadt.* The rigid regularity and the wide streets of the *Neustadt* contrast sharply with the irregular spontaneity of the *Altstadt,* the one dominated by the church and the other by the palace.

154. Hanau in 1790.

Mainz, Palatinate. This town stands at the northern end of the lowland plain of the Upper Rhine almost opposite its confluence with the Main, on a moderate elevation that gently slopes down to the river. The site is naturally protected against floods and enemies, and has been the crossing point of the ancient routes from Italy through the Rhine Valley and from Bohemia through the regions of the Elbe and the Weser to Gaul. When the Romans occupied the banks of the Rhine, they found on this site a Celtic settlement whose name referred to the Celtic deity of Mogo, the God of Light. In 38 B.C., Agrippa established here the *castellum* Mogontiacum and on other side of the Rhine the *castellum* Mattiacorum, the present Kastel. Both were connected by a provisional

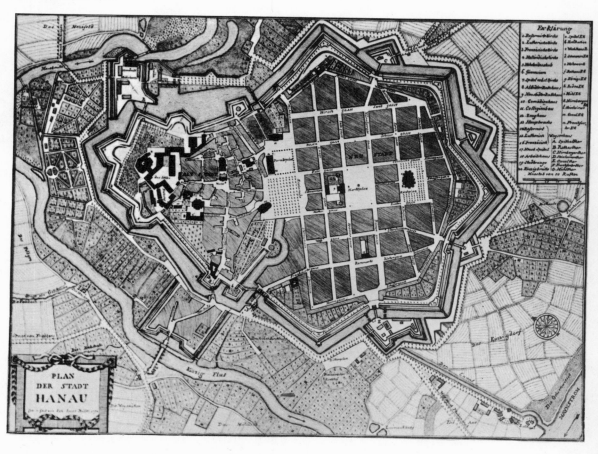

156. *Opposite:* Central section of the great view of Mainz in 1633, by Matthaeus Merian. Note the open spaces near the walls behind the houses and churches.

bridge. Mainz became the military base of the Roman campaigns on the right bank of the Upper Rhine. Around A.D. 400 the Romans left Mainz. It shared the lot of almost all Roman towns: It was inhabited by only a small number of people, its buildings became dilapidated, and its large open spaces were used as fields and pastures.

Gradually, however, life and work revived, and in the Carolingian period Mainz regained something of its former urban character. The Roman streets had disappeared, but in the center of the Roman layout the nucleus of the medieval town with the oldest church began to take shape. Archbishop Willigis' building of the cathedral ushered in the temporal reign of the spiritual rulers over the hitherto royal town. Market and

155. Sectional view of Mainz in 1565, showing its central part, the cathedral, and other churches. The peripheral row of houses forms a wall on the riverside. On the embankment are piers and other installations.

157. Mainz in 1784, showing the complicated girdle of bastions, the citadel, and the detached forts with their outworks.

church were the symbols in whose signs medieval Mainz, the Golden Mainz, attained its greatest glory. Around 1300, ten churches and numerous monasteries were built. But this spiritual, artistic, and economic prosperity was shattered by internal conflicts. The decline had set in by the middle of the fourteenth century. The ruin of the town was sealed when merchants and traders emigrated because they regarded the situation as too precarious and, therefore, without favorable prospects.

The center of the highest point of the town was occupied by the Cathedral. It was surrounded by the burghers' houses, these being interspersed with numerous churches and confined within the *enceinte*. Great civic buildings were lacking, and not even a town hall, as a worthy manifestation of independence and pride of the citizens in their town, was erected. The physical embodiment of this spirit of impotence and lethargy was the Martinsburg. It was built after the destruction of the town in 1462 that concluded the centuries-old feud of the burghers among themselves and with the elector with the loss of all civic liberties and the expulsion of the patricians. The Martinsburg occupied the northern corner of the town, which was easily defensible. It had the unequivocal func-

274

tion of a stronghold from which the territorial lord could keep his subjects obedient and issue his commands. The siting of the Martinsburg was characteristic: The elector followed, although certainly unconsciously, the old practice of other tyrants who preferred to build their fortified castles near the periphery, not in the center where they would have been surrounded by their subjects on all sides and where defense was more complicated. The peripheral site of the Martinsburg is in itself an accusation of the ecclesiastical rulers of Mainz.

Up to the seventeenth century, the fortifications of Mainz consisted of the medieval walls with towers and a moat which had been built partly on Roman foundations. During the Swedish occupation from 1632 to 1635, the fortifications were rebuilt as a starlike girdle with modern bastions. But even this system proved insufficient. In 1704, the elector decided to call in the most famous German military engineer of the time, Maximilian von Welsch, and to charge him with the modernization of the fortifications. The new system was built from 1713 to 1740, and consisted of detached, advanced forts in front of the continuous *enceinte* and its bastions. The invention of these detached forts was an epoch-making achievement that determined the fortification technique up to World War I.

Speyer, Palatinate. Speyer stands on the Rhine on the site of the Celtic *oppidum* Noviomagus. Around 10 B.C., Drusus built a *castrum*. This was later enlarged, but in the middle of the first century A.D., it was destroyed by a flood and thereafter abandoned in favor of a new one in a less exposed position. Both these *castra* stood in the immediate vicinity of the medieval access road to the ferry. In about A.D. 74, when the Roman frontier was advanced beyond the Rhine, this military post was given up and a small town was established. After the Roman retreat, the remaining population concentrated in the peripheral areas of the urban territory, and the town proper remained empty. When the Franks occupied the region, Speyer became the administrative center of the district. Later, a *Pfalz* was built—first mentioned in 1090. It stood in the northern part of the town within the earliest walls. The medieval market extended over the whole length of the main street from the cathedral to the walls—in this case to the gate called Altpörtel. Before this time, there had been a triangular market on the northern side of this street. Near its confluence with an old branch of the Rhine to the north of the *Pfalz*, the Speyerbach served as a harbor. Here, timber and other goods were stored and the fish and timber markets were held.

The first walls were built in the second half of the tenth century. An extension took place in the middle of the eleventh century which included a rectangular area north of the earlier extension. Here a Jewish ghetto was established by the bishop.

The nucleus of the town lies on the terrace that rises above the Rhine, on the site of the later Roman *castrum*. From here, three radial streets lead to the West where they are crossed by two curved streets. Within this part, the Merovingian-Carolingian *Pfalz* with the chapel protected by walls and a moat

158. Development of Speyer: *A.* nucleus of the *Altstadt*, with the bishop's residence and the Cathedral; *B.* the town as it was during the eleventh century; *C.* extension during the thirteenth century; *D.* extension to the northeast during the fourteenth century.

275

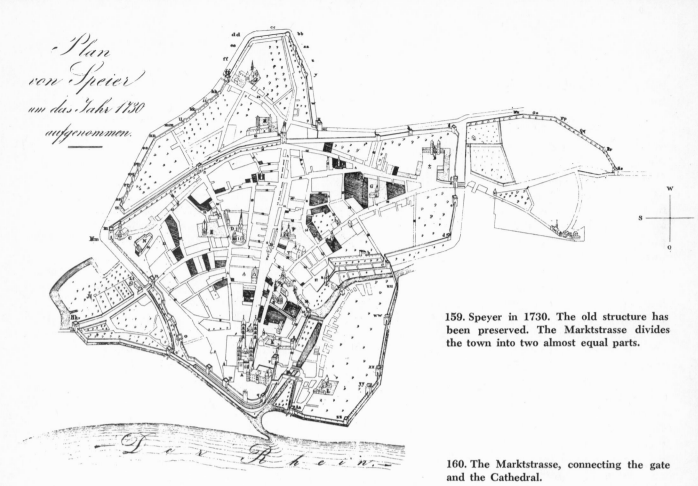

Plan von Speier um das Jahr 1730 aufgenommen.

Der Rhein.

159. Speyer in 1730. The old structure has been preserved. The Marktstrasse divides the town into two almost equal parts.

160. The Marktstrasse, connecting the gate and the Cathedral.

was situated. The wide Marktstrasse, the market street connecting the gate and the cathedral in a straight line, is unique—perhaps the only medieval example of a perspective view deliberately planned and preserved as an expressive prelude and approach to the Cathedral where generations of German kings were buried. Speyer and especially the Cathedral were, as Erasmus of Rotterdam said, ennobled and exalted as the burial place of the kings of Germany. The perspective view toward the Cathedral is in striking contrast to the basic medieval conception of space that was expressed in a coordination of individual elements and, therefore, in a multiplicity of viewpoints. The restriction to and concentration on one viewpoint, the Cathedral, and the introduction of movement as a spatial factor (a perspective view stimulates motion toward the building at the end of the axis) is diametrically opposite to the restful spatial compositions that are predominantly characteristic of medieval towns. In Speyer, however, the way to the altar seems to begin at the gate, as soon as the town is entered.

Mannheim, Baden. In comparison with Speyer and Mainz, Mannheim is a young town. Not until the beginning of the seventeenth century did it develop from an old fishing village, first mentioned in 766, into an urban community. The site on which the twin cities of Mannheim-Ludwigshafen stand today was unfavorable and without natural attractions until technical progress and changing ideas were in a position to transform the environment in accordance with new needs and new possibilities. Mannheim is situated at the edge of a terrace that rises above the flood-plain of the Rhine. The advantage of this situation, especially under primitive technical conditions is obvious: The lower terrain was used as pastures, and the fish in the river added to the food supply; on the higher and drier land, cultivation could be carried on undisturbed by the

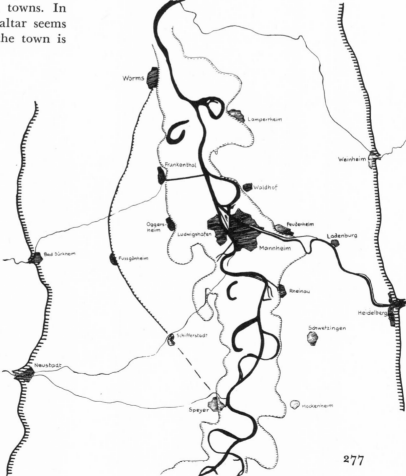

161. The region of Mannheim.

277

danger of floods. The limited rural economy of the village community was therefore more varied and lucrative than in uniformly dry areas. Mannheim's situation between the Rhine and the Neckar, later to become its greatest asset, remained for almost a thousand years a serious disadvantage. Here, at the confluence of the two rivers where the flood plains are widest and the danger of flooding is greatest, Mannheim's earlier inhabitants lived in constant fear that their small urban island might be destroyed by the floods in spite of the river regulations that had been going on for centuries.

The value of this semi-amphibian terrain changed when, in the seventeenth century, the territorial princes made the Rhine their strategic line of defense. The triangle between the Rhine and the Neckar could easily be defended since it was difficult to approach; it was thus the ideal site for a water-fortress. The Elector of the Palatinate first built a toll station and a mint directly on the bank of the Rhine, and in 1606 began constructing the citadel, Friedrichsburg, and building the town of Mannheim. Dutch water engineers and military engineers were called in, and

pamphlets in four languages were sent out extolling the unusual privileges of the new town and the absence of medieval guild-institutions in the hope of attracting liberal-minded burghers. But the combination of the citadel and the peaceful town of the citizens, later to affect the developing trade and commerce, proved to be a dangerous illusion. The citadel soon became the object of hostile reactions. A fortress of this size and strategic importance could not be left behind the advancing enemy armies. It was destroyed in 1622, and afterwards rebuilt. In 1688, the population had increased to 12 thousand inhabitants.

The citizens were forbidden to resettle on the terrain of the leveled fortress town or to restore their destroyed houses. Not until a decade later, after the Peace of Ryswick in 1697, could the rebuilding of the town again be undertaken. Citadel and residential town were enclosed in one powerful ring of fortifications with strong walls and bastions and protected by a moat. The citadel disappeared as did the walls that had separated it from the town. On its site a palace was erected. Mannheim became a residence town and

162. Engraving of Mannheim in 1645 by Matthaeus Merian.

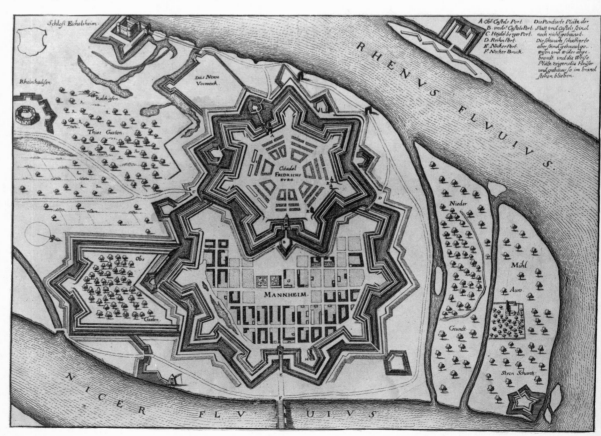

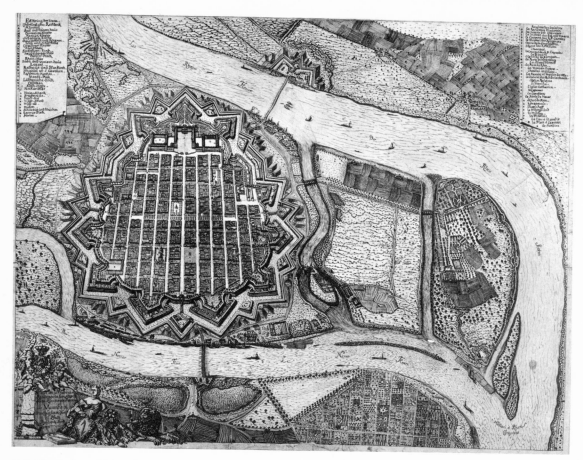

163. Engraving of Mannheim in 1750 by Baertels.

the court the center of cultural activities. Although the excessive cost of rebuilding the town and the extravagant expenses of the court imposed a heavy burden on the population, Mannheim was counted at this time among the most famous, though not the most important, cities of Europe.

This brilliant period was short-lived. It came to a sudden end when the court moved to Munich. The handicrafts, which for two generations had worked almost exclusively for the court, decayed, and the enterprising spirit passed away. But as a fortress, Mannheim remained the "lightning rod on the Rhine." During the revolutionary wars (1794–1820) it attracted bombardments, billetings, requisitions, and foreign troops from many countries who passed through the town from France to Russia. For decades Mannheim just managed to exist. It lived on tourist traffic and insignificant trade with the surrounding territory. It lost its character as a fortress, remaining for several decades a strange mix-

ture of idyllic small town and abandoned residence of faded grandeur whose upper classes had not yet been reduced to dull philistines.

A new era began when the regulation of the Upper Rhine was begun and the numerous river tolls abolished. From 1840 on, the port of Mannheim, the "inland seaport," was developed and steadily enlarged. This, together with railway building and the introduction of steamboats, created the basis for the industrial twin cities of Mannheim-Ludwigshafen.

The checkerboard plan has dominated Mannheim since its foundation in 1606. It was, and has remained, a "planned" town, conceived and built as a whole by the prince whose intention was clearly expressed in the inscription at the Neckar Gate. This proclaims that he had founded the town *"justa spatiorum dimensione nobilem urbem."* When the town was rebuilt after the Thirty Years' War, the old one-storied houses were

279

no longer regarded as adequate. The prince therefore issued an order that new houses with at least two storeys should be built. Four models were worked out by the local authorities, each having two or three stories and a front of three or more windows. Building lots were mostly allocated without payment. Houses were built on speculation by contractors and bought by capitalists as investments.

The third rebuilding proceeded after 1709, the former street system being partly preserved and adapted to the new requirements. The streets leading to the palace divided the area into building blocks about 160 feet wide while the distance between the side streets varied from 240 to 330 feet so that the blocks had a different depth. The building lots were also allotted without payment. Strict observance of the building line and a uniform height of the houses were requested. Symmetry and regimentation were the order of the day. At this time, the continuous block-front was born, and with it the division of the houses into flats.

The development of Mannheim is historically interesting, but why it has become one of the most famous examples of city planning is difficult to understand. The plan is rather unoriginal and is hardly a creative contribution to the art of building cities. Rather, it is the expression of a dull military rigidity where the blocks and the houses are lined up like soldiers on a parade ground. It was a reaction against medieval spontaneity and irregularity, but it lacked the *élan* of the Italian Renaissance and Baroque and the elegance of French compositions. True, the palace was the focal point of the layout and, as such, expressed the spirit of a period in which the prince was the undisputed apex of the social pyramid and identical with the state. But aesthetically it was unsatisfactory. Only seven streets led directly to the palace (in the plan of 1750), impeding its perspective value and producing only partial effects. Karlsruhe is a much more impressive example, more logical, more concentrated, and a more creative solution to the same problems.

Wimpfen, Württemberg-Baden. The Romans built a fort near the confluence of the Kocher and the Jagst with the Neckar—a strategically important situation. Outside the fort, a settlement of traders and craftsmen developed. The fort lost its importance when the frontier was advanced toward the northeast, but the settlement continued to grow and, at the end of the second century A.D., became a Roman *vicus* with walls and a moat. This is the origin of Wimpfen im Tal. It was surpassed by and finally absorbed into Wimpfen am Berg where a *Pfalz* was erected, probably by

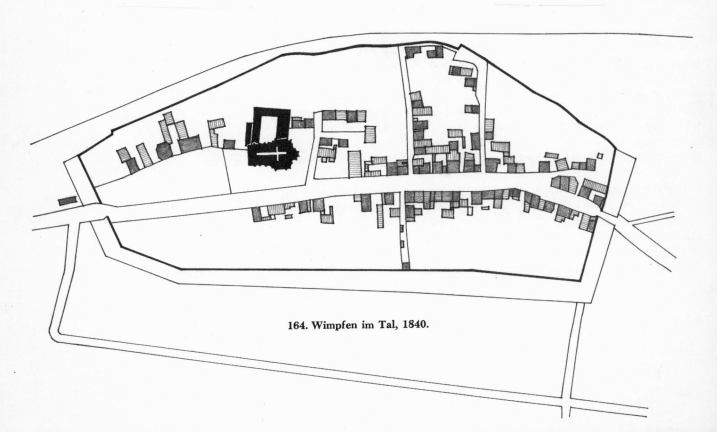

164. Wimpfen im Tal, 1840.

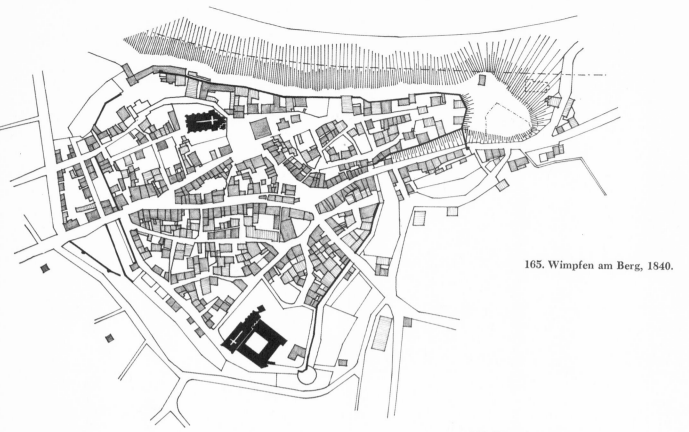

165. Wimpfen am Berg, 1840.

166. Wimpfen and the Neckar.

the Emperor Frederick I. Around this, a town grew up, separated from the *Pfalz* by a moat and protected on two other sides by the steep slopes of the hill. The layout of the hill town is irregular, following in part the contours of the terrain. At its narrowest end, it is focused on the *Pfalz*. The main road leads directly to the gate of the *Pfalz* entrance, passing, not intersecting, the market square.

167. The *Pfalz*, the Imperial Palace, and the silhouette of the town.

168. The Marktstrasse, Wimpfen, leading up to the *Pfalz*.

Weinsberg, Württemberg. This small town stands on a Roman site southeast of Wimpfen. It claims no exceptional artistic values, but is an excellent and representative example of the numerous towns in south Germany that have grown up at the foot of a castle hill. Its unpretentiousness is its beauty. The gently changing relief of the site, the smoothly curved streets, the easy harmony of the houses with their high gables, and the pure conical form of the hill, all these single elements create a union of form and purpose that by virtue of its modesty is more convincing than many more imposing achievements.

169. Castle hill and town of Weinsberg.

170. Dornfeldstrasse.

283

171. Market square in Weinsberg.

Heilbronn, Württemberg. Heilbronn stands on the Neckar, on the site of a Frankish farmhouse, the *villa* Heiligbrunna (deriving its name from a *heiligen Brunnen*, a holy fountain). The nucleus of the town is the *Deutschherrenhof,* successor to the *Pfalz* built by the Franks in the center of the southern part. It is separated from the larger and more regular northern section by a wide street which is characteristic of many towns founded by the Hohenstaufen. This market street did not serve the through traffic; originally it had no continuation over the Neckar. Here, in the northern part, lived the economically important people, the merchants; here was the market square with the town hall famous for its clock by clockmaker Isaäk Haprecht, who had also made the clocks for the cathedral at Strasbourg and the town hall at Ulm. The clock as the agent of precision and rationality symbolized the spirit of the Renaissance and a new rhythm of life— the beginning of a work-centered existence.

172. Plan of Heilbronn: market square with 1. town hall; 2. Kilian's Church; 3. Deutschherrenhof; 4. present-day bridge; 5. site of the medieval bridge.

284

173. Town hall and market square in Heilbronn.

174. Ludwigsburg's market square.

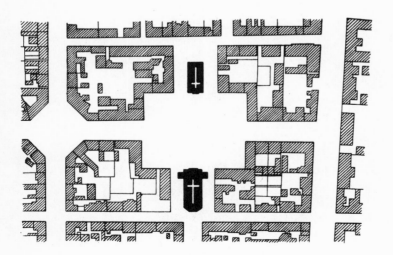

Ludwigsburg, Württemberg. This town stands near the Neckar about 9 miles north of Stuttgart. It was founded in 1709. The town has straight streets and is the adjunct of the palace and the park. The market square is surrounded by uniform low houses with continuous arcades that form a striking contrast with the two churches in the middle of the longer sides of the square. Italian influences are obvious, especially in the way the churches are set in the building line of the house front.

175. Ludwigsburg's market square, after a plan of 1859.

Stuttgart, Württemberg. Stuttgart, on the Neckar, owes its origin and name to a stud farm, *Stuten Garten,* that the early counts of Württemberg established around 950 in the circular widening of the valley of the Nesenbach. It was first mentioned in a record of 1229. In the course of time a manor and a village of vinegrowers developed. They were fortified around 1250, and in about 1270 they became a town. In 1320, Stuttgart became the capital and residence of the counts of Württemberg—their last refuge after a lost war against the Empire. Thereafter, Stuttgart was important as the market center of the fertile Filderebene, but for a long period retained the character of a small vinegrowers' town.

The original town was concentrated on the left bank of the Nesenbach in a trough that joined the Neckar about 2½ miles downhill. This compact nucleus had an oval shape that measured about 1575 by 750 feet. On the northeastern side, which was particularly exposed to attack, it was protected by the fortified castle of the counts. Nearby rose the collegiate church and the houses of the canons. Three main streets led from the market square to the three gates. The town was fortified by walls with gate towers and wall towers and by a keep with strong walls, a moat, and an embankment.

The topographical conditions of Stuttgart were unusually unfavorable. According to information supplied by the mayor, a privy councillor named Meiners remarked in 1793, when the development of the twentieth century could not even faintly be predicted, that "there is hardly any other bigger city in Germany whose situation has been influenced in every respect by chance and is so unfavorable as that of Stuttgart." An unrestricted growth on level terrain as in other cities was impossible. The inner districts were closely pressed together, wedged in between the slopes of a narrow valley and cut off from traffic. The surrounding hills formed a rugged hilly landscape of Keuper Marls and rose about 900 feet above the lowest parts of the town.

Two suburbs were laid out in the fifteenth century. The Esslinger suburb was developed at the southeast on the left bank of the Nesenbach around the Church of St. Leonhard, with a very wide main road as the market street. About 1450, soon after the inhabitants had begun building the walls of the Esslinger suburb, work started on the Upper, or *Turnieracker,* suburb on the opposite side of the town, with the Dominican monastery and its church in the center and a checkerboard ground plan. The Esslinger suburb was approximately equal in size to the original inner town, whereas the Upper suburb roughly corresponded to the combined area of the Esslinger suburb and the inner town; this remained for a long time much more densely built-up and settled.

176. Topography of Stuttgart.

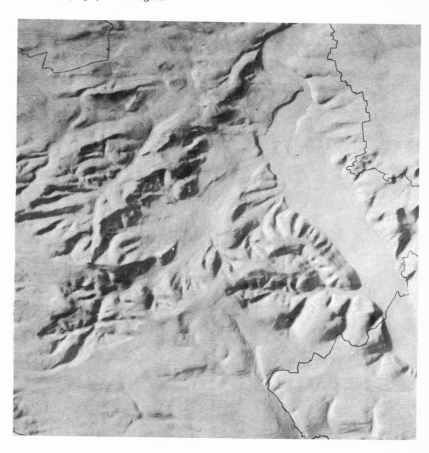

177. The Pleasure Gardens of the princes, 1616. The town of Stuttgart is in the background and the castle at right of center.

178. Engraving of Stuttgart in 1638 by Matthaeus Merian. The old castle and the new Residence are at right, the two suburbs at the top and bottom, and the old medieval nucleus in the center.

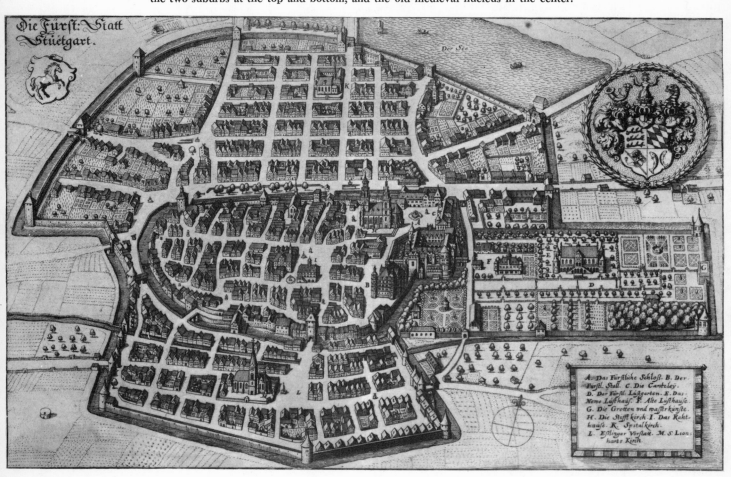

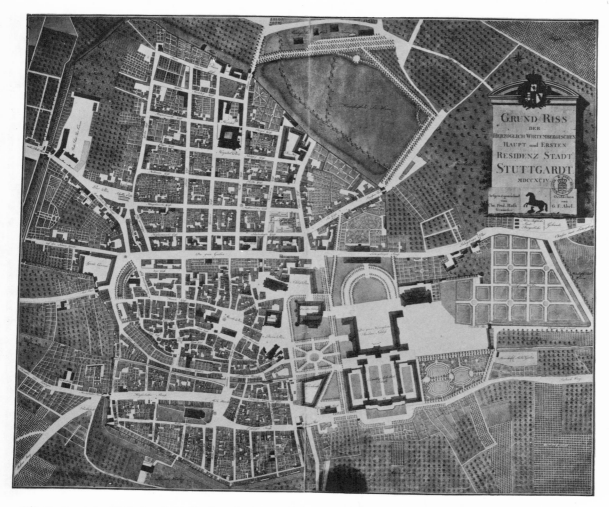

179. Stuttgart in 1794, by C. F. Roth and G. F. Abel. The city still covers almost the same area as in the Middle Ages.

To this medieval nucleus of Stuttgart were added—in the second half of the sixteenth century, as the contribution of the Renaissance—the old castle at the north and the pleasure gardens of the dukes with buildings that adjoined the town. This grouping, which can clearly be seen in Merian's engraving of the year 1638, was preserved until the beginning of the nineteenth century. Only the gardens had to give way in 1746 to the erection of the New Residence.

The absolute rulers of the seventeenth century, who had been elevated to dukes, followed the trend of the times. Like other Baroque princes, they were eager to enhance

their prestige, and they believed that this could best be done by the splendor of their residence city. Their ambitions demanded ostentation, wide spaces, free views, and grand designs—conditions that Stuttgart with its unimpressive narrowness could not satisfy. They decided, therefore, to abandon their old residence and to build the town and palace of Ludwigsburg; there they remained for many decades. But when the grandiose ideas of the Baroque had begun to lose their hold over the minds of the potentates, and when the less ostentatious architectural forms of classicism and the more modest conceptions of city planning gained general accept-

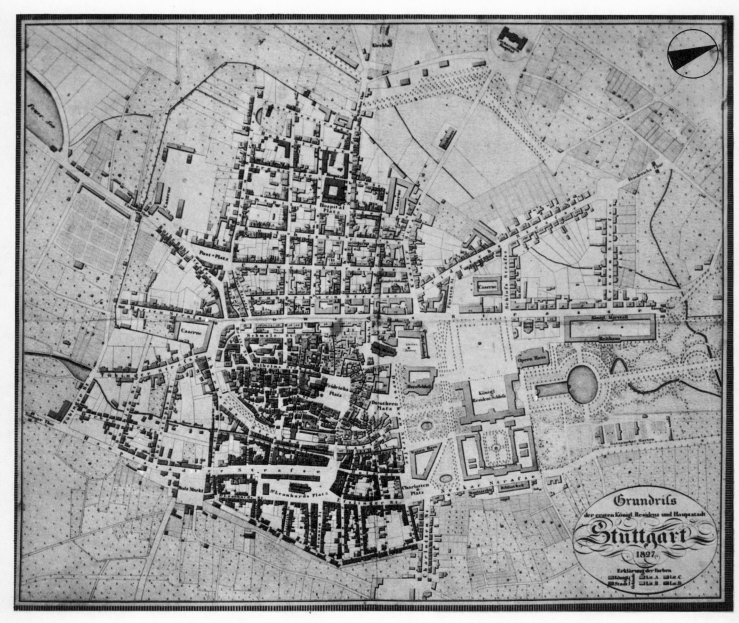

180. Stuttgart in 1827, with the new extensions to the south and northeast. According to the inscription on the medallion, "The First Royal Residence and the Capital."

ance, the rulers of the late eighteenth century discovered again the charm and attraction of the landscape of the Stuttgart valley. They moved their residence back to the old capital, thus initiating the city's modern period.

In 1806 Württemberg became a kingdom and Stuttgart the capital of a now considerably larger country. This political change was expressed in visible form when the old walls and gates were demolished and certain improvements were carried out. A new suburb for the wealthier citizens was built at the northern end of the widened and modernized principal street—now called the Königstrasse by the king's architect, N. Thouret; palace gardens were laid out in "the English style," and were later extended down to the Neckar. In 1817 work on the Tübinger suburb in the south was begun. This new district was soon settled by tradespeople and craftsmen who established their houses and workshops in this more modest part of the growing city.

After the customs union, the Deutsche Zollverein, had come into force in 1834, and especially after the opening of the first railway to Stuttgart and the end of the Franco-German War in 1871, the industrialization of the city proceeded rapidly, and the population increased so fast that the municipal administration had to be content with purely utilitarian and expedient remedies like the provision of land for new houses, site development, and street building. The quality of these new enterprises was subordinated to misunderstood demands of economic prosperity. Considerations of progressive city planning and architecture were brushed aside in consonance with the *laissez-faire* spirit of the times. New nondescript

districts, homogeneous only in their ugliness and without any architectural and cultural attractions, began to cover the slopes of the surrounding hills. At the turn of the century the first reactions against this travesty of city planning made themselves felt. The upward trend culminated in the Weissenhof Siedlung. This exhibition, built by the Deutsche Werkbund in 1927 and intended for permanent use, was a major event in the history of modern architecture. It was a break-through of great consequence, and established new ideas and new architectural forms with a programmatic clarity and an irrefutable insistence.

Esslingen, Württemberg. This town stands on the Neckar a short distance downstream from an Alemannic village. In the sixth century it grew together from several hamlets. Downstream was situated the hermitage of St.

181. Esslingen, after an eighteenth-century plan by R. Schmidt. I. A. Nucleus, founded by the Hohenstaufen; B. Market squares, with 2. Church of Our Lady and 3. St. Paul's Church and the Dominican monastery. II. Suburb in the late thirteenth century. III. Suburb in the first half of the fourteenth century. IV. District incorporated during the fourteenth century.

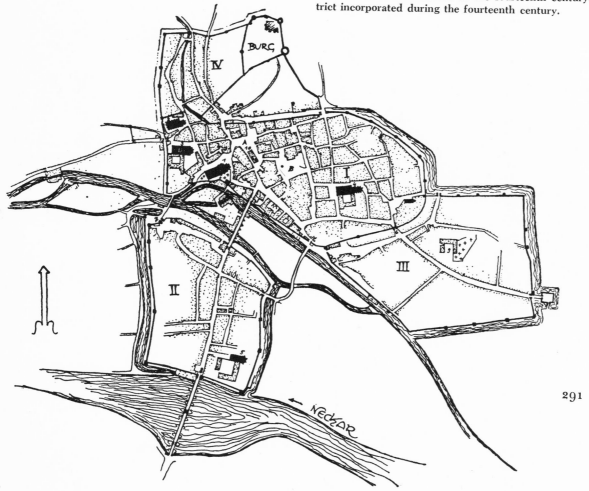

182. Esslingen's old town hall, the *Steuerhaus*, originally a half-timbered building between two streets in the eastern part of the *Altstadt*. This arrangement is rather common in many towns in southern Germany.

Vitalis where an annual fair was held. In the course of time this fair became a weekly market and the hermitage turned into a small settlement The place was first mentioned as a town in 1219. It lay near the ford, where the important road from Ulm to Speyer crossed the Neckar. The early town covered an oval area. Its western part was the quarter where the oldest churches and monasteries and also the market square were located. The unusual situation of the latter at the periphery of the *Altstadt* can be explained by the fact that it had developed from the original annual fair held at the church of the hermitage. The *Altstadt* adjoined the *Burg,* which protected it in the north. A bridge crossing an island in the Neckar connected the *Altstadt* with the oldest suburb, which was walled in at the end of the fourteenth century. The eastern suburb was the last to be included in the fortifications.

183. Schwäbisch Gmünd. The clock tower (*right*) and choir of the Heiligkreuzmünster and a fountain.

Schwäbisch Gmünd, Württemberg. This town in the Rems valley developed, like Esslingen, from a market village near a hermitage. Situated in the middle of the Hohenstaufen possessions, it became the administrative center of their royal domain. It was mentioned in the twelfth century as a fortified town, and after the downfall of the dynasty was made an Imperial City. The *Altstadt* covered an oval area with the market square as the focal point.

The present market square, a long, wide street dividing the *Altstadt* into two unequal parts, belongs to the later systematic extension. Here were situated the church and monasteries, the hospital, the houses of the patricians and merchants, and the warehouse. As in many cases suburbs where peasants and craftsmen settled grew up outside the walls along the roads. These suburbs were not fortified until the fifteenth century.

293

Böblingen, Württemberg. Böblingen, south of Stuttgart, originated from a *Burg* and a village. The *Burg,* built after 1100, was afterwards the seat of the bailiff of the counts of Württemberg. The exact date when it became a town is unknown. It remained a small town; for many centuries it had a population of hardly more than a thousand inhabitants. Böblingen was built on a hill, and the main street with the market square was laid out on the ridge of the hill. It did not follow the contours of the terrain. The side streets enter the main axis at right angles and connect it with the peripheral streets that run parallel to the walls. These streets and walls are adapted to the contour lines. This layout was unusual. The side streets were extremely steep and traffic was therefore difficult. The system was forced upon the natural configuration. This was in striking contrast to the nearby Herrenberg where the conditions of the terrain were quite similar: The main streets followed the contour lines all around the hill.

The town of Böblingen was laid out on the western slopes of the Schlossberg below the *Burg* and above the village which was, at the time of the foundation of the town, almost a thousand years old. In all proba-

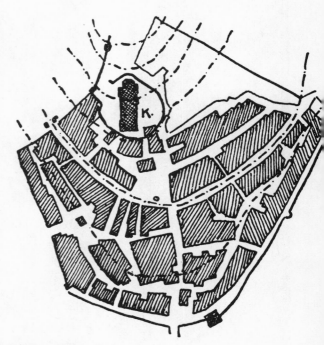

184. Herrenberg, showing street pattern and the contours of the terrain.

185. Böblingen in 1643. Engraving by Matthaeus Merian.

186. General view of Herrenberg.

187. General view of Böblingen.

bility, the fortifications of the town had been completed by the middle of the thirteenth century. The town was separated from the old village by wide approaches. The walls were protected in the south by the lakes, in the north by marshy meadows, and in the east by the *Burg*.

The houses within the walls huddled together. The reddish sandstone walls contrasted sharply with the rich green of the fields and meadows, and above the walls the roofs of the houses glimmered in many colors. Here and there, the golden yellow or silver grey of a newly-covered straw or shingle roof stood out from the mass of the houses. Later the bright red of the tiled roofs added a more conspicuous note to these subdued and discreet colors. The town council had ordered this change because the danger of fires was great and the building density had increased.

The walls were reinforced in the sixteenth century, but Böblingen remained a small town like others in Württemberg. There were possibly too many within a small area, and perhaps their spheres of influence overlapped, a situation somewhat similar to the numerous small places in the Aargau in Switzerland.

188. The *Altstadt* of Tübingen.

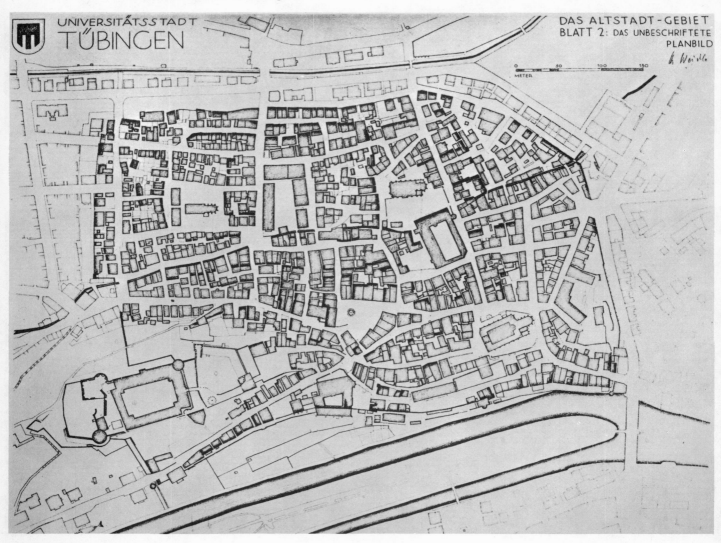

UNIVERSITÄTSSTADT
TÜBINGEN

DAS ALTSTADT-GEBIET
BLATT 2: DAS UNBESCHRIFTETE
PLANBILD

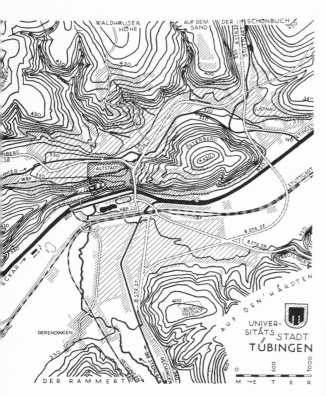

189. Plan of Tübingen and environs.

190. Tübingen's market square.

Tübingen, Württemberg. The *Altstadt* of Tübingen stands on a ridge between the valleys of the Neckar and the Ammer Rivers. It extends beyond the valley floor of the Ammer but does not quite reach the bottom of the Neckar valley. The shape of the *Altstadt* was determined by the walls erected in the 1580's, and enclosed an area 1800 by 1600 feet. In general, their course followed the configuration of the terrain. The *Altstadt* consisted of a level northern part, the "lower town" with an agricultural character, and the "upper town."

Its entire layout was, and still is, unsystematic. The main street wound its way with numerous bends from the bridge over the Neckar in a wide curve to the old Roman road along the Ammer. Tübingen has gradually grown together from these two halves, the *Ammerstadt* and the *Neckarstadt,* but how this has happened is unknown. It has developed without any apparent system, although this does not mean that its growth was without organic adaptation to the difficult terrain or without regard to the coalescence of the two nuclei.

192. The former Inn zur Traube during the second half of the eighteenth century. Gouache by J. C. Hoffmann.

193. Hirschgasse in 1835.

191. *Opposite:* View of Tübingen from the Neckar.

Karlsruhe, Baden. This city was founded under the name of Carolsruhe in 1715 by the Margrave Karl Wilhelm who resided in the nearby Durlach. Originally the palace was to be built only as a retreat in the Hardtwald. But soon the town was added and the palace was made the layout's focal point.

194. Region of Karlsruhe.

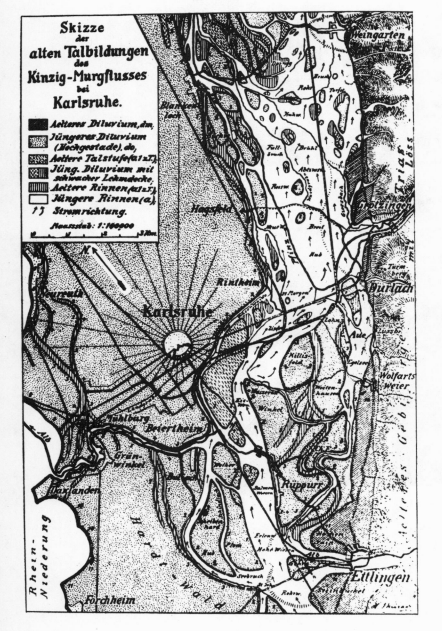

The palace stood in a circular clearing of the forest. In the exact center, the palace tower was erected. Thirty-two avenues radiated from this point; twenty-three of these led through the forest, and the other nine in the south to the town. The park extended behind the palace in the northern sector. A main road running east to west to the south of the palace had to be connected with the radial system; thus, the road was retained and the radial avenues crossed it at different angles. A circular avenue surrounded the central part, and on the main avenues toward the east, a round and a rectangular square, special accents of the landscape architecture of the gardens, followed each other. The main north-south axis led from the central tract of the palace, through a forecourt with a garden parterre, to a square adjoining the east-west road, and farther on to a church closing the perspective view in the south.

Symbolically, aesthetically, socially, and economically, the town was the appendix of the palace. It was only under the reign of the grandson of the founder of Karlsruhe that the whole plan was completed: Timber houses were replaced by stone buildings, and the palace was reconditioned and rebuilt by the Würzburg architect Balthasar Neumann who acted as consultant. French and Italian influences, theoretical designs for ideal towns, geometrical landscape architecture, and the new techniques of military engineers—all manifold and new conceptions—played a part in shaping the rigid geometrical layout of park and town. It was a veritable pattern-book of ideas and prototypes ranging from the radial pattern of Palma Nova, the starlike design of new fortresses, and the diagonal streets of the Piazza del Popolo to the gardens of Versailles. It was a drawing-board plan, rigid, logical, and somewhat disingenuous, but it was a perfect symbol of the time, of the *l'état c'est moi* spirit of the absolute rulers.

The subsequent period is of particular interest. Baroque and Classicism, the old and the new, clashed when the next stage of development began to take shape. In the

195. Old engraving of Karlsruhe, showing the view from the palace.

196. Pedetti's design for the market square, 1788.

last decade of the eighteenth century, the old Protestant church with the tomb of the founder of Karlsruhe was still standing on the main axis. The old town hall was still in use. Behind the church was the cemetery, and to the west and east houses with gardens adjoining the church. An extension of the town was under way. It was decided to lay out a market square on the site of the church and the cemetery and to build a new town hall and a new church. Renowned architects, mostly French and Italian, were consulted. Pedetti's designs met with approval but were not selected, for they represented the established ideas of the Baroque: an

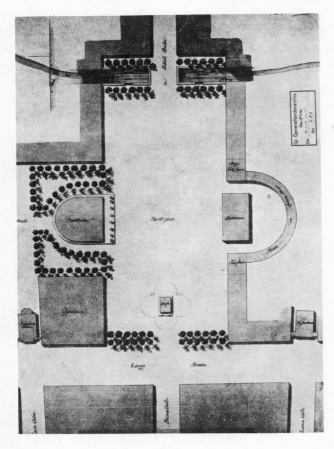

197. Weinbrenner's design for the market square.

198. *Opposite:* Weinbrenner's second design for the market square.

oval place flanked by continuous block fronts of stately buildings and culminating in two monumental groupings, the town hall at the right and, at the left, the church with towers, cupolas, and arcades as propylaea to the avenue leading to the palace.

At the same time an unknown young architect presented his plans. He was Friedrich Weinbrenner. His design suggested a rectangular square with the town hall and church in the middle of the long sides. Verdure was introduced as an integral part of the architectural composition. This classicistic and contemporary design was not approved, although encouraged by the margrave who paid the architect 200 louis d'or as a reward. It was not accepted because the city architect, as so many officials before and after him, regarded it as too modern, as the work of one of those disturbing innovators

who wanted to imitate the French inventors of fashionable styles who create every moment new fashions but produce more often than not very shapeless things. When young Weinbrenner seems to rely in some respects on his own principles which deviate from good proportions and genuine beauty, one is inclined to believe that these aberrations could have a relation to the Tower of Babel and the confusion of tongues.

However, Weinbrenner was not discouraged. In 1797 he submitted a new design that served, essentially unchanged, as the basis of the building of the Via triumphalis that continued for the next thirty years. This design showed the market square in its present form. It consisted of two space units of different dimensions. The rectangular *forum*, the open-air festival hall, was flanked by the church and town hall; here, "the timber and cattle market may be held." The town hall formed one block with the stalls for the butchers and the magazines, whereas the church was built

199. *Opposite:* Weinbrenner's design for the Lange Strasse.

302

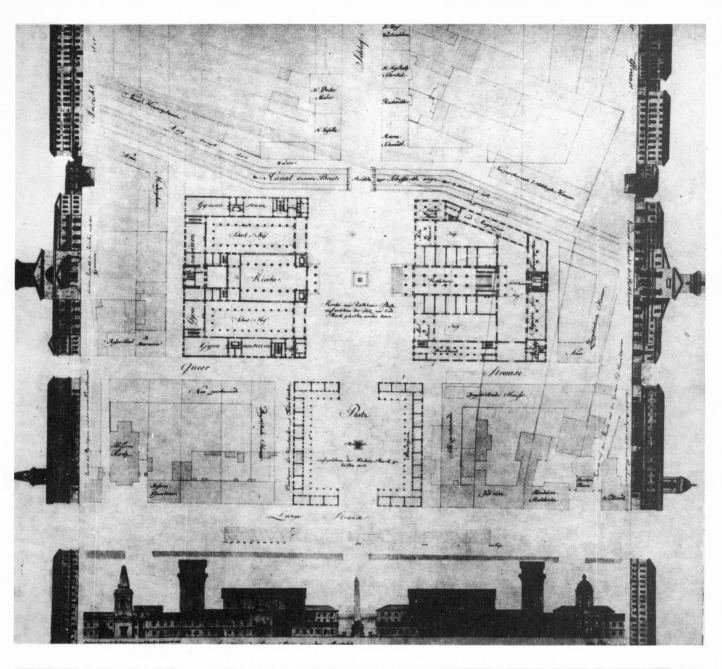

200. The palace, with the tower, and the beginning of the central axis.

between two *gymnasia* connected by open arcades leading to two courts. The other square was surrounded by two U-shaped market halls enclosing an open space for the weekly market. In its center a monument to the founder of Karlsruhe was to be erected. The whole was a strange combination of ceremonial seriousness and everyday functionalism. After the city architect's death, Weinbrenner succeeded him, but his ideas were still so unconventional that a school of architecture had to be established where a sufficient number of collaborators could be educated.

201. Arcaded houses on the Circle.

202. A *rond point*.

Rastatt, Baden. Rastatt is situated on both sides of the Murg on the western edge of the terrace that follows the eastern bank of the river. On its site stood originally a village for fishermen and raftsmen. This developed into a modestly prosperous community under the margraves of Baden. It was destroyed by the French in 1689, together with the old palaces. The *Neue Schloss* in Baden, which had been built in the fifteenth century on a hill above the town, had to be ruled out as a residence for two reasons: The terrain would not have permitted rebuilding on a large and more opulent scale, and, above all, the taste and style of the period demanded a level site for a princely residence having avenues and gardens. The contrast of the castle on a hill and the burghers' town at its foot, this symbolic expression of subordination and authority,

had given way to a side-by-side arrangement on the same horizontal level. However, the social contrasts persisted, and arranging the palace and town on the same level was merely another way of increasing social antagonism and of hardening the frontier that separated ruler and ruled.

Rastatt fulfilled all the conditions for the erection of a new residence. It is not clear whether the new palace was to be a hunting lodge or a permanent residence. In any case, it was intended, *ad venationem commoditatem,* for the hunting comfort of the margrave. This was a modest building consisting of three small sections and a rectangular forecourt. It dominated the old settlement of Rastatt and formed the background for the gardens at the other side. This plan was the typical product of the Viennese school. It was designed

203. Rastatt and environs. Engraving by E. Voysard, 1798.

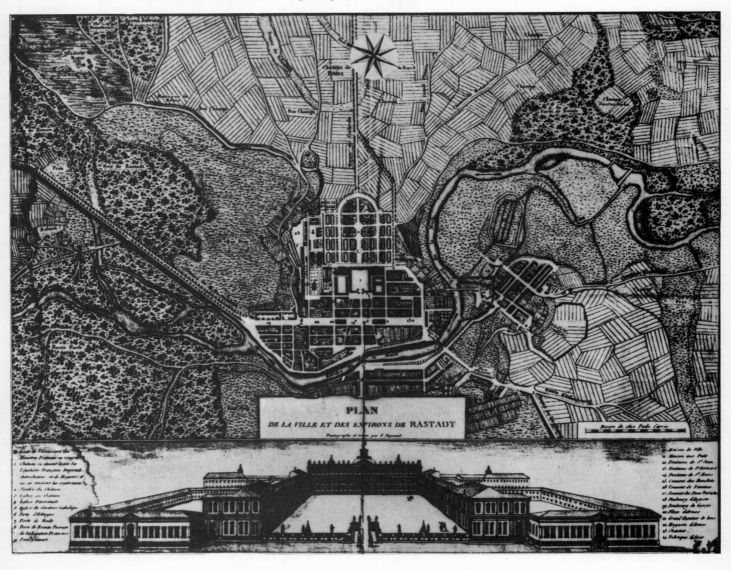

by Matthia da Rossi, a member of an Austrian family of architects. The oval outside staircase with the portico, the accentuation of the central part by collossal pilasters, the open-roof pavilions, and the crowning gallery of statues were all requisites of the Italian architects who had come to Austria in the seventeenth century.

Before this first palace was finished it was decided to make Rastatt a fortified residence. With a carelessness and reckless determination of which only an absolute ruler of the Baroque was capable, the hunting lodge as far as it had been completed was pulled down; in Rossi's words, "As it was regarded as totally useless, it was decided to demolish it completely." This happened in 1700. The fortifications enclosed a more or less circular area with the new palace in the northeastern section near the periphery. The plan for the palace and the town copied Versailles and the wedgelike layout of the Piazza del Popolo. The palace stood on a slight elevation and was the apex of the new street system, which penetrated the original checkerboard layout of the streets. The architect's intention was to continue the main axis beyond the fortifications as a straight avenue leading directly to Ettlingen.

Freudenstadt, Württemberg. This city in the Black Forest is the only "Ideal City" that has been built in Germany. It is unique in as much as it was square in outline—a contrast with the circular or polygonal plans of all other schemes. It had two counterparts, one designed by Albrecht Dürer early in the sixteenth century, and another one described by Johann Valentin Andreae in his *Christianopolis* (1619). While no connection existed between the plans for Freudenstadt and Christianopolis (the later date of Andreae's scheme rules this out), it is not impossible that Dürer's design had a certain influence upon the conception and the layout of the town in the Black Forest. What is important is that these theoretical speculations were in the air occupying the minds of the architects and their patrons and that Germany had gone her

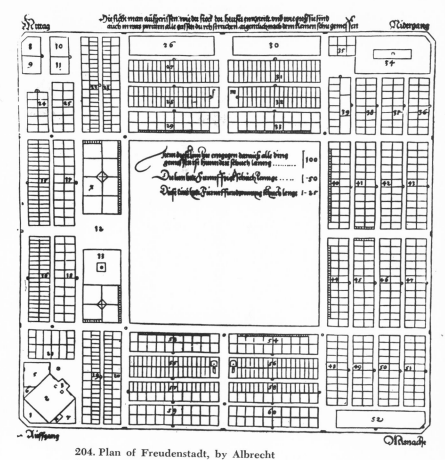

204. Plan of Freudenstadt, by Albrecht Dürer.

205. Schickhardt's first plan, 1596.

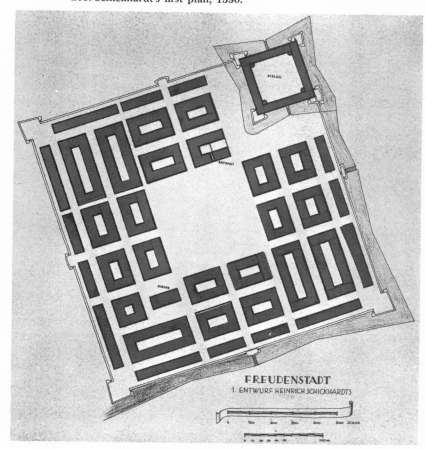

FREUDENSTADT
1. ENTWURF HEINRICH SCHICKHARDTS

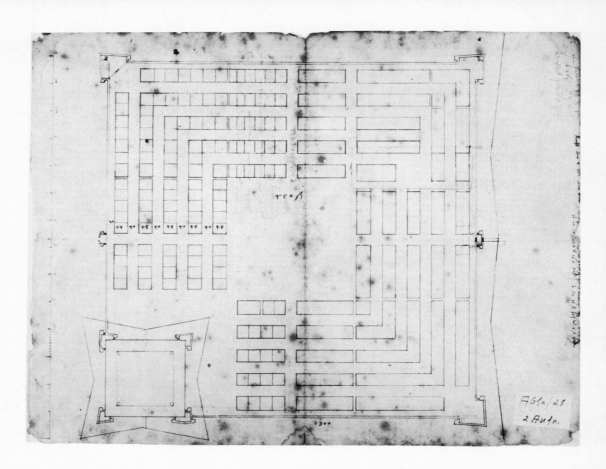

206. *Above:* Schickhardt's second plan. *Below:* Another version of Schickhardt's plan.

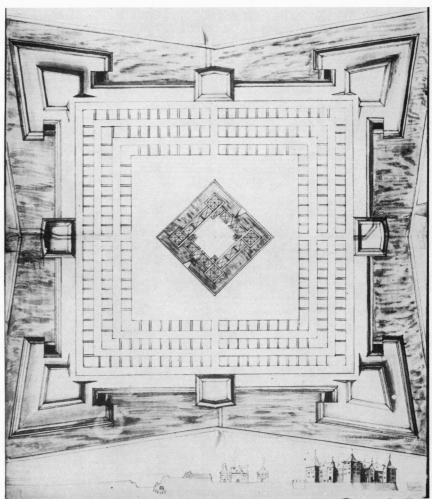

own way by inventing a square "Ideal City." Andreae, born in 1586, was a German scholar-humanist and reformer, a sort of Robert Owen. His city was small and compact and perfectly symmetrical.

Its shape is a square whose side is seven hundred feet, well fortified with four towers and a wall. . . . Of buildings there are two rows, or if you count the seat of government and the storehouses, four; there is only one public street, and only one market place, but this is one of a very high order. . . . All buildings are in three stories. . . . About four hundred citizens live here. . . . Outside the walls is a moat.

Freudenstadt was designed by the architect Heinrich Schickhardt (1558-1634). It was founded in 1599 by Frederick, Duke of Württemberg, not for religious refugees as most modern authors assume, but as a mining town. In 1596 the Duke issued an order to all his bailiffs to announce on two consecutive Sundays from all pulpits that rich rewards would be paid to all who could indicate one or several places where mineral resources were to be found. An intensive search began, and foreign experts and miners were brought in from the Tyrol, the Erzgebirge, and Hungary. In 1597, a *Bergfreiheit* (mining rights) were issued and publicized; this was followed in the next year by a *Bergordnung* (mining regulations). At this time the plan to build a town for the miners, not in the narrow valley of the Forbach, but higher up on the hills had doubtlessly reached a more advanced stage. Schickhardt's first plan of about 1596 still has several medieval features: The castle stands on the highest point in one corner of the town; the church is surrounded by houses, and stands in a narrow space off the main square; the building blocks have inner courtyards; and there is no continuous block front. Like another compromise solution in which there were five rows of houses instead of closed building blocks, this design was rejected. And a further plan, although corrected by the Duke himself, was also abandoned as "not modern." Finally, patron and architect visited Italy and Paris to study the newest achievements of city building and fortress de-

sign. The trip resulted in another plan. The castle was in the center, the church in the corner, and there were three rows of houses consisting of narrow dwellings. The final design, used at the beginning of the building of the town, shows even more than preceding ones the influence of theoretical speculations about ideal fortresses: The castle in the center is surrounded by moats and placed diagonally, and its four corner-towers face the firing line through four streets leading to the gates. For political and economic reasons the castle was never built and the rows of houses were not finished.

The last plan shows the extent to which the original Schickhardt plan had been carried out. In 1632, a fire burned the residential quarters that consisted of half-timbered houses. Only the church survived. Schickhardt made an entry in his *Investarium,* a record of all he had built in forty years, of which the following is a rather free translation:

Freudenstadt. I inspected the site for the first time when it was still covered by forest, and had the soil investigated to a great depth in many places. But since not much good was found I humbly submitted that it would not be advisable to build a town on this site. However, I designed a plan for a large town and a castle because it was the gracious wish of His Highness, Frederick, the high-born prince and Duke of Württemberg. I arranged for every house to have a courtyard and a small garden, and the castle was to be situated at the corner of the town. But His Highness decided that every house should directly adjoin a street and wanted the castle to be placed in the center of the market square. Therefore, in accordance with the orders of His Highness for a square town, I made a new plan, each side of which was 1418 feet in length and the market square 780 feet. The castle was to be erected in the middle of the market square. On this layout the town was built, but the castle has not yet been executed.

Thus, in the presence of His Highness and in the name of God, I, Heinrich Schickhardt, marked out on March 22, 1599, a part of the said town with a number of houses and streets. During the next few years much was built. Out of the privy purse of His Highness alone more than 100,000 guilders were spent on building, excluding the burghers' houses of which there were 287 by January 8, 1612.

On May 24, 1632, a terrible fire broke out at Freudenstadt. Three persons perished and 144 houses were burnt down. The fire started in the inn which had been the first building to be erected in the Town.

Except for a few larger three-storied buildings, most of the houses turned their gables to the street and had only two stories. Refugees did not settle in Freudenstadt until 1602, but from then on, more and more began to arrive. Around 1604, an extension of the town was planned and partly carried through: instead of three, five rows of houses were projected but not completed. In relation to the original plan, Freudenstadt remained a torso and never played a role as a fortress. The mines, the actual *raison d'être* of the town, proved to be insufficiently productive.

Freudenstadt is particularly interesting because it was a belated example of a colonial town of the Middle Ages and, at the same time, an Ideal Town of the Renaissance. It stood at the dividing line between these two periods, continuing the pragmatic principles of deliberately planned colonial towns and foreshadowing the theoretical drawing-board schemes of the following centuries.

207. Freudenstadt before its destruction in World War II, showing the dissolution of the periphery and the silhouette of the town after the walls were dismantled at the end of the nineteenth century. Note the chaos in the unnaturally large market square.

Rottweil, Württemberg. Rottweil stands on a tongue of land sloping from west to east about 90 feet toward the valley, the *Au, Owe*, around which the Neckar flows in a wide horseshoe-shaped bend. The oldest traceable settlement within the urban area was a neolithic village (about 2000 B.C.). In A.D. 73-74, the Romans founded on this site a *castrum* with wall and moat, of which the *Arae Flaviae* (The Flavian Altars) were the center. These altars were shrines in memory of the incorporation of the region on the right bank of the Rhine and visible symbols of the successful arrival at a final destination. Two *castra* have been identified: a large, early one with a north and south wall apparently serving as a transit camp, and, within it, a smaller and later one for an auxiliary force of a thousand equestrians. In the last quarter of the fourth century, the place was conquered by the Alemanni, who established themselves on the right bank of the Rhine near a dispersed Roman civic settlement. On the site of the Roman camps a *Königshof* with a large domain was erected. It covered a considerable area, almost twice as large as the Roman *castra*, and was fortified with a wall and a moat.

A short distance to the northwest, the town of Rottweil was founded around 1140. It took its name from the village, which henceforth was called *Altstadt*. It followed the scheme of the Zähringen layout that had in its turn been adopted from the *Königshof*. The new town was a planned market place for craftsmen and traders. It was a square area of about 37 acres, characterized mainly by the following:

1. A checkerboard street pattern,
2. Regular building blocks of about 40 by 24 feet,
3. Houses turning eaves to the streets and forming a continuous block front,
4. A market street, instead of a separate market square, using the main south-north axis,
5. Only the main streets originally having houses on either side.

The town was protected on three sides by steep slopes, and on the fourth by the rising

208. Reconstruction of an earlier (1564) plan of Rottweil.

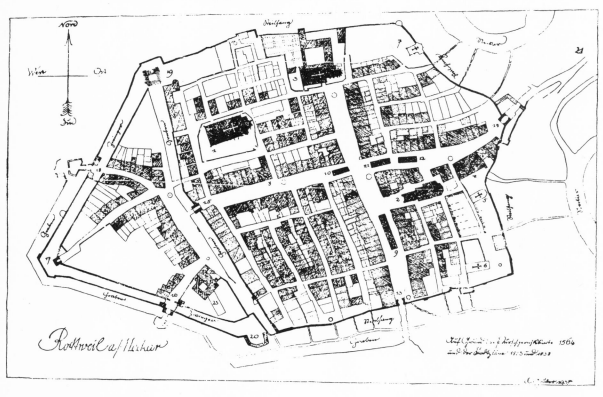

209. Aerial view from the southwest of the old nucleus of Rottweil.

210. The oldest houses of Rottweil. They form a compact group of great variety in volume, articulation, style, structure, and accents, all pressed together within a narrow space.

211. Houses at the old cattle market, forming a continuous block front and turning their eaves to the street. Modern alterations on the ground floors have destroyed the unity and scale that were enhanced by the oriels and by the loft windows, equipped with hoisting beams for lifting and lowering goods.

plateau on whose spur Rottweil was built. The first fortifications consisted of three gates that defended both the roads leading into town and of the unprotected earthen wall and palisades on the west side. The Hohenstaufens' further fortifications provided a solid stone wall 24 feet high with three strong gates and a drawbridge over the 52-foot-wide moat. After 1410, a simple wooden passage with circular and semicircular towers along the inner side of the walls was added, and at the end of the sixteenth century redoubts and bastions were built. Suburbs developed outside each gate.

In 1441, the town's taxable citizens numbered 1330; in 1563, 1133; and in 1666, 625. By 1794 it had a population of 3 thousand, and in 1852, of 5200. These considerable fluctuations resulted from wars and partially from economic decline.

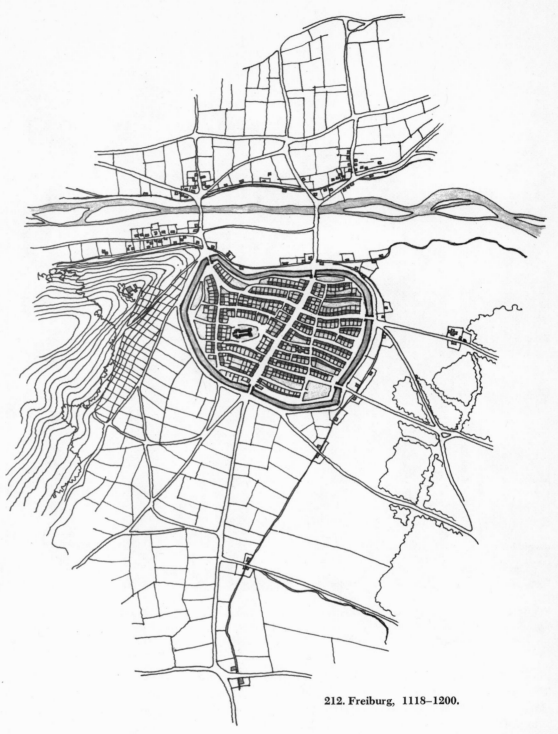

212. Freiburg, 1118–1200.

Freiburg im Breisgau, Baden. This was the first of the numerous towns founded by the dukes of Zähringen. Building began in 1120. The main highways were not originally included in the urban area; this was done only later. Freiburg, situated at the foot of the castle of the Zähringen Dynasty, which had been erected in 1090, was a market town having far-reaching privileges. As the seat of craftsmen, traders, and merchants, its economic function was to exchange the agricultural products of the surrounding countryside

213. Freiburg, 1638–1677.

for the goods produced in and imported to the town. Silver mining, and in the later Middle Ages cutting and polishing precious stones, were the specialized industries carried on in the neighborhood or in the town.

The plan shows the typical characteristics of all Zähringen foundations (as described for Rottweil): a walled-in oval; two main streets and parallel side streets, all crossing each other at right angles; and the parish church, the present cathedral, standing in the cemetery (later the market square) off the main

315

214. The market square and *Kaufhaus*, the warehouse, of Freiburg, as seen from the cathedral tower.

axis. The houses stood with their eaves to the street and were mostly built of stone. This regular layout was originally adapted to the terrain and the existing roads. The oval covered an area of about 1600 by 2000 feet, and the building blocks had a depth of 450 feet —that is, for one or two dwellings with courtyards. The land remained in the possession of the dukes, to whom the burghers paid an annual rent. Consequently, buildings and land were legally separated. The walls had five gate-towers.

The town grew rapidly in the thirteenth century. The suburbs were incorporated, each with its own municipal law, walls, and parish church—in the north, the *Neuburg* with an area as large as the *Altstadt* but with fewer inhabitants; in the west, the Prediger and Lehener suburb on territory of the Reich with numerous monasteries and gardens; in the south, the Schnecken suburb with the *Gerberau* and *Fischerau* for craftsmen and settlements for tanners, dyers, and all activities based on water power.

Around 1300, the town had reached its greatest extension—9500 inhabitants, about the same number as Frankfurt am Main. After a retrogression the town recovered, and in about 1500 a second period of prosperity followed with a considerable building activity. In 1677, the northern and western suburbs, which had suffered greatly during the Thirty Years' War, were completely demolished. This led to a grave and unhealthy overpopulation of the *Altstadt* because the town area, which had grown to about 193 acres in the thirteenth century, had been reduced to approximately 91 acres. Around 1700, Vauban modernized and rebuilt the fortifications. But in 1744, they were dismantled, and Freiburg became an open city. Since 1825, Freiburg has expanded—at first slowly, but after the middle of the nineteenth century more rapidly beyond the *Altstadt,* at first along the arterial roads, but later filling the intermediary zones.

Radolfzell, Baden. This town stands on a tongue of land projecting into the Untersee, the southwestern inlet of Lake Constance. The site has been settled since the Mesolithic Age (8000 B.C.) by hunters and fishermen who had been attracted by the fertility of the soil and the abundance of fish in the lake. They erected their reed and brushwood huts on the sunny moraine of the bay. In A.D. 826, the Bishop Radolf built a *Zelle* (a small group of cells for monks) and a chapel that he called Cella Ratoldi, Radolfszell. Around this nucleus developed the town.

It received the right to hold a market in 1100 and became a town in 1267. At this time it was fortified with walls, five gates, and seven towers. All gates had drawbridges and the towers were 40 feet high. The irregular rectangle of the town was protected in the south by the lake, and in the west and north by the marshes. If necessary, the terrain could be inundated, as it was in 1673 when the French threatened the town.

The church occupied the center, together with the town hall which also served as a warehouse. The streets were tortuous and winding with innumerable corners, nooks, and broadenings. The building density was very high, so much so that very narrow houses were squeezed into the *Bauwich,* the space between the sides of two neighboring buildings that was left free because of the danger of fire. The narrowest house had a width of only 5 feet. Near the *See-* or *Dammtor,* stood the *Salzhof* and the *Gredhaus,* storehouses with jetties that could be adapted to the changing level of the lake. The craftsmen, traders, and merchants were part-time farmers and wine-growers, a combination that lasted until the end of the last century.

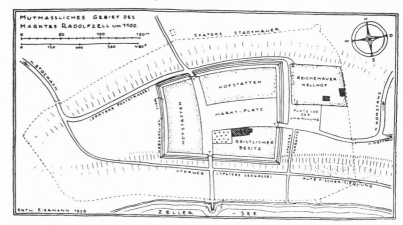

215. Probable site of Radolfzell's market place in 1100.

216. Plan of Radolfzell about 1800.

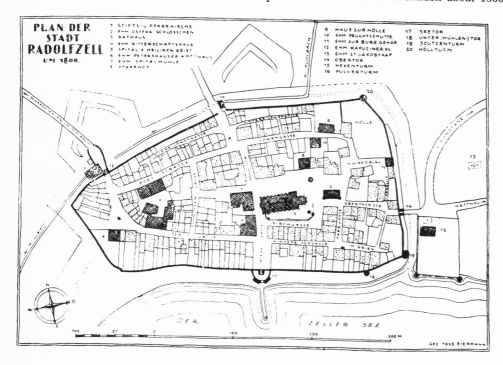

317

Radolfzell was involved in the hazards of history. Wars and contributions, sieges and billetings, good and bad vintages alternated with each other. It had the typical fate of a small town; it survived just because "it was there," and as such it is representative of innumerable other towns that were the unwilling tools of historical ups and downs.

217. Radolfzell's old town hall, demolished in 1847. Note the small windows for storerooms on the ground floor. This simple, functional, solid building was located at the market square.

218. Aerial view of Radolfzell. The compact *Altstadt* is near the lake shore (*right*), and the snow-covered mountains of Switzerland are in the background.

318

Konstanz, Baden. On the south bank of Lake Constance between the Untersee and the main lake, Konstanz stands on the site of the Roman *castrum* Constantia. Since bishops were allowed to reside only in towns, not in open places, it may be assumed that Konstanz had already a certain importance when it became the center of the Alemannic bishopric right of the Rhine. This may have happened between 629 and 639. The existence of the Roman *castrum* may also have influenced this decision, for the bishop established his residence within its still standing walls. A few houses had been built outside the walls along the old Roman road, and annual fairs had been held in connection with religious holidays. After the time of Charlemagne, its importance grew. It became necessary to extend the small area occupied by the residence of the bishop; thus a second wall shaped like an irregular square was built, increasing the precincts of the *Bischofsburg* by two-thirds. To the south, separated from the residence, lay the bishop's *Fronhof* (the socage farm): this was where his large estates were administrated, and where the farm buildings and houses for the villeins stood.

The precincts of the *Bischofsburg* formed the nucleus of the medieval town to which were added in the tenth century two new settlements: in the north, the Niederburg, and in the south, the market settlement. The latter was also shaped like an irregular square, and had a gridiron pattern of streets. It was inhabited by craftsmen and merchants who enjoyed their own administration and special privileges granted by the king. It was first mentioned in 1152. At the beginning of the twelfth century it had an earthen wall and a ditch. Stone walls were built, but not until the second half of the twelfth century. The market settlement was considerably extended in the first half of the thirteenth century. The new walls were finished around 1250. While they were being built, a long, broad street was laid out as a market, leading at its eastern end to the lake and the landing place. The rapid growth of the town was a sign of its economic progress. Very considerable extensions of the fortifications completed by the middle of the fifteenth century testify to the continuous prosperity that was based, above all, on the wholesale trade in linen and silk with Italy, Switzerland, and the fairs of the Champagne. The decline set in when Konstanz accepted the Reformation and was therefore outlawed.

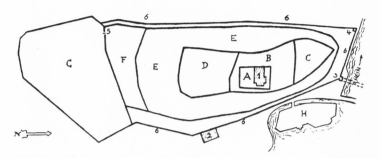

219. Development of Konstanz: *A.* Roman camp with cathedral; *B.* bishop's residence, eighth and ninth centuries; *C.* Niederburg, tenth century; *D.* market settlement, tenth century; *E.* extension of the town during the middle of the thirteenth century; *F.* Niedergassen district, second half of the thirteenth century; *G.* Stadelhofen district, beginning of the fourteenth century; *H.* Dominican monastery on the island.

220. The Schnetztor, the main gate at the exit to Switzerland.

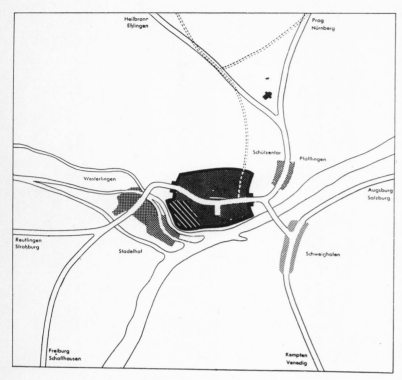

221. Ulm, 1140–1316.

Ulm, Württemberg. Ulm, on the Danube, owes its development to its situation on a river crossing that has been used since prehistoric times. Its situation has made it the nodal point in a net of important routes. The Carolingian *Pfalz,* Hulma, first mentioned in 854, consisted of the *palatium,* the residence of the king, and the estates with the seat of the administrator, the *villicus,* the mill, and the workshops. Above all, it served military purposes: the protection of the river crossing and the administration of the conquered

222. Ulm, 1336–1800.

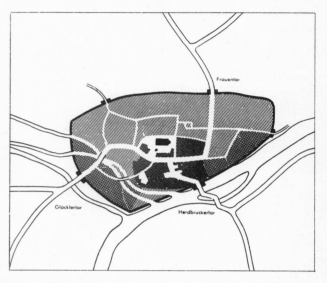

223. Ulm at the time of the Thirty Years' War. Engraving by Matthaeus Merian.

224. *Masters of the Black Dyers' Guild*, the Schwarzfärberzunft, painted about 1600. The Black Dyers' was one of the influential group of guilds that determined the economic life of the medieval town.

Alemannic territory. Its favorable location furthered the surrounding settlement, which soon received a market and a mint. This early Ulm was almost completely destroyed in 1134. Around 1140, the inhabitants began rebuilding the town and the fortifications, and in the following decades, the market settlement developed into a more and more important traffic and trading center. Around 1165 Ulm became a town, a *civitas*. At the beginning of the fourteenth century it was enlarged fourfold, and the fortifications were again rebuilt. This extension was sufficient until the nineteenth century. In intervening periods, modifications were carried out, among them a reinforcement in 1527 after the ideas of Albrecht Dürer and a far-reaching modernization in 1616–1623 by Furttenbach and the Dutch military engineer, Johann van Valckenburg. There were few public squares at this time; but this was changed in the following decades by systematic demolitions. The fish market, the *Judenhof,* the western part of the cathedral square, the haymarket, and others were laid out. The streets were narrow and the building blocks small and densely built-up, but the whole was admirably suited for the pedestrian traffic of the seventeenth century.

225. Part of the cathedral square in Ulm, 1677.

226. *Opposite:* View from the Wallfischgasse toward the cathedral. This picture gives a good idea of the relation of the houses to the cathedral. They are huddled together around its foot, their small scale enhancing its vertical uplift, which is majestically expressed not only in its height but in the long windows and the multiplicity of perpendicular lines in the tracery.

322

227. Southwestern view of Ulm's town hall and the cathedral, with a succession of interrelated squares. Note the effective contrast between the scale of the burghers' houses and the cathedral.

229. The old Tanners' Quarter on the Blau.

228. *Opposite:* Silhouette of Ulm in which a polyphony of contrasting accents culminates in the cathedral spire.

325

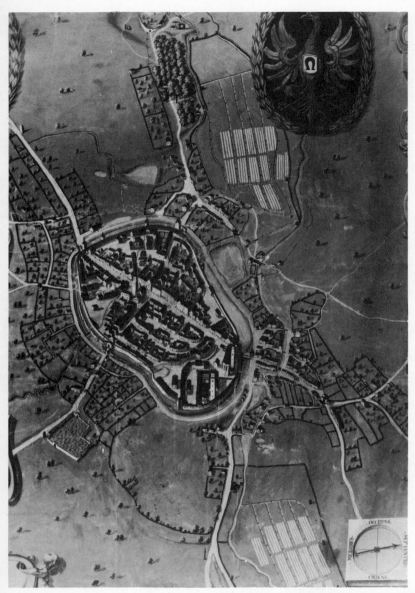

Isny, Württemberg. A small town at the crossing of several roads, Isny developed from a dispersed settlement that gradually grew into a market and church village. By the second half of the thirteenth century it had become a town, with walls, a moat, and four gates. The town hall stood in the center of the market square where the main streets that ran to the gates of the oval area crossed. The building density was moderate, and many open spaces remained within the building blocks and near the walls.

230. Old plan of Isny.

231. Aerial view of Isny. The inner town is now surrounded by a ring of verdure. The original street pattern has been preserved, although modified in detail.

326

232. Lindauer Street, with Blaserturm, at the market square. The street narrows to a passage with arcades on one side and the broken building line on the other. This variation enlivens what would otherwise be an uninteresting composition.

233. Plan of Wangen.

Wangen, Württemberg.　Wangen grew together from a number of dispersed farms. By the second half of the twelfth century it had a market, and soon after 1200 it became a town. When the town had been systematically planned, the original village was absorbed into it. The broad market street running north–south formed its main axis.

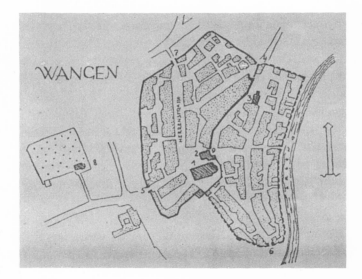

Kempten, Bavaria. Kempten consisted originally of two separate units: the town and the monastery at its northern periphery. After 1560 the *Neustadt* developed around the latter and has remained without walls. It did not receive town status until 1712. However, it continued to be a separate community under the monastery until 1818 when it was finally united with the town of the burghers. The reason for this long coordination of two individual urban settlements situated in close proximity lies in their origin. Both had grown up from two independent estates whose internal structural coherence persisted because both were organically sound and strong.

Kempten derived its origin from several sources: a pre-Christian Celtic *oppidum;* the Roman Cambodunum of the third and fourth centuries A.D., whose civic settlement was situated on the right bank of the Iller; and the citadel on the left bank. The town stood at the crossing of Roman roads to Vemania (Isny) and Brigantium (Bregenz), to Augusta Vindelicum (Augsburg), Celiomonte (Kellmünz), Abodiacum (Epfach), and further to Salzburg. The Alemanni established a settlement in the fifth century. A Benedictine monastery and a *Königshof* were founded in the eighth century.

The origins of the later Kempten were the Alemannic village at the river crossing, the monastery, the *Königshof,* and, after its destruction, the settlement of traders and craftsmen. By the end of the twelfth century it had become a market center, and was surrounded by earthen walls and a ditch. The abbot was the lord of the estate and the market. The antagonism between the settlement around the monastery and the town was perpetuated by certain privileges that Rudolph of Habsburg had granted to the town in 1289, and not to the clerical settlement over which he had no jurisdiction.

Centuries later, during the Thirty Years' War, the old discord between the temporal and the clerical parts and parties again erupted: The town burghers joined the Reformation in 1527, and in 1633 their community was besieged and destroyed by the imperial troops and a third of the population was killed. One year later, when the Swedes had arrived, the Catholic parish church and the monastery were demolished. Thus, the difference in origin that had sown the seeds of discord between antagonistic and rival attitudes toward life outlasted generation after generation untill, after centuries of a lack of cooperation, it flared up in violence and murder.

235. Plan of Kempten: 1. *Burg;* 2. square; 3. town hall; 4. monastery; 5. site of the Roman civic settlement, Cambodunum; 6. *Neustadt.*

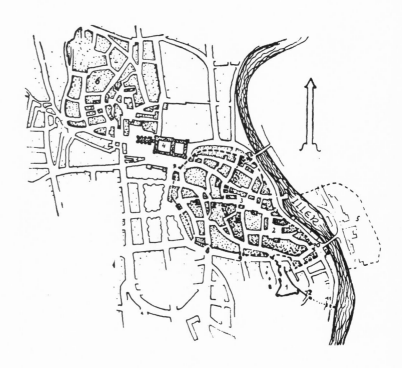

234. *Opposite:* Wangen's Ravensburg Gate and the houses closely adjoining it. The fountain, to one side of the street and against the background of the buildings, is excellently placed.

236. Town hall and market square of Kempten, the Free Imperial City. The hall was built in 1474 and rebuilt in 1562–1568. The fountain is one of the most charming and graceful metalworks of the German Renaissance. The coats of arms are those of the town and eight patrician families.

Augsburg, Bavaria. Augsburg, on the Lech, stands at the northern end of a high terrace. The old town descended the eastern and northern slopes of this terrace. Its highest southern point lies over 150 feet above the lowest in the north. Traces of the first settlement, dating back to the eighteenth century B.C., reveal that agriculturists of the early Bronze Age had already begun to cultivate the fertile loess soils of the Augsburg Field. We also know that at the end of the last pre-Christian millennium, a trade route led from the northern Lech valley to Italy, and that in the eighth and seventh centuries B.C., peasants had settled on the loess area of the western margin of the high terrace.

It is possible that the Veneto-Illyrians were the first to occupy the area of the *Altstadt*, but no exact data are available from which the original name of these people can be deduced with certainty. The Celts, who arrived after 450 B.C., were the first tribes whose name is known. They came from the middle Rhine, eastern Gaul, and Switzerland, and mixed in the course of time with the indigenous people of the late Hallstatt period. From this mixture developed the subtribe of the Vindelici; their center lay in the great ring-wall at Manching near Ingolstadt, to the east of the confluence of the Lech and the Danube.

Like the other Celtic tribes, the Celts of the Augsburg region were possibly prepared for the attack by the Romans; they had protected their farms with square earthworks—one of these *Schanzen* has been found southeast of Augsburg. But the Vindelici had to quit the field before the superior Roman armies. Their fortified refuge at Manching was destroyed, and the Celts east of the Inn surrendered voluntarily to Roman rule. The conquerors established a base camp for a legion on the Wertach near its confluence with the Lech, about 18 miles south of the Danube, still far enough from the frontier to serve as an assembly point for larger formations of their army and for advances further north. This first camp was abandoned in A.D. 15 and a new town was founded around

A.D. 30, this time immediately between the Wertach and the Lech at their confluence.

Like all Roman towns, Augsburg was systematically laid out. It covered an area of 2250 by 1800 feet on the high terrace. Its north–south axis, the *via principalis,* was the *Via Claudia Augusta* leading south to the Alps, while the east–west axis connected it with Kempten, Bregenz, and Switzerland. The town was surrounded by a wooden wall and was probably the seat of the *procurator Caesaris Augusti in Vindalicis et Raetis et in valle Poenina.* It received the name of *Augusta Vindelicia* in the middle of the second century. It was a *municipium,* a self-governing town with *cives* (fully qualified citizens) of Italian or Celto-Roman descent, and *incolae* (natives with the right of residence). In the fifth century, this town was destroyed by the Alemanni and deserted; only an impoverished portion of the former population stayed on within the walls, which slowly fell into ruin.

The Alemanni were defeated by the Franks in 742, and the town, together with the whole region, fell under the administration of a Frankish count who seems to have established his *Königshof* in Augsburg. Bishop Sintpert laid the foundations for the cathedral, which was consecrated in 807. This was probably the origin of the *Bischofsburg* and the *Fronhof,* the names of which have been preserved up to the present day and which, together with the cultivated land within the Roman walls, provided the means for maintaining the bishop's household. When the Hungarians threatened the town at the end of the tenth century, the bishop built a provisional earth wall with stockades and later, a stone wall consisting of rough sandstone and limestone mixed with Roman tiles and dressed stones. After the defeat of the Hungarians, a brisk building activity set in. The destroyed buildings were restored and the churches repaired. At this time the town consisted of the walled-in *Bischofsburg* with the cathedral and the residence, the monastic precincts with the school and a small hospital, a chapel, the *Fronhof,* and the houses for the bishop's officials and his bondsmen and the dwellings of

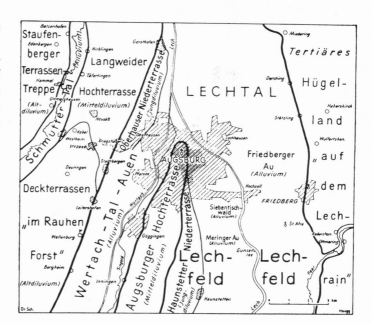

237. Augsburg region.

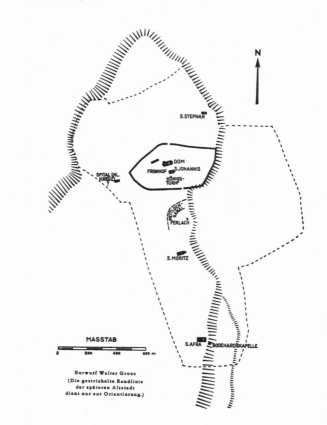

238. Augsburg about 1050.

331

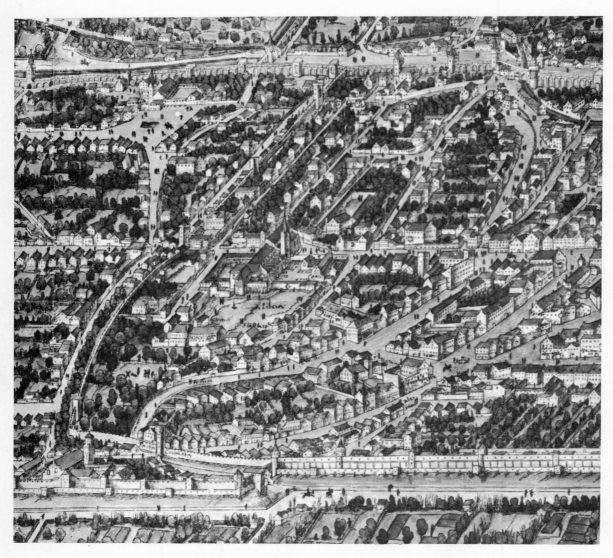

239. Section of a plan of Augsburg, by Hans Weiditz, 1521. It shows the center of the *Altstadt*, the distinct organic street pattern, and the still moderate building density. House gardens and open spaces for the public are interspersed among the buildings.

the peasants and craftsmen. There were, in addition, the Church of St. Afra, with houses for the clergy, and a third religious community of nuns north of the *Bischofsburg* at the Church of St. Stephen. Life was frugal and had a rustic simplicity. Augsburg had survived the storms of the Great Migrations and the Hungarian invasions. It was the seat of a bishop. It had retained the name of *civitas*. It was no longer a town in the Roman sense, and not yet a real medieval town. But the

seeds had been sown from which a new urban community could grow.

The nucleus of this Augsburg, the *Bischofsburg,* covered an oval area of about 37 acres. It was inhabited by the *canonici,* the *cives,* and the unfree peasants, servants and craftsmen who were possibly part-time farmers. The merchants who enjoyed particular privileges granted by the King remained outside these groups. The first small traders' settlement seems to have consisted of a row of houses and a market square on the old *Via Claudia* outside the walls, and to have been surrounded by wooden palisades. Augsburg was one of the main footholds of the Hohenstaufen, and under their protection it experienced an era of economic and cultural prosperity that found its expression in new buildings, a growing population, and an extension of the town. The guilds gained in importance, although they were not formed until the second half of the fourteenth century. New powers came to the fore; the burghers challenged the bishop's authority; and their community was what eventually determined the development of the town.

At the end of the Interregnum, around 1273, Augsburg stretched as a long settlement over a considerable part of the terrace. It had already begun to occupy the slopes at the eastern margin. It now covered an area of about 205 acres, 4800 feet long and 1800 feet wide. The town of the bishop and that of the burghers had grown together—the terrain did not allow for physical separation as it did, for instance, in Salzburg or Würzburg. New suburbs had developed in the northern and eastern parts of the old Roman town. Churches, monasteries, and other public buildings were dispersed over the whole urban area. The fortifications had been greatly strengthened with 115 towers and numerous gates. The *Stadtbuch*, the collection of municipal records, has preserved interesting details of the work and life of the craftsmen and artisans. It records that some of the *antwaerke*, the *Handwerke*, the trades such as tanners had settled at the four Lech-canals that traversed the town.

There were many trades, each living in its own quarter or street: cobblers; makers of fine linen, woolen felt, and woolen cloth; tailors; cutlers; goldsmiths; furriers; and many others. At the top of the social pyramid stood the merchants and the drapers. The structure of the *Altstadt* was changing: the building plots that had been leased were repeatedly subdivided or sold without paying any rent to the bishop. Thus, short lanes with narrow and deep houses were cut through the building blocks, a procedure that had a most unsatisfactory effect upon the sanitary conditions and which made hygienic counter-measures necessary, although these were, owing to the times, still rather rudimentary and primitive.

By the end of the Middle Ages, Augsburg had consolidated its civic liberties and its position as an Imperial City. It could not yet compete with the economic importance of Regensburg or Nürnberg or with the artistic achievements of Cologne, Lübeck, and Ulm; but the groundwork had been laid from which for several decades the fabulous ascent of the "Golden Augsburg" could begin spreading its ideal and material goods to faraway countries. Its splendor was proverbial. A well-known epigram of the time ran:

Hätt' ich Venedigs Macht,
Augsburger Pracht,
Nürnberger Witz,
Strassburger Geschütz,
und Ulmer Geld
so wär' ich der Reichste in der Welt.[1]

1. If I had the power of Venice, the splendor of Augsburg, the cleverness of Nürnberg, the cannons of Strassburg, and the money of Ulm, I would be the wealthiest man in the world.

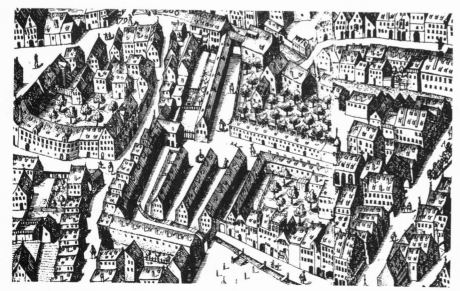

240. The Fuggerei, as shown in a contemporary drawing.

241. The Fuggerei, as rebuilt after destruction in World War II.

Around 1480, the two great business houses of the Fugger and the Welser began to dominate Augsburg's trade and commerce. The Fuggers had interests in Hungary and in the mines of the Alps, and were the bankers for princes and emperors. The Welsers had similar investments and connections. But these merchant princes also patronized the arts and social enterprises, of which the *Fuggerei* proved to have perhaps the most outstanding and revolutionary legacy. The plan for the *Fuggerei* materialized in 1514 when Jacob Fugger decided to build a miniature town for the poor citizens of Augsburg "in honor of God and as proof of gratefulness for the success of the House of Fugger." Of the 106 houses that had originally been planned, 53 were erected. They were two-storied two- or three-room flats, one on the ground and the other on the first floor. Each had its own kitchen and a separate entrance from the street. Three gates closed the *Fuggerei* against the town. The annual rent was one Rhenish Guilder, which is still today not quite equivalent to 40 cents.

Within two generations Augsburg had become a metropolis, although one that had to exert its greatest efforts to maintain its position in the world market; it also had to overcome the limitations of its situation, which was favorable only as far as the transit trade of central Europe was concerned. When the wealthy burghers gained their full share in the "splendor of Augsburg," the time of the great merchant princes had passed. The following period has been called a "splendid decline." The failure of Augsburg's external policy and territorial ambitions had weakened its political influence; but this was a blessing in disguise, for the energy and interest of the burghers turned inward. Enormous

242. The Hercules Fountain, designed by Adriaen de Vries, and the Church of St. Ulrich.

243. The wide Maximilianstrasse, with two fountains, lined with high and gabled houses. The town hall is in the right background.

sums were spent on new buildings, sculptures, and paintings—generally on the artistic enrichment of the city. The fountains of Augsburg are famous. They were the works of brilliant sculptors, among them Hubert Gerhard and Adriaen de Vries. They have become synonymous with the city's name, and are like syncopes in the flow of the unusually wide streets with their high buildings and ever-changing perspectives. They stand in the middle of the streets, not at the side or against the background of a façade. Their arrangement is not very subtle, it is rather pompous, but they suited the "Golden Augsburg."

However, the fountains were merely a beginning and only part of the great artistic activity. In 1602, Elias Holl became the city architect. His work and influence changed the face of Augsburg more than anything else. He designed numerous public buildings, above all the Town Hall; but even more important, he broke with the medieval tradition. He had the courage to be "modern," to be an architect of the Renaissance, although his works were somewhat dry and disproportionate versions of Italian prototypes. He took part in building the new fortifications, and especially in the design of the powerful bastions which were added in 1632. This period was a sunset of great beauty, but a sunset it was; and the decline of the city after the Thirty Years' War, this "splendid decline," was an irrevocable reality.

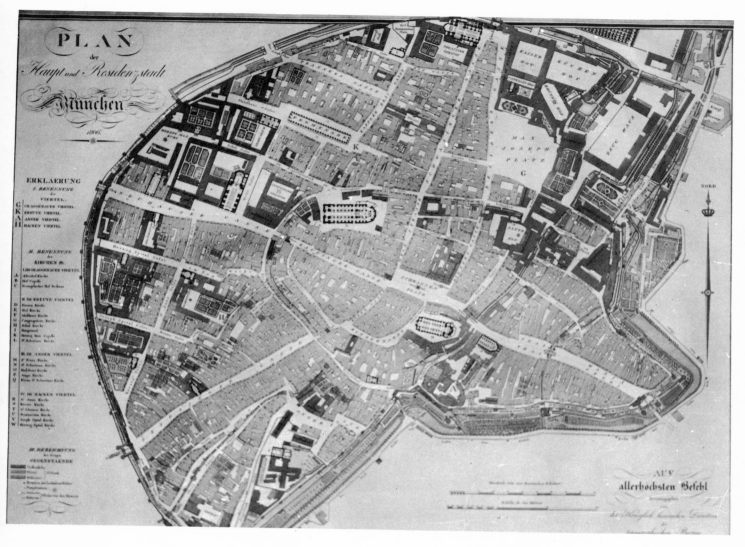

245. Munich in 1806.

München, Bavaria. Munich stands on the river Isar, some 20 miles north of the foothills of the Alps. It was founded in 1158 near the site of a dispersed settlement, *ad monachos,* so called after the owners of the land who were monks. The deed that settled the dispute between Duke Henry the Lion and Otto, Bishop of Freising, stipulated that market, mint, and bridge should in future be established *apud Munichen* and that the Duke had to pay to the Bishop one-third of all taxes raised from these sources. The foundation of Munich was inspired by the commercial ambitions of Henry the Lion who wanted to profit from the salt trade that was carried over the old route from Reichenhall and Hallein to western Upper Germany, Swabia, and Switzerland, and in general from the favorable situation at the meeting point of the east–west and north–south connections over which flowed the steadily increasing goods traffic with the cities of western Germany and northern Italy. The old town formed a semicircle, its diameter resting on the left bank

244. *Opposite:* Munich, 1618–1640, showing the new fortifications and bastions. Engraving by Matthaeus Merian.

Prospectus magni mercatus versus Ecclesie B.V.M. Vue du grand Marché vers l'Eglise de Nôtre Dame a Mun-
ad Monachium.

246. The Marienplatz about 1730, with the towers of the Frauenkirche. Engraving by G. Gottfried Winkler.

248. *Opposite*: Gärtnerplatz.

247. Asamhaus and St. John's Church.

338

of the Isar. It was surrounded by walls and a moat before 1255. In 1253 it was made the capital of the House of Wittelsbach. It was almost entirely destroyed by fire in 1327.

The plan of the Munich of Henry the Lion, with its systematic layout and its more or less equal building plots, has survived the centuries up to the present day. The market square, a broadening of the east–west axis, the main artery of the foundation, the area around the Church of St. Peter, the *Alte Hof,* and the Church of St. Mary were the nuclei of the early settlement. At the beginning of the fourteenth century the town was enlarged, and experienced its first great prosperity. For a short time it was one of the most important centers of the Empire. After 1429, as defense against the Hussites, a second *enceinte* was built. At the end of the fifteenth century the population reached over 13 thousand inhabitants, while most of the other German towns had hardly more than 5,000. During the Thirty Years' War a third ring of fortifications was built.

Munich suffered heavily when it was occupied by Gustavus Adolphus. The population decreased by a third and the flourishing trades did not recover until the Baroque and the Rococo again stimulated artistic activities on a large scale. Munich's so-called "classical" period began with the reign of Louis I (1825–1848). The university was transferred from Landshut to Munich. Innumerable classicistic buildings were erected by the architects Leo Klenze and Friedrich Gärtner who had been given the task of rebuilding whole districts—a wise and foresighted decision that enabled them to create a harmonious and beautiful unity instead of isolated and individual showpieces.

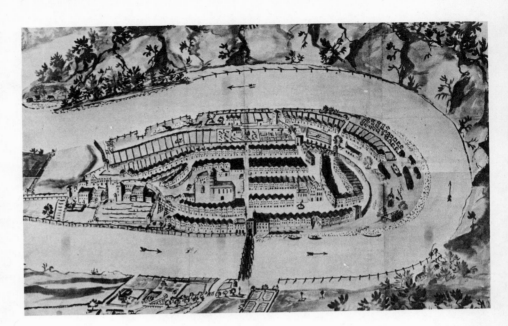

249. Old plan of Wasserburg am Inn.

250. The *Burg* and town of Wasserburg, seen from the north, as they were at the beginning of the seventeenth century. Engraving by Matthaeus Merian.

Wasserburg am Inn, Bavaria. This town is surrounded by the Inn, which flows around it in a wide bend. It was founded in 1137 and received its name from the *Burg* that guarded the Inn crossing of an old overland route from Freising to Salzburg. During the early Middle Ages, this road separated the castle and the settlement that, after 1137, had developed under the castle's protection. The layout of the small town followed the contours of the peninsula. The outer roads form an oval that encloses the inner town. The inner town is divided by a few parallel streets, and has no building blocks with inner courtyards, only continuous rows of gabled houses that on one side form the wall. On the other side, open spaces with gardens lie between the walls and the river.

251. The Brucktor, built in 1470.

252. Aerial view of Wasserburg. The town has preserved its old form, with open spaces on the periphery and continuous house fronts on the river bank.

253. Plan of Landshut, 1811.

Landshut, Bavaria. Landshut stands on the Isar. It was founded in the thirteenth century as a ducal residence. It was first named in 1150, but did not become a town until 1204. It grew up around the Trausnitz Castle of the Wittelsbach family. After 1339, it obtained the right to hold an annual fair. It has been involved in the usual dynastic rivalries and wars. The town has spread over an island in the Isar to the other bank. The *Altstadt* is

254. Part of the *Altstadt* and the two branches of the Isar.

divided by two wide parallel streets from which side streets branch off. The street nearer the river curves before it reaches the bridge, and here stands the Church of the Holy Spirit. Near the other end of the road is the Church of St. Martin. Both churches are recessed from the street, but project into it slightly; they are the perspective dominants that hold together the succession of the numerous small units of the houses and the jagged silhouettes of their gables. The spatial effect is that of a lively movement, foreshortened, broad, and arrested by the two higher buildings of the churches at either end. It is a continuous flow of the ups and downs of gables, which is partly accompanied by arcades and arches bridging the entrance to the narrow side lanes.

255. St. Martin's Church and the main street of Landshut.

256. The Dreifaltigkeitsplatz at the end of the main street of Landshut, which is called the *Altstadt*. The square, a continuation of the street, is formed by a slight concave curve of houses on one side and a sharp angular recession of buildings on the other. It is an outstanding example of the instinctive and unsophisticated assurance with which a multitude of individual elements of different character and size has been welded together in a masterful composition.

Passau, Bavaria. The "Town on Three Rivers" —the Danube, the Inn, and the Ilz—occupies a site settled by Celtic peoples before Roman times. Its name was Boiodurum, the *Burg* of the Boii. During the Roman period the Inn was the frontier between the provinces of Raetia and Noricum. At the time of Domitian (A.D. 81-96), a fortified camp, *castrum Boiodorum*, was built opposite the confluence of the three rivers. It was surrounded by a wall and a moat, and guarded the access to the province of Noricum. At the beginning of the second century, a second fort was built on the peninsula between the Inn and the Danube and was named after its garrison, *castra* Batava. This fort protected the important Inn crossing of the route along the Danube. At this time the place received its name, Passau, which was derived from *Batavis*. This twin town, Boiodurum-Batavis, traded with the frontier peoples, and was an Illyrian custom barrier.

During the storms of the Great Migrations, Passau was probably occupied by Thuringian tribes. It was destroyed in 476. But life never wholly came to a standstill. The town became the seat of a bishop in the eighth century. Three nuclei came into being: the *Bischofsburg;* the convent of Niedernburg, an independent-imperial abbey; and the town of the burghers. Niedernburg was later handed over to the bishops, and a wall was built on the western side of the town (1209), which remained the boundary between Bavaria and the bishopric until 1803. It included a suburb that had grown up in the west and had repeatedly been attacked by the nobles of the neighborhood. In 1143, another settlement, the *Innstadt,* on the southern bank of the Inn was connected with the *Altstadt* by a wooden bridge. A fortified castle, the *Oberhaus,* was built by Bishop Ulrich on the Georgsberg between the Danube and the Ilz. It was the stronghold of the ecclesiastical rulers in the following centuries, and from there they tyrannized the burghers and directed their

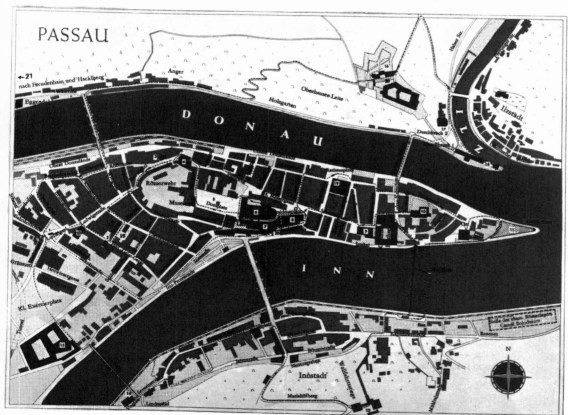

257. Plan of Passau.

345

oppressive rule over the town. It is characteristic that a town hall was not built until the fifteenth century. Bishop Ulrich fortified the hitherto unprotected districts of the *Innstadt, Ilzstadt,* and *Anger,* more as a haughty demonstration of their incorporation into his domain than out of consideration for the security of the inhabitants.

Passau reached the height of its economic

goldsmiths created first-rate products. Prosperity, self-assurance, as well as the burghers' pride had reached a very high degree.

Passau was spared the horrors of the Thirty Years' War, but two devastating fires in 1662 and 1680 destroyed large parts of the medieval town. This was a turning-point in the town's architectural history. Italian architects and artists introduced ideas and forms of the

258. Aerial view of Passau, with the Danube and the Inn at their confluence with the Ilz in the right foreground, where the bishop's castle rises on a hill. Note the *Innstadt* (*left*) and the *Altstadt* (*center*).

and cultural influence at the end of the Middle Ages. Stretching from the Isar to Hungary, it was the center of the Empire's greatest diocese. It enjoyed a very considerable income from its trade with foreign countries, especially in wine and salt. Staple and custom rights yielded large profits. The trades, organized in guilds, flourished. The blades of Passau were famous and, like those of Toledo or Damascus, in great demand; the *Dombauhütte* was one of Germany's leading groups of architects, artisans, and craftsmen, and it influenced the architecture of numerous churches. Shipbuilders, bellfounders, and

Italian Baroque, making Passau a "Second Salzburg"—an "Italian town with a German Soul," as it has been called. The prince-bishop who reigned between 1664 and 1673 rebuilt the cathedral and his residence after their designs; but his plan to surround the *Altstadt* by a tree-lined promenade along the banks of the Danube and the Inn was abandoned after his early death. This was a novel idea— an invasion of nature into the stone desert of a town—and a break with the rigid tradition that had excluded verdure as an instrument of city planning.

346

259. The Residence Square with the choir of the Gothic cathedral and the bishop's Residence (*left*). The fountain is the focal point of the perspective views through a narrow lane and a street on either side of the Cathedral. This convergence of the perspective views has determined the location of the fountain, which dominates the square in spite of its lateral situation. Its flowing Baroque contours and vertical composition introduce an element of motion and contrast to the more rigid perpendicular accents of the cathedral and the Residence.

260. The curved canyon of the Pfaffengasse, sloping down the hill, seen through the arch that spans its upper part.

347

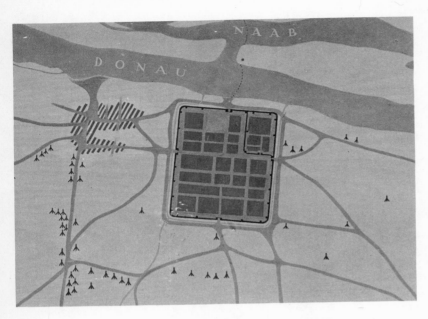

261. Regensburg about 350.

262. Regensburg about 1100.

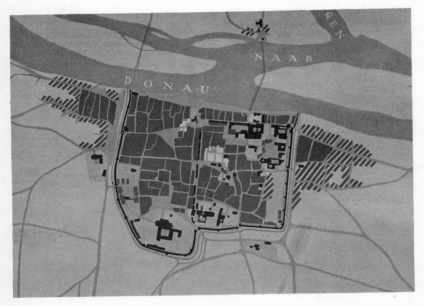

Regensburg, Bavaria. This town is situated at the northernmost point of the Danube where it is joined by the Regen River. The marshy plain with its numerous islands made the crossing easy, and the valleys of the northern and northwestern landscapes leading to Franconia and Bohemia directed the flow of

small and large groups naturally toward the wide bend of the Danube. Therefore, trade and traffic favored this site for settlements since early times. The Celts established an *oppidum* at the old ferry south of the Danube and called the place Rathaspona, a name that, as Ratisbona, remained synonymous with Regensburg and was used by the Romans for their first *castrum*.

This first fortified camp was founded between A.D. 77 and 80 on an elevation south of the Danube, from which the surrounding country could be overlooked. A new camp was built in A.D. 179 by Marcus Aurelius opposite the confluence of the Regen and the Naab. It was called Regino, according to ancient records, Castra Regina being a later humanistic reconstruction. The name Regino is derived from the nearby river, the Regen. The intention was to make Castra Regina not only a fortress but also a depot and trading center. It fulfilled the first task, but the more peaceful purposes were thwarted by the death of the Emperor. The third period of the Roman history of Regensburg coincided with the military reforms under Diocletian around A.D. 300. The camp was reinforced and became the strongest fortress in this region of the Empire. The walls were rebuilt to a height of about 24 feet and with enormous square, hewn stones; the gates were strengthened by semicircular towers; but the garrison was reduced to a sixth of its former strength. It was abandoned by the Romans in 470 and then used by the inhabitants of the camp villages as a refuge in the dangerous times that followed the Roman retreat. Castra Regina was the easternmost outpost of the Roman Empire in Germany after the middle of the first century.

The first Christian community in Castra Regina dates back to the time of Constantine. During and after the 8th century, the town grew beyond the Roman walls toward the west and the east. From A.D. 700–900 only the King or the Duke lived in the old Roman fortress; no burghers did. A certain stabilization was reached around 920 when the new fortifications had been completed.

"Die Stadt Ratisbona ist alt und neu zugleich. Sie ist die erste unter allen grossen Staedten und liegt im Nordgau, in der Mitte zwischen dem oberen Pannonien und Alamannien, den Blick der böhmischen Grenze zugewandt. Keine Stadt Deutschlands ist berühmter. An ihrer Nordseite bildet die Donau eine Schutzwehr. Gross ist ihr Ueberfluss an Gold, Silber und anderen Metallen, an kostbaren Geweben, Purpur und Waren aller Art. Ihren überragenden Reichtum verdankt die Stadt der Schiffahrt und den Zöllen und dem Zustrom wertvoller Handelsgüter aller Art."[2]

2. The town of Ratisbona is old and new at the same time. She is the foremost of all great towns and is situated in the Nordgau, midway between Upper Pannonia and Alemannia with a view toward the Bohemian frontier. No town in Germany is more famous. At her northern side the Danube forms a bulwark. Her surplus is great in gold, silver, and other metals, and in precious textiles, purple, and goods of all kinds. She owes her eminent wealth to shipping and tolls and to the influx of valuable merchandise of all kinds.

Thus began the description of Regensburg by the monk Otloh, written around 1050. He then goes on to explain the inner structure of the town. There were three quarters. To the east of the Roman area was the *Königshof*, the *pagus regis;* in the western half, the *Pfaffenstadt*, the *pagus cleri,* with the Cathedral and the bishop's residence; in the south, two convents where priests and monks with their servants and craftsmen had settled; and finally the *Neustadt* with the Abbey of St. Emmeran and the merchants' quarter, the *pagus mercatorum*. The town continued to grow. New suburbs developed in the east and west along the Danube for craftsmen and traders. Here monasteries and convents were built by the mendicant friars. Following the rules of their orders, they had to settle near or outside the walls, that is, among the poorer people.

Around 1300 Regensburg had reached its greatest extension, which was to remain the

263. View of Regensburg from the north, by Jakob Hufnagel, 1594.

same for 500 years. The center of the town was the market square at the northwest corner of the Roman *castrum*. Here were the buildings of the administration and the ancient Church of St. Mary. This complex had not been planned; rather it grew spontaneously, yet organically. It was a representative symbol of the wealth, energy, and independence of the burghers, just as the fortified towers and the residences of the patricians near the town hall and the river expressed the domineering and violent spirit of the powerful leading families. However, in contrast to almost all cities founded in the twelfth and thirteenth centuries, Regensburg, already had several market streets by the sixteenth century; there buying and selling was carried on, and only the small square at the town hall was called "The Market." It is likely that at least parts of the early town grew up along narrow lanes that began at the Danube and were gradually extended upward.

An unusual organization, which began in the sixteenth century, should be mentioned. This was the so-called *Baumannschaft*. It consisted of the landowners who also had interests in the land outside the walls. This organization owned all parts of the *Allmende* within the *Burgfrieden,* the jurisdiction of the town, and was responsible for the maintenance of roads and bridges within this area. It was a sort of guild of the "urban peasantry," and is proof of the agricultural activities of the burghers and their intimate relationship to the countryside.

After the Thirty Years' War, Regensburg was selected as the seat of the "Long Diet of the Empire," which may be regarded as the first—though very tame—parliamentary institution of Germany. After 1663 the electors and princes did not attend in person but were represented by ambassadors whose presence changed the character of the town. Regensburg became a residence city, a court with all the mannerisms, idiosyncrasies, and peculiarities of this not all too rational institution. But the multitude of newcomers, the foreign and German ambassadors with their large retinues, had to be content with the narrow and simple framework of the medieval town. They had to adapt themselves to this atmosphere, which had nothing in common with the residence cities of the Baroque. In general, Baroque and Rococo had no in-

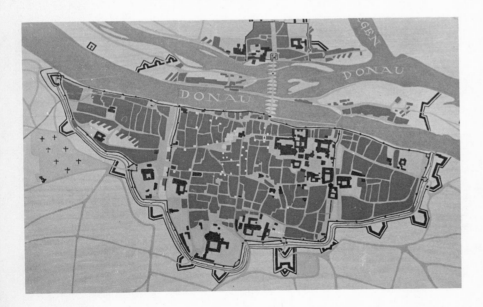

264. Regensburg about 1700.

265. *Opposite:* One of the most beautiful ensembles created in a German town. The massive ancient bridge leads to the gate, which is flanked by a tower. The compact, solid mass of the old houses, with their high roofs and strong walls, is transcended by the Cathedral—by the ethereal filigreed tracery of the spires that rise above the substructure of the towers and finally fade into space.

350

fluence on the city. No new streets or squares were laid out, and only a few new buildings were erected. Not until the last decade of the eighteenth century did life grow more relaxed, more graceful, and more lighthearted for the participants of the diet. Italian opera, French comedy, and German drama competed with the theater of the Jesuits. On the surface foreign influences were supreme. The physical embodiment of this spirit were the promenades that encircled the medieval wall instead of the Baroque fortifications.

266. View from the Cathedral to the east. This part of Regensburg is entirely different from the residential and trading quarters. Here, within a narrow space, are crowded together the ancient parish church (*foreground*); the Römerturm, connected by an arch with the Ducal Residence; and, behind it, the Kornmarkt and two other churches.

267. *Opposite:* View of the Neupfarrkirche from the cathedral. The square occupies the site of the ghetto that was destroyed in 1519. The Church stands on the site of the former synagogue.

Eichstätt, Bavaria. Situated in the valley of the Altmühl at the foot of the Franconian Jura, this town was occupied by Roman legions around A.D. 90. The Rhaetian *limes* ran but a few miles north of the Roman settlement. Eichstätt was first mentioned in 740 and was elevated to a bishopric by St. Boniface in the same year. In 1042 it was first named a *civitas*. After the transformation of the original Benedictine monastery, founded by the first bishop, Willibald, into a cathedral seminary, and after the abandonment of the communal way of living by the cathedral canons in the first half of the eleventh century, *curiae*—each with its own residential "towers," chapel, and *Wirtschaftsgebäude* and surrounded by a wall—were built for the members of the cathedral chapter. "The Ottonian City of God," as it has been called, was surrounded by numerous monasteries and convents.

At the end of the twelfth century the town of the clerics began to merge with the town of the burghers, which was laid out systematically around the market and surrounded by a wall with four gates and numerous towers. After grave conflicts with the stewards of the bishops, the first charter was granted in 1291 to the citizens, among whom the clothmakers and the furriers were especially prominent in strengthening the civic pride and prosperity of the inhabitants. When the line of the local lords, who had been bishops' stewards, became extinct, the way was free for the formation of an episcopal territory, whose capital and residence city was Eichstätt. In the middle of the fourteenth century the bishops

268. Baumberger Turm, Regensburg, one of many fortress towers that served as patrician residences. Such typical features of the fortified castles in the countryside as the chapel and the keep have been transferred to this town house. In Germany, these tower residences were unusual. Whether or not they were stimulated by Italian prototypes, especially the towers at San Gimignano, is not clear. More than fifty of these towers, with up to nine stories, were built during the thirteenth and fourteenth centuries in various parts of Germany.

transferred their household to a fortified castle on a hill outside the town. Henceforth Eichstätt represented the typical medieval community with its two focal points, the town and the *Burg,* as contrasting symbols. After destruction and pillage in the Thirty Years' War, the town was rebuilt, and Eichstätt became the town of the Baroque that we know today with its squat and horizontal dwellings and graceful public buildings, with its homogeneous streets and intriguing vistas and squares.

269. Eichstätt's market square.

270. The Residenz Platz in Eichstätt, with the cavaliers' houses and St. Mary's column.

Ellingen, Bavaria. The Town Hall, built in 1746, stands at the broadening of a gently curved street at the end of the perspective view in splendid contrast to the modest and low-gabled houses.

Situations such as those at Ellingen—modest in scale, inconspicuous in their means, yet impressive in their simplicity—are not uncommon in the small towns of southern Germany.

271. Ellingen's town hall.

Ansbach, Bavaria. The town dates back to the private foundation of a Benedictine monastery in 748. It was later given to Charlemagne who handed it over to the Bishop of Würzburg. This was a typical development: the successive ownership first by a private lord, then by the king, and finally by the bishop. Around the monastery a settlement called Onoldsbach grew up which, in the eleventh century, received the right to hold a market; in the twelfth century it was accorded civic rights. It was first mentioned as a town in 1221. Since 1456, Ansbach has been the seat of a margrave and has become a capital and residence town.

272. General view of Ansbach, with the *Altstadt* in the foreground and the Residence in the center.

273. Martin Luther Platz, Ansbach, with the town hall and the Church of St. Gumbertus. The asymmetrical positions of the town hall and the fountain permit a free view of the entrance to the church, absorbing it into the square and increasing the impression of depth.

Nürnberg, Bavaria. Nuremberg stands on both banks of the Pegnitz near that river's confluence with the Rednitz. It is not one of Germany's oldest cities, although the Pegnitz Basin has been occupied by small groups of settlers since the mesolithic era. The present city of Nuremberg was founded by King Henry III in 1040–1041, and was mentioned for the first time ten years later as *Nuorenberc* when the king built a *Burg* on the Felsberg near the old *Königshof* of Fürth. That site was chosen because it was favorable for guarding the Pegnitz Valley and the roads from Bavaria, Franconia, Swabia, and Bohemia. The former meeting-point of these roads near Fürth lost its importance and was transferred to the new foundation. A small settlement developed at the *Burg* and received the right to hold a market. The market was withdrawn from Fürth where it had previously taken place.

The new settlement was originally inhabited by ministerials who had to render military service to the king, and by bondsmen who worked in the *Burg* and on the adjoining farm. They were peasants, craftsmen, and small traders. Another settlement was added to the market town at the beginning of the twelfth century with the Church of St. Sebaldus, and its name was transferred to this district.

About this time, a royal manor was independently established, separated from the former group. Here, a second settlement was systematically laid out with a wide market street as the main axis. From it, parallel and narrow lanes, also used as markets, branched off. Its longish oval shape, the characteristic form of foundations by the Hohenstaufen during the twelfth century, is clearly distinguishable in the general plan of the town. It was called the *Lorenzerstadt* after one of the principal churches, St. Lorenz. It was fortified in the first quarter of the thirteenth century. Thus, early Nuremberg consisted of two parts, each with its own walls, separated by the marshy Pegnitz Valley. Around 1320, both parts were joined, and the walls were extended to cross the river. The *Altstadt* of Nuremberg had come into being.

274. Nuremberg in the Reichswald, a self-contained island in the vast forest. Watercolor, 1516.

275. Engraving of Nuremberg's market square by Lorenz Strauch, 1599. The Frauenkirche and the Schöne Brunnen are the main accents. Note the buying and selling of food that are going on at booths and in the open market. The houses in the background are simple and unadorned.

276. Plan of Nuremberg, by Matthaeus Merian, 1648. A clear and simplified view of the town.

Der grosse Marckt in Nürnberg.   La grande place du Marché à Nuremberg.

277. Nuremberg's market square. Engraving by I. A. Delsenbach about 1700. The Schöne Brunnen is in the right foreground and the Frauenkirche at the left. Booths cover a large part of the square. Shops have been installed under the roof on the ground floors of the buildings in the background.

278. The *Burg*, with houses at its foot. Engraving by I. A. Delsenbach, 1718. The architecture of the buildings is simple, a variety of half-timbered and stone houses. One Renaissance dwelling has moderate decorations around the windows.

Vorstellung der Kaiser. Burg gegen den Berg hinauf, zu Nürnberg.   Representation du Château Imp. du côté du chemin qui y mene a Nuremberg.

279. Nuremberg's market square today. Large umbrellas cover the whole area. Some of the original houses are still standing.

During the thirteenth and fourteenth centuries, suburbs gradually developed in the east and south outside the walls. It became necessary to build new fortifications that would enclose the whole town. The task was an enormous one, and was begun and completed in the second half of the fourteenth century. The fortifications were elaborate and extremely strong, consisting as they did of double walls, a deep moat, five double gates, and numerous towers. The introduction of firearms in the first half of the six-teenth century necessitated a further change: Bastions, gun emplacements, and new projecting towers were built. The *Burg* was also strengthened by new and modern fortifications.

The town, ruled by patrician families, attained great wealth. It traded with Italy and the East and northern Europe. Its sphere of influence covered a territory of nearly 500 square miles. Nuremberg's greatest claim to fame lay in its contribution to German art. Adam Kraft, Veit Stoss, Peter Vischer, Wohl-

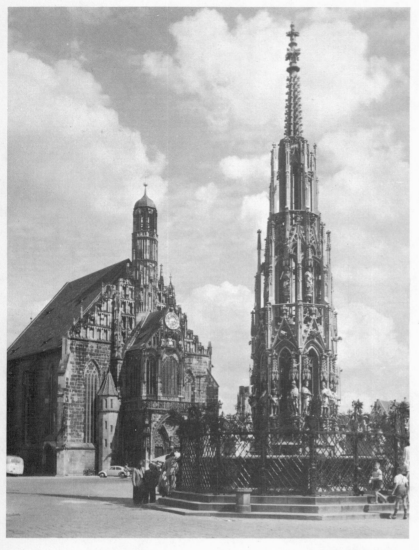

gemut, Dürer, Hans Sachs and other *Meister-singer,* as well as a high standard of arts and crafts, made it the great center of artistic achievement. Regiomontanus, Pirckheimer, and Behaim, to name only a few of the Humanists, made Nuremberg prominent as a seat of cultural progress.

The *Altstadt,* with its hilly quarters rising to the *Burg,* its gently curved streets, its relatively large and spacious squares, and its narrow lanes, testified to the wealth of the city. The burghers' houses were a modification of the peasants' farms in Franconia. They consisted of the main dwelling and a courtyard with buildings on both sides and at the rear. Originally they were built as half-timbered houses, later in sandstone; their façades were simple and divided only by windows and gateways. This changed in the course of time when ostentatiousness and delight in decorations gained the upper hand. The façades and the courtyards were covered with ornate embellishments; the front and rear buildings were often connected by galleries; and the high roofs and gables were loosened up by dormer windows, scrolls, and finials.

280. The Frauenkirche and the Schöne Brunnen in Nuremberg.

281. The fortifications at the Neutorturm in Nuremberg.

Nördlingen, Bavaria. Nördlingen stands on the site of a Roman military post that was abandoned under Emperor Trajan when the frontier was further advanced. The post was replaced by a *vicus* that was soon overrun by the Alemanni who established a settlement on the site. Nördlingen was first mentioned in 898. Owing to its favorable situation at important traffic routes it became a market, and toward the middle of the thirteenth century a town. The nucleus of the Carolingian settlement lay outside the first walls built by the Hohenstaufen. The circuit of the walls is clearly visible in Fig. 283. Within the inner circle an oval can be distinguished that may be an indication of the extent of the old market settlement. The first fortifications, of which no vestiges have remained, were replaced in the fourteenth century by the circular walls that enclosed the *Altstadt* and the suburbs that had grown up along the main routes leading into the town.

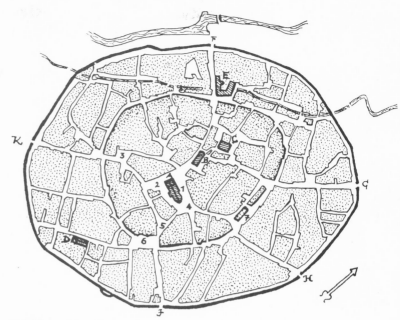

282. Plan of Nördlingen.

283. Aerial view of Nördlingen, showing the sharp contours of the circular fortifications, the Church of St. George in the center, and the compact mass of houses pressed together within the circumvallation.

363

284. Nördlingen's town hall, near the market square in the center of town, was originally a town house of the territorial counts. Used as a town hall since 1382, it has been repeatedly enlarged. The ground floor once served as a storeroom.

Dinkelsbühl, Bavaria. The town lies on the right bank of the Wörnitz, a tributary of the Danube. The terrain rises toward the south and west so that from the valley, the town's skyline stands out clearly—not even partly hidden behind natural features in the foreground. The powerful silhouette of the Church of St. George dominates everything: the walls with their numerous towers and the roofs and gables of the houses. The layout of the town approximates a triangle, the longest side of which follows the river. The oldest part of the town, an oval, is placed roughly in the center of the walled-in area. The hospital lay, as usual, outside the town. St. George's Church stands at the intersection of the main streets near the northern periphery. The first market square at the old town hall was replaced by a succession of market streets beginning at the church. It stood on the site of a former cemetery that was later moved to another place.

Dinkelsbühl owed its existence as a town to its favorable situation at the crossing of important south–north and east–west routes. It belonged to the family possessions of the Hohenstaufen and was mentioned in 1188 as *Burgum Tinkelspuhel—burgum* was the word used for a town in the legal sense from the middle of the twelfth to the thirteenth centuries. It is probable that at this time it had already become a larger settlement with walls and a moat. By the fourteenth century, Dinkelsbühl had reached a certain importance as a trading and manufacturing town, and especially as the seat of clothmakers and

285. Plan of Dinkelsbühl: *A.* leather market; *B.* wine market; *C.* pig market; *D.* timber market; *E.* harbor market; *F.* bread market; *G.* lard market.

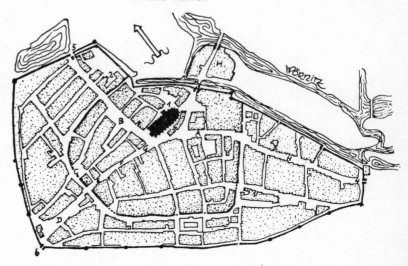

286. Aerial view of Dinkelsbühl, dominated by the mighty roof of St. George's Church.

287. Nördlinger Gate and the town's water mill at the southeastern corner of the walls. The mill was part of the fortifications and had embrasures and a half-tower for guns.

288. Exterior of the Wörnitz Gate, with the bridge over the moat.

of smiths who made scythes, sickles, and other iron goods. Trade was in the hands of the few wealthy, patrician families. They composed the ruling minority, craftsmen being excluded from any participation in the administration. The patricians not only had large houses in town but estates in the country; they even owned whole villages. This one-sided social preponderance changed when, in 1387, after the craftsmen and artisans had united in guilds, the municipal council was equally divided between the patricians and the guildmasters.

In 1387, Dinkelsbühl was not yet fully fortified. Its suburb was still without walls. The fortifications enclosing all suburbs were completed around 1500. Dinkelsbühl, with its wide street-markets on which were situated the merchants' houses and the comfortable inns and which offered ample space for vehicles and goods, is one of the most significant examples of a town laid out by the Hohenstaufen.

290. Church of St. George, a hall-church with a massive roof, closely surrounded by low houses. The market streets begin in the foreground.

291. Rothenburg's fortifications, with a covered passage for the defenders. Note the round and square towers and the interior street that follows the course of the walls.

Rothenburg, Bavaria. Rothenburg developed around a fortified castle situated on a steep slope on the western bank of the Tauber. In the Hohenstaufen period, the castle was a center of the Hohenstaufen power policy in southern Germany. After the fall of that dynasty in the thirteenth century, the market settlement was enlarged to cover more than twice its original area. In the late fourteenth century the southern suburb and the hospital were incorporated. With its street cross and market streets, the layout of Rothenburg is a typical product of the Hohenstaufen era.

292. Klingentor, with covered stairway and passage.

293. Gateway with fortifications.

367

296. *Opposite:* Engraving of Rothenburg's market square by J. F. Schmidt, 1726. The new town hall is at the right. The streets enter the square at the corners or run along one side, thus preserving its unity as a self-contained entity.

294. Plönlein with Siebersturm. The main street leads to the gate, while a side street slopes down to a lower part of the town. Between them is a narrow house, the gable of which blends with the stronger accent of the gate, as can be seen in the perspective view toward the gate.

295. Markusturm and Röderbrunnen. Gables, towers, roofs, and the vertical lines of the half-timbered structures and the fountain create a unity in diversity within a narrow space. In its intensity, it is unique even among the many similar architectural compositions of southern Germany.

368

297. A general view of
Ochsenfurth.

Ochsenfurth, Bavaria. A former frontier fortress of the bishopric of Würzburg on the Main, Ochsenfurth is a regular square—a rather unusual shape in this part of Germany. The main streets lead to the central market square. The building density of the *Altstadt* is high; there are hardly any open spaces left. The town's *raison d'être* was the ford where the river could easily be crossed.

298. General view of Frickenhausen. The church stands in the center at the market square, with the town hall nearby. Behind the town rise the vineyards, which gradually merge into the open country.

299. Oberes Tor (Upper Gate), with wooden stairway to upper floor.

Frickenhausen on the Main, Bavaria. There are innumerable small towns that, in all lands and at all times, have the same characteristics and atmosphere: the world forgetting, by the world forgot. Nevertheless, when taken together such towns house a very considerable number of people. They are inconspicuous; they have been passive objects of historical changes; they border between towns and villages; and their inhabitants are deeply embedded in the rhythm of nature, nearer to the countryman than to the townsman. Yet they often contain jewels of architecture and city building that are more expressive of a deep-rooted culture than the famous showpieces of large cities.

Frickenhausen is such a town—or village. It was first mentioned in 903. It belonged to the Counts of Babenberg, under whose rule it remained for over five hundred years. In 1406, the Bishop of Würzburg sold it to the cathedral chapter. The walls were begun in 1462 and finished one hundred years later. They have been well preserved up to the present day.

300. Mühltor (Mill Gate.)

301. A gate in Sommerhausen, another of the small Main towns. Note how compact, simple, strong, and purposeful it is.

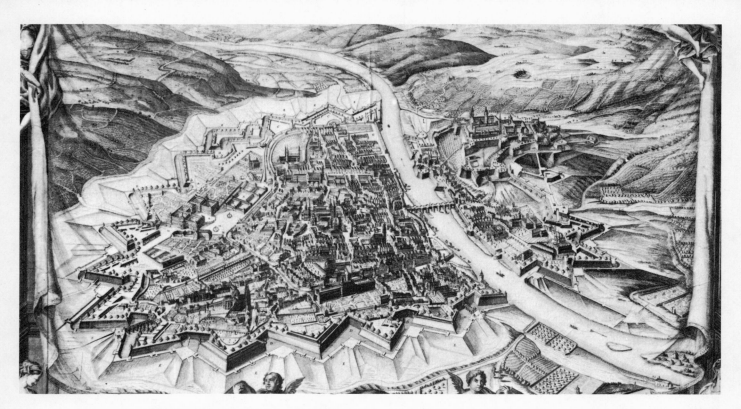

302. Engraving of Würzburg by Balthasar Neumann, 1723. A great view of the city in all its Baroque splendor. The Residence is at the left near the fortifications, the Marienberg fortress at the right on the hill that rises above the Main. Also shown are the *Altstadt*, with its church, chapels, monasteries, small and large houses confined within the inner walls, and the outer *enceinte*, with open spaces between the bastions and the old ring of fortifications.

303. View over Würzburg from the fortress.

Würzburg, Bavaria. Würzburg on the Main is the center of a region that has been settled for several thousand years. Around 1000 B.C., the present Marienberg had probably been a refuge, a *Volksburg,* and many centuries later Celtic tribes may have built their huts at the foot of the hill. Around A.D. 500, the lands on the Main became Frankish, and the region in the vicinity of Würzburg was soon densely settled. In the seventh century it became the seat of Frankish counts who established their residence in the center of the present *Altstadt.* By 750 it became the see of a bishop, and it is likely that Charlemagne gave the old ducal castle to the bishops. Together with the *Pfalz* of the bishop it formed the *Domfreiheit* (the cathedral precincts). It was surrounded by the farms, houses, stables, and barns of the peasants, fishermen, vine-growers, and craftsmen. Trade and commerce began to develop. The center of settlement shifted to the right bank of the Main. This coincided with the general trend of this period when the hilltop *Burgen* were abandoned in favor of strong sites near important roads. Thus the settlement grew up along the highway, which offered a more attractive site around the nuclei of the *Königshof* and the bishop's residence. Around A.D. 1000 the Ottonian town was more or less consolidated. Several *vici* had developed, one for cloth-makers and drapers, perhaps from Flanders, and another one inhabited by ministerials.

The population grew and a modest prosperity set in. Würzburg was now a market, and soon it was granted the right to have its own mint, customs, and jurisdiction. The town was now ruled by the sovereign bishops to whom the kings had transferred their royal privileges. It is characteristic of the domineering position of the ecclesiastical princes that the town in the valley and their old residence did no longer satisfy their ambitions. Around 1200 they built a new residence, a fortified castle, on the Marienberg, from which they ruled as bearers of the "crosier and the sword." At this time about five thousand people may have lived in the town, which still had many

open spaces within the walls—including several suburbs—and had been finished shortly before 1200. New ecclesiastical buildings were erected and the cathedral was finished in 1237. Within two generations, Würzburg had become a town of monasteries and churches, of chapels and hospitals, the reason being that the great Frankish abbeys had acquired large farms within the walls that were dispersed over the urban area like religious islands.

Although grave internal conflicts between the burghers and the bishops filled the time from 1250 to 1400, the cultural and spiritual life flourished under the rigid guidance of the ecclesiastical rulers. The Ghetto was burned down, but as an "atonement," a Chapel of St. Mary was built on the old Jewish square. A decline set in about 1400, after the prince-bishop had destroyed the army of the burghers in the battle of Bergtheim. In 1398 the town had 2600 taxable inhabitants, but by

304. View from the market fountain to the Falkenhaus. Note the contrasting succession of spatial elements framed by vertical and horizontal, projecting and receding volumes.

305. At the Mühltor. The street narrows toward the higher level, and the stairs repeat the one-sided accentuation of the street at the projecting house—asymmetry at its best.

306. Würzburg's town hall, with Vierröhrenbrunnen (*left*).

307. Aerial view of the fortress of Marienberg, crowning a hill that rises almost 400 feet above the Main and slopes steeply down on three sides. Its eastern and western slopes are covered with vineyards.

1412 the number had fallen to 1400. With the introduction of a new municipal constitution in 1590 the absolutism of the bishops was unchallenged. Around 1600 the fortress of *Marienberg* was renovated and enlarged, and its fortifications were strengthened. A hospital and a university were founded, the first secular monumental buildings to be offi-cially sponsored. Between 1642 and 1673, the rebuilding of the fortifications around the town and castle began. This enormous work was finished in 1786. It exhausted the munici-pal finances but the town had the satisfac-tion of having mighty bastions and ramparts, starlike outworks, and advanced gun emplace-ments. It is amazing that in spite of these

308. The Fürstengarten of the fortress. It covers a narrow oblong area that is open on three sides. On the fourth, it is bordered by the walls of the *Burg*. The contrast between the open and closed long sides forebade an exclusive emphasis on the oblong character of the garden. Furthermore, the fine view over the town and the river demanded that the layout be oriented toward it. Consequently, a platform was built to project over the slope in the middle of the long side, and on its axis a fountain was erected to separate two identical *parterres*. Terraces close the garden at either end. Stairs lead down to the lower level around a niche with another fountain. A marvelous composition, which is, because of intelligent and congenial subdivision of an originally unfavorable site, a masterpiece of landscape architecture and carefully related to the town below. The garden is still essentially the same as it was in the eighteenth century.

great expenses—the burdens of billeting and the compensations for expropriations of terrains—Würzburg reached its greatest splendor and prosperity. However, the explanation of this miracle may be that the town had to spend money, whereas the coffers of the Church remained well filled. Moreover, the ecclesiastical authorities did not share in the expenses that the town council had to incur. The Church was, therefore, free for other tasks.

At this time the Baroque Würzburg was born. The bishops led this movement which was in essence the work of the Church and of the Counter-Reformation. They invited architects and artisans, painters and musicians, poets and scholars. Religious establishments and monasteries emulated each other in erecting new, splendid buildings, in executing dazzling façades that would hide old houses, and in covering medieval vaults with a stucco sham-architecture of exciting vitality. Nobles and burghers were anxious to follow the example of the clergy. The culmination of this building fever, the embodiment in stone and mortar of this spirit, was the new Residence outside the walls of the old town, built by Balthasar Neumann, the greatest genius of the German Baroque.

Würzburg had now joined the elite of the Residence Cities of the absolute rulers of this period—under a prince bishop, not a temporal prince, but the final result was the same: the Residence dominated the city. It was its center and focal point, and the town of the burghers was a mere annex.

309. Aerial view of the Residence, the most perfect secular eighteenth-century building in Germany and the very essence of the Baroque spirit. The Residence closes the perspective view from the cathedral and stands on the axis, which leads, although interrupted and broken by the church, to the old bridge over the Main. It dominates the city, not because of a rigid and geometrical pattern of streets focused on its center as at Mannheim or Karlsruhe, but merely by its placement at the edge of the *Altstadt*. The *cour d'honneur* absorbs the movement that surges up from the city and spreads out over the large outer square. Behind the palace extend the gardens. A relationship between city and palace, though unsystematic, does exist, more through impromptu interdependence than through carefully thought-out design.

Erlangen, Bavaria. Erlangen is situated on the Regnitz, which joins the Main at Bamberg. The region west of the Regnitz is gently rolling country, whereas in the east the cliffs of the *Fränkische Alb* slope steeply down to the river plain. The town of Erlangen was founded around 1364 near an old village of the same name. It remained an insignificant small town for centuries. Before the Thirty Years' War it had hardly more than 1000 inhabitants; and in 1634, it was completely destroyed. When it was rebuilt after the war, the population had fallen to about 500. In 1706 a devastating fire razed the place to the ground. At about the same time the Margrave of Brandenburg-Bayreuth opened his land to the Huguenots and founded a new town a few hundred yards south of Erlangen where they could settle. Thus the old, German town became the *Altstadt* and the new, French town, the *Neustadt*. Each place retained its individual independence and made this fact unmistakably manifest by closing its gates at night against the sister-town. The first groups of refugees, about 600, arrived in 1686. Like the later arrivals, they had to be accommodated in the neighboring communities before they could move to their new homes.

The plan of the French town was designed by the architect J. M. Richter. Its layout was regular, rectangular, and divided in two equal halves by a main street (the road Nürnberg-Bamberg) and three side streets, the whole surrounded by a peripheral road following the course of the walls. The building blocks were also rectangular. The center was occupied by a square open space and the southern part by a rectangular open space. The whole plan was a typical drawing-board scheme—symmetrical, rectilinear, and dull—but it offered the refugees all they needed: their own church, *le Temple;* a *grande maison des manufactures* (never built); a building for storing and selling their goods; a market and meeting place; dwellings; the protection of walls that had to serve less for defense than as customs boundary—for the frontiers of Nürnberg and Bamberg were very near; and, last but not least, their private cemetery. The *Neustadt* with its regular rigidity was nothing unusual. It had its predecessors in Freudenstadt and Neu-Hanau and its successors, among others, in the Dorotheenstadt and Friedrichstadt in Berlin, all of which were built for Huguenots. Richter's plan for Erlangen was, however, a serious attempt to instill a certain *élan* into his work and to create a few architectural focal points, but he hardly succeeded. The symmetrical rigidity is too uncreative and too obvious. He tried all sorts of tricks: change of rhythm and proportion, symmetry and contrast, and perspective views. But his main materials were the groups of identical houses, which he interrupted by somewhat larger and higher corner buildings. Erlangen is a typical colonial town, it is an uninspiring and sterile demonstration of certain "recognized" principles. The architect worked under difficult conditions: he had to satisfy his patron that the new town was simple to build, for he never had enough funds at his disposal.

The palace was erected on the eastern side of the central square between 1700 and 1704. The Huguenots' town became a residence city, although on a very small scale. The rebuilding of the *Altstadt* after the fire of 1706 led gradually to a growing together with the *Neustadt*. The final merger of the two took place in 1812.

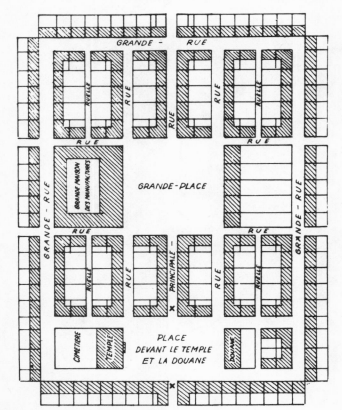

310. Richter's plan for Erlangen.

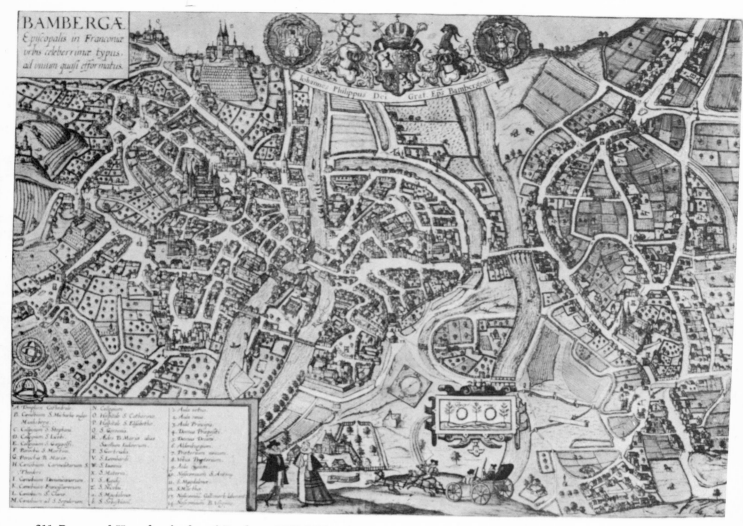

311. Braun and Hogenberg's plan of Bamberg, 1608–1609.

Bamberg, Bavaria. Bamberg consists of a *Talstadt*, town in the valley, and a *Bergstadt*, town on the mountain. The former lies on the two main branches of the Regnitz; the latter on the spur of the Steigerwald. It is the meeting place of several important roads. The Upper Main and the Regnitz were used in the Middle Ages as waterways. The early development of Bamberg from about A.D. 900 followed the usual stages: *Burg, Königshof,* bishop's see, civic settlement. The narrow, sandy strip on the banks of the left branch of the Regnitz may have been the nucleus of the later town. It had no cultivable land,

and may have been settled in the tenth century by fishermen, sailors, craftsmen, and manorial bailiffs, the predecessors of the later patricians. In the south it was adjoined by a Jewish colony. As the small original settlement seems to have been insufficient for the growing population toward the end of the eleventh century, a new and larger market place was founded on the island in the Regnitz. This was the work of Bishop Otto (1102-1139), among whose pious deeds was mentioned the acquisition of "the market with farms on both sides of the river."

The town grew from several nuclei—the

379

312. View over the *Altstadt*, showing the four towers of the Romanesque cathedral towering above the compressed mass of houses. A branch of the Regnitz River is in the foreground.

Burg, monasteries, the settlement on the left bank, and the island—a development that resulted in an unequal legal status of the citizens and a lack of unity in town planning. This must have been very obvious and not just a passing shortcoming, for the Swedish Fieldmarshal Horn characterized Bamberg during the Thirty Years' War as "one large widespread place, as it were, of different towns." The interest and the beauty of Bamberg lie more in the individual medieval and Baroque buildings than in its general appearance or layout. It is difficult to explain why this is so. The most likely reason may be human incongruity—and this is a very excusable reason in any case.

313. The old town hall on the Obere Brücke (Upper Bridge), with a group of the Crucifixion—one of the marvelous Baroque compositions that abound in Bamberg.

Erfurt, former Province of Saxony. A commercial town of the Middle Ages, Erfurt owed its rise to its site on important trade routes that met at a ford through the Gera River, hence the origin of the name *Erphesfurt,* or *Erpesfurt.* Numerous river branches provided a natural protection and were the basis of the dyers' trade, which used the woad, the medieval blue dyestuff that was cultivated in the neighborhood. Erfurt consisted originally of the *Domhügel,* the cathedral hill, with the parish Church of St. Mary and the Church of St. Severus, and the Petersberg, presumably the site of the *Pfalz* and the Church of St. Peter.

The oldest settlement dates back to the eighth century. St. Boniface regarded it as sufficiently important to make it a bishopric in 741. He mentioned it as an "old settlement," *iam olim urbs paganorum rusticorum*

under the protection of the *Pfalz.* This earliest settlement may have stood on the site of the present Domplatz. It received market rights in 805. The first walls of 1066 may have enclosed this first market place. The center of the next market settlement, east of the Domplatz, was the market square, the present *Fischmarkt* with the old town hall. The market street was its axis connecting it with the Gera ford. In 1168, both of these earliest settlements, together with the Petersberg and the *Domhügel,* were walled in. Gradually the original settlements expanded and suburbs grew up in the southwest, the south, and the north.

The *Domhügel* with the two churches is the crowning accent of the whole town. The natural configuration of the terrain has been convincingly and marvelously used. The group of the Cathedral and the Church of St.

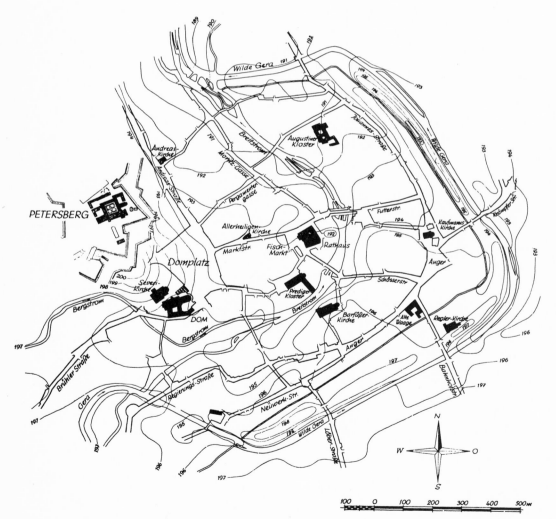

314. Contour map of Erfurt.

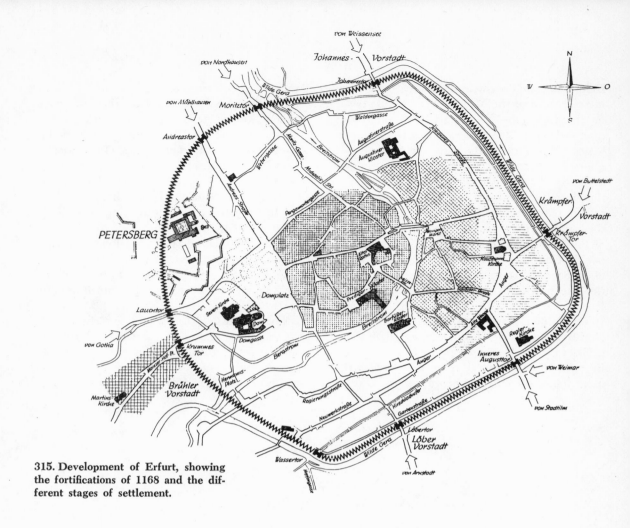

315. Development of Erfurt, showing the fortifications of 1168 and the different stages of settlement.

317. Cathedral and Church of St. Severus as they are today.

Severus, the stairs filling the whole space between their diverging volumes, belongs to the most impressive and beautiful achievements of city building in Germany. The low and modest houses huddled together at the foot of the stairs heighten the scale of the churches. The strong vertical lines of the Cathedral, its towers, and the three spires of St. Severus create a powerful contrast to the horizontal lines of the cathedral terrace, the stairs, and the horizontal accentuation of St. Severus, which is unique in its strength and concentration. The original impression has been spoiled: the old buildings on the *Domplatz* have been pulled down. As in numerous other cases where a misunderstood monumentalism, one of the misguided ambitions of the last century, has created large open spaces around ancient churches, the scale has been destroyed. The Domplatz is now much too large; instead of being a preparation for the buildings on the hill, it is just an empty space.

316. *Opposite:* Cathedral and Church of St. Severus in 1795. Engraving by J. J. Ramée.

318. Aerial view of the *Burg*. The main gate in the foreground leads to the courtyards, the church, and other buildings. The keep is in the center background. The medieval irregularity and loose grouping of a "Residence" are in sharp contrast to the Renaissance and Baroque palaces, with their regimented, compact, and symmetrical groupings—different in form and spirit but fulfilling the same basic function.

Friedberg, Hesse. Friedberg, in the *Wetterau,* lies on the important route from Frankfurt to Hamburg. It was first mentioned in 1219. At this time the walls were still unfinished. The town was built as a trading center that guarded the trunk road. It flourished in the thirteenth and fourteenth centuries; it was a member of the *Rheinische Städtebund;* and later it joined Frankfurt, Wetzlar, and Gelnhausen in the *Wetterauer Städtebund.* By the end of the thirteenth century suburbs had grown up in the south and north of the town, which received the same rights as the *Altstadt* and were, therefore, probably also walled in. The *Burg* Friedberg was erected by Emperor Frederick I before 1216 on the site of a Roman *castrum,* which was followed by a Frankish *Königshof.* The count who resided in the *Burg* was originally also the highest judicial and military authority in the town; but the burghers contested his claim, and long disputes followed, ending in 1483 with the submission of the town and its duty to swear allegiance to every *Burggraf.* The town's dependence on the feudal lords was accompanied by a gradual decline and the loss of its importance as a trading center and a fair. Friedberg's layout, consisting of a rectangle with a wide street where markets and fairs were held, was well adapted to its function. Narrow streets ran parallel to this main street and were connected with each other by small lanes.

319. The town and the *Burg* of Braunfels. The market square is in the left foreground.

Braunfels, Hesse. South of the Lahn, Braunfels originated around 1100 in a small street village, St. Georgen, at the foot of a hill on which a *Burg* was built in 1246. It was inhabited by peasants, soldiers, servants of the feudal lords, gentry, officials, craftsmen, and miners. All these people, apart from the peasants who were, of course, full-time farmers, had a few fields and pastures in addition to their main jobs. There were guilds of tailors, shoemakers, masons, carpenters, blacksmiths, bakers, butchers, and others. It had the usual social and economic structure of a typical small town.

320. Braunfels's market square with gate.

321. General view of Rosenthal.

Rosenthal, Hesse. Southwest of Kassel, Rosenthal is particularly interesting because it is one of the few small places where repetition of identical building elements has not degenerated into a dull monotony. A rectangular street system, a central church, gables alternating with eaves, and half-timbered houses all having almost the same height were the means with which a coherent diversity was achieved. This is an instructive counterpart to the developers' settlements of our own time with their soulless, stereotyped, and profit-centered "mushroom" houses.

322. Plan of Kassel, by Matthaeus Merian, 1646.

Kassel, Hesse. Kassel on the Fulda, founded
before A.D. 913, became a town in the thirteenth century. By the middle of the seventeenth century it consisted of the *Unter-
neustadt,* the lower new town, on the right
bank of the Fulda and the *Altstadt* on the
left bank; both were connected by a stone
bridge.

Between 1690 and 1710 the *Oberneustadt,*
the upper new town, was laid out by the
French architect Paul du Ry who had been
connected with the planning of Karlshafen
on the Weser originally intended for Huguenots. Like the *Oberneustadt* at Kassel, this
one consisted of a rectangular street pattern.
The *Oberneustadt* adjoined the *Altstadt* in
the southwest and was composed of building
blocks extending to a terrace above the Kleine
Fulda. The center is occupied by a small
square with a Protestant church. One of the
building blocks has been shortened in order
to gain sufficient space for the church and to
place it in the axial perspective of the main
street. The difficult connection of the *Oberneustadt* with the *Altstadt* was solved by the
insertion of a square, the usual recourse that
was used by du Ry's predecessors and successors in similar circumstances. This articulation consisted of a large, rectangular square,
the Friedrichsplatz—one of the largest in
Europe—with an area of 1000 by 450 feet. A
second circular square, the Königsplatz, with
a diameter of 560 feet, was added by the
grandson of Paul du Ry on the northern side
of the *Altstadt,* whose fortifications had been
dismantled after the capture of Kassel by the
Germans in 1662. It was the point of departure for six streets, a small version of the
Place de l'Etoile. French influences were
even more obvious in the layout of the gar-

387

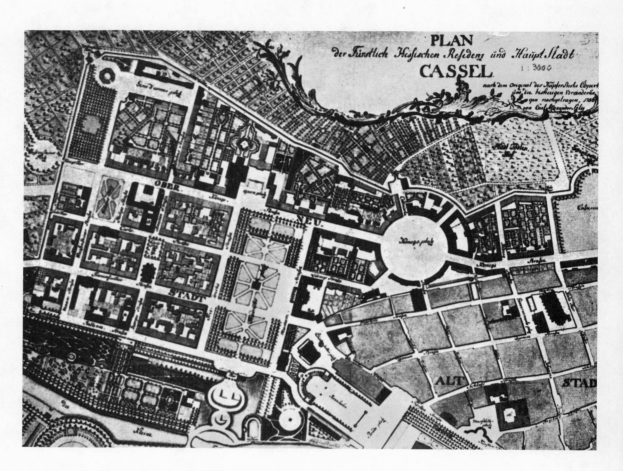

323. Plan of Kassel in 1786 by Carl Alexander Selig.

dens between the Fulda and its branch, the Kleine Fulda, for the architect, Louis du Ry, had visited Paris in 1748 and worked there under J. F. Blondel. The tip of the peninsula was occupied by the Orangery; on it converged three streets. An oval esplanade, two *ronds points,* and a pond were the main features of this miniature Versailles.

The delight of the rulers of Kassel in pleasure grounds was a marked characteristic of their activities. Soon after 1700 the gardens at Wilhelmshöhe, near Kassel, were designed and laid out by the Roman Giovanni Francisco Guernieri for the *Landgraf;* they were reminiscent of the gardens at Rome and Frascati. They were perhaps the most grandiose venture upon which the Baroque had embarked and the most audacious attempt at blending architecture and landscape. The

gardens were connected with Kassel by a magnificent avenue almost one mile long. Guernieri intended to build a palace at the foot of the hill. A double stairway curving round a fountain led up to the main floor. An open portico in the center, consisting of five arches, opened the view over the gardens. A long line of cascades interrupted by nine basins, each with a fountain, rises along the slopes to a terrace at the center of which stands a small pavilion. Paths radiating from it divide the pond that surrounds it in fanlike sectors. A second line of cascades with five basins completes this water avenue, which ends in an octagonal water castle 120 feet in diameter and three stories high. Its lower part, as also the terraces that accompany the cascades, is built of natural or very rough ashlar stones. The water pours down in cascades from the highest point, which is crowned by an enormous copy of the Farnese Hercules, feeding the fountains and water-falls and streaming through the grottoes with their numerous statues. Parts of this ambitious demonstration of an absolute prince have been preserved. No period but the Baroque could have created this fantastic monument, born of the whims of a little potentate fascinated by the splendor of the court of *Le Roi Soleil* and craving for self-glorification. It was a childish amusement but, at this time, an all too human temptation to have something unusual, something not utilitarian. Let us not forget, however, that this was the period of the labyrinths, which expressed the same desire, the same contempt for the "practical" use of the financial resources of the state; which also worked with repetitions, illusions, and an extension in depth and movement. These gardens certainly achieved one thing: They were unique; they were the distant focal point of Kassel and a conspicuous landmark for a wide region.

324. Plan of the fortress of Kassel in 1717. Although this date is indicated on the plan, it is probably incorrect. The gardens were laid out later but are shown in this plan.

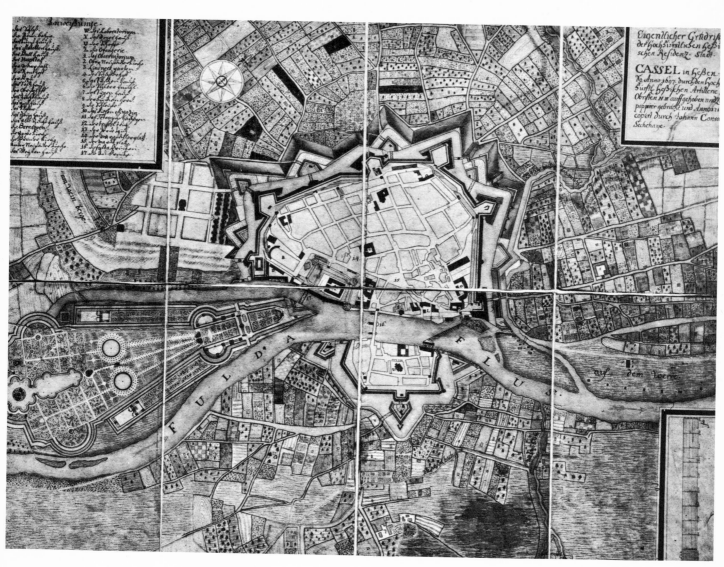

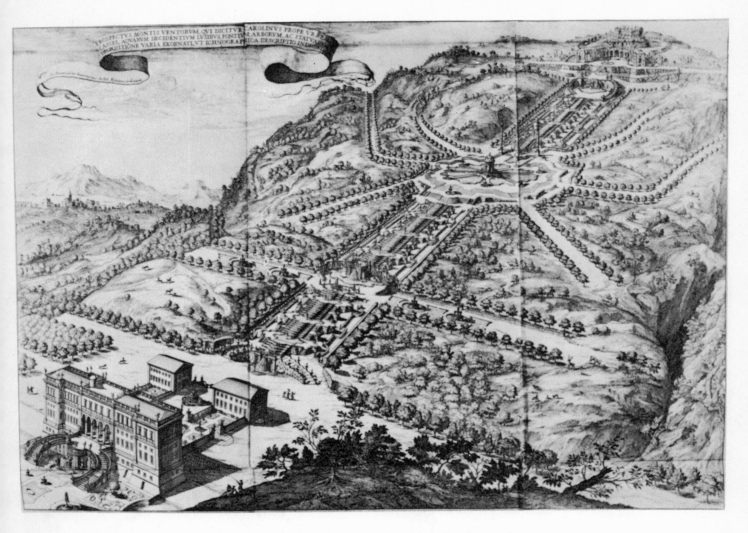

325. The cascades at Wilhelmshöhe in Kassel, 1706. Guernerius. *Delineatio montis.*

Goslar, Lower Saxony. Goslar, on the Gose, at the northern foot of the Harz Mountains, was probably a foundation of Henry the Fowler (A.D. 920). It gained in importance under Otto the Great when minerals were discovered in the neighborhood. It was repeatedly the meeting place of German diets, and it joined the Hanseatic League about 1350. At the end of the twelfth century it was surrounded by walls. It has preserved much of its previous charm and many old buildings, streets and squares, which are of particular interest as landmarks in the development of city planning. The early nucleus of Goslar was the imperial *Pfalz* with its surrounding area. There the feudal lords and their retainers settled, whereas the traders, artisans, and craftsmen established their homes around the market-church.

326. *Opposite:* Peterstrasse in Goslar, part of an ever-changing perspective of facades, projecting upper stories, rows of windows between the vertical lines of the half-timbered structures, and the undulating rhythm of the roofs.

327. Monastery of the Grosse Heilige Kreuz, a religious establishment, at the corner of a gently curved street in Goslar. There is a veritable polyphony of roofs, dormers, chimneys, and doors.

Hildesheim, at the northern foot of the Harz Mountains, originated in a *vicus* that was situated near a ford through the Innerste on the ridge of a hill. Like all *vici,* it was a street market with one row of houses. It got its name from an old Saxon farm that had been founded by a Hiltwin; it was therefore called Hiltwineshem, later to become Hildensem and finally Hildesheim. In A.D. 815 it was made the seat of a bishopric, a fact indicating that the place already had, at this time, a certain importance; for according to a canonical decree by the Council of Sardica held in 344, bishoprics had to be established only in populous regions. Consequently, market settlements were preferred because the bishops and their retinue could easily acquire most of the goods they needed to maintain their accustomed standard of living. Around A.D. 1000 the *vicus* Hildesheim was elevated to a market, to a *mercatus.* The road from the *Domburg* to the Church of St. Michael, which today is still called Burgstrasse, crossed the old west–east trade route, the *Hellweg,* at a point where the *vicus* developed. This part of the route was the *Alte Markt,* a name it has retained to the present day; this was the earliest nucleus of Hildesheim.

By the middle of the twelfth century the *Alte Markt* and its settlement had become too small for the growing population. A new market square was laid out at the Church of St. Andreas where important roads met. Here the first town hall was built in 1217. Although the *vicus* was originally an open settlement, later possibly protected by palisades, the second market place around St. Andreas was fortified from the beginning.

Hildesheim's economic prosperity seemed to have aroused the envy of the feudal lords who wanted to take part in the profits of the lucrative trade of the town. They built, therefore, two new settlements on the main trade routes but in advanced positions, obviously in the hope of cutting off trade and traffic before they reached the town. In 1196 the canons of St. Moritz auf dem Berg invited clothmakers from Flanders and settled them west of the *Altstadt* on both sides of a dam

328. *Opposite:* Am Liebfrauenberg in Goslar, a secluded square of miniature dimensions. The streets enter it almost invisibly at the corners. Although of a later period, it has the multiplicity of points of view characteristic of the Middle Ages. Each house has its own individuality.

329. *Opposite:* A different impression of Goslar's Am Liebfrauenberg. More open, but still intimate, this view shows a less serene blending of nature and architecture.

393

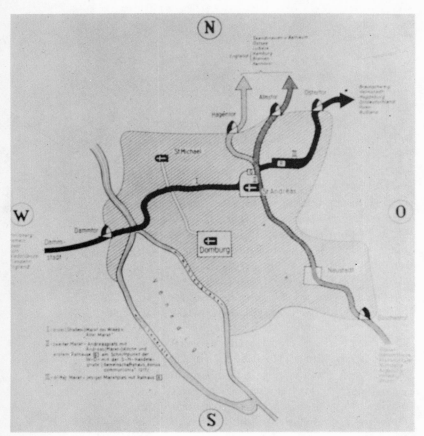

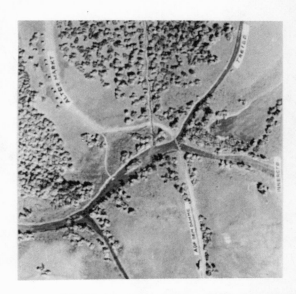

331. Model of the earliest development of Hildesheim. The Alter Markt (Old Market) is probably the earliest focus of the town.

330. The three markets of Hildesheim.

332. Engraving of Hildesheim in 1654 by Matthaeus Merian.

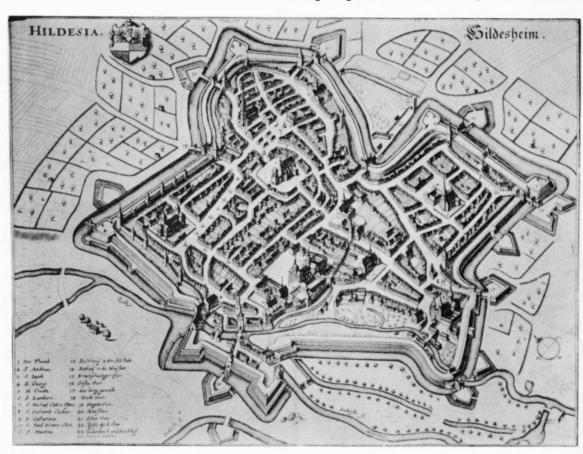

333. View of Hildesheim from the tower of the Church of St. Andreas toward the Church of St. Godehardi. This and the following pictures were taken before the city's destruction in World War II.

that connected Hildesheim and the Moritzberg; this was the *Dammstadt*. The other settlement was founded by the prior of the cathedral in the southeast; this was the so-called *Neustadt*.

The third market, the present *Altstadtmarkt*, moved the development of the town farther to the east. Shortly before 1200 the bishop prohibited the market at the cemetery of the Church of St. Andreas on the grounds that it was interfering with the divine service and was incompatible with the respect due to the dead. This was the beginning of the new development: The west–east road was systematically enlarged immediately to the east of its intersection with the south–north road. At this square, which was originally a long rectangle, the present town hall was built between 1268 and 1290.

By the end of the thirteenth century the essential features of Hildesheim had assumed their final character: Three nuclei existed, which were gradually to grow together; and the position of the burghers had been strengthened by a constitution that, though created by the patricians, was the basis upon which the guilds slowly but steadily rose to influence and wealth. The whole area of the town was fortified by walls, towers, and strong gates. A *Landwehr*, more than a mile away from the walls, ran in a wide semicircle in the east from river to river; it was a low wall with a ditch covered with thick thorn hedges that could be crossed only at a few points, which were guarded by watchtowers. Toward the end of the sixteenth century the fortifications were modernized and strengthened; bastions were built; massive earthen walls were added; and the moats, which were used in peacetime as fish ponds, were deepened and broadened. Most of the magnificent half-timbered houses—almost all have been destroyed by bombing—belong to the decades before the Thirty Years' War.

334. Market square in Hildesheim, with the Knochenhauer Amtshaus (*left*), the "most beautiful wooden house in the world." Built in 1529, it was originally the butcher's guild house.

335. *Opposite:* Hildesheim's Andreas Square, showing the Church of St. Andreas and the beginning of a narrow, curved street. The houses stand very close to the church, enhancing its height and massive grandeur.

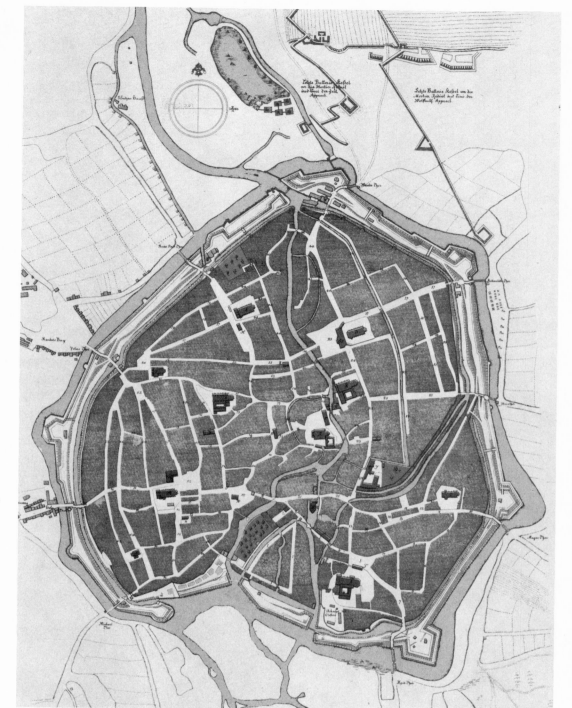

337. Braunschweig in 1671.

336. *Opposite:* Zuckerhut (Sugar Loaf House) and Pfeilerhaus (Pillar House) in Hildesheim, making a daring composition on a small site. Note the extreme utilization of space; the powerful contrasts of surfaces and openings, of receding and projecting volumes, of light and shadow; the structural audacity; and the purposeful adaptation to the streets.

Braunschweig, Lower Saxony. Braunschweig, on the Oker, was founded in A.D. 861. The *Burg* with a market, the Kohlmarkt, and a harbor were the oldest nuclei of the town. The Kohlmarkt provided for the *Burg,* and the harbor on the Oker with a *Wik,* where the name Brunswik originated, loaded and

338. Burgplatz and Lion, the symbol of Braunschweig.

unloaded the goods to and from Bremen. At the Kohlmarkt, the earliest growth of the settlement began shortly before A.D. 1000. Soon after 1200 Braunschweig had reached a size that remained more or less the same until the nineteenth century. By 1100 the settlement at the Kohlmarkt had spread westward; this was the *Altstadt*. By the middle of the twelfth century two new districts had been added: the *Neustadt* west of the *Altstadt* and the *Hagen* on the eastern bank of the Oker. Then followed the settlement of the *Sack* west of the *Burg*, which was now enclosed on all sides by these urban communities. The first nucleus was then called the *Alte Wik*. The name Brunswik was applied to all these cells as a whole. There were, thus, five townlets, which were originally independent self-contained units—*Altstadt, Hagen, Neustadt, Altewik,* and *Sack*—each having a street system with a character of its own. This was unique in Germany. Each town built its own town hall, its own parish church and market, and had its own constitution and coat of arms, and its own wall and moat within the large and common fortifications.

Braunschweig reached a leading economic position in the time of Henry the Lion (1129–1195), especially as a reloading point for the iron ores from Goslar at the Harz Mountains. As lord of the town, Henry granted it important shipping privileges. He was the founder (1160) of the *Hagen* where weavers and wool and cloth merchants from Flanders settled, while the majority of the inhabitants of the *Altstadt* were metal merchants. The duke also founded the *Neustadt* with the collaboration of the merchants of the *Altstadt*, fortified the *Hagen* with palisades and a moat, and later built a common wall around the *Altstadt*, the *Neustadt*, and the *Hagen*. In 1269, these three townlets formed a common council, but this attempt at an administrative union came to nothing. It was destroyed by a revolt of the guilds in 1293. In the fourteenth and fifteenth centuries, despite the existence of a common council that was eventually set up, each of the five *Weichbilder* (as the townlets were called) had retained its own council. Braunschweig was a leading member of the Hanseatic League and, at one time, was the greatest commercial town in the inland trade of northern Germany, with connections to Flanders, England, Denmark, the Baltic, and Hungary. In about 1500 it had 20 thousand inhabitants. Trade was mainly carried on in the market squares in each *Weichbild*. The three annual fairs were held in the *Altstadt*.

Apart from the fortifications around the whole town and the *Weichbilder,* the *Landwehr* with toll booths existed far outside the walls. A new *enceinte* was built in the sixteenth century, and in the eighteenth century bastions were added. The fortifications, dismantled in 1797, have given way to a girdle of gardens and promenades.

339. Braunschweig's old weighing house (Alte Wage) and the Church of St. Andreas behind it.

340. Old street leading to the Cathedral in Braunschweig.

Eisleben, former Province of Saxony. This small town was first mentioned in 974. By the middle of the eleventh century it received the rights to hold a market, coin money, and levy tolls. It was the birthplace of Martin Luther, who also died there.

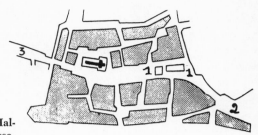

341. Plan of Eisleben: 1. market; 2. Hallesche Strasse; 3. Sängerhauserstrasse.

342. The market, a slight broadening of the main street that ran through the town from one end to the other. Eisleben was a road town, and the road was the obvious place for all market activities. The town hall divides the main road into two smaller streets. The church standing behind the town hall in a lateral widening of the road closes the perspective view. A spatial impression in depth and interrelated volumes and shapes was created, using simple means.

Hamburg. It is still unknown whether the earliest settlement was a permanent village, a halting place for traveling merchants, or both existing side by side on the narrow ridge between the Alster and Bille valleys. However, this was not the nucleus of the later development that began with a *Burg,* as the name Hammaburg implies. The name means a *Burg* at the village of Hamma or Hamm. It was possibly a Saxon refuge against the Slavs. It was protected in the west by a wall, the *Heidenwall,* and the low-lying lands of the Elbe, the Alster, and the Bille, which were difficult to pass. It was open in the east, the actual danger point where an attack could be expected. Another hypothesis is that the site on the hill was occupied by a *Königshof* of Charlemagne and that the refuge belongs to a considerably earlier time. In 831, the seat of a bishop was established within the walls of the *Burg,* and a *Domburg* with its usual fortifications was laid out. In its charter, Louis the Pious speaks of it significantly as a foundation *"inter has utrasque gentes Danorum sive Winedorum ultima in regione Saxonica trans Albiam"* ("between the two pagan peoples of the Danes and the Wends at the outermost border of the land of the Saxons beyond the Elbe"). This means that Hamburg became the center of religious propaganda directed toward the North and the East, a fact that corresponds with its geographical position. Its position restricted its role as a traffic center of overland routes to Schleswig, Holstein, Mecklenburg, and Pomerania where Hedeby, Oldenburg, Rethra, and Jumme were the targets of missionary expeditions. As an inland waterway, the Elbe was still undiscovered and too dangerous in the violently disputed frontier districts.

In the immediate vicinity of the *Domburg,* an open civic settlement, a *suburbium* or *vicus proximus,* came into being. It was both a halting place and a market settlement. In 845, *Burg,* church, and *vicus* were razed by the Danes. After this catastrophe, there is no information on the development that took place during the next hundred years. But by the middle of the tenth century Hamburg was again mentioned as a market and a har-

bor, protected on one side by palisades that joined the walls of the *Domburg.* After an attack by the Wends in about 1020, the archbishop restored the *Domburg* and settled "a large number of clerics and burghers"; this "large number" consisted of twelve canons, a few deacons, and some auxiliary priests. The concentration of the clergy had a surprising effect: On the archbishop's orders all questionable women to whom the priests had been sneaking away from their seclusion— *e claustro egressi*—were expelled from the *civitas* and distributed among the neighboring villages. Apparently because of this, the *Altstadt* of Hamburg was born. Sedentary citizens, instead of traveling merchants, now dominated the picture. The *Altstadt* was approximately circular, and was surrounded by new palisades in place of the destroyed walls. The smaller eastern part was reserved for the clergy, the larger western half for the laity. From the central market square on an eminence the streets led in all directions like the spokes of a wheel. Numerous trades were established, each confined to its own street. The building plots were narrow and not deep; they remained more or less the same until 1842. On the average they were 16 to 20 feet wide and about 30 to 35 feet deep.

Next to this half-clerical and half-trading town developed a settlement of merchants, the *Reichenstrasse,* whose character was entirely different from the *Altstadt.* Where the *Altstadt* had been, as it were, hydrophobic, the new town preferred water courses; where the former had occupied an elevation safe from flooding, the latter chose an endangered island in the marsh; where the former had a spokelike system of narrow, short streets with small plots, the latter consisted of one long street with houses on one side only, on a dikelike eminence with large and deep plots; where the former had been fortified, the latter remained without walls and moat, gates and towers. The *Reichenstrasse* island was a long rectangle. The plots extended from one long side to the other, *ab aqua ad aquam,* and the street ran along the elevated dam parallel to the northern long side. On the average, the plots were 320 feet deep and 48 feet wide. The houses on the southern edge of the dam were one-storied. On a lower level behind them lay the courtyard and the garden, which were susceptible to flooding. In front of the northern side of the dam, on the short, outer dikes, there were storage places and booths of the auxiliary trades of the merchants, especially of the coopers who were small holders dependent on the merchants. The original number of settlers was perhaps twenty. The whole conception and layout of this island settlement was adapted from the *Marschhufen* villages; it had one row of houses facing a dike in a tidal marsh where the strips of land were laid out at right angles to the dike. It was an application of rural colonial methods to urban conditions.

The successful advance of German colonization in the East since the middle of the twelfth century fundamentally changed the situation. The precarious existence of Hamburg as an outpost on a hostile frontier came to an end. The marsh settlements were filled with Saxon, Frisian, and Dutch immigrants, and the middle Elbe was settled by German and Flemish peasants and burghers. New economic possibilities opened. An extension of the existing town became imperative, and a *Neustadt* was added to the *Altstadt* of Hamburg. This was carried through by a group of contractors under the leadership of a certain Wirard of Boizenburg. The Count of Holstein, the feudal lord, granted these men, *Wiradus et sui cohabitatores*, permission to develop an area west of the *Altstadt* and to establish there a free trading settlement and a port with a weekly market and two annual fairs. The land that was given to them consisted of an oblong area surrounded by the Alster in the north, east, and south. Because it was the former *Neue Burg*, which had fallen into disuse, it was enclosed

343. Plan of Hamburg by Matthaeus Merian, 1633.

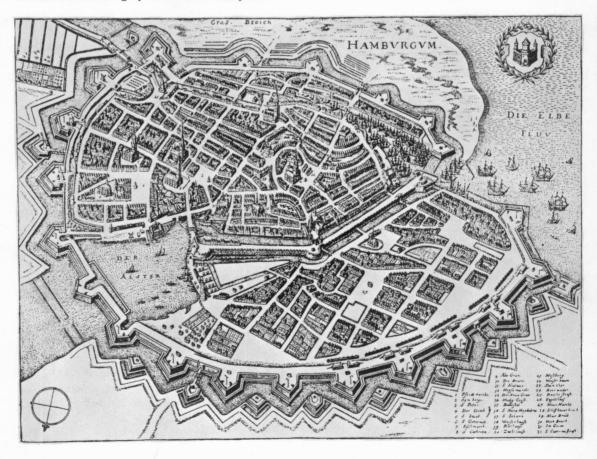

344. Hamburg's third town hall in 1671.

345. Sectional plan of Hamburg in 1800.

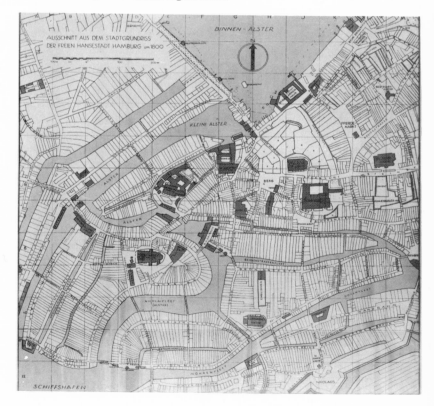

by a wall. Its 8 acres were divided into fifty equal sectors; the western part was reserved for public purposes. The houses were erected on the former walls' inner side, which was leveled and then used as a road, a layout that was like a ring-fence village turned outward. Only a small market square, the *Novum Forum,* later the *Forum Humuli,* the hop market, was laid out, a certain proof that collaboration, not competition, with the *Altstadt* was intended. When new settlers arrived, they received lots in the adjoining marshlands. This part was called *Deich-strasse,* or simply *Deich,* dike. Soon the market square was enlarged, and a small town hall was built. Because this new foundation was to be a port, the not yet built-up land at the Alster was used for quays. At the end of the twelfth century the episcopal *Altstadt* had 600 to 800 inhabitants, and the *Neustadt,* 400 to 500. In contrast to Braunschweig, both hitherto separate towns were combined into one community with one council, one town hall, and one law court; and the walls between them were pulled down. After the liberation from the Danes, Hamburg grew rapidly. Its area increased threefold and the population fourfold, to over 5 thousand around 1300.

405

346. Merchants' houses at the Rödingsmarkt in Hamburg.

Now the expansion of Hamburg proceeded apace. Two larger *Werder,* islands in the river, in the south of the town were settled, again systematically using the example of the *Marschhufen* villages. About 1300 Hamburg covered approximately 198 acres, roughly the same as Bremen, Hildesheim, and Regensburg but still less than Lübeck, Braunschweig, or Mainz, not to mention Augsburg, Cologne, and Nürnberg. This early "Greater Hamburg" had grown together from nine small units. The subsequent development proceeded along similar lines; that is, it was an organic and cellular growth. Each of the cells retained for a while its own privileges and structure, and was absorbed only later into the larger community through constitutional and building transformations. By the end of the thirteenth century Hamburg had reached a size it did not surpass until the period of the Hanseatic League 250 years later. However, its internal structure underwent considerable changes. As in other towns the fortifications were improved, churches were completed, and the Gothic replaced the Romanesque style. The houses grew higher, the building density increased, small houses and dwelling units were built, and even cellars and booths were used for housing the poorer population.

But in one respect Hamburg followed a different path. It was not only a river town like Lübeck, Bremen, or Cologne; it was a town "in the waves." Since the twelfth century it had spread from the higher *Geest* to the low-lying marshland and turned its face toward the innumerable larger and smaller watercourses that traversed the marshes like

406

347. Warehouses on the Mührenfleet in Hamburg.

348. Breweries at the Grimm.

a vascular plexus. For a long time, however, most of the settlements remained behind the dikes. This changed in the fourteenth century when Hamburg became the "brewery of the Hansa." There were 457 breweries in 1376, a number that rose in the following century to more than 500 with a total production of more than 12,000,000 gallons. These 500 breweries changed the face of Hamburg. They stood out from all other buildings, for they were much larger; they had enormous halls on the ground floor and several low stories for storing grain and malt; and they were situated directly on the watercourses. These spacious buildings, which reached from the street to the water (*a platea usque ad aquam*), were peculiar to Hamburg. Since then, uninterrupted rows of high-gabled houses have lined the narrow and wide *Fleete,* the canals.

Hamburg has often been compared with Amsterdam; yet the differences are interesting. Hamburg is nature refashioned; Amsterdam's canals wash directly against the buildings, which turn their backs to the water; Amsterdam is more rational, more artificial —in the best sense of the word.

Lübeck. Lübeck, on the Trave, is 14 miles from the Baltic. Seagoing vessels can reach it through the river, which has been deepened. The inner town stands on a hill surrounded by the Trave and its tributaries.

A German trading settlement had grown up close to the old, Slavic Lübeck, which was destroyed by the Wends in 1138. In its place a *Burg* was founded south of the peninsula between the Trave and Wakenitz. The settlement grew and soon had several street markets. This place was ceded to Henry the Lion, who made it a religious center and began building the cathedral in 1173. The new town was transferred to the middle of the island. Each settler received a plot of 25 by 100 feet.

Henry granted far-reaching privileges to

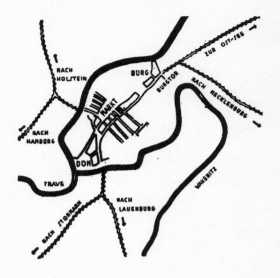

349. Lübeck about 1100.

350. The oldest surviving plan of Lübeck. Watercolor, 1705.

353. *Opposite:* General view of Lübeck.

408

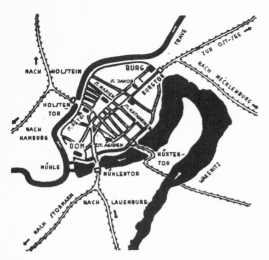

351. Lübeck about 1200.

352. Lübeck about 1700.

the new town—the most honorable legal position, *jura honestissima,* as the chronicler Helmolt called it—for he was determined to attract the influential and wealthy merchants to trade with the Scandinavian countries and Russia. For them he built a market and a residential district near the port, and also fortified the town with earthen walls and palisades. From the very beginning, the merchants seemed to have formed a guild-like corporation and to have played a decisive role. They were, according to Helmolt, the *patres rei publice Lubicanae.* He also called Lübeck a *civitas,* a town, a confederation created as a community for peace. The motives of the duke were obvious. He recognized that the great economic prosperity of

the towns in western Germany had been born and was maintained in a spirit of freedom; now he adopted their liberal constitutions for his own new foundation and thus released forces that were to dominate the trade and commerce of the Baltic region.

The town's population remained fairly constant during the Middle Ages; it may have numbered 20 thousand to 30 thousand people. For a long time it did not grow beyond its natural limits between the rivers. The principal streets roughly followed the contours of the terrain; the main street ran along the ridge of the hill and the side streets branched off at right angles. The sites for the three main churches were chosen with that admirable and instinctive empathy of

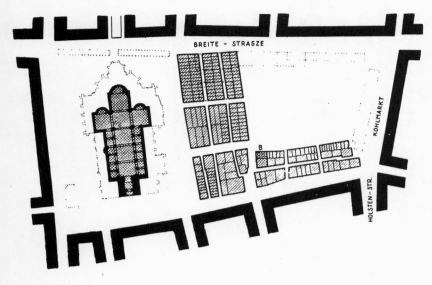

354. Lübeck's market square about 1200.

which only medieval architects were capable: the Cathedral at the southern end of the town, St. Mary's in the center, and St. Peter's at the other end on a steep terrace—a beautiful triad reverberating over the roofs of the town. The original market square covered a large area of 8.3 acres. There a wooden church was built, later a Romanesque basilica, and eventually a Gothic church. A cemetery was laid out, and the rest of the square was occupied by booths. The first stone buildings were halls of the cloth merchants, the most distinguished members of the trading community. The town hall was not built in its present form before 1570.

Lübeck was a trading town from the beginning, a characteristic expressed in its dwellings with high gables. For the merchant the street front was the showpiece of his trade. Because the street front was expensive, the plots were narrow and deep. The workshops were badly lit, but the great height of the hall provided enough light through the higher windows for him to sort and pack his goods. Little space was needed for the office and living rooms, but the storerooms were large, and since they required no light or air, were low and deep and connected with the street by a windlass. Thus narrow buildings about 60 to 75 feet deep developed naturally out of the particular and functional needs of the inhabitants. The wealthier the merchant, the higher the house—hence the gables with their blind windows and walls projecting far above the roofs.

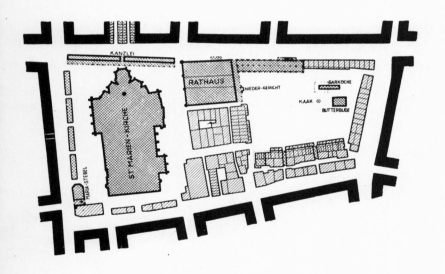

355. Lübeck's market square about 1620.

357. *Opposite:* Lübeck's town hall. *Left:* the old part (1220–1226), with high screening wall, round openings to reduce wind pressure, and Renaissance arcades built in 1570. *Right:* the two additions, finished in 1244 and 1308 respectively. It is the most impressive town hall built in Germany during the Middle Ages. The wings, at right angles to one another, close the market square on the east side.

356. Storehouses for salt in Lübeck.

358. General view of Ratzeburg.

Ratzeburg, Schleswig-Holstein. This town stands on an island connected with the mainland by dams. The church occupies the northern tip and is now separated from the town by a park. The town was founded in 1154 by Henry the Lion. The site was probably chosen because it offered natural and excellent protection.

359. General view of Mölln.

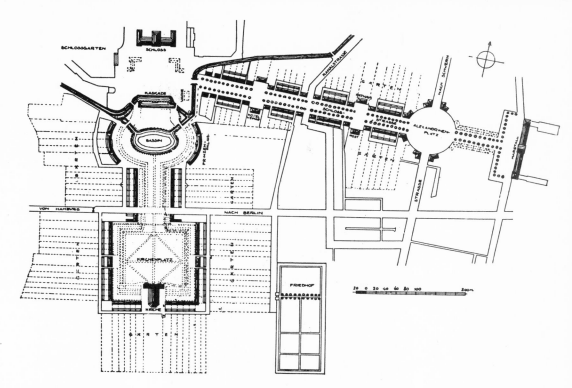

360. Plan of palace and gardens at Ludwigslust.

Mölln, Schleswig-Holstein. On a peninsula between two branches of the lake of Mölln stands a perfect model of a unifocal town. Its church stands on a hill in the center, and streets and houses follow the contours at its base. One small square (center foreground) joins this part to the extension (right foreground), and another one (behind it in the air view) connects it with the rest of the town. It is a solution adapted to the natural conditions: uncomplicated, organic, and full of attractive views.

The lake was first mentioned as *stagnum Mulne* in 1188, and the village of Old Mölln, in 1194. The fact that the available evidence refers to "Old" Mölln may be adduced as proof of the existence of a "New" Mölln, which can only have been the town of the same name. Mölln was a resting place for the long-distance traffic from the South over the great salt-route from Lüneburg and over other roads to the East, North, and Southwest. This favorable location explains its importance.

The town was fortified at the middle of the sixteenth century. Throughout its history it remained a small and rather insignificant place as far as the number of inhabitants was concerned. In 1581 it had fewer than 300 households.

Ludwigslust, Mecklenburg. This is a modest, yet charming, version of the ostentatious residences of western Germany. It was founded in 1747 with 6,950 inhabitants. Its small palace, finished in 1775, is the focal point for a composition that works with simple means. There are no round points, no star patterns, no excessively broad or long avenues. The palace is at the end of an axis, at the other end of which stands a church. The whole is relatively compact with a squat forecourt; a round basin and a cascade; a short and tree-lined avenue; and a square, also tree-lined, with the church. The low houses are at a distance from the palace and follow roughly the outline of the open space around the basin. The Schlosstrasse, which leads diagonally to the palace from a circular square, connects it with the town, an asymmetrical solution that does not diminish in the least the unity of the composition or the situation of the palace as the heart and *causa causans* of the town.

413

361. Rostock's New Market square.

362. Development plan of Rostock, showing the two oldest nuclei, the *Mittelstadt* and the *Neustadt*.

Rostock, Mecklenburg. Rostock, on the Warnow, occupies a site that is distinguished by the variety of its terrain. The old market square lies 36 feet above the level of the embankment. The hill slopes steeply down in the east to the Warnow. To the west, the elevation continues to the new market square and beyond to the Church of St. Jacob. The earliest settlement of the Wends with a *Burg* probably stood on the right bank of the Warnow protected by the marshes. German traders settled around the old market square before 1218. A few decades later craftsmen and merchants from Lower Saxony, Westphalia, and Holstein began to occupy a second nucleus further south around the Church of St. Nicolas.

The two nuclei with their squares were connected by two parallel streets following the contours of the ridge. Each square had a church, St. Peter's and St. Nicholas' respectively. The foundations of the nuclei of Rostock followed each other in short intervals: the *Altstadt* in the east in 1218; the *Mittelstadt* with the new market square and St. Mary's in 1232; and the *Neustadt* with the *Hopfenmarkt*, the hop market, and St. Jacob's in 1252. The street system is simple: A few streets run almost parallel from east to west, and are crossed at right angles by parallel side streets. With the exception of the triangular *Hopfenmarkt*, the squares are more or less rectangular.

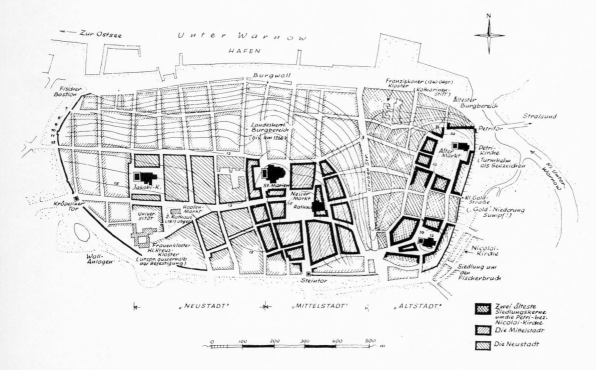

Potsdam, Brandenburg. Potsdam, on the Havel, was a Slavonic fishing village. It was first mentioned in a record of the year 993. It became a town in 1220, and was surrounded by walls. It remained unimportant until the Great Elector built a palace between 1660 and 1682, but even then it had only 3 thousand inhabitants. He enlarged the town, and on his orders the main axes of the street pattern were laid out. But the actual founder of Potsdam, the very embodiment of the Prussian spirit, was Frederick William I, the creator of the Prussian army. He rebuilt the *Altstadt* "according to his lights," that is, he followed his instinct and the mode of his time by applying the rigid regimentation and ruthless equalization of the parade ground to his new foundation. The main street was the canal, the *Gracht*. The other streets were adapted to the existing axes. The houses had Mansard roofs and two stories, except at the market where they had three stories. In some other streets Dutch row-houses were copied. A town hall and churches were built; the *Lustgarten* (the pleasure grounds) was turned into a drill square, the Orangery, into a riding school. The main purpose of this royal effort was to create a sufficient number of billets for the king's life guards, his giant grenadiers, who were his personal plaything with which he amused himself. Of the eleven thousand inhabitants every fourth was a soldier. Most houses had a five-window front—only occasionally seven or nine windows. The whole town was surrounded on three sides by a brick wall and on the fourth by a palisade. Since defense purposes had to be ruled out, this was virtually a prison wall to prevent the soldiers from escaping, inasmuch as the king had paid large sums for them.

Frederick the Great, who followed his father in 1740, began rebuilding Potsdam on a monumental scale. By the end of his reign its population had grown to 28 thousand inhabitants. He replaced the half-timbered houses by solid stone buildings, which he distributed as free gifts among the citizens. About 600 houses had been built at the time of his death. His plans could not be finished; this explains why the *Altstadt* and a part of the *Neustadt* show late Baroque and Rococo forms, while the rest retained the simpler houses of the time of Frederick William I. The name of the great dilettante Knobelsdorff, who was an officer, is intimately connected with the time of Frederick the Great. He was a friend of the king. Both men

363. View of Potsdam from the Garnisonkirche.

415

were innovators, almost revolutionary in their taste. They did not think very highly of the architectural qualities of the Germans —a complete misjudgment in view of the great achievements of both the past and their own time: Frederick's first buildings were contemporary with the last works of Balthasar Neumann, Zimmermann, and Fischer. These men preferred Italian architecture— not the Baroque of Italy but Palladio, or rather a Palladio interpreted by the English and somewhat anemic and dry. Knobelsdorff designed a number of dwellings; the French Church; a part of the Stadtschloss; and, above all, Sanssouci and its park. The town hall was built by one of his pupils. The second building period after the Seven Years' War was dominated by the architect Karl von Gontard, who was followed after 1815 by Friedrich von Schinkel and his pure classicism. The latter built the Church of St. Nicolas, private houses, and a few small palaces.

Potsdam is Prussian *par excellence.* Why is this so? Its plan is nothing particular; it is rather indifferent and could be found anywhere. Regimentation in building was *le dernier cri* of the time. The opposition to Baroque forms was a sort of revolution, but not particularly Prussian. What then is the

364. Canal and houses in Potsdam, dating from the time of Frederick the Great.

366. Sanssouci, by G. W. von Knobelsdorff.

365. *Opposite:* Stadtschloss, by G. W. von Knobelsdorff, and the dome of the Nicolaikirche, by F. von Schinkel.

explanation of this phenomenon that can be sensed more than it can be clearly defined? Is it the atmosphere, the intangible spirit history and adulation have woven around the town? The houses of Potsdam are not dissimilar from those in Karlsruhe, Mannheim, and other Residence Cities; the palaces are possibly even better and more refined. The continuous block fronts emanate the same monotony found in many other towns. And yet Prussian rigidity is the label that has been affixed to Potsdam. And Prussian it is, not because its buildings are particularly Prussian, but because history and legend have made it so in the minds of all generations from Frederick William I onward. The imponderables of history are more potent than the realities of architecture.

417

Berlin. The Berlin landscape belongs to the zone of the large abandoned glacial stream channels, the *Urstromtäler,* east of the Elbe. This part of the North German Plain is divided by four *Urstromtäler* running approximately east–west in large regions consisting mainly of ground moraines, which are again subdivided by smaller north–south channels. Berlin lies in the Warsaw-Berlin *Urstromtal,* the second one from the north, today the valley of the lower course of the Spree. That part of the country with its marshy valleys and sandy heath has never been particularly inviting to urban settlement. Berlin is the product not of favorable natural conditions but rather of historical accidents, especially of those connected with the destiny of the Hohenzollern family. It is therefore a political creation, artificial as far as the selection of its site is concerned. Its rise and eminent position as the capital of Germany have resulted exclusively from political combinations, international influences, and the staying power of the early settlers who clung with an almost mystic tenacity to this desolate land.

About 1230, after the plateaux of the Barnim and the Teltow had been occupied, the margraves of Brandenburg founded the twin city of Berlin-Cölln. The origin of the name Berlin is unknown; but Cölln means *colonia* —either the colony of Berlin or in memory of Cöln in the Rhineland, the home of the first arrivals. Cölln was first mentioned in 1237 and Berlin in 1244. It is probable that Cölln was originally a settlement of Wendish fishermen, a *Kietz,* on the southern part of the small island between the branches of the Spree and that the trading settlement of Berlin, north of the island, was founded later.

367. The oldest surviving plan of Berlin, about 1650. Engraving by J. G. Memhardt.

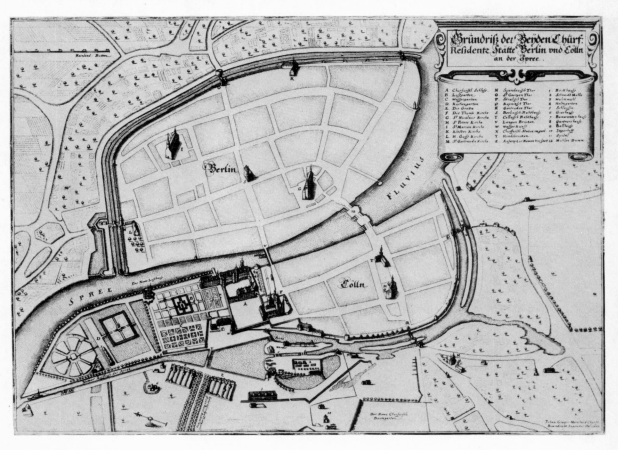

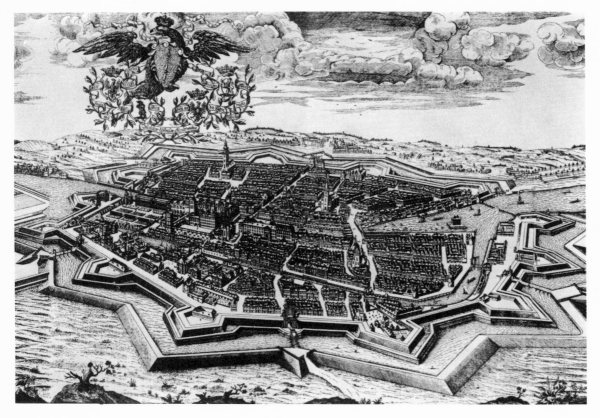

368. Berlin and Cölln in 1688. Engraving by Bernhard Johann Schziltz.

The site may have been chosen for two reasons: Crossing the Spree valley, here only 3 miles wide, was relatively easy, and it was the only passage for many miles upstream and downstream; also, two important routes met at this point, one from the Elbe to the Oder, and the other one from Saxony and Bohemia. Cölln showed the typical features of an east German colonial town—a large central square with town hall and church, and a simple rectangular street pattern— whereas the part of Berlin around the Church of St. Nicholas may belong to an earlier period, although it too was laid out as a colonial town. The Church of St. Peter, belonging to the fishermen, and the Church of St. Nicholas, belonging to the traders, are the oldest buildings in Berlin and Cölln. Both parts were connected by a dam over the Spree, the Mühlendamm. Since the river and road crossings were the actual reason for founding Berlin-Cölln, it was only natural that traffic and trade determined the growth and layout of the towns: The market squares were established near the river crossing. Here was

the nucleus of the Berlin of the future. The town hall, the Church of St. Nicholas, and the Church of St. Mary were built on the three dunes that traverse Berlin, and the oldest streets were laid out along their base. This was also the case in Cölln where the town hall and the Church of St. Peter were erected on a dune. Both towns were enclosed by fortifications with a double moat, a wall, towers, half-towers, five gate-towers, and bridges. Originally the fortifications were much less elaborate than that. In 1251 they consisted of palisades and earthworks. The stone walls belonged to a later period, to the beginning of the fourteenth century.

The two towns concluded a treaty in 1307, which established a closer cooperation, although each retained its own council. During the fourteenth century both acquired, by purchase, villages in the north and south and estates of territorial lords, and both tried to secure their independence and freedom and, if possible, to become subject to the Emperor only. This dream was shattered by the Elector Frederick II in 1448. He

419

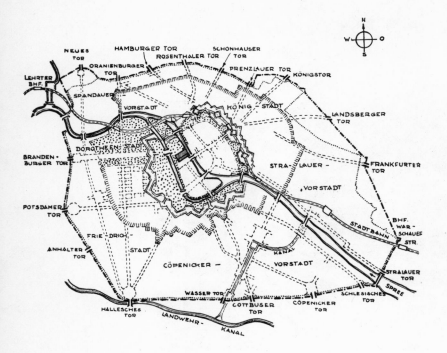

369. Development of Berlin from the Middle Ages to the early nineteenth century.

deprived the towns of their independence, incorporated them into his state, and erected his *Burg* on an island in the Spree. At this time each town had about 6 thousand inhabitants. This was the end of the "burgher town" of Berlin-Cölln and the beginning of the Residence City of the Hohenzollern. After the loss of their independence, the development of both towns stagnated for 2 hundred years. The suburbs that had grown up were destroyed in the Thirty Years' War. Although Berlin itself was spared, the economic situation was so bad that the citizens seriously considered emigrating *en masse* and abandoning the town.

This desperate situation ended when the Great Elector ascended the throne in 1640. Under his guidance Berlin was fortified from 1658 to 1685 after the plans of the Dutch military engineer, Johann Georg Memhardt. An inscription at the Leipzig Gate commemorated the completion of this work: "The Elector Frederick William, the fortunate, the pious, the brave, who has extended the frontiers of the electoral provinces, has enlarged this city through new settlers for the protection of the citizens, the fear of the enemies, the delight of foreigners, surrounded it with fortifications, adorned it with this gate in the year 1683." The *enceinte* consisted of thirteen bastions at regular intervals, which were connected by *courtines,* a Dutch earthwork, and the main wall, which was 25 feet high, and moats. As far as possible, the new gates remained near the old gates. Within the walls the *Werder,* the river island, personal possession of the Elector near his palace, was the first district to be settled; it was called Friedrichwerder. Soon afterward the first suburb, the Dorotheenstadt, was laid out. It received its privileges in 1674. In 1688 a second suburb, the northern Friedrichstadt, followed. Both districts were built on a grid-iron plan and were connected by the avenue, Unter den Linden, of which the first parts were finished in the 1670s.

Numerous French refugees settled in Berlin. About 1700 almost 25 per cent of the population was French. Between 1650 and 1710 the total number of inhabitants rose from 10 thousand to 60 thousand. The Great Elector's successor continued the work. He employed Schlüter, Eosander, and Nering as architects. Under his reign the five towns of Berlin, Cölln, Friedrichwerder, Dorotheenstadt, and Friedrichstadt were combined into the Residence City of Berlin. From 1721 onward, the Friedrichstadt was enlarged, first to the south and then to the west, and new squares were laid out—the Quarré, the Pariserplatz, the Oktagon, the Leipzigerplatz, the Rondell, the Belle Alliance, and later the Mehring Platz. To protect the flourishing urban industries a customs barrier was built in 1737—a stone wall in the south and a palisade fence in the north. The city continued to grow and to prosper. Under Frederick the Great, the Unter den Linden was completed; the opera house was built by Knobelsdorff; the Gendarmenmarkt was begun by Gontard and finished by Schinkel, who then erected the Schauspielhaus. New gates were built in the customs barrier, among them the Brandenburger Tor by Langhans.

420

370. Engraving of the old Brandenburg Gate in 1764 by Chodowiecki. This and the other gates shown here were part of the customs barrier.

371. Colored engraving of the Hamburg Gate about 1800 by Serrurier.

372. Colored lithograph of the Potsdam Gate about 1830.

373. Colored drawing of Unter den Linden in 1691 by Johann Stridbeck the Younger. The view is toward the Tiergarten.

374. Engraving of Unter den Linden in 1780 by Johann Georg Rosenberg. The opera house and the palace of the crown prince are at the left and the arsenal (Zeughaus), by Nering and Schlüter, at the right. These buildings are part of the *forum* planned by Frederick the Great.

375. The Quarré, the Pariser Platz, at the Brandenburg Gate, with the Guardhouse at the right and the Unter den Linden in the center, about 1800.

376. The square at the Zeughaus, with the New Guardhouse, 1828. Oil painting by Wilhelm Brücke.

In 1815 the population had grown to 200 thousand; in the next thirty years it doubled. This increase produced a great housing shortage. Between 1841 and 1861 considerable extensions took place, and hitherto outlying districts were incorporated. The fortifications were dismantled in 1867; and, at the same time, the building of the *Ringbahn,* the circular railway, was begun, laying a new constricting girdle around the city. Between 1875 and 1897, the *Stadtbahn,* the east–west connection, followed. Industries moved out from the inner city to the zone along the *Ringbahn,* but a generation later a redistribution began again. The city grew too fast. By 1880 it had 1.2 million inhabitants. Berlin's organic development had come to an end. A general redevelopment plan was worked out by Hobrecht around 1860. It was a complete failure. It missed all opportunities and created the prerequisites for the overcrowding of the inner city, for the erection of tenement houses of the worst type with several interior backyards, and for disastrous social conditions. The private speculator and developer reigned supreme. After 1880 more than forty private agencies existed, which bought up the land outside the city, divided it into lots, and sold their jerry-built houses. The nadir had been reached.

377. Colored drawing of Friedrichsgracht and Jungfernbrücke, 1690, by Johann Stridbeck the Younger.

423

378. The Rondell, the Belle Alliance Platz (*center*), at the southern end of the Friedrichstadt, and the old Hallesche Gate (*foreground*). Faint Italian and French influences in the general conception mingle with the puritanic Prussian character of the buildings.

379. Engraving of Klosterstrasse and Parochialkirche in 1780 by Johann Rosenberg. The street follows the old walls. Built about 1700, the church is part of the continuous block front that accentuates the changing perspective view of the gently curved street.

380. Gendarmenmarkt. Drawing by Hennig, engraved in steel by Hausheer about 1840. German Church, Royal Theater by Schinkel, and French Church. The square covers an area of 523,000 square feet. It was surrounded by three-storied private dwellings. Gontard designed the church towers.

381. Lustgarten. Drawing by Schröder engraved in steel by Hausheer about 1840. View from the Royal Palace. In the background is the Old Museum and at the right the cathedral, the *Dom*—both by Schinkel. This square adjoined one side of the Royal Palace.

382. Lithograph of the old Berlin town hall in 1827 by L. E. Lütke.

425

383. Painting of the Parochialstrasse, as it was in the middle of the nineteenth century, by G. Gaertner. A typical old Berlin street, with workshops, high and narrow houses, overcrowded flats, and no light or air.

384. Oil painting, dated 1830, of an elegant shop near the palace, by Johann Erdmann Hummel. The arsenal is in the right background.

Leipzig, Saxony. Leipzig lies at the junction of three small rivers, the Pleisse, the Parthe, and the Elster, which flow through and around the town. It owes its origin to the favorable location at the crossing of trade routes and two rivers. A Slavic village *Lipzk, Lipa,* from which the name of Leipzig was derived, existed before A.D. 1000. It was probably situated at the northwest periphery of the later *Altstadt.* A settlement of German colonists developed near this spot under the protection of a *Burg.* Early in the tenth century another settlement and a new *Burg* with a church were established on a more favorable site free from flooding, which was called *Lipzi* and was first mentioned in 1015. This was the nucleus of the medieval *Altstadt.* It was enlarged by a second settlement around the *Neumarkt* and later by a third around the "new *Neumarkt*" toward the south. Leipzig was mentioned in the eleventh century as a fortified place. In the second half of the twelfth century it received some municipal privileges.

The early medieval nucleus and the two extensions gradually grew together and covered, after several centuries, the whole area within the walls. The large market square was the meeting point of the traffic arteries. A few other squares with churches were distributed over the town. The *Burg* occupied the southwest corner of the fortifications. The town

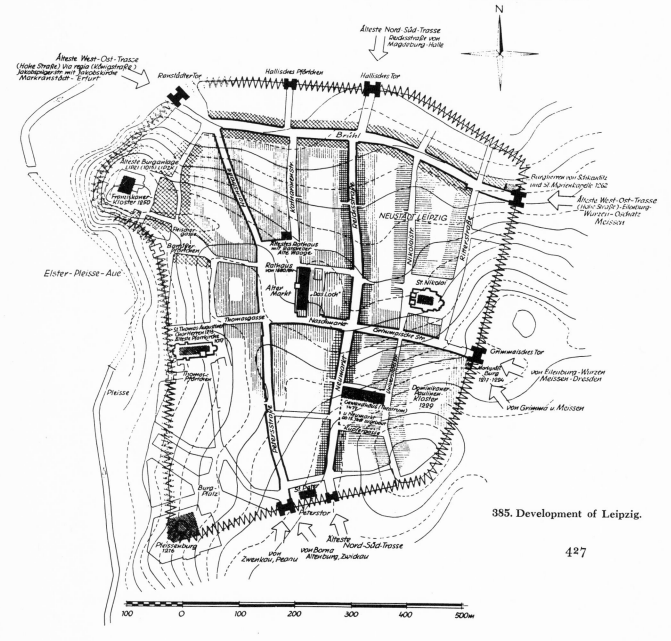

385. Development of Leipzig.

427

hall stood on the eastern long side of the market square. With its octagonal tower it was the dominating perspective view, not only from the square, but also from the streets that converged upon it. The building density was high; there were hardly any open spaces left within the building blocks. The gridiron street pattern and large market square are the typical product of the colonial movement. Within the network of the primary streets was a labyrinth of narrow lanes, alleys, and covered courtyards with large warehouses and cellars.

386. Plan of Leipzig, 1650.

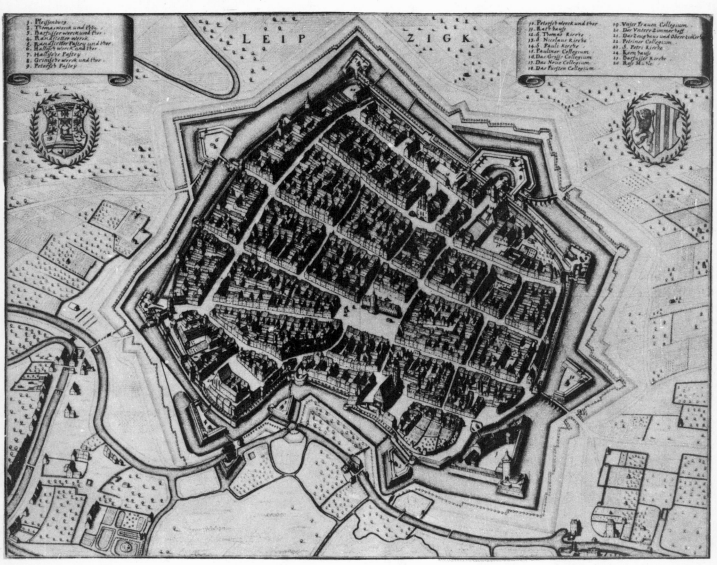

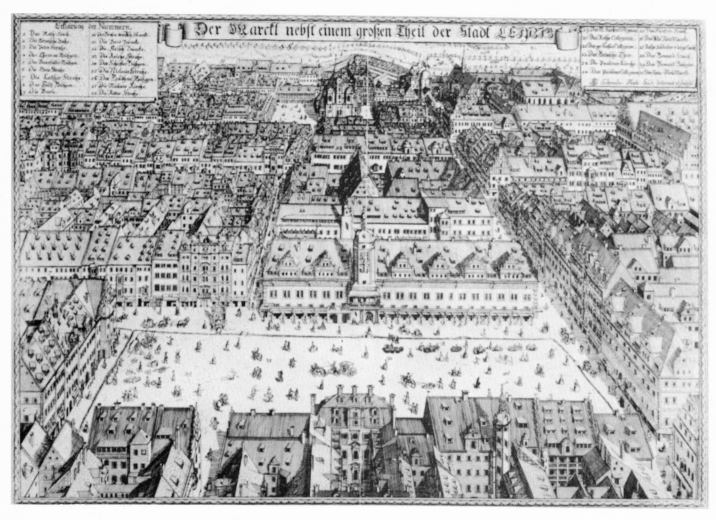

387. Leipzig's market square in 1712. Engraving by J. G. Schreiber.

388. Leipzig's market square in the nineteenth century.

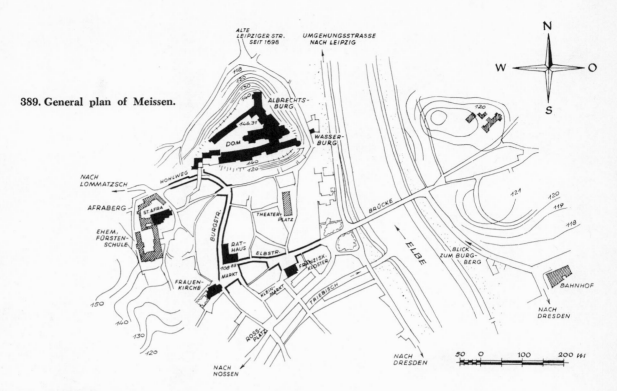

389. General plan of Meissen.

390. General view of Meissen.

Meissen, Saxony. Meissen, on the Elbe, was founded about A.D. 920 by Henry I, who erected a stronghold on the *Burgberg* and a *Wasserburg* on the bank of the Elbe to guard the river crossing. In the tenth and eleventh centuries a settlement south of the *Burgberg* attracted much of the traffic and trade of the Via Regia, the important route that connected Franconia and Thuringia with Silesia and Poland. Founded by colonists from Franconia, Thuringia, and Hesse, the new medieval town was systematically laid out on a plateau, with the market square as the center, to the southwest of the earlier settlement. Within the relatively small area there were several squares: the present Theaterplatz; the market square with the town hall and the *Frauenkirche,* the Church of Our Lady; the square at the Franciscan monastery; the *Kleinmarkt* and the *Rossmarkt*—the little market and the horse market—respectively. The traffic from the west was directed through the Burgstrasse to the market square and thence through the Elbestrasse to the oldest bridge over the river. The market square with *Frauenkirche* and town hall is a particularly good solution of a difficult problem. The square is the link between the Burgstrasse and the Elbestrasse, that is, the main traffic artery, which is here broken at right angles. The church stands in its own space annex, not on the highest point, but on the lower side of the market square with the choir projecting into the field of vision. The town hall occupies the opposite corner. All streets that converge upon the square are bent, thus preserving the spatial coherence of the square and the streets. This multiplicity of individual elements has been perfectly united into one balanced and homogeneous composition.

391. First stage of the settlement of Dresden, on the right bank of the Elbe.

Dresden, Saxony. Already known by 1206, Dresden lies in a broad valley on both banks of the Elbe. Its Slavic origin has been preserved in its name, from *Drezga* meaning forest, and *Drezgajan* meaning forest dwellers. A site on the right bank free from flooding may have favored the establishment of the first settlement. The right bank was probably chosen because the west–east road ran on this side upstream and changed over at this point to the left bank. About the same time, possibly a little later, a second nucleus came into being around a triangular square, a form that was typical of the settlements created by the needs of traffic in the early Middle Ages east of the Harz Mountains. The depression between these two settlements remained free of buildings; it was not filled until 1738.

The third stage was the earliest German settlement on the left bank of the river. Its center was a market square with the Chapel of Our Lady, the *Frauenkirchenkapelle*. The building blocks and the square were regular, a layout taken over from other colonial settlements. Here, not far from the square and the chapel, at the narrowest point of the Elbe may have been the first passage to the other bank, either a ford or a bridge. Traffic considerations must have played a considerable role in the development of the town on the left bank. Important trade routes had to be organically connected with the interior layout, and adequate crossing facilities had to be provided.

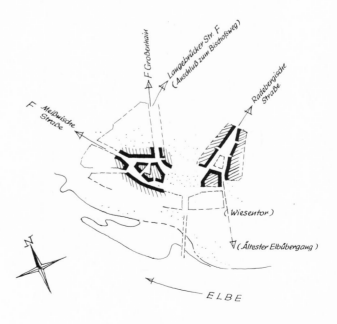

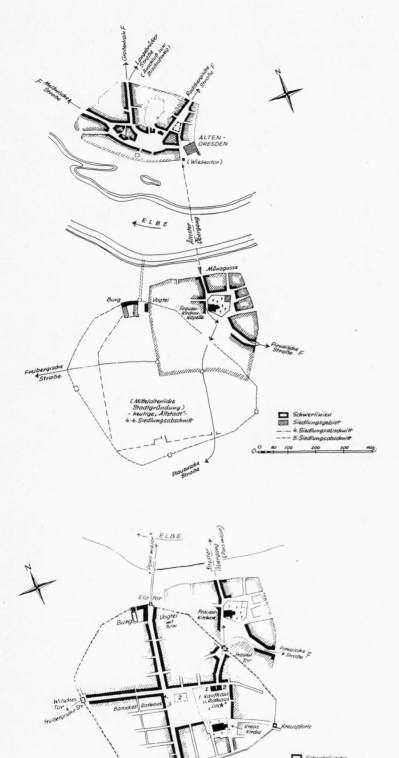

The execution of these far-reaching plans, which were most probably carefully worked out beforehand and made possible by the authoritative decisions of the territorial prince, Henry the Illustrious, took decades; for they were part of the general traffic and settlement policy that aimed at the systematic opening-up of the *Mark Meissen* and its connection with the Via Regia by the foundation of new towns and the building of new roads. An enterprise on a large scale, it was the basis of the later prosperity of Saxony. The erection of a *Burg* that protected the river crossing was, therefore, of the greatest importance. It seems that a *Vogtei,* the fortified residence of a bailiff, existed around 1300 as the oldest seat of the administration of the margrave even before the new bridge was built.

The fourth stage belonged to the fourteenth century. The trade route from Meissen in the north to Pirna, south of Dresden, was the natural artery on which depended the further development of the town on both banks. A large and irregular square, the first market square on the right bank, at the meeting point of the overland routes and the river crossing was the obvious solution of the pressing traffic problems. Here was sufficient space for the market with its manifold activities and for the numerous vehicles of the traders and merchants. Dresden's economic development was, above all, dependent on the river traffic. Meissen, the economic and political capital, attracted in the tenth and eleventh centuries the bulk of the transit trade and the through traffic of the Via Regia. Pirna was the eastern terminus of the navigation and the transhipment point for the salt trade. Dresden lay halfway between these two trading centers, about a day's journey by boat or vehicle. The silver-mining town of Freiberg, only 20 miles southwest, also contributed to the growth of Dres-

393. Third stage of Dresden's settlement, the oldest nucleus—*Altstadt* with market square.

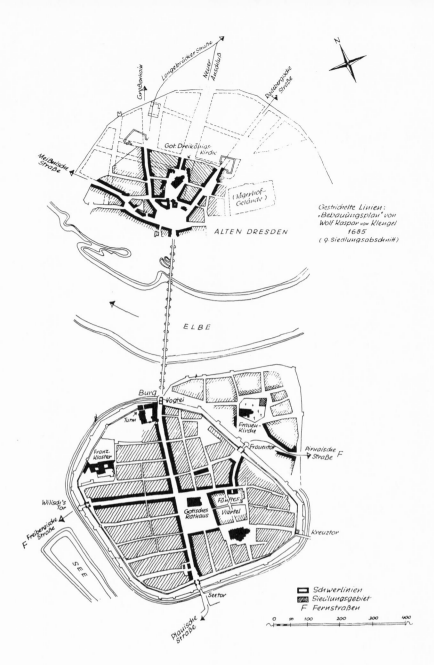

den: the route from Franconia, which touched Freiberg, crossed the Elbe at Dresden; and the more silver mining developed, the more the traffic on this road increased. Thus the rise of Dresden was intimately connected with the "regional planning" and city development in the *Mark Meissen.*

The fifth stage was mainly an interior consolidation of the town on the left bank. The building density increased; streets were laid out; the fortifications were completed. At the beginning of the sixteenth century the time had come to surround both towns with one common circumvallation, which one century later received its more elaborate structure in accordance with the needs of the new techniques of warfare.

After a fire in 1685 that destroyed large parts of Dresden on the right bank, the medieval limitations disappeared. A new plan was worked out by Klengel in 1685. His design should be considered together with a later plan of 1731. The main feature was a wide street broadening toward the river, which it reached not in the axis of the bridge but at the side where an isolated monumental building, the *Blockhaus,* built by Longuelunes, closed the perspective view. A second axis was developed at the northwest periphery of the *Neue Königstadt*—as the town was called by the Elector—which had as its viewpoint the Japanese Palace. The moving spirit behind the modernization of Dresden was Augustus the Strong, Elector of Saxony and King of Poland. His ambitions were in consonance with the ideas of the time. He said that he had found a Dresden, small and wooden, but he would leave it great, of stone and splendid. He made it the easternmost Baroque Residence of Germany.

The Elbe was the connecting link that joined the two parts in one grand composi-

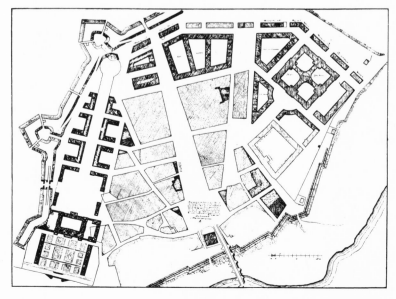

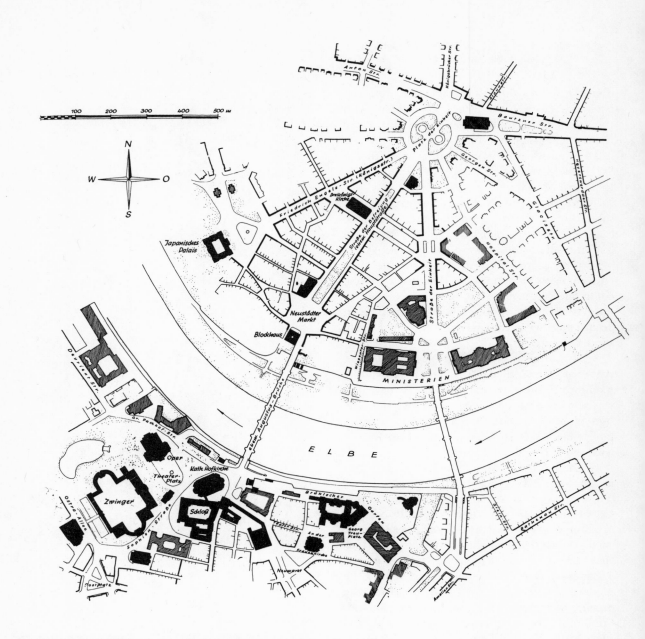

396. The Elbe with the two most significant parts of Dresden.

434

397. The Elbe with the Zwinger, the Museum, the Theater, the Frauenkirche, and the Hofkirche.

tion. On both banks the architectural high points were concentrated at the river. On the concave left bank the old center of the palace was surrounded by the *Frauenkirche* and the *Hofkirche,* the *Zwinger* and the newer buildings of the museum and the opera. On the convex right bank the *Blockhaus* and the Japanese Palace, the towers of the *Dreikönigskirche* and the old *Jägerhof* responded to the polyphony of cupolas and towers on the other side. The situation and skyline of Dresden were one of the most characteristic creations of the German Baroque. They expressed all the ambitions of this period; all the unconcerned harnessing of the financial resources of the country; and all the passing glory of an epoch in which the obedient subjects of the prince were nothing, the ruler everything. The core of Dresden with most of its buildings was destroyed in World War II.

APPENDICES

Notes on Settlements of the Earliest Period

Pile dwellings, refuges (*Fluchtburgen*), and strongholds (*Volksburgen*)

The pile dwellings on the Bodensee and the Federsee were standing at the beginning of the history of settlement in Germany. On the Bodensee the settlements extended out as far as 210 feet into the lake, the level of which was 9 to 15 feet lower in prehistoric times than today. They were made up of permanent colonies of sedentary people who had developed a common culture and a certain degree of social stratification. The average temperature in the neolithic era was probably 2 to 3 degrees higher than now. This resulted in a dry period that reached its maximum in the early Bronze Age. The settlements of this latter age were farther away from the shore than those of the Stone Age.[1]

The lake dwellings were not mere fishing villages or temporary summer retreats or refuges; they were built into the lakes, for after the end of the Ice Age, as Swiss archeologists suggest, the warmer climate with the still continuing humidity produced a luxurious forest with larger open spaces on the rivers and lakes. The early settlers had hardly any other choice than following the lines of least resistance by establishing themselves on or near the water where they could move easily; for overland communications were still difficult. Moreover, a large area of water exerted a moderating influence on heat in the summer and cold in the winter, and the fish in the lake and the animals on the shore gave the settlers a double source of food supply. About forty settlements have been discovered on the Bodensee (Lake Constance), some of them fairly large—for instance, one at Bodman on the southwestern end of the lake

was 1200 feet long and 150 feet wide. They were built only where there was solid ground, on sandy or red clay soil. The pile village of Sipplingen is of particular interest. When more detailed investigations were made possible by pumping out the water within a large caisson so that the investigators could work on dry ground, it was found that a long double palisade had protected the settlement against the shore. The inner line, about 4 feet wide, seems to have been accompanied on the inside by a sort of narrow parapet. The height of the main palisade was about 12 feet. The outer line was about 12 feet wide and 7 feet high.

The settlements on the Federsee in Württemberg, a contracting swampy lake, belong to different periods. They consist of several types of houses; for instance, the round hut with sloping reed walls without inner supports and a rather shapeless hip roof, and the rectangular Nordic hut with posts, a hearth in the center, an entrance hall, the whole being covered by a saddle roof and having an open platform. The entrance hall served as the working place.

The settlement at Köln-Lindenthal is situated in a region that must have been particularly attractive for the prehistoric tribes when they moved through the Rhine Valley in search of new land. Their scouts, for whom a loess landscape was the most desirable area for a settlement, found here a wide and fertile district that fulfilled all their expectations and needs.[2] Nine neolithic places have been discovered where excavations were made.

1. C. Schuchhardt. *Vorgeschichte von Deutschland,* 1943, pp. 35 ff. See also for the following.

2. W. Buttler and W. Haberey, *Die Bandkeramische Ansiedlung bei Köln-Lindenthal,* Römisch-Germanische Forschungen. 1936, pp. 5, 13, 161-164.

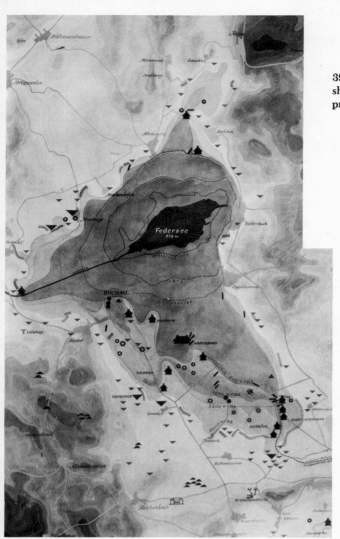

398. Settlements at the Federsee Swamps, showing the shoreline from 8000 B.C. to the present day.

In the first period the settlement consisted of a number of barns with a few temporary shelters in the form of shallow caves in the ground that served as huts for the watchmen, while the houses to which the barns belonged were probably dispersed in small groups over the nearby terrain. In the course of time the inhabitants of these oldest huts moved nearer to the barns, and as the old barns deteriorated and became gradually unusable, new ones were built near the newer huts; this was the second period. The third period introduced an entirely new feature: There were fewer huts because the older inhabitants had left and a new group had moved in. It is likely that the inhabitants of the third village were the first precursors of the people who later built the large fortifications. The apparently violent destruction of the third settlement may be an indication of the exodus of these settlers who abandoned the place and left it to the next group. These people built their

399. Reconstruction of Lindenthal in the final stage of its development.

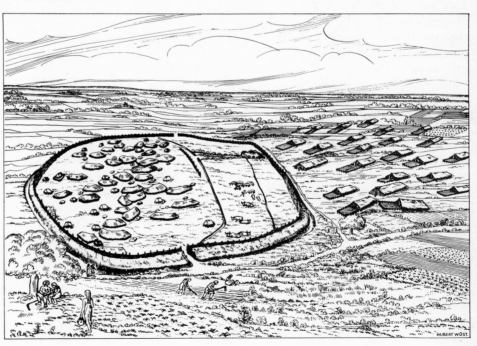

440

huts close together and fortified the village with palisades, a wall, and a moat. The barns were erected near the village on the other side of the valley. During the second period the population may have consisted of 160 to 200 people who lived in twenty-six to twenty-eight huts. This number decreased during the third period to fifty to eighty people living in eight to ten huts; it increased again in the following period to 250 to 350 inhabitants, living in twenty to twenty-five dwellings. All these numbers are only conjectures although they are based on very detailed spadework.

The duration of the settlement consisting of five to six subsequent groups of buildings may have lasted for about three hundred years. It is remarkable that the site of the Lindenthal settlement was occupied time and again by different groups in an almost uninterrupted sequence. It is difficult to attribute this to one definite reason; perhaps it was because of the favorable terrain or the strategic location of the site with reference to the traffic routes: The north-south road through the Rhine Valley was joined near Cologne by an old road to the West so that the village may have had a certain importance in this respect.

The social structure rested on the biological family as the basic unit. But beyond this, more extended social units existed, a fact that can clearly be deduced from the large village of the last period. What is certain is that a developed community spirit and, therefore, a social order was at work. The settlers were free peasants with no outspoken accent on the leader principle. Economically the settlement was based on cultivation, but it is uncertain whether hoe or plow cultivation predominated. In any case, it may be assumed that the fields were worked extensively in a sort of three-field system or something similar.

Our knowledge of the earliest German settlements is scanty. However, some information is available on sites of the Bronze Age. The distribution of tumuli serves as a clue to the location of inhabited areas since the dead were buried near the place of residence of the living: When the tumuli were isolated

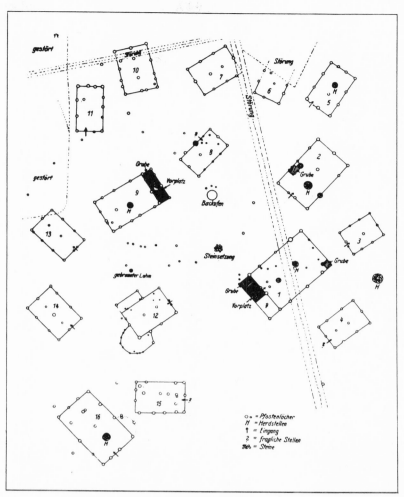

400. Germanic settlement at Perleberg, Mark Brandenburg.

and widely dispersed, the individual homesteads would also be dispersed; when they occurred in groups, compact villages would exist. In this way the distribution of settlement was mapped for parts of northern Germany, especially for Schleswig and Jutland. The inference is that the sandy and light soils were preferred and that a wide belt of settlement stretched roughly from the north to the south of this region. Another conclusion is that the settlements followed as nearly as possible the main roads of this period, in Schleswig and Jutland the north–south road, and further south the east–west communications also. In general, small and dry elevations on the margin of humid and low-lying ground—valleys, boggy land, rivers, and lakes—were chosen for farmsteads and villages.

Possibly the best example of these early settlements is the village discovered near Perleberg in eastern Germany, about 70 miles northwest of Potsdam. The houses were loosely and irregularly grouped around a central open space. The largest house with a porch, which may have been the residence of the village headman, adjoined this square. The other houses were smaller, decreasing in size toward the periphery of the settlement, thus indicating a certain stratification in social status and wealth. These villages were surrounded by gardens and fields and probably by pastures, although the actual area of the animal husbandry of this period was the forest: the oak forests served as pastures not only for hundreds of pigs but also for cattle and horses.[3]

Fluchtburgen and *Volksburgen* existed in

3. H. Reinerth, *Vorgeschichte der Deutschen Stämme,* I, pp. 29 ff.

the Stone Age in France and Spain and gradually penetrated to the western margins of Germany. They did not exist in Thuringia and the northern regions during this early period since methods of conquest and protection were still in their infancy. The terms *Fluchtburgen* and *Volksburgen* denote different functions: the former served as refuges in times of unrest, and the latter, sometimes called *Gauburgen,* as refuges and places of administration and religious and political assemblies. The terminology is somewhat vague, and both terms are often used rather loosely. Dionysius of Halicarnassus, the Greek historian who lived during the reign of Augustus, describes in his *Roman Antiquities* (IV, 15) refuges built by Servius Tullius. We may assume that the basic features of these places were the same in Germany as in ancient Italy.

After Tullius had divided the country into a certain number of parts . . . he built places of refuge upon such lofty eminences as could afford ample security for husbandmen, and called them by a Greek name, *pagi.* . . . Thither all the inhabitants fled from the fields whenever a raid was made by

401. The *Fluchtburg* at Fielsenberg in the Swabian Alb.

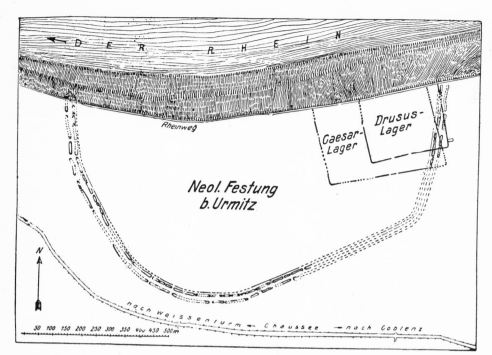

402. Neolithic fortress at Urmitz, Rhineland.

enemies, and generally passed the night there. These places also had their governors, whose duty it was to know not only the names of all the husbandmen who belonged to the same district but also the lands which afforded them their livelihood. . . . He ordered them to erect altars to the gods . . . and directed them to assemble every year and honor these gods with public sacrifices.[4]

Pagus is a pre-Indo-Germanic word for citadel or stronghold—the citadel of Smyrna was also called *Pagos*—and was later used to mean district, *Gau,* thus assuming a wider meaning similar to the word *polis,* which originally also meant the citadel, later the city, and finally the city-state in Greece. The *pagus,* the *Burg,* was therefore the refuge and administrative center where the register of the inhabitants of the district was kept, taxes levied, and troops conscripted.

The largest of these *Burgen* was situated near Urmitz in the basin of Neuwied in the Rhineland. Strategically, it must have been an eminently suitable place, for Caesar and Drusus built their fortified camps there, and it is likely that Caesar crossed the Rhine at or near Urmitz where the river flows quietly

4. Loeb Classical Library.

403. *Burgen* of the Lausitz Culture.

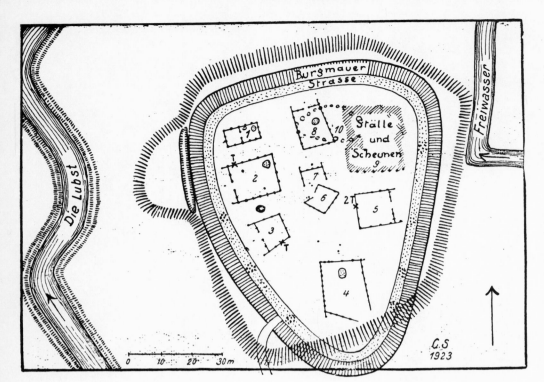

404. The Baalshebbel at Starzeddel, Poland.

405. Model of the Baalshebbel.

and the crossing is made easy by an island. But its importance was first discovered in the neolithic period. The *Burg* was 3825 feet long and 2520 feet wide and had room for 20 thousand to 30 thousand people. The fortifications consisted of two moats, each 24 to 27 feet wide, and of a palisade located 18 feet behind the inner moat. It is probable that there was a wall between the moats. There were numerous passages over the moats and through the palisade into the interior, about twenty-five over the outer and fifty

over the inner moat. The great number of these openings may have been necessary to permit an easy and swift influx of people and animals in case of raids by an enemy.

The *Burgen* of the Lausitz Culture fall into two categories: Those in the interior were *Gauburgen*, serving administrative and religious functions, while those near the frontier were strong points for the defense of the country. In the northern part there were relatively few of either type, but in the original and old southern part, in Upper and Lower

444

Lusatia, their number was considerable. In general, they follow the Oder-Neisse line, the old divide between Germanic and Slavic influences. Most of the *Burgen* of the Lausitz Culture were founded in the eighth and seventh centuries B.C.

The Baalshebbel near Starzeddel in the southwest of the Poznan Department in Poland, formerly in Brandenburg, Germany, is a representative example of an old Germanic *Burg* of this period. It stands on a sandy island in an alluvial plain and is almost free from Slavic influences. It covered an area of 240 by 300 feet, and was surrounded by an earthen and timber wall about 24 feet thick. On the inside, a 15-foot-wide road ran along the whole length of the wall. The houses were irregularly grouped around an open space. A barn and some stables occupied the northeastern corner near the gate. None of the houses was distinguished by size or layout, apparently indicating that the Baalshebbel was inhabited by equals.

The excavations of the Wasserburg Buchau, a fortified refuge surrounded by water at Buchau in the Federsee Swamps in Upper

406. Wasserburg Buchau. Earliest settlement, about 1100 B.C.

407. Later settlement of Wasserburg Buchau, about 1000 B.C.

Swabia, have revealed two periods of occupation. The older settlement dates back to about 1100 B.C. and the later one to 1000 B.C.; it was burned down in about 800 B.C. The fortifications enclosed an oval area with an east–west diameter of 450 feet and consisted of strong palisades. Two gates led into the interior. In both periods the center of the settlement was left free for refugees. When the climate grew milder after the end of the

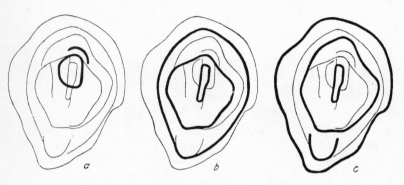

408. Three periods in the development of the Steinsburg at Römhild, Thuringia.

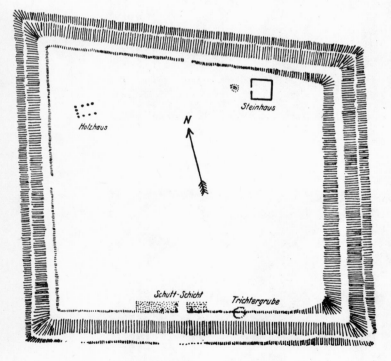

409. Fortified farmstead at Gerichtstetten, Baden.

Ice Age, fishermen and hunters rested on the shores of the lake, which at this time was still fairly large. Gradually the lake contracted, and swamps covered the marginal areas. Toward the end of the third millennium peasants built their timber and clay houses on slightly raised mounds in these swamps. By 2000 B.C. numerous villages had grown up around the lake. Cultivation had made the nomadic population sedentary. It demanded not only more hands but also larger buildings and granaries. The houses were rectangular and had mostly two rooms and a hearth. They were connected by log footpaths.

During the La Tène Culture (eighth to first centuries B.C.), many *Burgen* were built in southern and central Germany on mountaintops and were surrounded by strong walls. Two types may be distinguished: If the *Burg* was built on a spur with steep slopes, a wall was built only on the narrow side and the rest was protected by a lighter palisade; if a mountaintop with gentle slopes was chosen, the fortifications surrounded the whole area on all sides. To this type belonged the Steinsburg near Römhild not far from Meiningen in Thuringia. It seems that toward the end of the La Tène period a simpler method of defense was introduced: Individual farmsteads were fortified by a quadrilateral rampart, about 300 feet long. To this group belonged, for instance, the *"Viereck Schanze"* near Gerichtstetten in Baden. It had a rhomboid shape, and was surrounded by a moat and a wall 4 feet high. Other similar enclosures were found in Bavaria and Württemberg. It has been suggested that they were part of the Roman fortifications; but more detailed investigations seem to have identified them as Celtic farmsteads—this had originally been assumed when the first excavation was made in 1898. They may have been the predecessors of the Roman *villae rusticae* and of the later *curtes regiae* of Charlemagne. It has also been suggested that these enclosures were sanctuaries of the Celts. The question is still open, and only further excavations can throw light on their origin and purpose.[5]

5. Schuchhardt. *Op. cit.,* pp. 223 ff.

Nodal Points of Settlement in Roman Times and in the Early Middle Ages

The military bases from which the Romans began their expeditions against Germany were Xanten and Mainz. Both were first-rate strategic starting points: Xanten for the invasion of lower Germany along the Lippe River to Paderborn and thence to the Weser; and Mainz for an advance along the Main, through the Taunus to Giessen and Marburg, and finally also to the Weser. The oldest settlement at Mainz and its name—Mogontiacum—are of Celtic origin. Between 14 and 9 B.C., Drusus erected a fortified camp; the *castellum Mattiacorum* was later built on the opposite bank and connected with the camp by a bridge. Natives and Roman traders and veterans settled around the camp. Mogontiacum became the capital of *Germania Superior*. The camp covered an area of about 2000 by 2100 feet and accommodated two legions. The town was one of the most important focal points from which the settlement spread in all directions.

The Roman camp of Vetera near Xanten on the Lower Rhine was originally built as an operational base for two legions on the Fürstenberg, which dominated the surrounding country.[1] Vetera was the name of an indigenous settlement in the neighborhood; it does not mean "the old camp," that is, *castra vetera*. The two legions had about 8 thousand to 10 thousand regular soldiers, apart from the auxiliary troops. At first, temporary buildings were erected because the camp served only as winter quarters; the other seasons were spent in operations against the Germans. The camp was surrounded by strong

palisades and an earthen wall. When the Romans abandoned the plan to conquer Germany and decided to make the Rhine the frontier and fortified demarcation line against the Germanic tribes, the camp was rebuilt as a permanent fortress. It covered 148 acres in the form of a rectangle almost 3 thousand feet long and 2 thousand feet wide. It had four gates and ramparts that sloped slightly at the outside and a log or plank wall faced with bricks. Then followed a moat with two rows of abatis—that is, felled trees placed lengthwise one over the other with their branches toward the lines of the enemy. The usual rectangular street pattern divided the interior. The main streets were 180 feet wide and met in the center of the camp at the *praetorium*, the headquarters of the two legions. To the right and left of the *praetorium*, separated by a street 54 feet wide, stood two palaces for the two *legati*, the officers in command of the legions. This complex was adjoined on the north side by the offices and residences of the *tribuni*, the officers next in rank to the *legati*. Outside the camp, a settlement of traders and craftsmen grew up with more or less permanent, though primitive, buildings and an amphitheater.

A Roman colony, a military and veterans' town, was founded by Trajan to the north of Xanten. Its name was Colonia Ulpia Traiana. Founded around A.D. 100, it was fortified, and covered 205 acres, a size that almost equaled the area covered by the Roman Cologne. Four gates led into the interior, which was laid out according to the usual checkerboard plan with regular *insulae*.

The *limes* was not only the demarcation

1. P. Steiner. *Die Anfänge Xantens.* 1928.

447

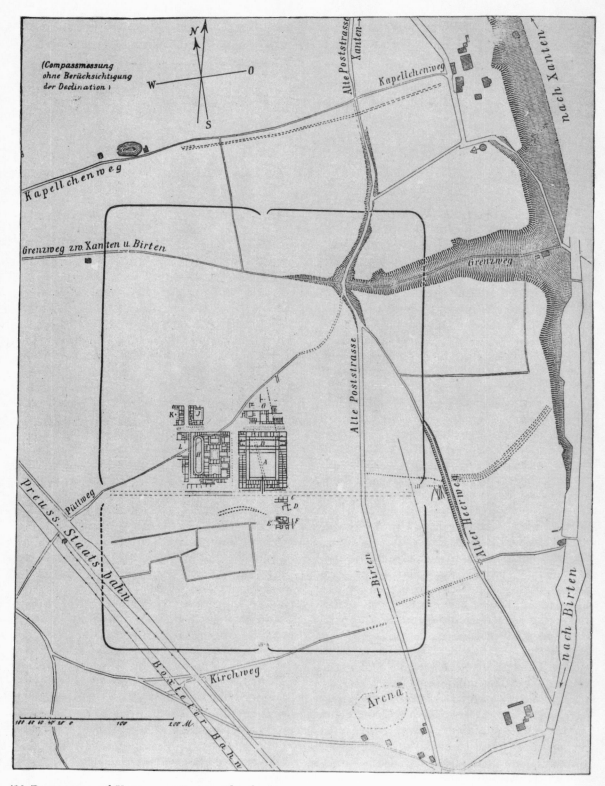

410. Roman camp of Vetera near Xanten, Rhineland.

448

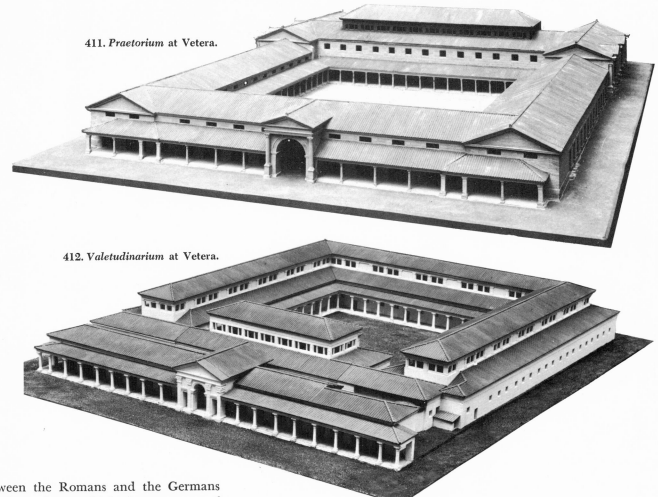

411. *Praetorium* at Vetera.

412. *Valetudinarium* at Vetera.

line between the Romans and the Germans but also the axis on which the structure of settlement was focused. Until about A.D. 70, the Rhine and the Upper Danube were the frontiers of the Empire, except for small parts on the right bank of the Rhine: the plain of Frankfurt, the southernmost slopes of the Black Forest, and a few bridgeheads. Under Vespasian, the frontier was advanced and shortened for geographical and military reasons. The bases for the advance beyond the Rhine were Mainz (Mogontiacum), Strasbourg (Argentoratum), and Windisch (Vindonissa) in Switzerland. Roads were extended to Rottweil (Arae Flaviae) and later to Cannstadt and beyond. Under Domitian, the rectified frontier was fortified with numerous blockhouses and forts in the rear. In connection with these movements forts were established under Caligula at Wies-

baden, Hofheim, and Gross Gerau, and later at Leddernheim, Okarben, Friedberg, Frankfurt, and Gernsheim. The original forts were small, square earthworks of about 1.8 acres, and they can still be identified within such later and larger forts as the Saalburg near Homburg. Hadrian reorganized the whole system. He built a continuous wooden palisade reaching in an almost straight line from the Rhine to the Danube, and moved the garrisons forward directly to this advance front. The old forts at Wiesbaden, Hofheim, Leddernheim, and Okarben were abandoned. This frontier consisted of two different defense systems: the so-called *Pfahlgraben,* an earthen mound with a ditch, and a stone wall beginning where the earthwork ended

449

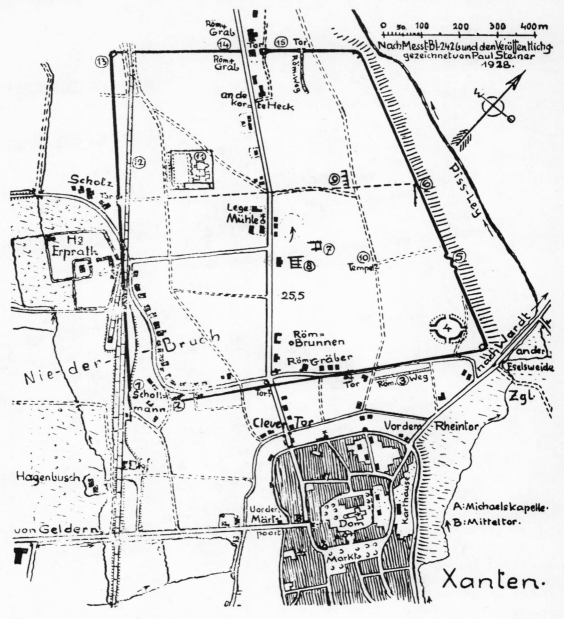

413. Colonia Trajana.

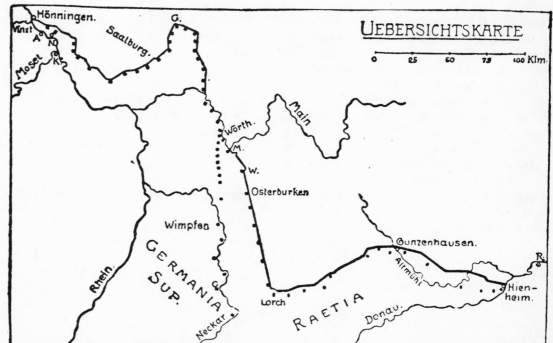

414. Map of the *limes*.

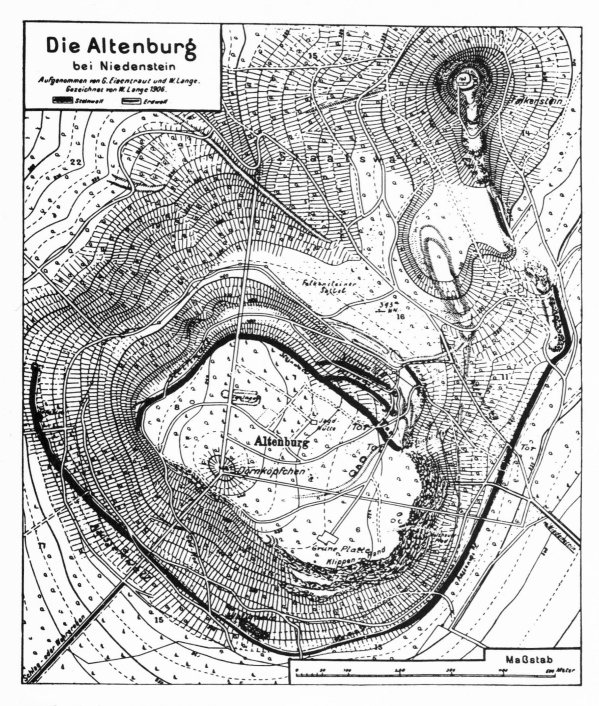

415. The Altenburg at Niedenstein, Hesse.

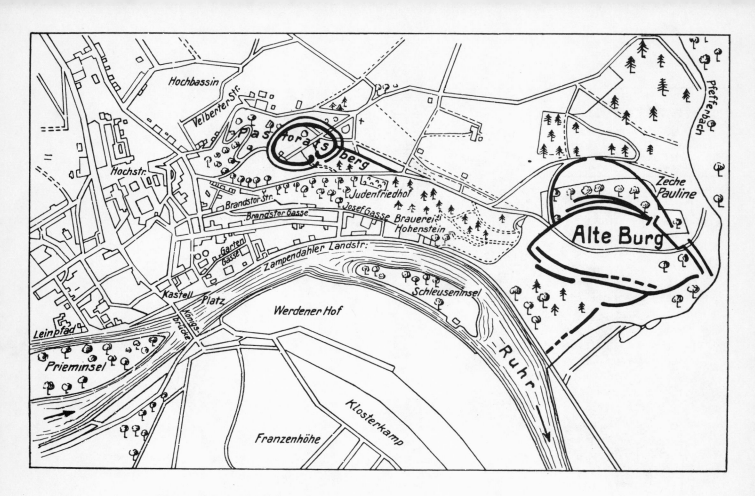

416. Werden on the Ruhr.

and running roughly parallel to the Danube. The Saalburg was one of the forts that had grown by various extensions around the small, earlier fort. It was strongly fortified with a crenelated wall, two ditches, and four gates.

The time from A.D. 100 to 260 was a period of peaceful Roman colonization along the *limes*. The population increased through immigration from Gallia and the settlements of veterans. At Ladenburg, Wimpfen, and Rottenburg, to name only a few cases, it spilled over the old walls and settled outside the towns; *suburbia* developed at all Roman camps where craftsmen and traders built their *canabae*. These settlements survived even when the forts were moved forward to the *limes* and often grew into large villages as, for instance, the *vicus* Ambitarvius near Koblenz. When the *canabae* were numerous and fairly permanent, the whole settlement was called a *vicus;* it extended in two long

rows of houses on both sides of the road. It is probable that the word *vicus* is derived from the Greek *oikos* meaning "house" or "group of houses." These *vici* were industrial, not agricultural, settlements. They often stagnated during the Roman period, especially in the region of the *limes,* although in some cases they became the nuclei of a later Roman town.

A good example of a fortified settlement on the Germanic side of the *limes* is the Altenburg at Niedenstein in Hessen, the *Volksburg* of Mattium in the land of the Chatti, situated on an almost rectangular and flat mountain 1620 feet long and 1000 feet wide. The gently sloping eastern side was strengthened by several walls of boulders. The Altenburg was a fortified refuge that could shelter many people. It was destroyed by Germanicus in A.D. 15. Its name of *Caput Chattorum Mattium* and the discovery of the remains of dwellings and outhouses and certain implements make it likely that it was not only a temporary refuge but also a permanent settlement.

Just as the Romans and their Germanic adversaries had built their strongholds as points of attack or defense, the Franks based their invasions of Lower Saxony on fortified places, and the Saxons defended their country from numerous strong points, their *Volksburgen*. The same methods were used for the same ends. The similarity is indeed striking, and the results were also similar, for in many cases the original and exclusively military establishments became the nuclei of civic settlements, villages, and, above all, towns. The Franks continued the Celtic tradition and protected their frontier through large *Volksburgen* on steep mountains, or hills as they knew them from France with her *oppida* of Alesia near the source of the Seine, Bibracte near Autun, Gergovia south of Clermont-Ferrand, and others. One of these Frankish *Volksburgen* was the Alteburg above Werden and the Ruhr, built about A.D. 700 against the Saxons. It rises high above the Ruhr and is protected by steep cliffs and gorges. It covered an oval area of 25 acres; toward the river it was surrounded by a wall 6 to 9 feet thick, and on the other sides by one or two more walls with ditches. At a distance of about half a mile, another oval but smaller citadel with wall and ditch was situated on a hill. This was the *curtis*, the fortified seat of the Frankish count, an important agent of the administrative and military system of Charlemagne, whose first invasion in the year A.D. 772 followed the route of Germanicus, beginning with the conquest of the Eresburg, the present Obermarsberg on the Diemel, south of Paderborn, Westphalia. It was half a mile long and about .3 miles wide, and its highest point rose to 420 feet above the river. The medieval ramparts follow the old Saxon walls along the edge of the plateau. The name of Marsberg is a contraction of "am Eresberg." In this case, the historical continuity has been preserved, and the excellent site with its natural and strong protection was used without interruption from the eighth century on.

The *Volksburgen* of the Saxons were the first objectives of the Frankish conquest. They were the starting points from which Charlemagne gradually spread his advance over the whole region of Saxony. In many cases a manorial farm was attached to the *Burg*. "This is the old Germanic type of settlement of Marbod with the *regia* and the *castellum iuxta situm* . . . and apart from the Saxon *Volksburgen* Charlemagne at first

417. The Eresburg on the Diemel, south of Paderborn.

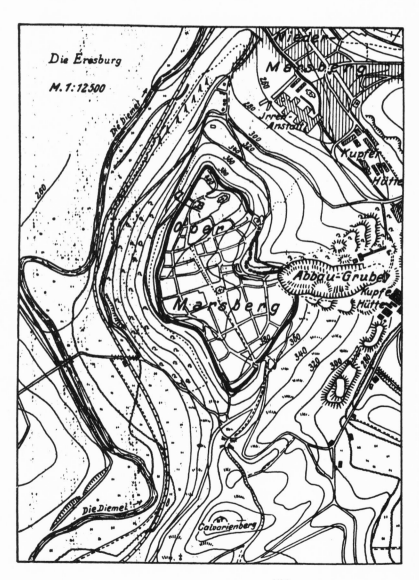

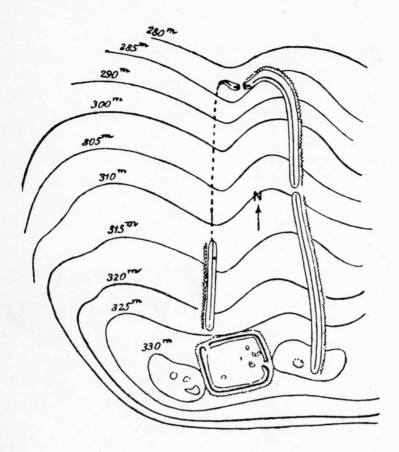

The Heisterburg on the Deister to the south of Hanover is a good example of the layout: the farm covered a square of 300 by 300 feet, about one-fifth of the whole area that was heavily fortified. In general, the walls were very strong, rising from 18 to 24 feet above the bottom of the moat. In the Heisterburg the buildings were situated at the periphery of the square farmyard so that the center remained an open space. The more important *Königshöfe* were equipped with more and better buildings.

Charlemagne had ordered a list of all his *Königshöfe* to be made, and a description of several of these fortified estates has been preserved. The first thing mentioned is always the type of the wall and the gate, whether they are of stone or wood or crowned with a wattle fence (*sepes*) or a thorn hedge (spinis); and in the interior it is always the *casa dominicata*, the manorial house where the king himself could stay overnight, that is mentioned first.[3]

The importance of the *Königshöfe* for the origin and development of urban and rural settlement can hardly be overrated. They were in many cases the nuclei of monasteries and bishoprics, such as Osnabrück, Paderborn, Hildesheim, Bremen, and Verden. In some cases the old *curtis* continued as the *Domfreiheit,* the precincts of the cathedral. In other places imperial or royal palaces, called *Pfalz,* arose on the old sites and, in the course of time, became the origin of an urban community. Ulm may serve as a representative example of this structural coherence. The *Stadelhof,* a farm of considerable size, was situated in the immediate vicinity of the *Pfalz.* It was large enough to house and provide for the royal retinue. The *Pfalz* was the seat of the *villicus regalis,* the highest official and judge who, with the help of subordinates, organized the administration, the military affairs, the collection of taxes and customs, and supervised the mint. In the eleventh century a settlement grew up around the *Pfalz.* The landowners, the *praestantiores,* the ruling minority in the

418. The Heisterburg on the Deister, south of Hanover.

occupied these manorial farms and converted them into Frankish *Königshöfe."*[2] Later he founded new *Königshöfe,* mainly on the lines of his advance into Saxony.

What were these *Königshöfe?* They were military administrative centers established by the king under his direct authority. They were occupied by counts, nominated by the king, and peasants, and received substantial land grants. Their principal function was to serve as stations on the lines of communications where troops could be provisioned and find quarters. They consisted, therefore, of a farm, mostly a square precinct, as the core of the whole compound, and a large enclosure where the army could camp. The whole was fortified with a ditch and a wall.

2. C. Schuchhardt. *Vorgeschichte Deutschlands.* 1943, p. 337.

3. *Ibid.,* pp. 339 ff.

new place, were feudal lords who originated from the royal ministerials of the *Pfalz*, the executive officers of the royal household. Thus, from the beginning there existed at Ulm, as in other towns, a social hierarchy: the representative of the lord of the town, in this case the king; the ministerials; and the common people without privilege. It may be assumed that a market and a traders' settlement existed in early times because the presence of a mint was usually the sign of a nearby market settlement.

The original Frankish *Königshöfe* were square or rectangular, a form that with but a few exceptions did not occur east of the Weser. In the region between the Weser and the Elbe it was replaced by circular defense works. Both types belonged to the Carolingian period, but the circular *Burgen* were the original Saxon *Gauburgen*. After many years of war against the Saxons, the Emperor adopted another, and more conciliatory, policy. He would be content if the Saxons recognized him as their king, paid the tithe to the Church, and allowed him to conduct the foreign policy and the decisions on war and peace. Apart from these matters, they would be free to retain their self-government with their own counts and their own jurisdiction. Thus, a certain amount of indigenous culture was preserved, and old forms survived, among them the circular shape of the original *Burgen*. The Pipinsburg near Sievern downstream from the mouth of the Weser and the *Burg* at Stöttinghausen near Bremen belong to this group. The former, about 200 feet in diameter, had a strong wall with a high palisade supporting it and a low terrace up to the ditch. The buildings of the interior were grouped near the wall leaving the center free for refugees and cattle. The Stöttinghausen *Burg* was similar in structure and layout but with an exceptionally strong gate tower. The *Burg* Werla near Goslar was founded by Henry I and was one of his fortresses and feudal strongholds against the Hungarian invasions, which owed their origin to his famous ordinance that nine *milites*

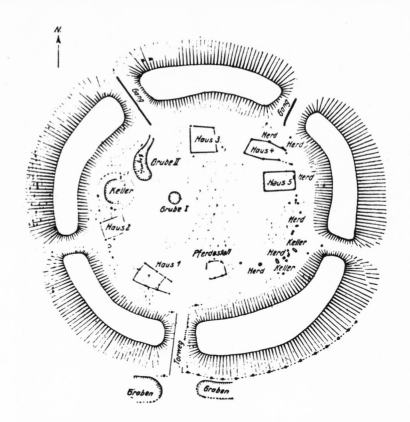

419. The Pipinsburg near Wesermünde.

420. The *Burg* at Stöttinghausen near Bremen.

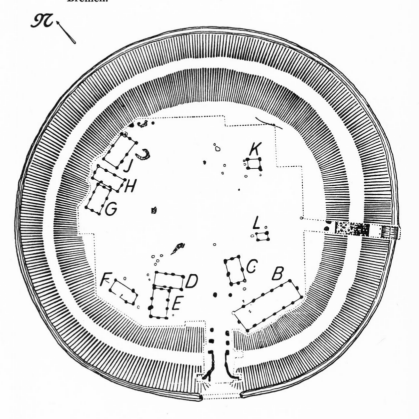

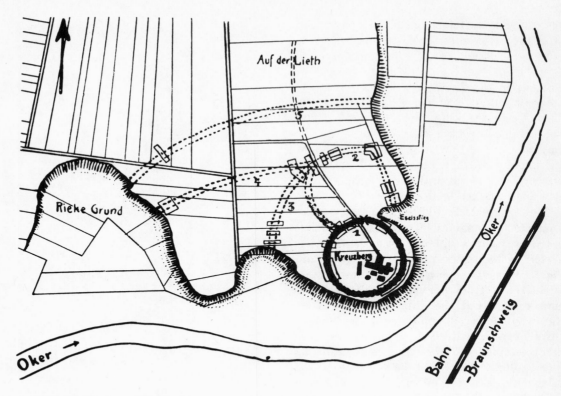

421. Burg Werla near Goslar.

agrarii, lower vassals, should build a *Burg* where one of them would live and maintain the grounds and buildings while the others took care of the food supply. The *Pfalz* of Werla covered an enormous area, almost 100 *Morgen* (149 acres), and consisted of one main *Burg,* and several outlying ones. It was situated on a spur jutting out into the plains of the Oker and was perfectly adapted to the terrain. The main circular stone wall was about 6 feet thick and was surrounded by a ditch 36 feet wide. The outlying *Burgen* served as additional protection and as accommodation for the numerous retainers, soldiers, and horsemen.

456

The Morphology of a Wurt

A *Wurt* is a mound in a flood-endangered area. These mounds are very numerous in the region between the Zuider Zee and the mouth of the Elbe. Today they have lost their importance as inhabited places, with the exception of some so-called active *Wurten* east of the Elbe and in Schleswig. The first stage of a *Wurten* settlement were groups of farms on the flat mainland built at a time when the danger of floods did not yet exist. Where and when the shore line began to submerge, the settlers raised the area on which they wanted to rebuild their farms by depositing a layer about 3 to 5 feet thick consisting of debris, refuse, and other material. The *Wurten* are either small—so-called "refuge" *Wurten*—or sufficiently large to accommodate a small number of houses. They are an impressive proof of the tenacity, and voluntary cooperation of sedentary people. Although the *Wurten* have not materially affected the structure and distribution of settlement in general, they are nevertheless a not negligible contribution to the history of colonization that existed before the building of large dikes protecting long sections of the coast line made most of them, although by no means all, redundant, preserving them only as interesting remnants of an almost forgotten past.

The *Wurt* Feddersen Wierde near Bremerhaven has been selected as a good example because very detailed and careful investigations have been published in one of the most recent reports on this subject.[1] The map shows the rest of the old mainland, which the invading sea has dissected into bays and islands. The tidal flats extended to the area in the northwest corner of the map. Two ocean currents have cut two channels that met in the eastern sector of the area. Between them a part of the mainland was preserved as an island; it was 960 feet long and 690 feet wide. At the beginning of the settlement the sea had again receded; the deep channels in the northwest had been filling up; and the other channels in the east, which surrounded the island, had narrowed. When the first settlers established their houses on the island, they selected the northwestern part on a narrow watercourse. The fields covered the eastern and southeastern portion. The whole settlement was protected on all sides by the surrounding water. The channels were the natural lines of communication, and the bays were the natural landing places. In the course of the centuries the settlement spread from the northwest to the southeast. The narrow and shallow watercourse, which, at the beginning, had limited the inhabited area, had been silting up and included in the settled area like its northern branch. Only the southern channel remained open.

The results of the excavations, as far as the first settlement period is concerned, are very meager. For the second period (first century A.D.), an extension of the settlement to the east and four houses surrounded by a rectangular ditch were identified. These houses stood on a common artificial elevation that was carefully prepared before the building began. The following period of settlement, still in the first century A.D., saw an eastern extension of 30 to 45 feet; the houses of both these periods were built one on top of the other and could be separated

1. W. Haarnagel, "Vorläufiger Bericht über das Ergebnis der Wurtengrabung auf der Feddersen Wierde bei Bremerhaven im Jahre 1956," *Germania*, 35. 1957, *Heft* 3/4.

457

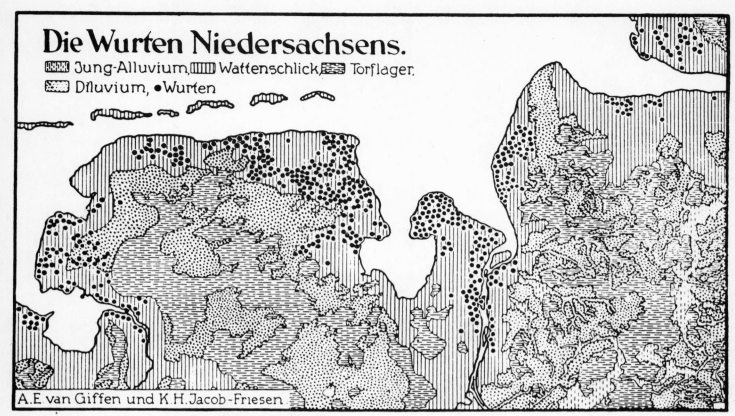

422. The _Wurten_ of Lower Saxony.

only with great difficulty. During the third period (end of the first and beginning of the second century A.D.), a further extension took place, and on this small extension a house was erected, which was surrounded by an earthen wall slightly over 4 feet high. This was obviously not a protection against men and animals—the wall was too low for this purpose—but a miniature dike that sheltered only this one building, not the whole village. This is the oldest dike that has been discovered to date and it clarifies the origin and development of dikes: at first they protected only single farms; then, whole settlements; and finally, in the Middle Ages, the entire coast line. The extension of the _Wurt_ had become necessary because the population had increased and room for new houses had to be added.

In the next period (second century A.D.) the longitudinal _Wurt_ and the separated _Wurten_ had grown together through repeated and new additions. The demarcation between the individual farms consisted now of wattle fences; the old trenches had been filled in. The extension of the settlement area was

effected not only through the connection of the _Wurten_ but also through the extension of the whole complex toward the northeast by the depositing of dung and earth. In this process when each house was rebuilt, it was erected on a separate, low, long hill so that the rain water could flow off and the houses stood on dry ground. Thus two sorts of additions are to be distinguished: large additions that raised the level of the whole _Wurt,_ and local additions that protected the individual house against dampness from the ground. During the fifth period (third century A.D.), the area was again enlarged to the northeast and the southwest and raised by 1½ feet. But this time the extension was obviously undertaken not because more houses had to be built—their number did not increase—but because a social reorganization seems to have taken place. The settlement, which, since the beginning, had been organized in extended family groups and was later subdivided into individual properties, grew during this period into a community.

The first four houses erected in the first century were arranged one behind the other

458

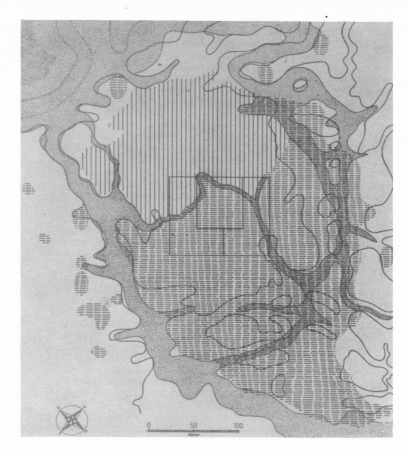

423. Feddersen Wierde. First settlement.

in one line stretching from west to east, and it seems that each farm was a self-contained unit. In the third period the number of houses had increased to seven; they stood in two rows with an open space between them. By the fourth period each farm had been surrounded by a fence, a possible indication that the large family group had disintegrated. At the end of this period the whole village was destroyed by fire and was rebuilt in a totally different way. The farms were concentrated in two areas and were separated by fences. The farms in the northwest were arranged radially, and apparently they had a sacklike layout.

The last period (fourth to fifth century A.D.) revealed, in spite of unfavorable conditions, that the economic structure of the settlement, as well as its layout, had undergone far-reaching changes. The houses were much smaller, irregularly placed, and the street had disappeared. This transformation must have been caused by events that imposed a totally different way of life on the inhabitants of the village. The most likely explanation is that the population had been reduced by poverty. The larger houses on the street had not been rebuilt; their owners had either left the *Wurt* or lost their livelihood. Whether this decline was due to war—a similar deterioration has been observed on the *Wurt* of Ezinge in the Province of Groningen in Holland, and has been attributed to the ravages of

the Great Migrations—or to the rising level of the sea and the inundation of the fields and meadows has not yet been clarified. In any case, the basis of the food supply seems to have been destroyed, and the inhabitants had to leave the *Wurt*. The place remained deserted until the early Middle Ages when it was reoccupied by a few dispersed farms.

424. Feddersen Wierde, first century A.D.

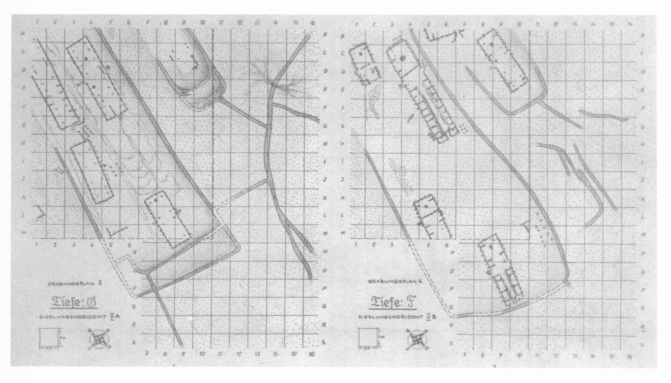

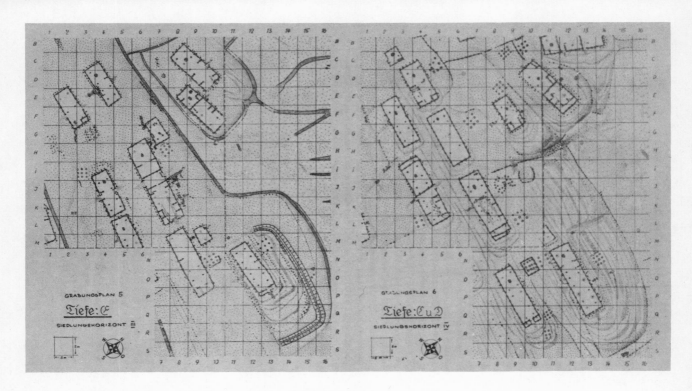

425. Feddersen Wierde, first and second centuries A.D.

426. Feddersen Wierde, third and fourth Centuries A.D.

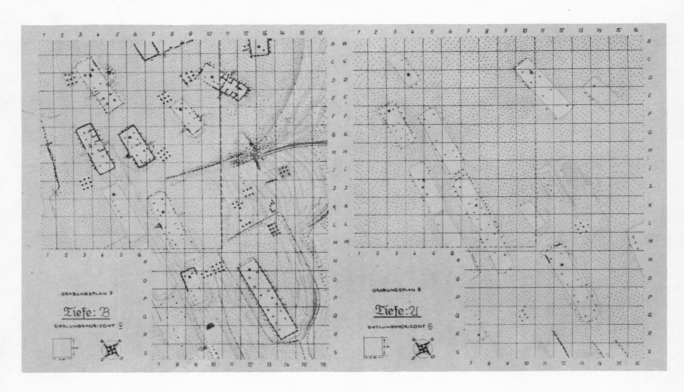

The Moving Frontiers of Settlement during the Middle Ages

The Carolingians advanced from the Rhine toward the East along the Main and the Danube. The found a country covered with woods almost untouched by human hands. The clearings interspersed in this vast extent of forest were occupied by small villages, hamlets, and isolated farmsteads where nobles, free peasants, or manorial serfs had settled. Soon, manors granted as fiefs by the king sprang up; and the Church, mainly represented by the bishops of Würzburg and Regensburg, acquired large estates through donations from the Royal Family and pious nobles. Monasteries were founded as the nodal points from which the transformation of the natural into the cultural landscape spread in all directions and which were especially valuable for the advancing Franks because these footholds served both peaceful and military purposes. Thus began the colonization of Bavaria between the upper Main and the middle Danube, spreading along rivers and the few existing roads.

The center of the colonial and political activities moved northward when Henry I, Duke of Saxony, ascended the throne in A.D. 919. Now it was the marginal region around the Harz Mountains and along the middle Elbe and the Saale, instead of the more centrally situated territory on the Rhine and the Main, from which the colonial expansion advanced and the frontiers of the realm had to be protected. The old Frankish strongholds and missions—for instance, Erfurt in Thuringia—were valuable assets as bases of the new expansion. Existing strongholds were rebuilt; gaps in the line of fortifications were closed; and peasant soldiers were settled in the frontier zone, though only rarely east of the Saale. These activities were directed by the state; they were not a spontaneous folk movement.[1]

Otto the Great, crowned king in 936, continued his father's work. His most important contribution was to found the town and archbishopric of Magdeburg, which was to become the center for the colonization of the eastern lands. The king acquired estates from the nobles in the already developed parts of the country in exchange for land in the still underdeveloped border regions, and transferred them to the ecclesiastical institutions. Numerous settlements grew up on river crossings and road junctions where the traveling merchants could interrupt their journeys. Here church and market developed, and in many cases these early and small places became the nuclei of towns. Broadly speaking, the eleventh century was more a period of consolidation in the West than one of expansion toward the East. New land was reclaimed in the West, on the lower Rhine and in the Netherlands, and peasants settled in the forests between the Rhine and the Weser.

The causes for the west–east movement are difficult to trace. There are hardly any original sources available to explain what drove people to leave their homeland and set out to unknown and unsafe regions. As far as can be conjectured one reason for the exodus of many people from the West may have been the increase of population and growing urbanization, which, together with economic

1. K. H. Quirin. *Die deutsche Ostsiedlung im Mittelalter.* 1954; and W. Kuhn. *Geschichte der deutschen Ostsiedlung in der Neuzeit,* I. 1955, and II. 1957. See both also for the following.

progress, created a fluctuating class of workers and craftsmen who were politically restless and whose loyalties were labile. At the same time the natural economy was gradually being replaced by a primitive money economy, and a more rational mentality was spreading, which undermined the attachment to old values and accustomed habits. After the disturbances at Bruges at the turn of the eleventh century, a part of the population emigrated to the Southeast. The appeal for a crusade against the Wends (about 1108) may also have induced people to emigrate to the East, the more so as the summons was couched in a highly emotional language.

We, archbishop of Magdeburg, by the Grace of God . . . to . . . the bishop of Halberstadt . . . Abbot of Corvey . . . bishop of Paderborn . . . and to all spiritual lords and laymen greetings and blessings. Afflicted for a long time by frequent deeds of violence and injustice, we appeal to your pity that you help to re-erect the destroyed edifice of your Mother Church. The heathen have risen against us with an unequalled cruelty and almost vanquish us; men without pity who are proud to boast of their maliciousness; who are devoid of any morality. Arise, thou Bride of Christ, and come. Thy voice shall sound in the ears of Christendom so that all rush to the war for the Saviour and render assistance to the fighters in Christ. The heathen are infamous but their land is astonishingly rich: there milk and honey are flowing. It yields harvests for which there is no comparison. Thus say all who know the country. Therefore, Saxons, Franks, men of Lorraine and Flanders, you famous conquerors of the world, rise up in arms! Here you can win your salvation and, if it pleases you, the best land for settlement in addition. He who has led the Franks through the strength of his arm from the outermost West to triumph over their enemies in the distant Orient will not fail to give you might and strength to conquer the inhuman heathen, your neighbours, and to be successful in all your enterprises.[2]

What a marvelous mixture of idealistic and realistic inducements! Pope Eugene III encouraged this crusade. He promised to all who were ready to march against the Wends

the same indulgences granted the crusaders to the Holy Land.

Eugene . . . servant of the servants of God. . . . You too want to take part in this work so pleasing to God and to go to war against the Slavs and the other heathen peoples of the North in order to convert them with the help of God to Christianity. . . . We promise therefore to all who have not taken the cross for the crusade to Jerusalem but are determined to march against the Slavs that indulgence for their sins which has been granted by our predecessor Urban to those who went to Jerusalem.[3]

We may assume that the combination of spiritual and materialistic gains produced the desired results and drew considerable numbers of not all too selfless crusaders toward the promised lands in the East.

Natural catastrophes drove people from their homes and induced them to begin a new life in other lands. During the twelfth century the whole coast of the North Sea, especially the Dutch part, was devastated by floods.

[The year 1144] brought a hard winter with much rain and storm. Strong trees were uprooted; churches, towers and other buildings which had been considered solid were for the most part destroyed. . . . A great famine oppressed many people. . . . Not only poor and moderately well-to-do ones but also those who were thought to be wealthy enough were forced by the all penetrating sword of hunger to emigrate.

[And of the year 1163 and 1183:] From St. Lorenz (10th August) to Martin's Day (11th November) it was raining incessantly so that almost all crops in the fields were ruined. . . . On St. Thomas Day (21st December) a colossal tidal wave broke in. In the coastal villages no house remained undamaged. . . . Even Friesland and Saxony were visited at the same time by such a flood.

[And] especially in the diocese of Utrecht and in the county of Holland many places were affected by a flood. It was intensified by incessant rains to such a degree that many people lost their life and property. Others driven by hunger abandoned hearth and home and emigrated.[4]

2. *Codex diplomaticus Saxoniae regiae* (1864), I, 1, 40; *Codex diplomaticus Anhaltinus* (1867), I, 112.

3. *Mecklenburgisches Urkundenbuch*, I. 1863, No. 44, p. 36.
4. *Monumenta Germaniae historica*, Scriptores VI, 388; XVI, 463, 469.

The first contract with Dutch settlers, which is dated 1106, refers to the reclamation of the marshes of the Weser. It begins as follows:

In the name of God . . . We, Frederick by the Grace of God, head of the Church of Hamburg, wish to make known the contract which Hollanders who live beyond the Rhine have made with us. These men came to us and begged to make over to them . . . for reclamation land in our diocese that until now has remained uncultivated and swampy.[5]

Another document refers to the settlement of Flemings by the archbishop of Magdeburg in 1159:

. . . that I have given the village of Wusterwitz with all its possessions of fields, pastures, meadows, water, forest, and fisheries to Heinrich and the other Flemings who came through him and with him to me. . . . Because the village is situated favorably to traffic, I have granted . . . that an annual fair may be held.[6]

Further:

In the name of the Holy Trinity . . . I, Gerung, Bishop of Meissen make known that I have settled able men from Flanders on abandoned land which has hardly been cultivated and has been deserted by its inhabitants.[7]

The kings were the main patrons of the towns, especially in central Germany. They furthered their development chiefly by granting special privileges to the merchants. Territorial policy, markets, and rural settlement were all essential instruments of the expanding economy and the advance toward the East. How important the market was for the growing settlements can be read from the subsequent stages of the layout of towns and large villages. At first in many places parts of the streets were widened, thus enclosing an elongated open space, which served as a market. Houses for the merchants and traders were built on these streets; churches followed. When this simple street pattern became in-

sufficient, new streets were added or old ones were diverted. Market squares developed through the crossing of streets and gradually the checkerboard plan, which is characteristic of almost all colonial towns, came into being.

Toward the end of the eleventh century the colonial expansion eastward underwent an essential transformation. Hitherto, this expansion had been restricted mainly to the south, while in the north the conflict with the Slavs had delayed or prevented an advance on a broad front. Now a more systematic colonization along the whole frontier from the Alps to the Elbe and the Saale set in. Large, compact, regular villages were built mostly by a *locator*, a sort of wealthy contractor and developer who supplied not only the buildings and the land but often also the peasants. On level country, in the Northeast and in the Alpine foreland and the basins of the Carpathian Mountains, the road village and the *Angerdorf* (a road village in which the road widens or divides to enclose a central green) were preferred, with the homesteads lined up along the road and the fields arranged in a few large *Gewanne*. On the Baltic Sea, in the central part of the Thuringian Forest and also in the southern region of the Bohemian Forest the settlements were preferably laid out as *Marschhufen* or *Waldhufen* villages consisting of one row of houses facing a dike or a road, respectively, with the strips of land laid out behind the houses at right angles to the dike or road.

After the second half of the twelfth century, colonial towns became more numerous. For the center of their regular layout a long, rectangular market place was preferred in the South, while in the North a square market place was more common. With growing experience large areas were systematically colonized from an urban focal point, and urban and rural expansion and development proceeded simultaneously and organically. By the end of the twelfth century a belt of 45 to 60 miles was opened up: eastern Holstein, western Mecklenburg, the Mark Brandenburg up to the region of Potsdam, the eastern half of present-day Thuringia, and Upper Saxony to

5. *Bremisches Urkundenbuch* (1873), I, 27.
6. O. von Heinemann, *Albrecht der Bär* (1864), App. 41.
7. *Codex diplomaticus Saxoniae regiae* (1864), I, 2, 254.

the Elbe. The Franks advanced through the forests to the north of the Erz Mountains and were the main colonizers of southern Saxony and Upper Lusatia, where they built large *Waldhufen* villages. The Thuringians settled farther north. The region east of the Elbe was occupied by people from Lower Saxony, who built their villages in clearings on the wooded boulder clay soils of the Baltic coast in Mecklenburg and later in Pomerania. These groups were joined by Hollanders and Flemings whose greater experience in technically more advanced forms of settlement and, above all, in irrigation and reclamation soon made them the leading experts among the less experienced pioneer settlers. During this period townsmen and peasants, nobles and monks went eastward. By looking at the years in which the towns were founded, the progress of the colonization can be read: Chemnitz, 1143; Leipzig, before 1170; Brandenburg, before 1170; Jüterbog, 1174; Schwerin, 1160.

At the same time, important towns came into existence that later, independent from the rural settlement, developed their own commercial and industrial bases. To this group belonged Lübeck on the Baltic Sea and the mining town of Freiberg in Saxony. Merchants penetrated farther eastward on the great continental highways and soon established their own companies in traffic centers and under the protection of the fortified castles of feudal lords, for example in Old Ofen, Prague, Cracow, (Krakow), Stettin (Szczecin), and Danzig (Gdansk). On the foundation of the town of Stettin (1187):

We, Siegfried, Bishop of Pomerania . . . make known that the layman Beringer . . . has erected a church in honor of God outside the fortified castle of Stettin.[8]

This was the beginning of the urban settlement under the protection of the castle. On the foundation of Greifenhagen in Pomerania (1254):

Barnim, Duke of the Slavs . . . Everyone shall know that we have given 200 hides towards the foundation of the town of Greifenhagen, namely 100 for wood and pastures, 100 for the fields. Four hides and the village of Damerow have been allotted by us to the Church . . . the citizens of Greifenhagen shall remain tax-free . . . the market of the town shall remain free for ever of taxes. . . . What the councilmen built for the common good within the sphere of influence of the town and within the walls the town shall own free forever.[9]

And finally on the town of Brieg in Silesia:

We [Duke Henry I] have handed over to the *Schultheiss* [head of the village] Henry of Reichenbach our town . . . to establish settlers according to the law that was valid for the foundation and settlement of Neumarkt. . . . The contractors [locatores] receive every sixth homestead with its revenues. . . . We allow the building of mills. . . . We promise to fortify the town within two years.[10]

During the first half of the thirteenth century it was, above all, Silesia that received the main attention of the advancing colonizers. German settlements approached this region from the West through Upper Lusatia and from the Southeast, that is, from Moravia. The towns founded in the course of this advance were, among others, Bautzen in 1213 and Görlitz about 1215, and in the South, Mährisch-Neustadt in 1213 and Troppau before 1224. At about 1250 two lines of towns encircled the core area of Silesia, following in the North the Oder and in the South the fringe of the Sudetic Mountains. A similar development took place in the North in the region of Mecklenburg and Brandenburg. Here Prenzlau was founded in 1235. By 1250 the German colonization had reached the Oder, extending almost its entire length from the mouth of the river to Ratibor. The northern advance along the Baltic had covered about 120 miles, while the center—that is, the Silesian colonization—had spread almost 240 miles eastward, thus approximately catching up with the expansion in southern Germany. This rather rapid advance slowed down in the second half of the thirteenth century; the

9. *Pommersches Urkundenbuch* (1868), II, No. 35, p. 3.

10. *Codex diplomaticus Silesiae* (1857), IX, 219.

8. *Codex Pomeraniae diplomaticus* (1862), I, 60.

464

newly occupied lands had to be consolidated and further developed. However, the colonization proceeded eastward, though more slowly and less aggressively. By the middle of the thirteenth century it had reached on a broad front the southwestern frontier of Poland where it was stopped by the densely settled population of Greater Poland. On the other hand, the western part of Poland could not resist the pressure from the west. Here Guben was established in 1235 and Cracow in 1257 by the initiative from Breslau and Neisse (Nysa). In the North, the Teutonic Order was active: Memel was founded in 1252 and Königsberg (Kaliningrad) in 1286.

The colonization of the East proceeded simultaneously as an urban and a rural expansion, and in this way it was the continuation and the equivalent of the corresponding development in the western parts of Germany. Both village and town were indispensable prerequisites for the great success of this movement. Before 1200, about a hundred towns were mentioned; in the first half of the thirteenth century about four hundred, and in the second half about the same number were founded. Then in the fourteenth century the intensity of urbanization decreased to one hundred, and in the fifteenth century to even fewer than that. In human terms this meant that the merchant and peasant were equal partners in the colonial adventure, and in economic terms that agricultural and industrial activities were complementary and formed an organic economic entity. Economic unity furthered a social community, and rural and urban law often merged into each other. An illustration of this can be found in the term sometimes used for the municipal court, *Burding,* which originally meant the court of a rural community where infringements of the community regulations for the common use of the pastures and the cultivation of the fields were adjudicated.

Similarly, the regular layout of villages influenced the plan of the colonial towns and vice versa. The combination of a community of citizens and a market was typically Germanic, unknown to the Slavs; or if rudiments of this sort existed it was further developed

by the German colonists. The law so characteristic of the German towns, the so-called *Weichbild-Verfassung,* the bylaws concerning the incorporated and contiguous area of a town, was repeatedly applied to Slavic towns. It was the legal basis for the unity of urban and rural settlement, and guaranteed to the urban communities an almost complete legal and economic preponderance. This area was clearly delineated by the *Bannmeile,* and within this area the town exerted its influence in accordance with the privileges it had received from a prince or a feudal lord. These privileges regulated the market, the sale of certain goods, brewing, and the keeping of inns, and later also trade and handicrafts. Its aim was to adjust the rural and urban activities; but in reality the countryside was a more or less passive partner in relation to the town. Toward the end of the colonial movement, *Bannmeile* adjoined *Bannmeile.* In the domain of the Teutonic Order these areas were surveyed from the very beginning: The towns were sited at a distance of 18 miles from each other as functional centers of the surrounding sphere of influence.[10]

By the fourteenth century, immigration from Germany had come to an almost complete standstill. The population had ceased to increase as a consequence of the Black Death in 1348 and the subsequent epidemics that had left great gaps that could not be filled. The progress of colonization, or rather its preservation on a level that would guarantee a continuation of its success, therefore rested mainly on the self-replacement of the local population, especially by the younger age groups. In general, the German territories, with the exception of Prussia, were fairly well settled at this time, and the two large Slavic areas—the Czech-Moravian on the Elbe, the Moldavia, and the Morava and the Polish on the black earth of the Kujawian region south of Bydgoszcz (Bromberg) and Torun (Thorn), and on the loess soils of Little Poland—were densely peopled.

The colonial expansion that spread from the west to the east over central Europe deep

10. Quirin. *Op. cit.,* p. 34.

465

into the present Czechoslovakia, Austria, and Hungary had, of course, its inevitable drawbacks. Numerous villages were abandoned and became *Wüstungen* (abandoned villages) after the end of the thirteenth century, and even more during the fourteenth. The reasons for this retrogression were manifold: the overeager pioneers had underestimated the natural difficulties, such as lack of a sufficient water supply, unfavorable soils, and climatic hazards; the peasants were unable to cope with financial and other problems and could not sustain their energy; or the settlers did not have the necessary skills and experience. Other reasons were the need for protection and security, which made it more desirable to live in larger and less isolated villages, and last but not least the general migration to the towns.

This latter, especially, had a detrimental effect on the efficiency of the agricultural districts. The sanitary conditions in the towns were utterly insufficient. The death rate was greater than the natural replacement rate. Immigration from the countryside was, therefore, essential if at least the normal level of the urban population was to be maintained. The percentage of the urban population in relation to the total population rose steadily until the fifteenth century. Not only did the cities and towns grow, but innumerable small country-towns came into existence. Moreover, the Black Death, epidemics, and famines hit the urban population hardest. This led to a decrease in the demand for agricultural products by the townspeople and, therefore, to a surplus of provisions held by the rural population and to a fall in prices, while the price of the goods the peasants had to buy in the towns showed a tendency to rise. The result was unfavorable for the rural population. Many peasants had no choice other than to leave their homes, to abandon their villages and fields, and to move either to more favorably situated villages or to migrate to the towns. But this period should not be regarded as one of decline. Rather, it was a transitional epoch that resulted in a certain concentration of settlement, a consolidation of what had been achieved, and a selective process in which the weak elements were eliminated or reformed in favor of the stronger and healthier members.

The decrease of the migration from the old German regions to the east after the middle of the thirteenth century resulted from far-reaching changes in the west, from a general decline in rural settlement, and from the abandonment of cultivated land and whole villages and groups of villages, not only individual farms. This process began in western Europe toward the end of the thirteenth century; it spread gradually to the East in the second third of the fourteenth century and continued with increasing intensity until the end of the fifteenth century despite energetic countermeasures by the territorial lords and the lords of the manors. Its climax in the West was reached at about 1450, and in the East, shortly before 1500. It has been estimated that almost one-third to one-half of the medieval peasant farms were affected by this development.[11] That is, of course, an approximate estimate, the more so as only the completely abandoned villages could be clearly identified. Farmsteads and fields were deserted and the forests spread again over the land. Fields that were not covered by the forest were often used for extensive cultivation by neighboring communities. At the end of the fifteenth century when the crisis had passed, the gaps in the partially abandoned settlements were soon filled, but the totally abandoned villages and fields remained covered by the forests in those cases where the lord of the manor preferred a systematic forestry and protected his woods from renewed clearing. In other cases, only the buildings remained unused and dilapidated, while the fields served as pastures; or the villages and fields were restored, the land systematically cleared, and the whole settlement with a new village and redistributed fields was rebuilt. The last was fairly common in eastern Germany during the sixteenth century because of the stronger position of the lords of the manor. In general, the large villages in the East with forty, fifty or more farms survived more easily than the smaller ones,

11. Kuhn. *Op. cit.,* I, 55.

466

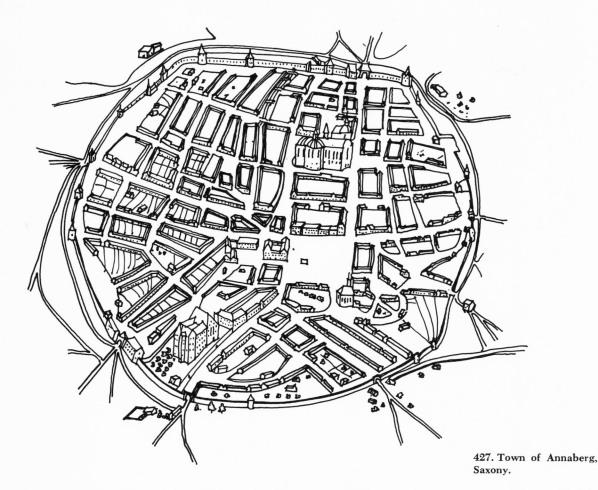

427. Town of Annaberg, Saxony.

and were abandoned only under particularly unfavorable geographical conditions.

Industrial settlements, especially mining towns, had a certain, though locally restricted, significance for the eastward spread of the colonization. The ore-bearing rocks, found mainly in the mountainous regions, were of relatively low quality. However, the silver found in the Harz and the Erz Mountains and in Upper Silesia attracted considerable numbers of adventurers and miners, and gave rise to several mining towns that survived the centuries. In 1471 rich silver deposits were discovered on the Schneeberg to the south of Zwickau. A silver rush, which has been compared with the California gold rush in the nineteenth century, set in. By 1478 over 160 miners were working. A town developed, at first unsystematically, until the Elector of Saxony intervened and granted civic and mining rights to the town of Schneeberg. Its layout was almost circular and had radial and concentric streets. Its population had reached 10 thousand by the end of the fifteenth cen-

tury. Other mining towns were Annaberg and Joachimsthal, with a total population of 18 thousand in 1533. During the sixteenth century many more mining towns were founded; and on the northern slopes of the western Erz Mountains a chain of mining settlements, a veritable conurbation, developed. These places were smaller than the three older towns and stagnated when the deposits were exhausted.

Most of the mining towns began as chaotic conglomerations, and may have been similar to modern shanty towns. This spontaneous growth was stopped when the authorities insisted on a more systematic procedure. In general, the checkerboard plan of the colonial settlements served as an example. For instance, at Annaberg a detailed plan was worked out even before it was elevated to a town in 1496; it was fortified in 1503. Marienberg is especially interesting: The mayor designed the plan, and a peasant drew on the ground with a hook the main streets and the circumference. It was a square of 1500

467

428. *Locator* and settlers. From the *Sachsenspiegel*.

feet, and had a market place of 375 by 375 feet in the center.

A few notes may be appropriate on the *locatores* who, after the twelfth century played a decisive role in the colonization of the East. They were the agents of the lords of the manor, and their tasks were to recruit the settlers, to convey them to the selected site, to allocate the hides, and in general to assist them during the first years. As compensation for their expenses and the considerable risk involved in these activities they received the hereditary office of *Schultheiss,* village head, in a new village, or of *Vogt,* bailiff, in a new town. In addition, they received a farm of several hides that was free of taxes; one-sixth to one-tenth of the current taxes from all the village lands; the judgeship in the lower court of the rural district with one-third of the

fines; and the exclusive right to run a mill, a forge, an inn, a bakery, a butcher's and a shoemaker's stall, and special hunting and fishing rights. With all these privileges guaranteed by inheritance the position of the *locatores* and their descendants was very influential and remunerative. The reason for the extraordinary procedure that devolved these important privileges and usufructs upon the agents of the feudal lords was the inefficient administrative organization of this period. The territorial lords, and even more the petty nobles, had no experts who could deal with the complex problems of colonization. This changed only toward the end of the Middle Ages and especially in the Southeast when some of the lords began to use their own officials for the foundation of new villages and towns.

The Morphology of a Region

The following is a condensed morphology of a characteristic and important region of Germany, Franconia, or Franken. It shows the development from the earliest time to the beginning of the eleventh century A.D., by which time its history and its rural and urban settlement had become more and more absorbed into the general trend of the events that are the subject of the main part of this volume. The principal purpose of the survey is to show the unfolding of the role of man in transforming the natural into a cultural landscape—his slowly increasing activity as a colonist and his efforts to establish permanent settlements in conformity with his social aspirations, his economic needs, and his technical ability. Franconia was the birthplace of some of the greatest German artists, of Grünewald, Dürer, Lucas Cranach, Veit Stoss, Adam Kraft, and Peter Vischer. On its soil rose cities and towns that occupy a leading place in the development of urban civilization. Nürnberg, Bamberg, Würzburg, Rothenburg, Dinkelsbühl, and many other small towns and villages testify to the historical continuity and cultural heritage of this region. Nature and man have shaped its character in a mutual adaptation stretching over millennia and growing in intensity over ever-widening circles in space, diversity, and achievements. This interdependent work of nature and man has changed the face of the landscape: It has cleared the woods, determined the distribution of the forested and cultivated areas, transformed the regimen of the rivers and the fauna and flora, and left its manifold imprint on the intricate web of existence that now spreads over this region. All this is not unusual; it has happened in all parts of the world. But Franconia has been selected because it is a typically German land that is not too large, though sufficiently diversified, to offer a sequence of historical and natural features of a representative development. However, the survey has been primarily restricted to the historical development of settlement, the proper study of this work.

The landscape of Franconia forms an organic whole within a cuesta topography—that is, low ridges of steep gradients on one side and gentle slopes on the other.[1] Its situation in a troughlike depression outside the relatively stable area that was less affected by all later movements of the earth's crust exposed it to the deposition of enormous masses of gravel, sand, and mud from the surrounding lands over millions of years, which, under the immense pressure, were cemented together into hard conglomerates. In the course of mountain-building and the consequent folding and faulting, molten granite rose from the deeper layers; after cooling and solidifying, it formed veins of gold, silver, tin, iron, and antimony, which in the Middle Ages gave rise to a mining industry in the Fichtelgebirge, the Franconia Mountains, and the Spessart. After the Jurassic period, the land masses in central Germany had risen along the northern margin of Franconia and pressed the waters back to the present Alpine foreland. At the same time a river system developed that during the following hot and humid Cretaceous period, cut deeply into the recently deposited layers. In the Tertiary, mountain-building spread to the Franconian region. Its tremendous pressure broke the old rock formations, the plutonic rocks deep down in the earth, and the superimposed

1. C. Scherzer, *Franken* (1955), Vol. 1, *passim*.

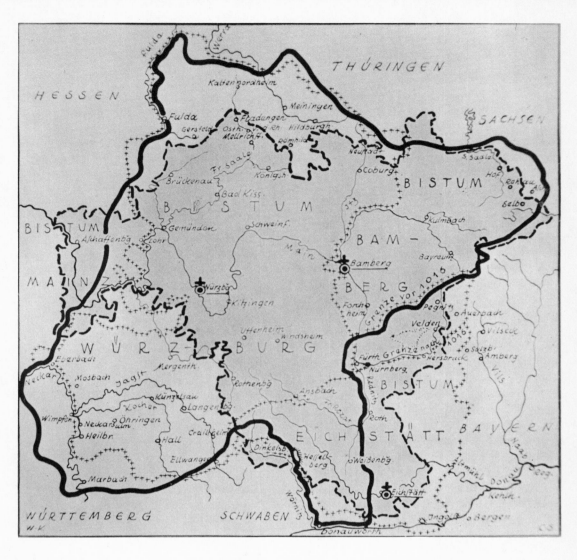

429. Historical development of Franconia:

Dukedom of Eastern Franconia after the eleventh century.

++++ Frontiers of the Bishoprics of Würzburg, Bamberg, and Eichstätt after 1016.

--- Present extension of the three Franconian districts after 1837.

layers into fragments, uplifting and depressing, tilting and overthrusting them, and forming a depression almost 6 thousand feet deep and 30 miles long in western Franconia. Compared with the large-scale changes since the Tertiary, the Ice Age was a period of small and more detailed reshaping of the relief of the landscape. The strong ice wedging overpowered even the granites of the Fichtelgebirge and the basalts of the Rhön, and disintegrated them into boulder fields and *Felsenmeere*. Soil erosion and denudation spread; the rivers could not carry away the great masses of debris that the melting snow deposited and transported for considerable distances, dispersing them over wide areas of the valley plains. The loose soil was blown

away, and accumulated in large wind-blown fields. The climate changed, and earth movements formed terraces along the rivers.

The great ice sheet that spread in the Quaternary over parts of Europe from the north reached its southernmost limits at the slopes of the Riesengebirge, the Thuringian Forest, and the Harz Mountains. A second ice sheet advanced from the Alps into the Alpine foreland and the plains. During this period Franconia remained an ice-free region between the glaciated northern and southern zones. Vestiges of human existence were found in the caves of the Fränkische Alb and of the open country, which may be regarded as the earliest settlements of this region. Hunting and fishing were the basic occupations. Hills

470

were also, though temporarily, occupied because they offered good posts from which the herds grazing in the plains could be observed. In the neolithic era, fundamental advances were made. Agriculture and the domestication of animals made people sedentary. Hoe culture developed. Permanent houses were built. Villages began to appear; and a certain amount of cooperation set in, as, for instance, in connection with the protection of the villages by fences, walls, and ditches. One of the great cultural changes during the Bronze Age (about 2000–800 B.C.) was the transition from the flexed burial of the dead to burials in tumuli, a method by which the dead rest deep down in the earth, and finally to burning the dead and preserving their ashes in urns. This was doubtless connected with a transition to new religious ideas and customs. Cave dwellings with fortifications seem to indicate that this protection was needed against invaders, possibly from the East.

The objects placed in the graves of the Hallstatt period indicate that cultural exchange with other countries existed and that Franconia was not a self-contained region in the strictest sense. Its eastern part and adjoining areas were densely settled. The elaborate fortifications of the hilltop settlements suggest that the times were full of unrest and violence and that the peoples had been stirred up and were on the move. Numerous settlements built on dominating heights and surrounded by fertile land have been discovered. It is still uncertain whether these places were rudimentary towns, seats of tribal chiefs, or merely strong points against invaders. In the late La Tène period (100–1 B.C.) the open country seems to have been favored for settlement; villages have been found whose names had survived until Roman times. Frequently Roman camps were laid out on the sites of Celtic settlements. It is not impossible that these places were markets or sanctuaries. The fortified places on hills were particularly important. The Romans called them *oppida*. They were also sanctuaries and seats of the chiefs. Within their sometimes very considerable enclosures, a smaller area was set aside for the residential quarter and a larger space

for cultivation. These *oppida* were the focal points for economic, industrial, and commercial activities.

In the first century A.D. the Romans advanced into Franconia. Behind the protection of the *limes* they founded their large and small *castra*, each with a civilian settlement outside the walls. Many of these camps and forts were the nuclei of later towns and villages. At the beginning of the third century, the Romans reached their northernmost line in Franconia, but they were forced back by the attacks of the Alemanni and had to evacuate the southern part of the country; and in the fourth century, the era of the Great Migrations, they evacuated the rest of the country. Roman influence came to an end; the military camps and towns were deserted. The sixth and seventh centuries A.D. witnessed the advance of the Franks. The rows of graves in eastern Franconia indicate a new stage of settlement and colonization in compact villages, while the few older graves are evidence of dispersed settlements and single farms. Our knowledge of the Carolingian villages, and of the military strong points and the administrative centers of the eighth and ninth centuries is still insufficient. But we do know that the eleventh and twelfth centuries were a period of an intensive clearing of the woodlands and of the foundation of numerous villages and towns, mostly near the fortified castles. The

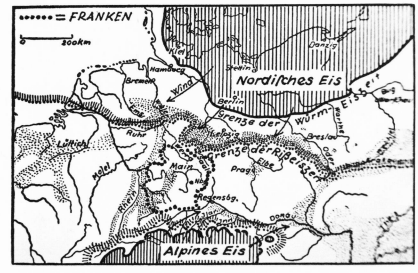

430. The *Lebensraum* of the settlers during the last Ice Age between the two ice-covered regions to the North and to the South. They lived in caves of the Franconian Alb or in the open country.

imperial policy and the administrative reorganization of the state resulted in the erection of *Burgen* in almost every village. They were the seats of the officials of the emperor or the territorial lord. At first, these buildings were very modest. They consisted of a tower as residence, a wall, and a moat. Excavations at Nürnberg and Würzburg have supplied interesting information about the earliest beginnings of these towns. They have revealed that within the nucleus of Nürnberg, for instance, the inhabitants had erected almost exclusively half-timbered houses in the early eleventh century. At the same time, the first fortifications were built, and the *Burgen* were enlarged and improved by adding a *Palas* with adjacent buildings and often a chapel.

Two main stages of the general structure of settlement may be distinguished: the Alemannic and the Frankish colonization. The Alemanni settled in villages, rarely in single farmsteads. They occupied a district and distributed the land among groups of a hundred men who settled in villages inhabited by members of the same family. They knew this type of settlement from the villages on the Main, which they had conquered from the Marcomanni, and it is probable that they adopted without change their village and field systems. When the Alemanni entered the area formerly occupied by the Romans to the south of the *limes,* they encountered an alien form of settlement in the single farms and in the partitioning of land, the *ager centuriatus,* the Roman centuriation, consisting of a gridiron layout of the fields. Here they had to redistribute the land according to their own custom in *Gemengelage,* a number of small, widely-scattered plots. This transformation can still be recognized today in some of the field boundaries. Before permanent settlements existed, that is, during the time of the migrations, the conquered land was owned by the chief; its annual distribution among the families was the concern of the community. When sedentary conditions developed, the need for permanent boundaries between the villages became necessary, and the areas of each village—including fields, pastures, forests, and built-up parts—were marked out. The whole land was divided in *Gewanne;* plots of about the same quality were given to each farmer in each *Gewann,* mostly as square fields. Forests and pastures were used and owned in common.

On the other hand, the advance of the Franks was dictated by a clear political program of their kings, by the needs of an organized conquest as the first stage of imperialistic expansion. The acquisition and distribution of the land was directed by royal officials and carried through by a militant nobility, the leaders, by enterprising peasants, and possibly also by craftsmen, the settlers. Forts and fortified castles on important roads protected this advance. They were erected—unlike the earlier castles, which were built on hills or mountains—on wide plateaux or plains, and resembled the Roman *castra.* Administrative centers of the Frankish kings were also the focal points from which the colonization and the clearing of the woods were organized in detail. As early as the eighth century, *Königshöfe* were built at distances of 12 to 15 miles along the road to Regensburg and Bohemia and on the road to Würzburg-Fürth—a clear sign of a determined military-political program.

431. Possible distribution of *Königshöfe* between Saale and Main during and after the eighth century. Beginning with the eleventh century, the protection of the important roads through the valley was taken over by *Höhenburgen,* fortified castles on hilltops, cliffs, and other elevations.

Residential Strongholds for Local Magnates

In describing the town of Regensburg a special type of residential tower, a *Wohnturm,* was mentioned. It is of particular interest. Such towers were not part of the fortifications of the towns but were owned and used by individual persons; feudal lords, ministerials, and later burghers and even peasants in the countryside. The towers were residential and protective; and, as such, they were an important element in some towns during the early and high Middle Ages. Their main and original purpose was utilitarian; but later, in about 1200, they were sometimes mere showpieces erected by patrician families as tangible symbols of their pride, wealth, and power. To date, these towers have been found only in the older and not systematically developed towns west of the Elbe, such as—in addition to Regensburg—Trier, Sangerhausen, Speyer, Eisenach, and also Meissen.

It seems that until the middle of the thirteenth century ministerials were the residents of these fortified towers, which, because of their location, dominated the town as the seats of the representatives of the territorial lord. This changed when the local self-government of the burghers gained the upper hand and the town hall became the expression of the civic freedom of the inhabitants. Neither the fortified towers nor the fortified town houses of the nobles were invented in the towns. They were feudal elements that had been introduced from the outside. As *burgus,* such a tower was first identified in the *Burg* Querfurt about A.D. 850, and later in the Saxon royal castles at Quedlinburg and Werla. We know of a considerable number of these towers in the smaller castles of the ministerials and nobles erected in the twelfth and thirteenth centuries. They were either habitable keeps or, with the increasing need for comfort, real *Wohntürme* consisting of comfortable rooms, fireplaces, and one main story with a larger hall and richly ornamented windows. In all cases the entrance to the tower was secured by a heavy door and a strong bolt, and lay several yards above the level of the courtyard.

In the countryside *Wohntürme* existed as part of farmsteads or as isolated individual buildings. They were owned by nobles, ministerials, or the peasant community. Today such towers can still be found in villages near Magdeburg, north of the Harz Mountains, and in Hesse. In Hundisburg near Braunschweig there still exist seven farmsteads with towers, adjoining the main village street.

Whether they were part of a fortified castle or of a seignorial town, the *Wohntürme* were an efficient instrument of the political and economic power of the feudal lords and their rule over the towns and villages. When the influence of the feudal aristocracy declined and the strength of the burghers increased, they became symbols of the independence of the urban communities.[1]

1. H. J. Mrusek, *Neue Ergebnisse der Forschung über Mittelalterliche Eigenbefestigungen in Deutschen Siedlungen,* Manuscript (1957); and K. Schuchardt, *Ursprung und Wanderung des Wohnturmes* (Sitzungsberichte der Preussischen Akademie der Wissenschaften), Philosophisch-Historische Klasse, XXXIII (1929).

473

Map of Central Europe

Acknowledgments for Illustrations

2. Photo by S. Presser, Black Star
3. Courtesy Freya Stark
4. Bildarchiv Foto Marburg
5. Courtesy Städtisches Fremden-verkehrsamt, Regensburg
6. Courtesy The American Geographical Society, New York
7. Courtesy Ministère des Travaux Publics
8. Courtesy Ministère des Travaux Publics
11. Courtesy Charles Singer
12. Courtesy Charles Singer
14. Courtesy K. L. M.
15. Courtesy Bildstelle der Stadt Karlsruhe
16. Photo: Toni Schneiders
17. Courtesy Nürnberger Presse Drexel, Merkel & Co.
19. Courtesy The Metropolitan Museum of Art, New York. Rogers Fund
20. Courtesy The Metropolitan Museum of Art, New York
21. Courtesy The Metropolitan Museum of Art, New York. Rogers Fund, 1922
22. After Haliczer
23. After Mielke
24. Plan und Karte, G. M. B. H., Münster
25. Plan und Karte, G. M. B. H., Münster
28. Courtesy Niedersächsische Landesstelle für Marschen- und Wurtenforschung
29. Courtesy Niedersächsische Landesstelle für Marschen- und Wurtenforschung
30. Plan und Karte, G. M. B. H., Münster
31. Luftbildtechnik G. M. B. H., Berlin
32. Luftbildtechnik G. M. B. H., Berlin
33. Luftbildtechnik G. M. B. H., Berlin
36. Luftbildtechnik G. M. B. H., Berlin
37. Luftbildtechnik G. M. B. H., Berlin
38. After Mielke
43. After Stein
44. After Stein
46. After Stein
47. After Stein
48. After Stein
49. After Stein
50. After Stein
55. After Schuchardt
56. After Scherzer
57. After Scherzer
60. Courtesy The Metropolitan Museum of Art, New York

61. Courtesy The Metropolitan Museum of Art, New York. Dick Fund
64. Courtesy The Metropolitan Museum of Art, New York
65. Bildarchiv Foto Marburg
66. Bildarchiv Foto Marburg
67. Bildarchiv Foto Marburg
75. Courtesy The Metropolitan Museum of Art, New York
80. Courtesy the administration of the Palace Gardens
88. Courtesy of the Staatsbibliothek, Munich
90. Bibliothèque Nationale, Paris
91. From D. Duret, *Architecture Religieuse*, 1950
115. Released by the Hesse Ministerium für Arbeit, Wirtschaft und Verkehr. Nr. 74/56
116. Photo: H. Saebens
118. Photo: H. Saebens
120. Photo: H. Saebens
121. Photo: H. Saebens
140. Courtesy Town Planning Institute, London
147. Photo: H. Hartz
148. Photo: U.S. Air Force
158. After R. Schmidt
172. After R. Schmidt
178. Courtesy Kulturamt, Stadtarchiv und Rathausbücherei, Stuttgart
179. Courtesy Kulturamt, Stadtarchiv und Rathausbücherei, Stuttgart
180. Courtesy Kulturamt, Stadtarchiv und Rathausbücherei, Stuttgart
181. After R. Schmidt
187. Released by the Innen-Ministerium Baden/ Württemberg. Nr. 2/424. Photo: H. Brugger
191. Photo: T. Schneiders
199. Courtesy Badisches General-landesarchiv, Karlsruhe
200. Photo: Kübler-Luftbild
206. Courtesy Hauptstattsarchiv, Stuttgart
207. Photo: Luftbild Strähle
219. After R. Schmidt
228. Bildarchiv Foto Marburg
235. After R. Schmidt
266. Photo: H. Retzlaff
275. Germanisches National-Museum, Nürnberg
282. After R. Schmidt
285. After R. Schmidt
296. Germanisches National-Museum, Nürnberg
314. After Rauda
315. After Rauda
318. Plan und Karte G. M. B. H.,

Münster
326. Foto-Walterbusch
327. Photo: E. Fischer, Hamburg
328. Photo: Tschira
329. Photo: Tschira
342. Plan und Karte, G. M. B. H., Münster
362. After Rauda
365. Bildarchiv Foto Marburg
366. Bildarchiv Foto Marburg
385. After Rauda
389. After Rauda
390. Plan und Karte, G. M. B. H., Münster
391. After Rauda
392. After Rauda
393. After Rauda
394. After Rauda
395. After Rauda
396. After Rauda
398. Courtesy Federsee Museum, Buchau
399. Courtesy Federsee Museum, Buchau
400. After Schuchardt
401. Released by the Ministry of the Interior of Baden-Württemberg. Photograph: Albrecht Brugger, Stuttgart
402. After Schuchardt
404. After Schuchardt
405. Museum at Mainz
406. Courtesy Federsee Museum, Buchau
407. Courtesy Federsee Museum, Buchau
408. After Schuchardt
409. After Schuchardt
410. After Steiner
411. Courtesy Rheinisches Landesmuseum, Bonn
412. Courtesy Rheinisches Landesmuseum, Bonn
413. After Steiner
414. After Schuchardt
415. After Schuchardt
416. After Schuchardt
417. After Schuchardt
418. After Schuchardt
419. After Schuchardt
420. After Schuchardt
421. After Schuchardt
423. After W. Haarnagel
424. After W. Haarnagel
425. After W. Haarnagel
426. After W. Haarnagel
428. Library of the University of Heidelberg
429. Courtesy Verlag Nürnberger Presse Drexel, Merkel & Co.
430. Courtesy Verlag Nürnberger Presse Drexel, Merkel & Co.
431. Courtesy Verlag Nürnberger Presse Drexel, Merkel & Co.

Bibliography

ATLASES AND MAPS

In addition to the books mentioned in the Bibliography, numerous detailed maps and plans of individual cities, towns, and villages have been used, as well as maps from the German General Staff.

Andrees Allgemeiner Handatlas. 1913.

Bartholomew, J. *The Times Atlas of the World.* 1962.

———. *The Citizen's Atlas of the World.* 1952.

Beihefte zum geschichtlichen Atlas von Schlesien. N.d.

Concise Oxford Atlas. 1958.

Der Grosse Weltatlas. Bibliographisches Institut A.G., Leipzig. 1936.

Grosser Historischer Weltatlas. Ed. Bayerischer Schulbuchverlag. Parts I (1957) and III (1958).

Meyers Handatlas. 1933.

Muir's Atlas of Ancient and Classical History. 1957.

Oxford Economic Atlas of the World. 1955.

Philip's Historical Atlas, Mediaeval and Modern. 1927.

GENERAL

Aristotle. *Nichomachean Ethics.* Loeb Classical Library, No. 73.

Beiträge zur Geographie Frankens. Würzburger Geographische Arbeiten. *Heft 4/5.* 1957.

Bode, K. *Agrarverfassung und Agrarvererbung in Marsch und Geest.* Abhandlungen des Staatswissenschaftlichen Seminars, Jena, 1910.

Bremisches Urkundenbuch, I (1873), 27.

Brinckmann, A. E. *Stadtbaukunst.* 1920.

———. *Deutsche Stadtbaukunst in der Vergangenheit.* 1921.

———. *Platz und Monument.* 1923.

———. *Schöne Gärten, Villen und Schlösser aus Fünf Jahrhunderten.* 1925.

———. *Baukunst.* 1956.

Bücher, K. *Die Entstehung der Volkswirtschaft.* 1926.

———. *Die Bevölkerung von Frankfurt a.M. im 14. und 15. Jahrhundert, Sozialstatistische Studien,* 1 (1886), XIX, 736.

Butterfield, H. *The Origins of Modern Science.* 1949.

Carl, F. E. *Kleinarchitekturen in der deutschen Gartenkunst; eine entwicklungsgeschichtliche Studie.* 1956.

Carr-Saunders, A. M. *World Population.* 1936.

Cassirer, E. *An Essay on Man: An Introduction to a Philosophy of Culture.* 1953.

Childe, G. *What Happened in History.* 1952.

Chronicles of Fredegarius Scholasticus.

Clapham, J. H., and E. Power. *The Cambridge Economic History of Europe.* 1941.

Codex Diplomaticus Anhaltinus, I (1867), 112.

Codex Diplomaticus et Epistolaris Moraviae, II (1836), No. 11, 219.

Codex Diplomaticus Saxoniae Regiae, I (1864) 1, 40; 2 (1864), 254.

Codex Diplomaticus Silesiae, IX (1857), 219.

Codex Pomeraniae Diplomaticus, I (1862), 60.

Creuzburg, N. *Kultur im Spiegel der Landschaft.* 1930.

Curschmann, F. *Hungersnöte im Mittelalter.* Leipziger Studien aus dem Gebiet der Geschichte, 1900.

Darby, H. C. "The Clearing of the Woodland in Europe," in *Man's Role in Changing the Face of the Earth,* ed. William L. Thomas, Jr., The Wenner-Grenn Foundation for Anthropological Research and the National Science Foundation, 1956.

D'Argenville, Antoine-Joseph Dezallier. *La Théorie et la Pratique du Jardinage.* 1709.

Dehio, G. *Handbuch der deutschen Kunstdenkmäler.* Vols. 1-5. 1905-1912.

———. *Geschichte der Deutschen Kunst.* 6 vols. 1921-1926.

Descartes, R. *A Discourse on Method.* First published in 1637.

Deutsches Land in Flugaufnahmen. Blaue Bücher, 1953.

Deutsches Städtebuch. Handbuch Städtischer Geschichte, ed. Erich Keyser. All vols.

Dickinson, R. E. *The German Lebensraum.* 1943.

Dietrich, B. *Der Siedlungsraum in eingesenkten Mäandertälern.* Schlesische Gesellschaft für vaterländische Kultur. 1917.

East, W. G. *An Historical Geography of Europe.* 1956.

Eberstadt, R. *Der Ursprung des Zunftwesens.* 1915.

———. *Handbuch des Wohnungswesens.* 1917.

Eulenburg, F. "Zur Bevölkerungs- und Vermögensstatistik des 15. Jahrhunderts," *Zeitschrift für Sozial und Wirtschaftsgeschichte,* III, 457.

Freidank. *Bescheidenheit [Practical Wisdom].* First published in 1508.

Ganshof, F. L. *Etude sur le Développement des Villes entre Loire et Rhin au Moyen Age.* 1943.

Gantner, J. *Grundformen der Europäischen Stadt.* 1928.

Geisler, W. *Die Deutsche Stadt.* 1924.

Gradmann, R. "Das mitteleuropäische Landschaftsbild nach seiner geschichtlichen Entwicklung," *Geographische Zeitschrift,* Vol. VII (1901).

———. "Vorgeschichtliche Landwirtschaft und Besiedlung," *Geographische Zeitschrift,* Vol. 42 (1936).

Griesebach, A. *Der Garten.* 1910.

Gruber, K. *Die Gestalt der deutschen Stadt; ihr Wandel aus der geistigen Ordnung der Zeiten.* 1952.

Gurlitt, C. *Geschichte des Barockstieles und des Rococo in Deutschland.* 1889.

Gutkind, E. A. *Creative Demobilisation.* 2 vols. 1944.

———. *Revolution of Environment.* 1946.

———. *Our World from the Air.* 1952.

———. *Community and Environment.* 1953.

———. *L'ambiente in espansione.* 1955.

———. *Architettura e Società.* 1958.

Haarnagel, W. *Die spätbronze- früheisenzeitliche Gehöftsiedlung Jemgum b. Leer auf dem linken Ufer der Ems.* Sonderdruck: *Die Kunde,* 1957. *Heft* 1-2.

———. "Vorläufiger Bericht über das Ergebnis der Wurtengrabung auf der Feddersen Wierde bei Bremerhaven im Jahre 1956," *Germania,* 35 (1957), *Heft* 3/4.

Haliczer, J. "The Population of Europe, 1720, 1820, 1930," *Geography,* 1934.

Hasenclever, A., ed. *Peter Hasenclever aus Remscheid-Ehringhausen ein deutscher Kaufmann des 18. Jahrhunderts (1716-1793).* 1922.

Heckel, A. *Der Runde Bogen.* 1952.

Heiligenthal, R. *Deutscher Städtebau.* 1921.

Heinemann, O. von. *Albrecht der Bär.* 1864. App. 41.

Helmold. *Cronica Slavorum, Scriptores Rerum Germanicarum,* I, 69, ed. B. Schmeidler. 1937.

Henne am Rhyn, O. *Kulturgeschichte des deutschen Volkes.* 1892.

Hessler, A. *Geschichte und Beschreibung des Kg. Hofgartens zu Veitshöchheim nach der vorhandenen Literatur zusammengestellt.* Würzburg, 1908.

Het Welvaren van Leiden. Handschrift Uit Het Jaar 1659.

Hoffman, P. Th. *Der Mittelalterliche Mensch.* 1922.

Hoops, J. L. *Reallexicon der germanischen Altertumskunde.* Unter Mitwirkung zahlreicher Fachgelehrten, Vols. 1-4. 1911-1919.

Jacob, G. *Ein arabischer Berichterstatter aus dem 10. Jahrhundert.* 1890.

Junghanns, K. *Der Frühmittelalterliche Städtebau in Deutschland.* Manuscript, Deutsche Bauakademie, Berlin, 1956.

Justi, J. H. G. von. *Staatswirtschaft,* Vol. I. 1758.

Keyser, E. *Städtegründungen und Staedtebau in Nordwestdeutschland im Mittelalter.* 1958.

Koepp, F. *Die Römer in Deutschland.* 1912.

Kötzschke, R. and W. Ebert. *Geschichte der Ost-Deutschen Kolonisation.* 1937.

Kuhn, T. S. *The Copernican Revolution.* 1957.

Kuhn, W. *Kleinsiedlungen aus Friederizianischer Zeit.* 1918.

———. *Geschichte der Deutschen Ostsiedlung in der Neuzeit,* Vol. 1. 1955, Vol. 2. 1957.

Lambert, A., and E. Stahl. *Die Gartenarchitektur.* 1910.

Lamprecht, K. *Deutsche Geschichte.* 1904.

Lavedan, P. *Histoire de l'Urbanisme.* 1941.

Le Corbusier. *The City of Tomorrow.* 1947.

Leixner, O. *Der Stadtgrundriss und seine Entwicklung.* 1924.

Leucht, K. W. *Die erste neue Stadt in der Deutschen Demokratischen Republik.* 1957.

Martiny, R. *Hof und Dorf in Altwestphalen.* 1926.

Maull, O. *Deutschland.* 1933.

Mecklenburgisches Urkundenbuch. I (1863), No. 44, 36.

Merian, M. Various topographies of German lands. First published during the first half of the seventeenth century.

Meurer, F. *Der mittelalterliche Stadtgrundriss im nördlichen Deutschland in seiner Entwicklung zur Regelmässigkeit auf der Grundlage der Marktgestaltung.* 1915.

Mielke, R. "Die Entstehung des Rundlings," *Zeitschrift für Ethnologie,* 1920.

——. "Entstehung und Ausbreitung des Strassendorfs," *Zeitschrift für Ethnologie,* 1926.

Mollet, Claude. *Théatre des Plans et Jardinage.* 1652.

Monumenta Germaniae Historica. Epistolae Selectae V. 1952.

Monumenta Germaniae Historica. Scriptores, VI, 388; XVI, 463, 469.

Mumford, Lewis. *The City in History.* 1961.

Niedersachsen, Wirtschaft und Kultur, ed. Vereinigung der niedersächsischen Industrie- und Handelskammern, Hannover. N.d.

Olbricht, K. "Die Gross- und Mittelstaedte des Deutschen Raumes zu Beginn des Dreissigjährigen Krieges," *Zeitschrift für Erdkunde,* 1938, p. 482.

Oncken, A. *Friedrich Gilly 1772-1800.* Berlin, 1935.

Otremba, E. *Die deutsche Agrarlandschaft.* Schriftenreihe: Erdkundliches Wissen, 1956. *Heft. 3.*

Ovid. *Metamorphoses.* Translation by M. M. Innes. London: Penguin Classics, 1955.

Paulsen, F. "Friedrich Gillys Städtebau," *Zeitschrift der Deutschen Akademie für Städtebau, Reichs- und Landesplanung,* 1936, 32 ff.

Penther, I. F. *Lexicon Architectonicum,* 1744.

Pfeiffer, G. "The Quality of Peasant Living in Central Europe," in *Man's Role in Changing the Face of the Earth.* 1956.

Pinder, W. *Deutsche Burgen und feste Schlösser.* 1913.

——. *Deutsche Dome.* N.d.

——. *Deutscher Barock.* 1940.

——. *Innenräume Deutscher Vergangenheit.* 1941.

——. *Grosse Bürgerbauten deutscher Vergangenheit.* 1943.

——. *Deutsche Wasserburgen.* 1952.

Planitz, H. *Die Deutsche Stadt im Mittelalter.* 1954.

Pommersches Urkundenbuch, II (1868), No. 35, 3.

Pückler-Muskau, Fürst von. *Andeutungen über Landschaftsgärtnerei.* 1834.

Püschel, A. *Das Anwachsen der deutschen Städte in der Zeit der mittelalterlichen Kolonialbewegung.* 1910

Quirin, K. H. *Die Deutsche Ostsiedlung im Mittelalter.* 1954.

Radig, W. *Die Siedlungstypen in Deutschland und ihre frühgeschichtlichen Wurzeln.* 1955.

Rauda, W. *Lebendige Städtebauliche Raumbildung.* 1957.

Read, H. *The Grass Roots of Art.* 1947.

——. *Icon and Idea.* 1955.

Reinerth, H. *Vorgeschichte der Deutschen Stämme,* Vol. 1. N.d.

Rietdorf, A. *Gilly, Wiedergeburt der Architektur.* 1943.

Rietschel, S. *Die Civitas auf deutschem Boden bis zum Ausgang der Karolingerzeit.* 1894.

Rosenau, H. *The Ideal City.* 1959.

Scherzer, C., ed. *Franken. Land, Volk, Geschichte und Wirtschaft.* Vol. I, 1955.

Schiller, F. von. *Gartenkalender.* 1795.

Schlenger, H. "Friederizianische Siedlungen rechts der Oder bis 1800," in *Beihefte zum geschichtlichen Atlas von Schlesien.* 1933. *Heft.* 1.

Schlüter, O. "Die Siedlungsräume Mitteleuropas in frühgeschichtlicher Zeit," in *Forschungen zur deutschen Landeskunde.* Vol. 63 (1952); Vol. 74 (1953).

Schmidt, R. W. *Deutsche Reichsstädte.* 1957.

Schmoller, G. *Die Preussische Kolonisation*

des 17. und 18. Jahrhunderts. Schriften des Vereins für Sozialpolitik, 1886.

——. *Deutsches Städtewesen in älterer Zeit.* 1922.

Schuchardt, C. *Die Burg im Wandel der Weltgeschichte.* 1932.

——. *Vorgeschichte von Deutschland.* 1943.

Siedler, J. *Märkischer Städtebau im Mittelalter.* 1914.

Sillibb, R. *Schloss und Garten in Schwetzingen.* 1907.

Singer, C. *A Short History of Science to the Nineteenth Century.* 1941.

Sombart, W. *Der moderne Kapitalismus.* 1921.

Speckle, D. *Architectura von vestungen; wie die zu unseren zeiten, an stätten, schlössern und claussen zu wasser, land, berg und thal . . . mögen erbawet . . . werden. Alles auss den fundamenten samt den grund rissen, visierungen und auffzügen für Augen gestellet durch Daniel Speckle. Jetzt aber . . . übersehen . . . verbessert, auch vielen anderen visierungen vermerket.* Strassburg, 1608.

Stein, R. *Die Umwandlung der Agrarverfassung Ostpreussens durch die Reform des neunzehnten Jahrhunderts.* Schriften des Königlichen Institutes für Ostdeutsche Wirtschaft an der Universität Königsberg; 1918. *Heft. V.*

Stephani, K. G. *Der älteste deutsche Wohnbau und seine Einrichtung.* 2 vols. 1902.

Stieglitz, C. L. *Encyklopädie der bürgerlichen Baukunst.* 5 vols. Published between 1750-1832.

Studien zu den Anfängen des Europäischen Staedtewesens, Vol. IV, Reichenau-Vorträge, 1955-1956. Edited by Theodor Mayer for Institut für geschichtliche Landesforschung. des Bodenseegebietes in Konstanz.

Tacke, B. and B. Lehmann. *Die Norddeutschen Moore.* 1912.

Toynbee, A. J. *A Study of History* (Abridged ed.), Vol. I., 1947; Vol. II., 1957.

Vitruvius, Marcus Pollio. *Baukunst.* Aus der Römischen Urschrift übersetzt von August Rode. 1796.

——. *Kupfer zu Vitruvius zehn Büchern von der Baukunst.* August Rode. 1801.

Volkamer. *Nürnbergische Hesperides.* Nürnberg, 1708-1714.

Wallner, E. *Altbayrische Siedlungsgeschichte.* 1924.

Weber, A. *Kulturgeschichte als Kultursoziologie.* 1935.

——. *Abschied von der bisherigen Geschichte.* 1946.

——. *Der Dritte oder der Vierte Mensch.* 1953.

Weber, M. *Römische Agrargeschichte.* 1891.

——. *Grundriss der Sozialökonomik.* 1925.

Whitehead, A. N. *Adventure of Ideas.* 1942.

Widukindi. *Rerum Gest. Saxonicarum Libri III, Scriptores Rerum Germanicarum.* 1935.

Wilhelmy, H. "Völkische und Koloniale Siedlungsformen der Slaven," in *Geographische Zeitschrift,* 1936, *Heft 3.*

Willebrand, J. P. *Grundriss einer schönen Stadt.* 1775-1776.

Wittich, W. *Epochen deutscher Agrargeschichte. Grundriss der Sozial-Oekonomik.* 1922.

CITY MONOGRAPHS

Ansbach

Ansbach. Special issue of *Bayerland.*

Augsburg

Deininger, H. F., ed. *Das Reiche Augsburg.* 1938.

Zorn, W. *Augsburg. Geschichte einer deutschen Stadt.*

Bamberg

Hofmann, M. *Kleine Bamberger Heimatkunde und Stadtgeschichte.* 1956.

Berlin

Assmann, P. *Der geologische Aufbau der Gegend von Berlin.* 1957.

Berlin. Planungsgrundlagen für den städtebaulichen Ideenwettbewerb "Hauptstadt Berlin," ed. Senator für Bau- und Wohnungswesen. 1957.

Jahn-Steglitz, H. *Die Reichshauptstadt,* ed. Reichshauptstadt. N.d.

Böblingen

Böblingen, Burg, Dorf, Stadt. 1953.

Bonn

Geliebte Stadt. Ein altbonner Bilderbuch. 1953.

Braunfels
700-Jahrfeier der Stadt Braunfels. Published by the Magistrat der Stadt Braunfels, 1957.

Braunschweig
Braunschweig. Tradition Trümmer Aufbau, ed. Amt. für Wirtschafts- und Verkehrsförderung der Stadt Braunschweig. 1954.
Göderitz, J. *Braunschweig, Zerstörung und Aufbau.* 1949.
Heidersberger. *Braunschweig.* N.d.

Bremen
Das Buch der Bremischen Häfen, ed. Gesellschaft für Wirtschaftsförderung, Bremen. N.d.
Gläbe, F., ed. *Bremen, Einst und Jetzt.* 1955.
Prüfer, F., ed. *Heimatchronik der Freien Hansestadt Bremen.* N.d.

Cologne
Baukunst und Werkform. 1957, *Heft* 5 (special issue on *Köln*).
Buttler, W., and W. Haberey. "Die bandkeramische Ansiedlung bei Köln-Lindenthal," *Römisch-Germanische Forschungen,* XI (1936).
Göbel, E. *Das Stadtgebiet von Köln.* Sonderheft der Statistischen Mitteilungen der Stadt Köln, 1948.
Tuckermann, W. "Die geographische Lage der Stadt Köln und ihre Auswirkungen in der Vergangenheit und Gegenwart," in *Pfingstblätter des hansischen Geschichtsvereins, Blatt* 14, 1923.

Dinkelsbühl
Doederlein, F. *Dinkelsbühl. A short guide through the thousand-year-old city.* N.d.
Horn, A. *Dinkelsbühl, St. Georgskirche und Stadt.* 1952.

Düren
Appel, H. *Wenzel Hollar in Düren. Die topographischen Darstellungen Dürens bis zum Jahre 1664.* 1957.

Emden
Diederichs, P. *Emden. Neuplanung einer deutschen Seehafenstadt im Lande Niedersachsen.* 1948.
Santjer, H., ed. *Emden. Stadt im Strom der Zeiten.* 1950.

Schöningh, W. *Emden vom Mittelalter bis zur Neuzeit.* 1956

Erlangen
Erlangen gestern und heute. Heimatverein Erlangen, 1954.

Frankfurt am Main
Baedeker, K. *Frankfurt am Main und der Taunus.* 1952.

Freudenstadt
Baumeister, February, 1955.

Frickenhausen am Main
Hochmann, A. *Dorfchronik von Frickenhausen.* 1952.

Goslar
Wiederhold, W. "Goslar als Königsstadt und Bergstadt," in *Pfingstblätter des hansischen Geschichtsvereins,* XIII (1922).

Hamburg
Reincke, H. *Forschungen und Skizzen zur Geschichte Hamburgs.* Veröffentlichungen aus dem Staatsarchiv der Hansestadt Hamburg, 1951.

Hildesheim
Merian, 1952, *Heft* 8 (special issue on Hildesheim).
Zoder, R. *Hildesheim.* 1956.

Karlsruhe
Baden. Südwestdeutsche Rundschau für Kultur, Wirtschaft und Verkehr. 1955. *Ausgabe* 4.
Baden Württemberg. Südwestdeutsche Monatschrift für Kultur, Wirtschaft und Reisen, 1957, *Heft* 6.
Das Karlsruher Rathaus, ed. Stadtverwaltung Karlsruhe. N.d.

Landshut
Hochwasserfreilegung des Stadtgebietes von Landshut. 1957.

Lennep
Stursberg, E. E. *Zur Älteren Geschichte Lenneps.* 1956.

Lübeck
Hansestadt Lübeck, ed. Senat der Hansestadt Lübeck. N.d.

Magdeburg

Schwineköper, B. "Die Anfänge Magdeburgs," in *Studien zu den Anfängen des Europäischen Staedtewesens.* ReichenauVorträge, 1955-1956.

Mainz

Published by the Altertumsmuseum der Stadt Mainz:
Vom Steinzeitmenschen zum Urkelten. 1958.
Kelten, Römer und Germanen. 1956.
Mittelalterliche Werke aus dem Mainzer Raum. 1959.
Aus Kurmainzer Zeit. 1957.

Mannheim

Mannheim im Aufbau, ed. Stadtverwaltung Mannheim. 1955.
350 Jahre Mannheim. Das Bild einer Stadt. 1957.

Munich

Bergmann, Michael von: *Beytraege zur Geschichte der Stadt Muenchen, von deren Entstehung an bis zur Regierung Kaiser Ludwig des IV.* 1780.
Dirr, Pius. *Grundlagen der Münchner Stadtgeschichte.* 1937.
Lasne, O. *Freie Plätze im Stadterweiterungsgebiet.* 1899.
Muffat, K. A. *München in seiner Entwicklung bis zum Anfang des fünfzehnten Jahrhunderts.* 1858.
Solleder, F. *München im Mittelalter.* 1938.
Steinlein, G. *Die Baukunst Alt-Münchens. Eine städtebauliche Studie über die Münchener Bauweise von der Gründung bis Ende des 16. Jahrhunderts.* 1920.
Weber, Carl. "München und seine Stadterweiterungen," *Deutsche Bauzeitung.* 1893.
800 Jahre München. Das Bild einer deutschen Stadt. 1958.

Münster

Das Bilderbuch der Stadt Münster. Städtisches Werbe- und Verkehrsamt der Stadt Münster, 1957.
Vernekohl, W. *Münster. Ein Kleiner Kulturführer.* 1956.

Nürnberg

Schultheisz, W. *Nürnberg. Die Schönheit der Noris.* 1957.

Osnabrück

Kamp, Martin auf dem. *Osnabrück. Die Zwischenlandschaft Osnabrück in ihren strukturellen Verflechtungen.* 1956.
Merian, 1951, *Heft* 12 (special issue on Osnabrück).
Osnabrück. Schöne alte Stadt zwischen Teutoburger Wald und Wiehengebirge. Published by Kultur- und Verkehrsamt der Stadt Osnabrück, 1954.
Poppe-Marquard, H. *Osnabrück. Ein Rundgang durch die Stadt.* 1956.

Paderborn

Stadt Paderborn. Ein Jahrzehnt Aufbau und Planung 1945-1955. Wirtschafts-Monographien, Folge 10. 1955.

Passau

Moritz, H. K. *Passau. The Ancient Episcopal Town on Three Rivers.* 1957.
Oswald, J. *Passau in Geschichte und Kunst.* 1956.
Wasserthal, G., ed. *Passau. Die Drei-Flüsse-Stadt.* N.d.

Potsdam

Baur, M. *Potsdam.* 1937.

Radolfzell

Berner, H. *Radolfzell. Das Tor zum Bodensee.* 1952.
Finckh, L. *Kleine Stadt am Bodensee.* 1951.

Rastatt

Kircher, G. F. *Die Einrichtung des Rastatter Schlosses im Jahre 1772.* 1955.
Kraemer, H. *Rastatt und seine Umgebung.* 1930.
Peters, G. *Das Rastatter Schloss.* 1925.
"Rastatt in Vergangenheit und Gegenwart," Sonderdruck der Zeitschrift *Baden, Südwestdeutsche Rundschau für Kultur, Wirtschaft und Verkehr,* No. 5, 1956.

Regensburg

Boll, W. *Regensburg.* 1955.
Das Bayerland. Special issue on Regensburg, 1925, 2, *Septemberheft.*
Klebel, E. "Regensburg," *Studien zu den Anfängen des Europäischen Staedtewesens.* Reichenau-Vorträge, 1955-1956.
Regensburg. Special issue of *Bayerland.*

Rottweil

800 Jahre Frei- und Reichssadt Rottweil. 1950.

Steinhauser, A. *Officina Historiae Rottwilensis oder Werkstätte der Rottweilischen Geschichte.* 1950.

Soest

Soest. Ein Heimatbuch und Führer durch Stadt und Börde. 1952.

Zeitschrift des Vereins für die Geschichte von Soest und der Börde, 1948, *Heft* 61.

Speyer

Doll, A. "Zur Frühgeschichte der Stadt Speyer," *Sonderdruck aus den Mitteilungen des Historischen Vereins der Pfalz,* Vol. 52 (Speyer, 1954).

Röttger, B. H. *Die Kunstdenkmäler von Bayern, Pfalz,* Vol. 3. Stadt- und Bezirksamt Speyer, 1934.

Zeusz, K. *Die freie Reichsstadt Speyer vor ihrer Zerstörung.* N.d.

Tübingen

Huber, R. *Tübingen.* 1955.

Merian, 1954, *Heft* 8.

Schefold, M. *Alte Tübinger Stadtansichten.* 1953.

Tübinger Blätter, December, 1955.

Weidle, K. *Die Entstehung von Alt-Tübingen.* 1955.

Ulm

Meynen, E. *Ulm/Neu-Ulm.* Sonderdruck aus *Berichte zur deutschen Landeskunde,* Vol. 16 (1956), *Heft* 2.

1100 Jahre Ulm. Published by the Stadt Ulm, 1954.

Wasserburg

800 Jahre Wasserburg am Inn. 1137-1937. N.d.

Wimpfen am Neckar

Arens, F., and R. Bührlen. *Die Kunstdenkmäler in Wimpfen am Neckar.* 1954.

Bad Wimpfen im Bild, ed. H. P. Eppinger. N.d.

Vassilliere, J. *Neues von alten Bauten in Wimpfen.* 1947.

Würzburg

Withold, K. "Die frühgeschichtliche Entwicklung des Würzburger Stadtplanes," *Studien zu den Anfängen des Europäischen Staedtewesens.* Reichenau-Vorträge, 1955-1956.

Xanten

Steiner, P. *Die Anfänge Xantens.* 1928.

Zell im Hamm

Kessler, E. *Zell im Hamm.* 1922.

Index

A

Aachen: *see* Aix-la-Chapelle
Absolutism, 190; *l'état c'est moi* spirit in layout and design, 190-191, 300; identity of ruler and state, 190
Africa: biological groups as originators of villages, 22; indigenous settlements, 25, 47-48
Aix-la-Chapelle (Aachen), 73, 138, 167, 258
Allmende, 88, 95, 98, 101, 261
Alps, 55; Alpine passes, 76
Alteburg, Werden, 453
Altenburg, Niedenstein, 136, 451, 452-453
Ammianus Marcellinus, 93n
Andrea, Johann Valentin, 307-309; *Christianopolis*, 307
Anger, 128, 130; *Kotla*, 130
Anger village (*Angerdorf*), 121, 130, 463
Animals, domestication of, 471
Annaberg, 467
Ansbach, 356
Arcades, 171, 286
Aristocracy, lay, 74
Aristotle, 177-179, 187; geocentric (Aristotelian) universe, 34, 177-178
Artisans and craftsmen, *see* Classes
Associations, Germanic, 94; trade, 192
Augsburg, 72, 76, 83, 137, 140, 330-336; Diet of, 81; Fuggerei, 169-170, 334; Elias Holl, 336
Augst, 137
Austria, 66

B

Baalshebbel near Starzeddel, 445
Babylon, 22, 46
Bach, Johann Sebastian, 84
Baden-Baden, 138
Balzac, Honoré de, 21
Bamberg, 379-380, 469
Bannmeile: see Urban
Bantu Negroes, *kraals* of, 33
Barcelona, 47

Baroque: attitude toward life, 184; essence of architectural composition, 182; gardens, 206-208, 213, 214-216; labyrinth, 214-217; layout of town houses, 201-202; period, 31, 83-84, 190-202; prince, 190, 289, 307; urge toward infinity, 185, 200; use of water in parks and gardens, 217; Wilhelmshöhe, Cassel, 388-389; *see also* D'Argenville; Dresden; Eichstätt; *Horror vacui;* Perspective view; Würzburg
Bath, 172, 219
Baumannschaft, 350
Bautzen, 464
Beethoven, Ludwig van, 84
Behaim, Martin, 362
Benedictines, 90
Berlin, 221, 222, 418-426; Eosander, 420; Gilly, 226-227; Knobelsdorff, 420; Nering, 420; Schinkel, 226, 420; Schlüter, 420
Bifang: see Forests
Bischofsburg: see Castle
Blockflur, 111; *see also* Field systems
Bodensee (Lake Constance), 439
Böblingen, 294-296
Bohemia, 64
Bonn, 72
Brandenburg, 83, 100
Braunfels, 385
Braunschweig, 399-401
Bremen, 83, 100, 239-246; Bremerhaven, 246
Breslau, 100, 465
Brieg, 464
Bromberg, 465
Bronze Age, 92, 330, 441, 471
Bruno, Giordano, 37, 177, 184; *Cena de le Ceneri*, 184
Buchau, Wasserburg, 445-446
Buildings: *Steinwerke*, 249; wooden, 173
Burding, 465
Burg, 136, 158; *Königsburg*, 142-143; *oppidum*, 136, 137; Steinsburg, 446; Wasserburg Buchau,

445-446; *see also* Baalshebbel near Starzeddel; *Pfalz;* and Strongholds
Burgher, 23, 30, 78, 135, 145-146; against feudal lords, 149; agent of a rational urban economy, 135; *Bürger, burgensis*, 158
Burgrecht, 158
Bushmen, windscreen settlements of, 33
Business, life, 201
Butterfield, Herbert, 29

C

Canabae, 140, 452
Cannstadt, 449
Capitalism, 191
Cardo, 140; *see also* Streets
Carnuntum, 137
Carolingian: period, 141-145; renaissance and urban culture, 145; revival of trade and municipal government, 141-142; urban economic life, 142
Cascades, 200, 217, 388-389
Castle: *Bischofsburg*, 331, 332, 345; fortified, 144, 162, 274-275; *Königsburg*, 142-143: *Wasserburg*, 268, 270; *see also Pfalz*
Catastrophes: Black Death, 465; famines, 90-91; natural, 462
Cathedral: Gothic, 77, 182, 185; Romanesque, 180-182; precincts (*Domburg*), 254-256, 403
Causality, concept of, 28-29, 39
Cave dwelling, 471
Celtic: clans, 94; settlements 272, 330, 345
Cemeteries, 163, 164
Central Europe, physical division of, 55-58
Central Uplands, 56
Chains of transformation, 27-40
Charlemagne, 72-73, 142-143, 247, 258, 453; Aix-la-Chapelle, 73, 258
Charles V, 80-81
China: adaptation of environment in, 33; biological groups as originators of villages, 22; consanguin-

Rhine, 76, 260, 261, 277-278, 279; frontier, 71, 72
Richter, J. M., 378
Riga, 64, 250
Rittergut: see Estates
Rococo, 83-84
Roman: camps, 111, 136-139, 348, 447, 471; centuriation, 472; forts, 449; frontier, 71-72; layout, 139-140, 265, 331; military and veterans' town, 447; ritual, 140; roads, 112-113, 139; Saalburg, 452; settlements, 136-141, 447-452; system of settlement, 111-112; trading centers, 140
Rome: fortified walls, 35; identification of city and state, 22; magical identification with environment, 25; Piazza del Popolo, 223, 300
Rosenthal, 386
Rostock, 161, 414
Rothenburg, 165, 367-368, 469; market place, 179-180
Rottenburg, 139
Rottweil, 139, 311-313, 449
Rural: home industries, 160-161; property, 103-104
Russia: space dimensions, 38; trading posts, 64

S

Saalburg, 452
Sachs, Hans, 362
Salhof: see Manor
Salland: see Manor
Scale: asymmetrical, 182; carriage, 188; harmony of, 171; human, 175; idea of, 182; relative, 38; sense of, 180-183; and space, 173-183; widening, 27, 34, 38-39, 41-42
Scandinavian Peninsula, 57
Schickhardt, Heinrich, 308-310
Schiller, Friedrich von, 84, 218
Schinkel, Friedrich von, 226, 416, 420
Schlüter, Andreas, 420
Schneeberg, 467
Schwäbisch-Gmünd, 293
Schwerin, 101
Schwetzingen, Baroque garden, 208
Semper, Gottfried, 226
Settlement: Alemannic, 472; earliest, 91-92, 439-446; of Flemings, 463; Frankish, 472; Huguenots, 270-272, 378; industrial, 467-468; Lithuanian, 132; and market, 463; Masurian, 130, 131; merchants', 144-145; Roman, 136-141; Roman system of, 111-112; rural, 67-69;

Slav, 63-64; structure of, 67, 91, 104; state promoted, 220-221; traders', 144; zones of 64; *see also* Teutonic; and *Vicus*
Settlers: Dutch, 270, 463; Dutch, Flemish, Frisian, 65, 404, 464; east and west German tribes, 60; French, 420; *see also* Monastic orders; and Settlement
Shops, 201
Silesia, 64, 464
Sipplingen, pile village of, 439
Slav communes, 94; settlement, 63-64, 120-121
Slavs, 63-64, 72, 120-121; crusade against, 68; rulers of, 64
Social: controversies, 188-189; forces, 24; principle of equality, 101; space, 173; structure of medieval towns, 156-157
Soest, 250-253
South Seas, relation to environment, 33
Space: changed conception of, 188; changing experience of, 27; contrast of spatial elements in gardens, 207; in depth, 171, 175; feeling of, 36, 38; hall churches, 224; idea of, 34, 176, 177, 178, 226; open, 130, 141, 163, 171-172; plurality of viewpoints, 176; preperspective, 176; primitive, 177-178; relations, 176; at rest, 177, 186; and scale, 173-183; sense of, 176, 177; social, 12-13, 173; time and, 39; urban, 173, 175, 178; *see also Anger*
Spaciousness, new, 188
Specialization: local, 42-43; of population and towns, 191; of towns, 192; of work, 189
Speyer, 72, 141, 275-277
Squares: central, 199; Friedrichsplatz and Königsplatz, Kassel, 387; Piazza del Popolo, 223, 300; *see also* Market, square; and Münster, Prinzipalmarkt
State, 23; centralizing tendencies, 192; identity of city and, 22; identity of prince and, 190; promoted settlement, 221; rise of, 23-24, 191
Statutes, road mileage and storage, 148
Steinsburg near Römhild, 446
Stettin, 161, 464
Stöttinghausen, 455
Storage privileges, 148-149
Stoss, Veit, 361, 469
Strasbourg, 72, 93, 449

Streets: *cardo*, 140; *decumanus*, 140; dirty, 172; layout of, 190; *Lexicon architectonicum*, 200; market, 164-165, 311; in medieval towns, 163-164, 169, 172; regulations, 172; traffic, 169; *see also* Cult, of the street
Strongholds: Alteburg, Werden, 453; Altenburg, 451, 452-453; *Burg*, 136, 158, 442-446, 472; Eresburg, 453; Martinsburg, 274-275; Pipinsburg, 455; residential, 473; Roman forts, 449; Saalburg, 452; Steinsburg, 446; Stöttinghausen, 455; Wasserburg Buchau, 445-446; Werla, 455; *see also Pfalz*
Stuttgart, 204, 287-291
Style, elements of, 45-46
Suburbs: incorporation of, 154-155; *suburbium*, 93, 452
Switzerland, 57-58
Symbolism, Greek, 29
Symmetry: and harmony, tenets of Renaissance aesthetics, 187; and regimentation, 280
Synoikism, 22

T

Tacitus, 112, 136
Teutonic, Order of the Knights, 64-65, 131
Thirty Years' War, 82-83, 124, 199
Thorn, 65, 465
Tiberius Gracchus, 90
Time, identity of space and, 39
Tolstoy, Leo, 9, 24
Town: and country, 13-14, 193-194; clocks, 284; and palace, 280, 300, 307, 413
Town planning: element of state policy, 197-199; elements of, 36, 202-203, 219; factors in medieval 168, 170-171
Towns: African, 33; ambition of German towns, 150-151; Chinese, 14, 33, 47; colonial, 378, 463; commercial, 83; eastern, 120; east German colonial, 419; economic development and growth of, 160; eighteenth century, 195; extension of, 153-154; fortress, 24, 189; foundations in eastern Central Europe, 64-66; functional transformation of German towns, 148-149; Greek, 46-47; Hanse, 76, 242, 250, 390, 406; hinterland of, 41; Hohenstaufen, 284, 293, 358, 364, 366, 367; Huguenots, 222, 378; Ideal Towns, 189, 199-200, 224, 226, 307-309; Indian, 33; lack of,

PRODUCTION NOTE

Urban Development in Central Europe, Volume I of the International History of City Development, was produced under the supervision of Sidney Solomon. Typography and picture layout are the work of Frank Comparato. The book was composed in Perpetua and Baskerville faces by Slugs Composition Company, New York, printed by Edward Stern & Company, Philadelphia, on Warren's Olde Style paper, and bound by The Book Press, Brattleboro, Vermont.